W9-CPK-353

DESCRIPTION OF BEARER.

43   Profession   Journalist

e & date of birth   Lithgow, New South Wales
                                          22.6.1875

den name if widow or
ed woman travelling }

ght   5   feet   9   inches

head   High   Eyes   Blue

    straight   Mouth   Large

    pointed   Colour of Hair   Brown

plexion   Fair   Face   oval

special peculiarities   left eyelid droops

tional Status   Natural born British

subject.

This passport has been cancelled

A new London passport No 12736

dated 25th March 1924 has been

granted. Hot...

FOREIGN OFFICE
67   25 MAR 1924   67

DESCRIPTION OF WIFE OF BEARER.

Age   Profession

Place & date of birth

Ma...

Heig...   feet   inches

Forehead   Eyes

Nose   Mouth

Chin   Colour of Hair

Complexion   Face

Any special peculiarities

PARTICULARS OF CHILDREN UNDER THE AGE OF 16 YEARS.

Name   Age   Sex

PHOTOGRAPH OF BEARER.

SIGNATURE OF BEARER.

W.H. Donald

Donald, William Henry

Durchreise

№   119   Geb. 5. Woolt zu Boo-
                                      Petan U.

Gut zur Durchreise durch Deutschland

nach   England

über jede amtlich zugelassene deutsche

Grenzstelle.

Gültig bis zum   10. März 1924

Aufenthaltsdauer   in   Deutschland

fünf Tage

Petersburg, den   21. Februar 1924
(Leningrad)
Deutsches Generalkonsulat Petersburg Leningrad

Paßkontrolle
24. II. 1924
Eydtkuhnen (B...

SHANGHAI FURY

AUSTRALIAN HEROES
OF REVOLUTIONARY CHINA

PETER THOMPSON

WILLIAM HEINEMANN: AUSTRALIA

A William Heinemann book
Published by Random House Australia Pty Ltd
Level 3, 100 Pacific Highway, North Sydney NSW 2060
www.randomhouse.com.au

First published by William Heinemann in 2011

Addresses for companies within the Random House Group can be found at www.randomhouse.com.au/offices.

National Library of Australia
Cataloguing-in-Publication Entry

Thompson, Peter Alexander.
Shanghai fury/Peter Thompson.

ISBN 978 1 86471 183 7 (hbk.)

Shanghai (China) – History – 20th century.
China – Foreign relations – Australia.
Australia – Foreign relations – China.

951.04

Front and back jacket photographs: Thomas Macauley Collection
Jacket design by Christabella Designs
Internal text and picture section design by Midland Typesetters, Australia
Typeset in Goudy Old Style by Midland Typesetters, Australia
Printed in Australia by Griffin Press, an accredited ISO AS/NZS 14001:2004 Environmental Management System printer

10 9 8 7 6 5 4 3 2 1

Random House Australia uses papers that are natural, renewable and recyclable products and made from wood grown in sustainable forests. The logging and manufacturing processes are expected to conform to the environmental regulations of the country of origin.

For Robert Macklin

CONTENTS

ACKNOWLEDGEMENTS

Shanghai Fury: Australian Heroes of Revolutionary China completes a trilogy on Australians at war. *Anzac Fury: The Bloody Battle of Crete 1941* focused on the Second World War in the Mediterranean, while *Pacific Fury: How Australia And Her Allies Defeated the Japanese* covered the broad sweep of the Pacific War.

This has been made possible only by the generosity of the many people who shared their personal experiences or expert knowledge with me and by Random House Australia's recognition that there was a place for such a trilogy in the military canon.

I am enormously grateful to Dorothy Lewis for permitting me to quote from documents in the archive compiled by her husband Winston G. Lewis at the Mitchell Library, Sydney. Professor Lewis, Professor of History at Macquarie University, dedicated 20 years of his life to 'Project Donald', contacting dozens of people who had known the Australian journalist in China and conducting a most informative correspondence with many of them. Winston Lewis died before he could complete his magnum opus. His painstaking work has proved invaluable in the writing of this book.

Wherever possible, I have combined the personal memories of Shanghai people with combat action. I have also returned to the original sources of many existing works on the revolutionary period and the memoirs and/or biographies of the main participants.

My sources include Alastair Morrison (1915–2009), second son of 'Chinese' Morrison, who shared his recollections of his father and his own experiences of wartime China with me at his Canberra home; Ivor Bowden, Shanghai-born son of the Australian trade commissioner V. G. Bowden who was murdered by the Japanese in 1942; Greg Leck, who published his comprehensive history of internment, *Captives of Empire*, in 2006, and internees William Macauley, Freda Howkins, Roy Fernandez Jr and his sister Stephanie Sherwood, all of whom lived in Shanghai during one of the most turbulent periods in its history.

I also consulted documents, private papers, diaries, as well as books and newspapers in the Shanghai Library, the Dazhong newspaper archives (Shanghai), the National Archives (Kew), the British Library (London), the New York Public Library, the Cosmos Club (Washington), the National Archives of Australia (Canberra), the National Library of Australia (Canberra), the Mitchell Library and State Library of New South Wales (Sydney), the State Library of Victoria (Melbourne), the Oxley Library and State Library of Queensland (Brisbane).

I am indebted to Dimity Torbett for her research at the Mitchell Library on the papers of George Ernest Morrison and Eleanor Mary Hinder; to Richard Rigby in Canberra for his guidance on the May Thirtieth movement; to Hugh Lunn for his memories of the Reuters correspondent Graham Jenkins; to Elizabeth Fay Woodfield for information about her great uncle William Charles Woodfield of the Shanghai River Police; and to Robert Macklin, my frequent co-author, for reading the work-in-progress and making many valuable suggestions.

Finally, I would like to express my special thanks to Nikki Christer, my publisher at Random House Australia, for her tremendous support during the writing and publishing of the

Fury Trilogy, and to Random House editors Kevin O'Brien and Patrick Mangan for their splendid work on these three titles. My agent Andrew Lownie of the Andrew Lownie Literary Agency, London, was closely involved in the development and writing of this body of work.

Shanghai Fury contains many exclusive photographs of Shanghai scenes donated to the author from the private collection of Thomas Jackson Macauley of the Chinese Maritime Customs Service. Ulsterman Macauley collected these photographs during the 1930s and took them into captivity when he was interned in 1941. Following his death, the photographs passed to his son William Macauley who has authorised me to use them for publication in this work.

Regarding style, I have used the spelling of names and places as they were rendered at the time in dialect pronunciations, for example Chiang Kai-shek and Mao Tse-tung, Peking, Tientsin and Canton. The modern pinyin equivalents are contained in the Appendices. Regarding currencies, the dollar sign ($) applies to the Chinese dollar at the time unless otherwise specified, such as US$. There is no difference between British and Australian pounds. I have also taken the liberty at times of using the present tense – for example, 'he says' or 'she recalls' – when a specific recollection may in fact have taken place years earlier. The sources of all interviews are clearly flagged in the references and notes section. In several instances, I have retained offensive terms such as 'Jap' and 'Chinaman' when they are used in direct quotations from the period.

Peter Thompson
August 2011

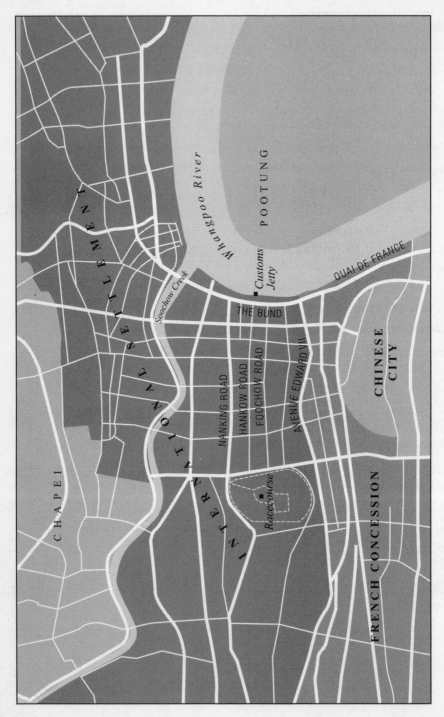

Shanghai in colonial times showing the Chinese City in relation to the Western concessions

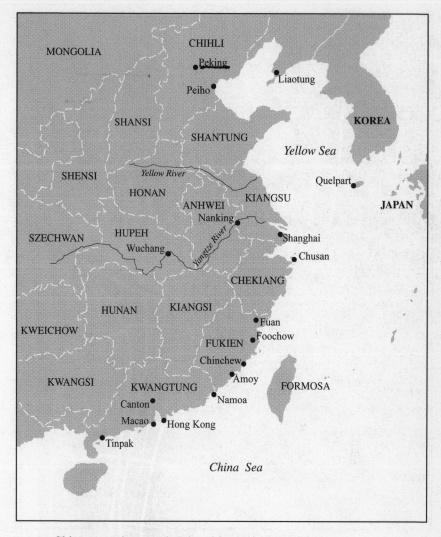

Chinese provinces and major cities in the late 19th century

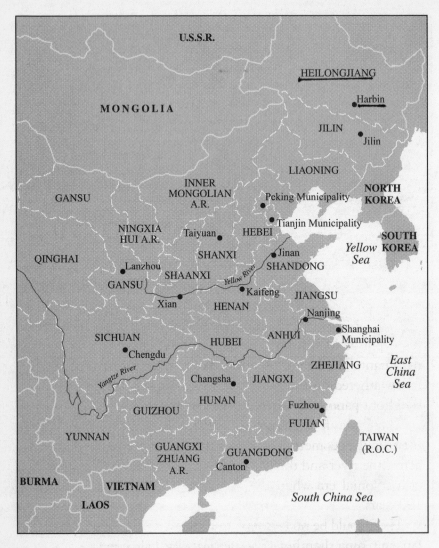

The People's Republic of China after October 1949

PROLOGUE

The Dragon's Head

It's 6 pm at M on The Bund, Shanghai's famous Australian restaurant. The heat of the day has passed and dozens of diners have gathered on the rooftop terrace to watch the spectacular riverfront panorama unfold in the soft evening light.

There are few greater architectural contrasts than that between the geometric modernity of Pudong (formerly Pootung) across the river and the classical beauty of The Bund, remnants of a colonial era when the West held sway over the East for 100 years.

There could be no better place to begin a story about Australians in China than here. M's founder Michelle Garnaut is from Melbourne and its corn-fed beef and the *maitre d'* are from Queensland. Yet it's doubtful if many of the Australians who patronise M are aware of other extraordinary Australian connections surrounding them.

Down below on the banks of the Whangpoo (now the Huangpu) River, George Morrison came ashore in 1894 as a 32-year-old traveller to take his first steps into Chinese history. It was here ten years later that his fellow journalist and friend

W. H. Donald landed on his way to the Russo-Japanese War and returned with his wife and daughter in 1911 to take part in the Chinese Revolution later that year. Morrison orchestrated the abdication of the Last Emperor, while Donald wrote the political manifesto of Sun Yat-sen, first president of the Chinese Republic.

And it was from The Bund during the ensuing Chinese civil war that Basil Riley, son of the Archbishop of Perth, set off on his journey up the Yangtze, only to die at the hands of the troops of General Feng Yu-hsiang, the so-called 'Christian General'.

To the left of the M vantage point is the old Hong Kong & Shanghai Bank building, the Honkers & Shankers, where Gordon Bowden had his office as Australian trade commissioner. Slightly closer to Nanking Road is the rooftop of the *North-China Daily News* building where Bowden and his six-year-old son Ivor watched the Chinese district of Chapei burning during the Japanese invasion of 1932.

From that same rooftop five years later William Arthur 'Buzz' Farmer saw the carnage of Bloody Saturday when a bomb exploded between the Cathay and Palace hotels at the intersection of Nanking Road and The Bund, killing hundreds of people at the start of the Sino-Japanese War (1937–45), known in China as 'the War of Resistance'.

To the right of M is Frenchtown and the Chinese district of Nantao where Harold John Timperley helped Father Jacquinot de Besange, a heroic French priest, set up a 'safety zone' that rescued thousands of Chinese refugees from the fighting. Just around the corner is the wireless and cable office where Timperley filed his reports on the Rape of Nanking when a similar safety zone failed to save thousands of lives.

And it was in Room 106 of the Palace Hotel that the treacherous trio of collaborators – Alan Willoughby Raymond, Wynette Cecilia McDonald and John Joseph Holland – launched the renegade Independent Australia League in 1942. At the fall of Singapore, when 14,000 members of the 2nd AIF were taken prisoner, Wynette McDonald drove down The Bund in an open-top car with a Japanese officer to celebrate the Japanese victory.

Indeed, Shanghai is a city defined by war. It is the 'dragon's head of the Yangtze', the starting point of a long and dangerous journey from China's imperial past to its astonishing present, a journey that culminates on 10 October 2011 in the 100th anniversary of the Chinese Revolution.

The Xinhai, or Double Tenth, Revolution of 1911 – hailed by Lenin as the 'awakening of Asia' – created the first democratic republic in North Asia and triggered other movements for reform and self-determination in the region. All too quickly, though, the hopes of Sun Yat-sen and his fellow revolutionaries were destroyed by the warlord regime of President Yuan Shi-kai.

Then in 1927 the Nationalists conquered South China, butchered thousands of Communists in Shanghai – birthplace of the Chinese Communist Party – and established a party-republic under the dictatorship of Chiang Kai-shek (Jiang Jieshi). The final phase of the revolutionary movement took place in 1949 when the Communists recaptured Shanghai and unified mainland China in the People's Republic of China under Chairman Mao Tse-Tung (Mao Zedong).

Mao's triumph heralded three decades of disastrous economic and political repression, which effectively sealed China off from the Western world. Only after the Great Helmsman's death in 1976 and the subsequent fall of the Gang of Four did Deng Xiaoping rise to the party leadership and begin the process of opening up the Chinese economy.

In the mid-1980s, his 'socialism with Chinese characteristics' gave free rein to the commercial and entrepreneurial instincts of his compatriots. The Bamboo Curtain was pushed aside and the sleeping giant awoke with a roar that echoed around the world.

In August 2010, China eclipsed Japan as the world's second

largest economy. At the current rate of growth, she will pass the United States as the world's largest economy by 2020. The importance to Australia's continuing prosperity through trade is self-evident.

The Bund, once the symbol of Britain's dominion over the Yangtze Valley, is a now a multi-lane highway called Zhongshan No. 1 Road East. Along its elegant curves the designer logos of Cartier, Zegna and Dolce & Gabbana have replaced angry Maoist wall posters denouncing American imperialism, while in the chocolate-and-white art deco Palace Hotel time now moves to an Omega beat.

The story of Australia in China is a thrilling one, peopled by many fascinating characters and packed with exciting events. And it begins right here.

PART I: 1842–1905

Chaos

'A foreign settlement has been established at Shanghai; a new
order of things has commenced in the Celestial Empire. The Indian
opium-growers and traders have flourished. London and New York
have a sure grip on Chinese commerce.'

JOHN STANLEY JAMES, WRITING AS 'THE VAGABOND'
IN THE MELBOURNE ARGUS, 1881

CHAPTER 1

Barbarians

Defying nature, the Yangtze flows 6380 kilometres from the mountains of Tibet, through the precipitous Three Gorges and across the rice-growing heartlands of central China to the rich delta plains around the most fabulous city to which it has given birth: Shanghai.

Known to the Chinese as 'the Chang', the Yangtze's watershed covers roughly half of China and includes almost half of her population. By rights, the terrain should take the river south-east to join the Mekong in Vietnam. Instead, it seeks out paths that head from west to east until it reaches the East China Sea.[1] To *yang guizi* ('foreign devils' in Mandarin), the river seemed as perverse as the people of the Middle Kingdom.*

In his 'Three Principles of the People' (nationalism, democracy, socialism),[2] Sun Yat-sen – the man revered in China today as 'the Great Forerunner of the Chinese democratic revolution'

---

* The name of China changed with each dynasty. During this period it was known as 'the Empire of the Ching'. But the common name among the Chinese populace was 'the Middle Kingdom' to signify that China was the centre of civilisation. It was also referred to as 'the Celestial Empire'.

– likened the republican struggle in China in the first part of the 20th century to the twists and turns of the Yangtze, 'sometimes to the north and sometimes to the south but in the end flows eastward and nothing can stop it. Just so the life of mankind has flowed from theocracy to autocracy and from autocracy now on to democracy and there is no way to stem the current.'

From the beginning, the Yangtze was the source of plenty and the maker of wild destruction as it traversed a dozen Chinese provinces. And in the twilight years of the Ching Dynasty it was the wealth of the Chinese interior that a grasping, colonising Britain sought to plunder in the first half of the 19th century. In August 1842, Sir Henry Pottinger, on the orders of the British Foreign Secretary Lord Palmerston and at the urging of the Scottish opium dealer William Jardine, sailed up the Yangtze with a fleet of Royal Navy warships (including the first steam-driven vessels) on the Victorian version of a trade mission.

Ten years earlier Hugh Lindsay of the East India Company had slipped into Shanghai and counted 400 junks entering the port each week in the middle of summer. 'The advantages which foreigners would derive from the liberty of trade with this place are incalculable,' he wrote in his report to the British Government. 'It is the seaport of the Yangtze River and the principal emporium of eastern Asia.'[3]

The Industrial Revolution had created huge demand among the newly emergent urban middle class in Britain for Chinese tea, silk, willow-pattern china, porcelain and other examples of *chinoiserie*. As a result, Britain had led the foreign pack in forcing the Chinese Government to permit the establishment of trading houses, or *hongs*, at Canton on the Pearl River just north of Hong Kong Island.[4] Rather than pay the Chinese in their preferred currency – the Mexican silver dollar – or indeed in any currency at all, the British insisted they exchange their products for Indian opium, the obnoxious 'foreign mud', which, although illegal in China, could easily be traded for goods or silver dollars through Chinese compradors (from the

Portuguese *compradores*) acting as intermediaries with Chinese drug syndicates.

Among the opium dealers of the early 1800s was Walter Davidson, a Scots-born Australian colonist, grazier, merchant and banker. This well-connected son of an Aberdeenshire manse arrived in Sydney as a 20-year-old in 1805 to take up a grant of 2000 prime acres (809 hectares) adjacent to John Macarthur's spread at Cowpastures between the Nepean and Georges rivers. Macarthur, the English-born soldier turned pastoralist, befriended the newcomer and they became involved in various commercial ventures.[5]

Hearing from his Scottish brethren of the immense fortunes to be made in the China trade, Davidson visited Canton in 1807 and saw the opium bonanza for himself. At that time, the East India Company was the biggest and most powerful of the drug traffickers. 'The Company', as it was known – and widely despised in Asia over its abuse of power as the virtual ruler of India – had the right to expel unauthorised British citizens from Canton. Davidson was refused permission to stay more than a few weeks.

He returned to Australia where he conceived a plan with Macarthur. On 26 January the following year, the Rum Rebellion ushered in Australia's two-year period as a rebel republic. Davidson and Macarthur defied the orders of the deposed Governor William Bligh and sailed for London with the rebel leader Major George Johnston. There, Davidson consulted the trading house of Baring & Company about how he might join the Canton drug cartel.

By coincidence, the governors of the East India Company had just ordered their staff to stop trading in opium. Davidson was invited to go back to Canton and run the narcotics business as a separate entity on behalf of The Company. Money changed hands. When Davidson set sail for the Orient in 1811, he was no longer a British citizen but a naturalised Portuguese.

Armed with his naturalisation certificate, he landed at Canton and worked there as an agent for Barings until 1816 when he established his own trading house, W. S. Davidson & Company. As he liked to say, he was 'Portuguese in Canton and British everywhere else'.[6] Davidson imported opium and cotton from India and exported tea and silver in collusion with another British trader, Thomas Dent, who passed himself off as 'the Sardinian consul'.[7]

'We were agents for all sorts of Indian produce but 90 per cent was cotton and opium,' Davidson told a House of Lords inquiry into the East India Company's role in the opium trade. 'The Company knew that I managed the opium trade. The arrangement was that every dollar I made from opium was mine and every dollar I made from cotton was theirs.'[8]

Meanwhile, the British Government, embarrassed by the East India Company's iron grip on India and points east, stripped it of its monopoly of the China trade in 1834. Gleefully, American opium dealers who had been kept on the periphery sought to compete with Jardine Matheson, Dents and the other British *hongs* for a share of the drug market. Russell & Company of Boston soon became the third largest opium house in China thanks largely to the efforts of Warren Delano II, maternal grandfather of the future president of the United States, Franklin Delano Roosevelt.[9]

The chance for Britain to seize Shanghai presented itself in 1839 when the Tao-kuang Emperor attempted to stamp out this insidious trade. 'Opium poison flowed into China and I instructed the people three times not to use it,' he wrote in an imperial edict. 'The foreigners brought it and they traded at Canton, so I gave special orders to Lin Tse-hsu to manage the matter.'

Commissioner Lin arrived in Canton with a mandate to seize all stocks of opium in the foreigners' 13 fortified 'factories' on the Pearl River waterfront. Over the next few months, he destroyed 20,000 chests containing 1.2 million kilograms of the drug, arrested 1700 Chinese opium dealers – and executed 400 of them – and confiscated 70,000 opium pipes.[10]

When Britain threatened military action, the Dragon Throne was assured by its military advisers there was nothing to fear: the United Kingdom was 'merely a handful of stones owned by Holland in the Western Ocean', the guns of barbarians' warships were too elevated to cause much damage to Chinese property, and British soldiers were so tightly uniformed that when they fell over they could not get up again.[11]

Ancient matchlocks, however, proved no match for the self-firing rifles of British troops, while Britain's armour-plated ships bombarded Chinese towns and destroyed China's cumbersome war-junks. British gunners watched in amazement as the suicidal Chinese battle fleet sailed into range to the beating of drums and the clash of cymbals, some of its ships mysteriously propelled by huge wooden paddle-wheels.

Shanghai, an ancient walled city on a mud-coloured tributary 20 kilometres from the Yangtze's estuary, fell to the British on 19 June 1842. For the next 100 years, the metropolis that would rise piecemeal out of the rich alluvial sludge would witness scenes of great drama and terrible sorrow.

Shanghai's name means 'on the sea'; indeed, it was a seaport until billions of tonnes of Yangtze sediment created a great swampy plain that extends eastwards for 16 kilometres to the East China Sea. At the confluence of the Yangtze and the Whangpoo, the island of Ching Ming, 60 kilometres in length, was built entirely by silt flowing through the river's 'nine bends of the intestine'.[12]

Shanghai had traded with Yangtze farmers, potters and weavers for two millennia, while its fishermen reaped a rich harvest from the salty waters of the Woosung and Whangpoo rivers. The Shanghainese lived peacefully, trading with Japanese junks that crossed the typhoon-tossed East China Sea. The city was far enough inland to be sheltered from the worst of the weather, while a high wall and a deep moat protected its citizens from the ravages of Japanese pirates.

Sir Henry Pottinger anchored his ships in the vast network of canals and waterways that fed the ricefields of the Yangtze Delta. The most important artery was the Grand Canal, a marvel of engineering that supplied most of Peking's rice. By blocking this canal at its crossing point with the Yangtze at Chinkiang, Pottinger had his foot on the Ching Dynasty's throat. He demanded an indemnity of three million silver dollars from Shanghainese merchants to move on. The money was scraped together and although most of the warships sailed upstream to Nanking, the blockade of the Grand Canal remained in place until the Chinese capitulated.

On 26 August 1842 the emperor's representatives signed the Treaty of Nanking on board HMS *Cornwallis* to end the First Opium War. HMS *Vindictive*, a 74-gun ship of the line, rushed the news to Australia in copies of a special edition of the *Hong Kong Gazette*.[13] Under the terms of the treaty, China ceded Hong Kong to Britain in perpetuity, opened five 'treaty ports' (Shanghai, Canton, Foochow, Amoy and Ningpo*) to British trading houses and agreed to pay 300 million taels (or ounces of silver) in reparations, including compensation to the foreign traders whose opium stocks had been destroyed in Commissioner Lin's purge.[14]

'In settling the barbarian affairs this time,' the emperor's chief negotiator wrote, 'we are governed at every hand by the inevitable and we concede that the policy is the least commendable. What we have been doing is to choose between danger and safety, not between right and wrong.'

The First Opium War was China's most ignominious defeat since the Manchu 'Tartars' crossed the Great Wall from Manchuria in 1644 and swept away the Ming Dynasty. As the treaty settlement made no mention of opium, it was still classified as contraband. 'The only object now to be desired is the legalisation of the drug trade,' Alexander Matheson, one

---

*   Canton (Guangzhou), Foochow (Fuzhou), Amoy (Xiamen) and Ningpo (Ningbo)

of the partners in Jardine Matheson, wrote on 31 July 1843, 'and of that there is no hope during the life time of the present Emperor.'[15]

Nevertheless, the opium traders were handed the perfect cover for their illicit operations. Britain demanded – and was granted – the right of extraterritoriality ('extrality' for short) under which foreigners could only be tried under the laws of their mother country.[16] They were therefore immune from Chinese justice for crimes committed on Chinese soil. Even more than Christianity and commercialism, extrality would incense the Chinese people as the ultimate abuse of the national polity.

Pottinger sent Captain George Balfour, an officer in the Madras Artillery who had proved himself an efficient administrator during the war, to Shanghai as British consul with the task of negotiating a set of Land Regulations to establish a British Concession on the banks of the Whangpoo River.[17] Balfour agreed with Pottinger's choice of a river frontage a little way upstream from the Chinese fortifications at Woosung. 'By our ships our power can be seen,' he said, referring to Palmerston's famous gunboat diplomacy, 'and if necessary, felt.'[18]

Shanghai was opened to foreign trade on 17 November 1843. Jardine Matheson, one of the instigators of the Opium War, was the first trading house to grab a piece of real estate on the waterfront. Its representative, Alexander Dallas, sailed up the Whangpoo in the fast clipper *Eliza Stewart* and registered Lot No. 1, a three-acre block next to the British Consulate on The Bund (named after the Hindustani word for embankment).[19]

Although other British companies soon followed, Balfour's bargaining with the Shanghai *taotai* Kung Mu-chiu, the Manchu's local administrator, had only just begun.[20] It was another two years before 138 acres of malarial mudflats crossed by a single wheelbarrow track were leased to Britain in perpetuity. 'The British occupation of 1842 was conducted with such tact that it left no resentment behind,' historian Arnold Wright wrote in 1908. 'Moreover, the inhabitants were naturally of a more peaceful type than the turbulent Cantonese.'[21]

The Jardine Matheson *hong* – known as the Ewo Building (meaning 'happy harmony') – didn't open for business until 1851.[22] By then, William Jardine, known to the Chinese as 'the iron-headed old rat', was well and truly dead – he passed away on 27 February 1843, three days after his 59th birthday.

The French and Americans swiftly followed the British lead with their own treaty arrangements for pieces of Shanghai. The French were ceded 164 acres between the British Concession and the walled Chinese city (then known as Nantao and now, minus the wall, as Nanshi) and the Americans 138 acres north of Soochow Creek (as the British called the Woosung River) in what became known as Hongkew. As all of these concessions were leaseholds, China theoretically retained sovereignty. However, the foreigners administered their concessions as though they were extensions of their own countries. Civilian volunteers were recruited to defend their borders.

The French treaty legalised Christianity, placing it on the same plane as Confucianism, Taoism and Buddhism. One seemingly innocuous clause granted missionaries permission to travel in the Chinese interior. The American treaty gave foreigners the right to buy land, build houses and factories and learn Chinese. The Manchu had hoped to play the European powers off against each other, but the introduction of the 'most-favoured nation' concept automatically entitled one signatory to any new privilege granted to another.

One by one the safeguards that had protected the Middle Kingdom from outside influence were violated, and with each act of surrender the Dragon Throne lost face with its Chinese subjects.[23]

George Balfour stayed in Shanghai until 1846 during which time he co-operated with Chinese officials in a vain attempt to stamp out the opium trade, even using British sailors to board a British merchant vessel and throw the bales into the

Whangpoo.[24] But there was no stopping the trading houses, which were making huge fortunes delivering opium and then filling the holds of their ships with Chinese silk or tea for the return journey. By the time the first Henley-style regatta was held on the Whangpoo in 1849, the oarsmen rowed past half a dozen British and American *hongs* which had joined Jardines on The Bund. Many of the names have since disappeared but they included Turner & Company, Dent Beale, Thomas Ridley, Dirom Gray, Holliday Wise and Gibb Livingston.[25]

During these frontier years Jardines and Dents operated a duopoly which effectively controlled the supply and price of all opium sold on the Shanghai market. The illegal trade flourished as never before, rising to almost 53,000 chests of imported opium in 1850. To the Confucian *literati* and members of the landed gentry, the opium pipe was, at least initially, a source of relaxation, a stimulus to the imagination and an aid to social intercourse. To the wharf labourer and farm worker, it was one of the few releases from a life of ceaseless toil and hunger. Inevitably, millions became enslaved by drug addiction.

The trade in misery extended to the people themselves. The least valued human life in China was the female child of a peasant family who would either be killed at birth, sold into the *mui tsai* bonded labour system to work as a servant in a Chinese household or as a prostitute in one of the 'singing houses', or at best married off for a small dowry.

After slavery was abolished in the British Empire in 1833, a lucrative traffic developed in Chinese coolies who were recruited (or when necessary 'shanghai'ed') by coolie-brokers and unscrupulous sea captains to work as indentured labour in Australia, California, Chile and Peru. Farmers in New South Wales who had access to a diminishing supply of convict labour after transportation ceased in 1840 welcomed the first shipment of coolies from Amoy to Sydney in October 1848.

Over the next six years Chinese numbers in the Australian colonies increased to 2500, with a coolie being paid £12 a year on a five-year contract, approximately half a white man's wage. During the gold rushes, the total jumped to 40,000 and by 1900 it had reached 100,000. As it was feared the Chinese would provide a pool of cheap labour which would put white men on the breadline, the importation of 'coloured' labour became a burning issue in Australian politics.[26]

On 3 August 1850 Shanghai's first newspaper made its appearance when the settlement's auctioneer Henry Shearman launched the weekly *North-China Herald*. 'It is the destiny of Shanghai to become the permanent emporium of trade between it and all the nations of the world,' Shearman observed in his first leading article. And he pledged, 'To aid by his humble efforts in effecting this grand object will be the one great aim of the editor's most strenuous exertions.'

The *Herald* was a four-page broadsheet printed on a little flat-bed press in a back street; it contained shipping movements, the names of all 157 full-time foreign residents and profiles of local Chinese officials, as well as some news items, mostly from 'the mother country'. It would soon have a very big story on its own doorstep.

The vast majority of China's 350 million people worked on the land and were vulnerable to the recurring natural calamities of flood and famine. Up to 90 per cent of the peasants owned no land at all and were prey to harsh landlords, unscrupulous rice merchants and loan sharks.

During the previous year the Yangtze had flooded in four provinces, Hupeh, Anhwei, Kiangsu and Chekiang, washing away whole villages and inundating thousands of farms. Most of the relief aid doled out by the Peking government disappeared into the pockets of Chinese officials. Millions were starving but the Manchu tax collectors still made their rounds and the usurers still demanded payment. Life for the peasants, always harsh, had become intolerable.

The pseudo-Christian Taiping Rebellion broke out in 1851 as a direct result of rural hardship. It would kill more people than any armed conflict except the Second World War – an estimated 20 million, although some modern scholars place the toll at twice that figure. With incredible ferocity, the Taiping Revolutionary Army headed north from Kwangsi province to the Yangtze, seizing the three Wuhan cities and the imperial southern capital of Nanking and putting thousands of mandarins, landowners, usurers and imperial troops to the sword.

War came to Shanghai on 7 September 1853 when the red-turbaned Small Sword rebels swept aside imperial troops and stormed into Nantao. The Small Swords were a branch of the Triad (*san he huior*), the Heaven, Earth and Man Society dedicated to destroying the Ching Dynasty and replacing it with Chinese rule. As such, they were blood brothers of the Taiping.

It was fortunate for Shanghai's foreign settlers that Hung Hsiu-ch'uan, the Taiping's Hakka leader,* refused a plea from his allies to drive the foreigners out of their riverside settlements. Instead, half a million terrified Chinese refugees fled from the countryside into the foreign concessions, sending land prices sky-high and triggering a building boom to provide accommodation for the new arrivals.

The Taiping were genuine revolutionaries whose blood-soaked legacy culminated in the Communist Revolution of 1949. Communism, Sun Yat-sen would claim in one of his 1924 lectures on the Three Principles, 'was applied in China in the time of Hung Hsiu-ch'uan. His economic system was the real thing in Communism and not mere theory.'[27]

In their manifesto, the Taiping rejected everything the Manchu had introduced to China and declared war on 'grasping

---

* The principal ethnic group of China are the Han Chinese, as distinct from her Manchu, Mongol and other minorities. Hakka people are Han Chinese who speak the Hakka language. Many settled in South China and provided revolutionary, government and military leaders.

officials and corrupt subordinates [who] strip the people of their flesh until men and women weep by the roadside'.

Taiping men eschewed the mandatory shaven head and woven queue or pigtail, and wore their hair in long tresses. They also practised a form of equality in which Taiping women had the right to sit for civil service examinations and thus become state officials. Foot-binding, opium-smoking, prostitution and slavery were strictly forbidden; land was confiscated and shared among the masses.[28]

The Taiping leader Hung Hsiu-ch'uan founded a state within the Celestial Empire, which he called 'the Heavenly Kingdom of Great Peace'. Hung had been introduced to the Gospel by a proselytising American named Issachar Roberts. He adopted the title of 'Heavenly King' and saw himself as one-third of the Holy Trinity with God and his elder brother, Jesus Christ.

Hung believed so totally in the resurrection of the soul that the word 'death' was banned from the Taiping vocabulary; people no longer died but rather 'ascended to Heaven'.[29] Some Europeans supported the Taiping on the grounds that they were semi-Christian until Roberts visited Nanking and – despite being offered a place in the Taiping hierarchy and three wives – denounced Hung's religious opinions as being 'in the main abominable in the sight of God'.[30]

Britain's aim in the Yangtze Valley was to extend trade 1000 kilometres from Shanghai to Nanking and Hankow, which would mean doing a deal with the Taiping. With their vast experience on the Indian sub-continent (and to a less successful extent in Afghanistan), no one was more adept at the game of divide and rule than Britain's colonial administrators. Sir George Bonham, the governor of Hong Kong, visited the Heavenly Capital and assured the Taiping leaders that Britain would remain strictly neutral in the Chinese civil war (and sell arms to both sides). He made it clear, however, that her armed forces would protect the lives and property of her subjects in Shanghai.[31]

Ironically, the first target of the British and American gunboats that appeared on the Whangpoo soon afterwards was not the Small Swords who were terrorising the Chinese inhabitants of the walled city, but a force of imperial troops who had camped on the muddy flats at the western extremity of the foreign concessions in defiance of an order from the British consul to keep a safe distance from the settlement.

On 4 April 1854 British and American naval forces, supported by the Shanghai Volunteer Corps, attacked the imperial encampment. Seeing a battle in progress, the Small Swords joined in – on the side of the foreigners. In the Battle of Muddy Flat, the imperial force was routed, with serious loss of face. It took another 17 months for local and foreign mercenaries hired by Shanghai merchants to expel the rebels from Nantao. The mercenaries then looted and burned down the northern and eastern districts of the Chinese city and murdered many innocent citizens, with British and French troops joining in the killing and looting.[32]

With mayhem taking place next door, British, French and American communities called a meeting at the British Consulate on 11 July 1854 to adopt a new set of Land Regulations governing the security and development of the foreign enclaves. Members were elected to the Shanghai Municipal Council, which assumed responsibility for running the concessions and maintaining law and order.

By 1857, considerable progress had been made. Many British merchants had abandoned Canton in favour of Shanghai where they felt safer than among the radical elements of South China.[33] The Bund – pronounced as it is spelled (*boond* is a later affectation[34]) – was described in that year by Wingrove Cooke, a visiting correspondent of the London *Times*, as 'a broad embankment, having on one side the wide river, with 70 square-rigged vessels lying at easy anchor in its noble reach; and on the other side the "compounds", or ornamental grounds each containing the *hongs* and the godowns of one of the principal European commercial houses'.[35]

Walking along The Bund one morning, Cooke noticed a curious meeting taking place between East and West at the Custom House, a traditional Chinese building in the *yamen* style with elaborate curved eaves. Twenty Chinese men, some with enormous plumes of pheasant feathers on their heads, had gathered outside the building. 'There are two executioners, conspicuous by their black conical caps, their dark costume, and their chains worn like a sword belt,' Cooke wrote. 'The larger one is said to be of wonderful skill in taking off heads; the smaller one excels in producing exquisite torture with the bamboo.'[36]

The *Times* man followed the *taotai*, Wu Chien-chang, into the Custom House. Incense was burning and priests chanted incantations, while mandarins in silk robes with white or red buttons on their caps knocked their heads on the ground in front of a little altar. The building had been turned into a joss-house in honour of the God of Wealth to ensure a good harvest of import and export duties.

While British officials in Shanghai smiled tolerantly at such pagan rituals, Palmerston ordered Lord Elgin, the corpulent son of the acquirer of the Greek marbles, to take another expedition to China to force the new Xianfeng Emperor, just 19 when he came to the throne, to accept the opium trade and permit Western ministers to live in Peking. In the Second Opium War, Elgin defeated the Chinese armies in the field and in 1858 concluded the Treaty of Tientsin.

Writing to his chum the Earl of Malmesbury on his return to Shanghai, he opined, 'The doctrine that every Chinaman is a knave, and manageable only by bullying and bravado, is, I venture to think, sometimes pushed a little too far in our dealings with this people.' Elgin changed his mind when an attempt to land Anglo-French envoys at Tientsin, the port east of Peking, was forcibly blocked by a brave Mongolian general, with considerable loss of European life. In retaliation, a combined force under the flags of Queen Victoria and the Emperor Louis Napoleon fought its way towards the Chinese capital in the summer of 1860.[37]

A mixed party consisting of the British interpreter Harry Parkes, the *Times* war correspondent Thomas Bowlby, five other Englishmen and 19 Sikh troopers rode ahead of the main column under a flag of truce to make arrangements for peace talks. On 18 September, they were seized by the Chinese and taken to the Forbidden City.[38] 'You instigate all the evil that your people commit,' one of his captors told Harry Parkes, who was known to the Ching Court as a hot-headed consul in Canton. 'It is time that foreigners should be taught respect for Chinese nobles and ministers.'

The 32-year-old Englishman was dragged before the Board of Inquisitors in heavy chains and interrogated, while four torturers pulled his hair, ears and whiskers. Parkes protested that he and his comrades should be treated as prisoners of war but were thrown into a filthy prison among common felons (who shared their meagre rations with them).[39]

By 6 October, the French advance had brought their forces to the gates of the Yuan ming yuan, the Garden of Perfection and Light a few kilometres east of the emperor's Summer Palace in the Western Hills outside Peking. Jesuit priests had laid out the exquisite villas, pavilions and colonnades as a showpiece of Italian baroque during the reign of the Emperor Chien Lung in the previous century.

In the absence of any resistance, troops began looting the Garden of Perfection and Light of its gold and jade and works of art.[40] When the British turned up, they joined in. 'The chief share of the plunder,' the Hong Kong-based *China Mail* reported, 'appears to have fallen to the French, who had the first ransacking of the rich ornaments, jewels, clocks and watches, the rich robes and embroidered silks, of the Son of Heaven.'[41]

The emperor fled outside the Great Wall to his hunting lodge in Jehol, leaving his brother, Prince Kung, to deal with the foreign devils. Hoping to avoid further pillage, Kung released Harry Parkes and some of his comrades. It was plain to see that the captives had been badly treated and 'unfavourable accounts' were received about the fate of the remaining prisoners. Indeed, four Englishmen, including Thomas Bowlby, and eight Sikhs, had been slowly tortured to death or beheaded.[42]

As 'a solemn act of retribution', Lord Elgin ordered the destruction of the Yuan ming yuan and the five surrounding palaces. More than 200 pavilions, halls and temples were systematically pillaged and then destroyed by fire.[43] 'You can scarcely imagine the beauty and the magnificence of the palaces we burnt,' one of the British officers, Captain Charles Gordon, wrote to his mother. 'In fact, these palaces were so large and we were so pressed for time that we could not plunder them carefully.'[44]

In Paris, Victor Hugo observed:

> One day two bandits entered the Summer Palace. One plundered, the other burned ... We Europeans are the civilised ones, and for us the Chinese are the barbarians. This is what civilisation has done to barbarism.[45]

At the same time as this special place was going up in flames, a pall of dense smoke from burning villages and farmhouses hung over the countryside around Shanghai. It heralded the approach of the Taiping Army, which had come south to find an outlet to the sea through which to receive fresh supplies of arms and ammunition. Barricades were erected at the extremities of all streets leading into the foreign concessions and the 100-strong Volunteer Corps was mobilised.[46]

The combined Allied force consisted of 1500 British, French and Sikh troops, and one small British gunboat. It was the policy of the commander-in-chief, Brigadier-General Charles Staveley, to defend Nantao, so despite the dramatic events taking place in Peking the Union flag and the Tricolour fluttered side by side with the blue dragon banners of the imperial troops.

'Happily for us, the rebels seem to have come with no other object than to get possession of the Chinese city,' the *New York*

Times correspondent reported from Shanghai. 'Wherever they met with a foreigner they treated him with marked politeness, and that even at the moment foreign troops were firing upon them from the city walls.'[47]

The Taiping were beaten back, largely by a mercenary force of foreign nationals consisting of 'runaway sailors, Manila-men [Filipinos] and foreign vagabonds', commanded by a 29-year-old American, Frederick Townsend Ward. This soldier of fortune from Salem, Massachusetts, had learned his soldiering with the mercenary leader William Walker in Mexico and the French forces in the Crimea.[48]

The Taiping, however, returned to Shanghai in strength the following year. Edwin Pickwoad, a journalist who had arrived from Melbourne the previous August to become the first secretary of the Shanghai Municipal Council, was probably the author of several dispatches published in *The Argus* at that time. 'We have had warlike and stirring times of it,' one article began.

> The imperialist troops stationed at Shanghai, together with a fleet of war-junks, proceeded up the creeks and river until they came up with the Taiping when several fights ensued, with great massacre on both sides. For a time they were repulsed but a strong band of marauders managed to approach within four or five miles of Shanghai, which roused the foreign residents from their lethargy, so that the naval and military authorities issued a notice to regulate the defence of the settlement in case of attack.[49]

Edwin Pickwoad originally hailed from St Kitts in the West Indies, where his family were sugar planters. He lived in style at the Astor House Hotel with his wife Janet and their children. In 1860, he had taken over the weekly *North-China Herald* following the death of Henry Shearman and would soon launch a daily edition, the *North-China Daily News*, for which he borrowed the *Herald*'s editorial slogan: 'Impartial Not Neutral'.

When rent payers complained that the council was too secretive in its deliberations, Pickwoad the municipal secretary agreed to hand reports of the council's proceedings to Pickwoad the publisher for inclusion in his newspapers. His readers then complained not only about the glaring conflict of interest but also about the brevity of the reports, which told them virtually nothing about the government of the settlement.[50]

There was unanimity, however, about the seriousness of the Taiping threat. Shanghai's defences were strengthened by the erection of three-metre-high redoubts placed in zigzag formation around the foreign concessions, while no fewer than eight British warships were anchored off The Bund.[51] Russia offered Li Hung-chang, a 39-year-old aide to the Manchu governor of Anhwei province, the services of 10,000 troops. Li declined the offer, evidently thinking the Russians might prove more dangerous than the Taiping.[52]

Instead, he raised a local militia of 6500 Chinese soldiers and with the help of the 'Foreign Army Corps' under the command of 'the notorious Colonel Ward, so-called',[53] routed the Taiping in January 1862 after the heaviest snowfalls in living memory immobilised their poorly clad soldiers. Ward led his force to several more victories, giving birth to the legend of the 'Ever Victorious Army' before being mortally wounded in a battle south of Shanghai in September of that year. He was buried with the full military honours of a Manchu bannerman.

Li Hung-chang's imperial army fought under the command of a Scottish surgeon, Dr Halliday Macartney, an able soldier who saved Shanghai from another Taiping raid in late 1862.[54] But Macartney had no interest in continuing the campaign, claiming he had 'only taken to military work to fill up my time while I am learning the language'.[55] Li Hung-chang asked General Staveley to recommend a British officer to take command of the Ever Victorious Army. He nominated Charles 'Chinese' Gordon, one of the soldiers who had looted and burned the Summer Palace. Gordon, now a major in the Royal Engineers, knew the

Shanghai battlefields well: he had surveyed the hinterland for the Taiping campaign and had been responsible for building the city's zigzag defences.[56]

Having taken over the 3900-strong EVA in February 1863, a few days after his 30th birthday, Gordon was appalled at its lack of discipline and immediately banned women and opium-smoking. Hundreds deserted rather than submit to his iron rule. To bring his force up to strength, he enlisted 2000 Taiping who had been taken captive and were willing to swap sides in exchange for their lives.[57]

Dressing his men in dark green jackets, knickerbockers and turbans, and arming them with American Remington rifles, hand grenades and trench mortars, Gordon led the revitalised EVA into battle carrying only a small cane which came to be known as 'Gordon's magic wand of victory'.[58] His army success-fully fought the Taiping in the myriad creeks and canals around Shanghai, employing pontoons to carry its artillery across the waterways. Altogether, it was credited with 33 victories against the rebels, although Taiping survivors claimed to have defeated them several times.[59]

By 1864, the Taiping capital of Nanking was besieged by the Manchu's Grand Battalions running into hundreds of thou-sands of troops, and the population was suffering from disease and starvation. Hung Hsiu-ch'uan, who had refused to permit the city to be provisioned in advance of the siege, issued an edict that people should eat a *pot pourri* of weeds and grasses, which he described as 'manna from Heaven'. After eating a handful of 'manna' himself, he fell ill and died on 1 June 1864 at the age of 50.[60]

In the Forbidden City, an artful concubine named Tzu Hsi had taken power as co-regent on behalf of her infant son Tsai-ch'un following the death of the Xianfeng Emperor in 1861. She awarded Li Hung-chang China's highest military honour, the Order of the Star, 'a yellow riding-jacket to be worn on his person, and a peacock's feather to be carried in his cap'.[61]

Charles Gordon was also decorated with a Yellow Jacket, whereas Halliday Macartney had to make do with the Precious Star medal and Double Dragon breast badge. With the help of Li Hung-chang, he then began a money-spinning career in the Chinese diplomatic service, just one of many Europeans who would prop up the decaying Ching Dynasty.

Meanwhile, the French had dropped out of the Shanghai Municipal Council and established their own *Conseil d'Administration Municipale* to advise the all-powerful French consul-general on matters concerning their concession. French-town (as the Anglo-Saxons called it) was intent on developing its own character, including the beautiful tree-lined boulevards that would give Shanghai its nickname 'the Paris of the East'. Like its namesake on the Seine, Frenchtown would become a combination of stately public buildings, comfortable villas and mansion apartment blocks, with a red-light district to rival Montmartre. 'Blood Alley', as the Rue Chu Pao San was known, became synonymous with nightclubs, prostitution and brawling sailors.

In 1863 the British and American zones were merged into the self-governing International Settlement.[62] Land which had sold for an average of £50 an acre in 1852 was now changing hands for £10,000. 'The present El Dorado of commercial men seems to be China,' *The Times* reported. 'More money has, it is said, been made in China during the last five years than in all the years of the East India Company's monopoly.'[63]

There were no barriers separating the concessions, so many British citizens moved into Frenchtown, where they patron-ised taverns with names like The Crown and Anchor and The Prince of Wales.[64] Foreign families also overflowed into the pleasant Chinese pastures west of Tibet Road, where they built mock-Tudor homes and antebellum mansions more often seen in the Home Counties or the Deep South of America.

During the Taiping Rebellion, foreigners armed with shotguns, rifles and revolvers had strengthened their grip on

Shanghai through methods which even the notorious Frederick Ward described as 'lying, swindling and smuggling'.[65] The boundaries of the foreign enclaves were redrawn and new treaty arrangements enforced to suit Western requirements.

The ending of the Taiping menace, however, heralded a downturn in Shanghai's fortunes when many thousands of refugees returned to their homes in the Yangtze Valley. Whole streets of newly-built houses in the northern districts of Chapei and Yangtzepoo suddenly emptied, new office buildings were left half-finished, godowns and wharves in Hongkew stood deserted. Speculators lost their investments and there was a period of financial panic.[66]

'In Shanghai, great destitution prevails among the lower classes of foreigners,' readers of the Hobart *Mercury* were informed in 1865. 'There being little or no outlet for rowdyism as formerly, and great stagnation in all branches of commerce, no means of relief are at hand and the distress is widely felt. Even the opportunities for crime are gradually being curtailed, and we can do no more than hope for better days.'[67]

Crime might have been curtailed but forbidden pleasures of one sort or another proliferated. Sir Harry Parkes, knighted for his bravery at Peking and installed as British consul of Shanghai, informed a meeting of rent payers in 1864 that out of 10,000 Chinese houses in the foreign concessions a total of 668 were brothels, 'while opium and gambling houses were beyond counting'.

The opium trade had been legalised in the 1860 Convention of Peking, which ended the Second Opium War. Fast opium clippers could now anchor off The Bund with impunity. Jardine Matheson's books for the financial year 1863–4 show that opium accounted for almost two-thirds of its business – little wonder the Duke of Somerset, following a visit to Shanghai, described the city in the House of Lords in 1869 as 'a sink of iniquity'.[68]

Shanghai was also a breeding ground for revolution. One anonymous Taiping survivor had moved into the International

Settlement, where he was safe from Manchu agents. He admitted to a visiting journalist that he was afraid to enter the Chinese city for fear of abduction and torture at the hands of the *taotai*. Dressed in a long blue brocaded garment, he offered his visitor a glass of Bollinger champagne and a cigar. 'We are the true owners of the land,' he said.

> We are the people of China and the Tartars should be our helots. Such traditions as ours sink deep into the hearts of the people – they are not obliterated or forgotten in a day; they go down from generation to generation. The grinding taxes, the squeezing which people suffer, are inflicted by aliens. The government mandarins are all thieves. No! We Taipings do not love the foreigners much, but we love the government less.[69]

Other Taiping veterans were scattered throughout South China. Many sought sanctuary in Hong Kong or the Western enclaves in treaty ports. Hung Chun-fui, a prince of the doomed Heavenly Kingdom, fled to the British colony when imperial forces captured Nanking. For almost 40 years, he plotted the downfall of the Ching Dynasty, joining forces with the Australian-born Chinese revolutionary Tse Tsan Tai in an anti-Ching revolt at Canton.[70] Known in Australia as James See, Tse was the son of a Grafton storekeeper, just one among the thousands of Chinese who flocked to the Australian goldfields and then returned home to fight the Manchu tyrants.[71]

The importance of the 14-year Taiping Rebellion in the history of modern China is rarely appreciated but cannot be overemphasised. The farming heartland of the Celestial Empire had been devastated during the civil war; government institutions, marketplaces and private dwellings in six provinces had been destroyed and the lives of their inhabitants shattered. Despite their twisted religious beliefs, the Taiping's ideas on agrarian reform had sown the seeds of revolution among the teeming peasant population of South China.[72]

Indeed, the ebb and flow of migration across the Pacific to Hawaii and North America and down to Singapore, the East Indies and Australia had been largely governed by the fortunes of the Taiping Rebellion. And it would be the commitment of these legions of 'overseas Chinese' – from tycoons to prospectors to laundry men and noodle makers – who would advance the revolutionary cause in the dangerous years ahead.

CHAPTER 2

Distorted Images

The first duty of Chinese immigrants once they reached the bewildering shores of the Australian colonies was to send money back to the homeland to help their families survive the deprivations of civil war, famine, flood and Manchu taxes. Sometimes they returned home for brief visits on the steamships that plied between Chinese and Australian ports.

These were the first tenuous links between two wildly disparate cultures. Long before George 'Chinese' Morrison, W. H. Donald, Eleanor Hinder, H. J. Timperley or any of the other white Australians who carved out their careers in China ever reached the Middle Kingdom, Chinese returnees were regaling their families and friends with stories about life among the foreign devils in Sydney and Melbourne, or in one of the many towns and settlements that had sprung up around the goldfields, notably Bathurst, Ballarat, Bendigo and Ararat.

In 1854 more than 10,000 Chinese miners joined the gold rush.[1] Indeed, a group of Southern Chinese miners en route from the South Australian port of Robe to the central Victorian goldfields discovered one of the world's richest shallow alluvial deposits in a spring near Ararat.

By 1858, the Chinese had set up a number of secret societies, or 'Yee Hings', the most popular of which was the Hung Men brotherhood, or the Chinese Masonic Society.[2] Despite the challenges presented by a strange and hostile land, members of the celestial diaspora were strictly divided into clans and the secret societies kept secrets from each other as much as from the authorities.

The most influential Australian Chinese of the early revolutionary period was Loong Hung Pung, who was born in Canton around 1831 and who left his wife and two young daughters to join the prospectors in 1858. Arriving on the Western Plains of New South Wales, he opened a store in Howick Street, Bathurst, to buy gold from his compatriots and provide a forum for his anti-Manchu views.

According to Taiwanese sources, he was 'the head of the secret societies in Australia and advocated opposition to the Manchu and restoration of the Han people while advocating fairness and freedom'.[3]

Loong would sit on a high stool in his store, 'a man of fine features, pale as wax, with only a light slanting of the eyes, a high forehead, surmounted by a silk embroidered cap, from which a long pigtail escaped down his back over his embroidered robe, a sparse moustache in which you could count the hairs and a long tuft of beard on the chin'.[4]

Loong wrote a pamphlet entitled 'The Reconstruction of China as a Modern State', which was circulated among anti-Manchu activists. Sun Yat-sen supposedly drew upon this work in drafting his famous Three Principles of the People in 1903. 'Sun Yat-sen procured a copy of Loong's great masterpiece,' Vivian Chow, an Australian-born Chinese journalist, claims, 'and started to copy and transpose it. He was unlucky to lose his copy in a fire, and could not procure another, though he tried hard.'[5]

While it is a fact that the library containing Sun's collection of books and manuscripts burned down around 1924, Chow's claim seems unlikely. Indeed, Sun indicated that the Three

Principles were based on Lincoln's Gettysburg Address with its characterisation of democracy as 'government of the people, by the people, for the people'. No copy of 'The Reconstruction of China' remains in existence, so it is impossible to compare it with Sun's famous work.

Nevertheless, Loong is an intriguing figure in the revolutionary pantheon and provides a link with the three most active Australian Chinese revolutionaries, Tse Yet Chong, known in Australia as John See, and two of his sons. Tse Yet Chong was born in Kaiping County, Kwangtung, in 1831 and settled in Sydney with his wife in the 1860s. He worked as a merchant for an import–export company called the Tai Yick (Taiyi) Firm at 39 Sussex Street.[6]

One of his sons, Tse Tsan Tai, published a memoir, *The Chinese Republic: The Secret History of the Revolution*, based primarily on extracts from his diaries for the years 1890–1911. The book strongly disputes Sun's claims to have fathered the revolution and gives much of the credit to the author and his family. He says that Chinese secret societies in Australia were in touch with the Taiping rebels and, following their defeat, joined forces with a variety of revolutionary factions in Hong Kong and Canton. Chesney Duncan, a British newspaper editor who wrote a biography of Tse Tsan Tai, had no doubts about Tse's place in revolutionary history. He called him '*the* Liberator of the Chinese people'.

Tse Tsan Tai, one of six children, was born in Sydney on 16 May 1872. The family moved to Grafton, where his father opened a general store and joined an anti-Manchu secret society founded by Loong Hung Pung. It was called 'the Revolutionary and Independence Society of Australian Chinese'.[7]

Tse Tsan Tai attended Grafton High School and was a member of the Anglican Church. He was baptised James See on 1 November 1879 in Grafton's Christ Church Cathedral by Bishop Greenway, son of the convict-architect Francis Greenway. The bishop was Tse's godfather and Tse attributes his 'strict moral rectitude and conduct in life' to Greenway's influence and his Grafton schooling.[8]

However, the revolutionary beliefs that were to bring him into contact with the exiled Taiping prince Hung Chun-fui and Sun Yat-sen himself were instilled at home. In his memoir, he says he was exposed from an early age to anti-Manchu thinking by his father who vowed to return to China and overthrow the Ching Dynasty.[9]

The most famous Australian Chinese of the period was another Cantonese, Quong Tart, who was born in 1850 at Hsinning in the Pearl River Delta. His father, a dealer in ornamental wares, had no intention of emigrating to Australia or anywhere else, but Quong was born with an unquenchable wanderlust. Although brought up to believe that every European was a ferocious, red-headed man-eater, he was determined to see the wider world, especially the Australian goldfields.

Quong was only nine years old when he was given permission to accompany his uncle who was taking a band of miners to Australia. The idea was that Quong would be trained as their interpreter. However, the little boy had made up his mind to try his luck as a prospector. In 1859, Percy Simpson leased the great alluvial area on the Braidwood goldfields of New South Wales known as Bell's Paddock, where he employed hundreds of Chinese miners. Quong Tart accompanied Simpson around the claims as interpreter.[10]

Friction between Chinese and European miners in New South Wales and Victoria culminated in the riots at Lambing Flat in 1860–61 in which thousands of Chinese were driven off the diggings in the belief that they were guilty of everything from muddying the waterholes to driving down the value of labour to working on the Sabbath.

Both Victoria and New South Wales enacted laws to limit Chinese immigration in defiance of Article 5 of the 1860 Convention of Peking which stipulated that Chinese 'choosing to take service in the British Colonies or other parts beyond the seas, are to be at perfect liberty to enter into engagements with British subjects for that purpose, and to ship themselves and their families in British vessels at the open ports of China'.[11]

When Quong Tart was old enough to swing a pick, he started work on the goldfields and found, in the words of his Australian wife Margaret, 'it was all work and very little gold'. He lived in Thomas Forsyth's store at Bell's Creek and was adopted by the family of Percy Simpson whose wife Alice taught him English and converted him to Christianity.[12]

Quong's Australian guardians encouraged him to acquire a share in some of the Braidwood gold claims and in 1872 the 'Mining News' section of the *Sydney Morning Herald* reported, 'We hear that a very rich reef has been discovered at Bell's Creek by Mr Quong Tart.'[13] Two years later, it said with reference to gold seams in the same reef, 'Some of these leaders, though narrow, are exceedingly rich: large returns have already been obtained from Quong Tart's claim.'[14]

Just four months later on 30 July 1874, the revolutionary Loong Hung Pung died in Bathurst at the age of 43. 'The deceased had been in business for many years,' the *Bathurst Times* reported, 'and, it is said, had accumulated a considerable sum of money. He was one of the most intelligent Chinamen that ever settled in the town and was altogether a man much respected among his brother celestials.' Sadly, that respect didn't extend to the town's larrikin element, which turned up in force at the cemetery to witness 'the strange ceremonies which prevail among the natives of the "flowery land" when burying their dead'. There followed 'about as disgraceful a scene as perhaps ever occurred in a Christian community'.

The six Chinese pallbearers had to fight their way through 'a body of ruffians who call themselves civilised men' to reach the grave. After the coffin was lowered into the ground, a couple of Loong's compatriots were almost pushed in after it. 'The crowd seemed to forget all decency and went forward on to one end of the grave when the Chinamen, evidently disgusted as well as frightened, abandoned all attempts to conclude their service and hurried away from the spot. It was a pitiable spectacle to see the poor Heathens thus prevented by Christians from paying their last tribute of respect to the dead.'[15]

Such were the conflicting images of Australia that were relayed back to China. While a young man like Quong Tart might make his fortune with the help of an Australian family, it was also a place where the Chinese were badly treated and needed to be on their guard.

Australians and Chinese faced each other across a great cultural and political divide. Many of the images presented to either side were distorted by ignorance and prejudice. In China, the people believed they were racially and culturally superior to their uninvited and unwelcome guests. They were amazed at the barbarians' sense of entitlement and their strange religious beliefs, which described Jesus Christ as the Son of God when it was known that the Son of Heaven resided in the Forbidden City. In a land of ancestor worship, it also seemed incomprehensible that the deceased could be burning in hellfire simply because they had failed to recognise Christ as their saviour.

The Nobel Prize-winning American novelist Pearl Buck, who was raised in China at the turn of the century, was as confused by the Virgin birth as the Chinese who 'had no sympathy for Mary, and felt sorry for Joseph', whom they regarded as a cuckold.

Li Hung-chang, the rising star of the Chinese diplomatic corps, admitted he found the belief in Jesus baffling. 'Why, that man's life was a failure, and he was actually crucified at the end of it,' he told a British army officer. 'Now, crucifixion is a very painful death, besides being a degrading form of punishment. How can you call yourselves followers of such a man?'[16]

Li looked up to no one: he was well over six feet tall, with long limbs, a drooping Manchu moustache, 'very small, bright and scrutinising eyes', and a brilliant academic mind. Born in 1823 in the province of Anhwei adjacent to Shanghai, he was China's leading moderniser in everything except politics. His motive was to uphold the Ching Dynasty while getting fabulously wealthy himself.[17] Li never hesitated to line his own pockets and the opportunity to do so on a grand scale came in 1870 when he was appointed viceroy of Chihli, the metropolitan or home province around Peking. As commissioner for the northern ports, he negotiated trade agreements with foreigners, particularly the Russians, who rewarded him handsomely.

Within the Confucian elite, Li became the prime mover of the 'Self-Strengthening' movement to restore the Ching Dynasty to its pre-barbarian glory. His strategy, as outlined in a memorial to the throne, was for China to bide her time, avoid war with the West and, with 'extreme and continued caution', build up her own armed forces for the final struggle. His first industrial venture in 1865 was to build the Kiangnan Arsenal upriver from Shanghai to provide the Chinese forces with arms and munitions. Seven years later, he founded the China Merchants Steam Navigation Company, which soon had a fleet of 18 steamships with distinctive yellow-and-black funnels flying the Chinese flag out of Shanghai.[18]

In the Great Famine of 1878, the crops of Chihli, Shansi and Honan failed for the second year running; people stripped bark from the trees and, *in extremis*, 'ate grass and one another'.[19] Li arranged for grain from the south to be shipped north to the stricken provinces in his steamers.

While fighting the Taiping around Shanghai, Li had bought several blocks of land in Huashan Road, one of the main arteries for transporting soldiers from the Whangpoo to the front and members of his family were soon residing there in Western-style mansions. He also accumulated big interests in mining, banking and the new electric telegraph system. He opened the first cotton cloth mill in Shanghai, and at one time owned all of the city's big stores and money-brokerage firms.[20]

Most Chinese, however, were slow to appreciate the gifts that the West was bestowing on them. The 'fire-wheel carriage', or railway engine, was the most monstrous of all foreign innovations.[21] In 1876, Shen Pao-chen, the viceroy then ruling Shanghai for the Manchu, purchased the first little 20-kilometre railway line opened by British merchants from Shanghai to Woosung and had the rails ripped up after the local people expressed violent opposition to the 'iron dragon' playing havoc with the *feng shui* (or geomancy) and disturbing the spirits of the ancestors. As Shen shrewdly explained to the emperor, if China were to control her own modernisation, the British must not be allowed to own even one Chinese railway line.[22]

When John Stanley James, a wandering scribe known as 'The Vagabond',[23] landed at Shanghai after a 73-day voyage from Sydney in the collier brig *Woodbine* in 1881, he found that the West was indeed challenging traditional China. 'A foreign settlement has been established at Shanghai; a new order of things has commenced in the Celestial Empire,' he wrote. 'The Indian opium-growers and traders have flourished. London and New York have a sure grip on Chinese commerce.'[24]

The 'new order of things' had forced the Chinese to allow foreign imports to flood the country, while the dour Ulsterman Robert Hart had turned the Imperial Maritime Customs Service – the Ching's main source of revenue – into a powerful instrument of foreign domination.[25]

John James was an extraordinary character who had exposed social injustice in Australia in a series of articles in *The Argus* and *Sydney Morning Herald* after living as an undercover reporter in migrant hostels, visiting the goldfields and even getting a job inside Pentridge Jail.

He had been in Shanghai just a few days and was enjoying the hospitality of the New York-born Dutchman DeWitt Clinton Jansen, mine host of the sprawling Astor House Hotel which occupied an entire block across Garden Bridge in Hongkew, when he noted more pleasing Western influences:

There is nothing 'shoddy' here. There have been no such sudden jumps as from bush shanties, from rough-and-ready station life, to Darling Point or St Kilda – from calico dresses, mutton and damper to Government House garden parties, diamonds and fine linen. Shanghai ladies dress most elegantly, and with exquisite taste. As one sees them go rolling by in their close broughams on the Bund, or Bubbling Well Road, of an afternoon, not New York, Paris or London can turn out better-dressed or more refined looking women.

One night James went in search of the kind of Chinese depravity that figured prominently in the minds of Western fiction writers and the sermons of evangelical missionaries. Armed with a revolver and accompanied by a Chinese guide, the intrepid reporter tracked down the opium trade, 'one of the cornerstones of Shanghai's prosperity', to a bazaar in the walled Chinese city where men lounged around in small cubicles smoking the drug, some singly, some in couples, others in parties.

'"Look, Chinee woman," said the guide. Well, it is true we did see Chinese women, but not one smoking,' James writes. 'They were merely accompanying their husbands, in some cases having their children with them, and partaking of tea and confections, while the lord of their bosom soothed his soul with opium.'[26]

Upstairs, James went through long galleries where men came 'to take a smoke as a refresher, the same as we go into a hotel for a brandy and soda'. He reached the conclusion that the majority of smokers 'did not take opium to an injurious extent, but that it is a habit which may become a vice like drinking'. He came away 'amused that the text for a moral lesson on Chinese depravity should have so lamentably fizzled out'.[27]

Manchu justice was an entirely different matter. James discovered that civil and criminal cases among the 300,000 Chinese citizens living or working in the International Settlement were settled with medieval ferocity at what was called 'the Mixed Court'. This judicial hybrid had been set up in 1864 by a man who had personal experience of Manchu methods – Sir Harry Parkes – and would later become the source of serious trouble between foreigners and their reluctant hosts. Beneath the baking hot tin roof of an unpretentious redbrick building on Chekiang Road, a Chinese magistrate officiated with the assistance of a Chinese-speaking European consular official acting as 'assessor'.[28]

The court could impose prison sentences up to 20 years and order up to one thousand strokes with a thin bamboo rod for men and up to 50 blows with a leather strap for women. Prisoners found guilty of capital offences were sent to the city magistrate for sentence, usually decapitation by sword. The most horrendous punishment – not abandoned until 1905 – was 'death by slicing', known as *lingchi* or 'the death of a thousand cuts', so precise that it requires no further description.

At the Mixed Court, Chinese policemen, plaintiffs, witnesses and prisoners milled around, while court officials called 'runners' served the magistrate with cups of tea, relit his water-pipe, browbeat witnesses and did deals with the prisoners' families and friends for preferential treatment.[29]

Some of the accused were caged in wooden pens on either side of a dirty passage, 'cooped up like fowls' in John James's words, with *kangs* – large square wooden collars – padlocked around their necks like a pillory.[30] The weight of the *kang* depended on how well the runners had been bribed by the prisoner's family – the wood might be quite light but could also be heavy enough to strangle him unless supported with both hands. Strips of paper were posted across the *kang* from back to front listing the prisoner's offence.

Male defendants accused of petty thieving were tied together by their queues, each carrying the article he was alleged to have stolen.[31] Throughout the proceedings, they knelt on the bare wooden floor in front of a hostile mob. If found guilty, the prisoner was placed in a *kang* and forced to walk up and down for several hours every day at the scene of his crime, plagued by flies in summer and icy winds in winter.

At night such prisoners – with the *kangs* still around their necks – were corralled behind bamboo bars at the city jail, dependent on relatives or friends for food and any extra comforts. Their wild, unkempt appearance as they crouched together for the night in their filthy, foul-smelling cage reminded one visitor of 'a den of wild animals'.[32]

The image of the devious, corrupt and barbaric Oriental was further inflamed in the Western mind by stories of infanticide, foot-binding, castration, teeth-filing and the *mui tsai* enslavement of young girls. The Australian journalist Dr George Ernest Morrison admits in his classic work *An Australian in China* that he went to China in February 1894 'possessed with the strong racial antipathy to the Chinese common to my countrymen'.[33]

Dressed in Chinese clothes with a pigtail attached to the inside of his hat, Morrison set off from Shanghai on an epic 2400-kilometre voyage up the Yangtze as far as Chungking on his overland journey to Rangoon. He spoke no Chinese, had no interpreter or companion and was unarmed. His life depended on the good faith of the Chinese people (and the expertise of his Chinese boatmen to run the rapids in the great Yangtze gorges). Morrison's experiences completely changed his mind: his antipathy towards the Chinese gave way to a feeling of 'lively sympathy and gratitude'.

China was such a novelty that Australians who visited Shanghai invariably had their experiences recorded in the press back home. Dr Walter Roth, protector of Aboriginals in Queensland and former science master at Brisbane Grammar School, described the twisted paradox of East–West relations after making the obligatory visit to an opium house. On the first floor he found Chinese playing billiards and ten-pin bowling, while the upstairs tiers were devoted to opium-smoking lounges.

'Here among the chattering crowds of men and women sweltering in the fumes of opium, many engaged in sipping less sensuous tea, were two Europeans, two "foreign devils" allowed to wander or to stay unmolested – two outcasts in the very midst of 500 of the elect,' he wrote.

> On my departure I could hardly refrain from wondering at the decorum exhibited throughout the building, as well as at the courtesy, forbearance and hospitality which these people extended to us: for the moment, reversing the conditions, I changed East for West, two Chinese among half-a-thousand Europeans, and alcohol in the place of opium – alas! the heathen by a long way had the advantage of the Christian.[34]

Outside the precincts of Shanghai city, Roth took drives to the Tea Gardens and the Bubbling Well (bubbling with marsh gas), and made a trip around the network of rivers, creeks and canals in a houseboat. On a raft in midstream, he watched a fisherman using cormorants to catch fish, 'speaking to them like so many children, sending them into the water, and after they dive, despoiling them of the fish they have been trained to procure'.[35]

To prevent the birds from swallowing the catch, a small ring had been placed around each neck, making the cormorant the perfect metaphor for the Chinese people – squeezed by the Manchu on the one hand and strangled by the foreign devils on the other. Roth's abiding memory of Shanghai was of the vivid contrast between the hard-working Chinese labourer and the European 'who indulged in all those comforts, pleasures and luxuries which his means deny him in the old country'.

Roth had just returned to Australia when the First Sino-Japanese War, the most traumatic event in Asia of the latter half of the 19th century, erupted on the Korean Peninsula. The conflict would have immense consequences for every nation on the Pacific Rim, including Australia and New Zealand. It provided the first proof that Japan, under the Meiji Emperor and equipped with the most modern army and navy in Asia, had embarked on a ruthless expansionist course, one that would ultimately lead to the loss of millions of lives.[36]

The war also confirmed what the Confucian *literati* and a growing number of Chinese merchants and students already knew to be true: that their Manchu rulers, once a proud, warrior race, were now decadent, foolhardy and fallible. China's defeat at the hands of the Japanese would deal a crushing blow to the nation's *amour propre*. It would become one of the main driving forces behind the Chinese Revolution.[37]

CHAPTER 3

Mission Massacre

The Hermit Kingdom of Korea had long been a Chinese vassal state but for many years Japan had persistently and deliberately challenged the Ching's position. Despite the best efforts of Li Hung-chang and his protégé General Yuan Shi-kai to find a compromise, war broke out on 1 August 1894 after Japan sent an expeditionary force of 8000 troops to Korea to support a Japanese-inspired rebellion against the throne.

Viceroy Li was ordered by the Dowager Empress Tzu Hsi to gather all of China's forces together 'to root the *wujen* [the 'dwarves', as the Manchu called the Japanese] out of their lairs'.[1] The very size of the Chinese population – 350 million compared with Japan's 46 million – should have ensured victory. There was a similar advantage in terms of men at arms: China's standing army numbered one million, compared with Japan's 270,000.

The Japanese, however, had invested wisely in the latest Western arms and warships, their army had been styled on the Prussian model and their navy on the Royal Navy, whereas the Chinese war machine was riddled with corruption at the highest levels. Members of Li Hung-chang's own family had pocketed funds allocated to buying explosives and had packed shell casings with sand, while Tzu Hsi had reputedly spent the naval estimates reconstructing the Summer Palace.[2] (With delicious irony, she built a marble houseboat as an entertainment pavilion. It remains there today.)

In the first battle of the war the Japanese routed a Chinese force of 3000 at the northern Korean city of Pyongyang. Two days later the Japanese Navy easily won the Battle of the Yalu on the Korean border with Manchuria. Chinese gunners found that sacks which should have contained gunpowder were full of rice and many of their cannon balls were made of wood and painted black to resemble the real thing. Japanese forces then crossed into Manchuria and attacked Li's favourite defence project, the strategic warm-water anchorage of Port Arthur, which fell with surprising ease on 21 November.[3]

Discovering the heads of Japanese prisoners with their noses and ears cut off, the Japanese massacred Chinese troops and some 2000 civilians. 'The defenceless and unarmed inhabitants were butchered in their houses and their bodies unspeakably mutilated,' Canadian war correspondent James Creelman reported in the *New York World*. 'There was an unrestrained reign of murder which continued for three days. The whole town was plundered with appalling atrocities.'[4]

Westerners in Peking and Shanghai speculated that China's crumbling military supremacy might bring down the Ching Dynasty and lead to the creation of a new royal line, the House of Li Hung-chang. Since 'the Great Li', as he was called, was too old at 71 to assume the Dragon Throne and his only son was retarded, the most likely candidate for emperor was his nephew, the self-styled 'Prince Li'.[5]

Tzu Hsi saw the danger and promptly made 'The Great Li' the scapegoat for the catastrophe that had befallen their country. He was stripped of his Yellow Jacket and dismissed from office.[6] Nor was he permitted to retire gracefully. When the Japanese crossed the Yellow Sea in February 1895 and seized the important port of Weihaiwei on the Shantung Peninsula, Li was ordered to negotiate an 'honourable' settlement with the enemy. Tzu Hsi reasoned that, if necessary, he could be blamed not only for having lost the war but also for having lost the peace.

In the Treaty of Shimonoseki of April 1895 China ceded the island of Formosa, the key port of Kiaochow on the Shantung Peninsula and the even more important Port Arthur in Manchuria to Japan. In addition, she lost control of Korea and agreed to pay an indemnity of 230 million ounces of silver, six times the annual income of the Japanese Government at that time.[7] The terms of the settlement would have been even harsher if Li Hung-chang had not been shot in the face by a Japanese fanatic while on his way to sign a draft of the treaty.

Even so, Japan's triumph was short-lived. In a blatantly racist response, France, Germany and Russia – the Tripartite Powers – forced the Japanese to relinquish most of their gains, including the Shantung Peninsula, which was colonised by Germany to give the Kaiser 'a place in the sun', and the great prize of Port Arthur, which the Russian fleet forcibly occupied soon afterwards.

Despite the so-called Triple Intervention, the Japanese had gained the same privileges as Western powers in China, including the right to manufacture products in the treaty ports.[8] Japanese immigrants swarmed into Shanghai and the district of Hongkew throbbed with the whirr and clatter of new Japanese-owned textile mills and factories producing goods with cheap Chinese labour. As a sign of the times, Hongkew was nicknamed 'Little Tokyo'. The Japanese were now a major force in Shanghai life and were soon agitating for representation on the Municipal Council.

The most immediate effect of China's humiliation in the Sino-Japanese War was the breakdown of law and order in many parts of the Celestial Empire, triggering outbreaks of violence against foreigners. The heaviest blows fell on missionaries who were spreading the Gospel in remote parts of the interior.

Between 1888 and 1900 a total of 81 missionaries – 41 men and 40 women – arrived in China from Australia to join hundreds of evangelists from Britain, the United States and Germany, and Catholics from France, Spain and Italy.[9] Two of the Australians were sisters, 24-year-old Nellie and 22-year-old Topsy Saunders, who arrived at the Anglican mission station at Kucheng, south of Shanghai, from Melbourne in December 1893 to join a third Australian, Annie Gordon, from Ipswich, Queensland.

The Saunders sisters made rapid progress in their Chinese language studies and were sent into the field. 'Your two ladies, Miss Nellie Saunders and Miss Topsy Saunders, are here and again at work,' the Reverend Robert Stewart, the superintending missionary at Kucheng, wrote to the Church Missionary Association in Melbourne on 18 June 1895.

> Miss Nellie is in charge of two classes of charming little boys from 12 to 16 years old, picked out from the whole district as giving special promise of future usefulness. Miss Topsy is located at a place called Sek-Chek-Du, about 12 miles north from here. Miss Elsie Marshall is with her. They are in charge of all the women workers, covering an immense area of about 300 square miles. She has women's classes, girls' and boys' schools, a little dispensary and any amount of visiting; people coming to her and she going to them. They are both very happy, and our only wish is that you will send us some more like-minded.[10]

Dr Stewart was pleased with the progress of the Kucheng mission, 140 kilometres from the treaty port of Foochow in the eastern province of Fukien. A total of 2212 Chinese had been converted to Christianity and 30 Chinese teachers recruited to provide a Christian education for their children. It was now the height of summer and to escape the punishing heat of the lowlands, Stewart had taken his family and a number of missionaries connected to the Anglican Church Missionary Society to live in bungalows collectively known as 'The Sanatorium' at the hillside village of Huashan.

The Taiping's successes of the 1850s had forced the Ching Court to grant a certain amount of autonomy to its viceroys in order to raise militia armies to defeat them. This form of regionalisation, coupled with defeat at the hands of the Japanese, had drastically weakened Peking's hold on the provinces. As its authority waned, even the lowest peasant became vocal about his dislike of the foreigner, who was suspected of casting spells to lure children into their mission schools.

'The continual spectacle of men and women going about among Chinese people in Chinese costume, and declaiming against the customs of these people, must have an irritating effect,' the *Sydney Morning Herald* noted.[11] Indeed, women missionaries caught up in anti-Christian riots three years previously in the same province 'drew much of the trouble upon themselves', according to the Foochow correspondent of the *North-China Daily News*. 'They dressed in native costume against better advice and went to the city [Foochow] to which they had been particularly warned not to go.' One source claims that the tragic events at Huashan in the summer of 1895 were triggered by 'the insistence of two Australian women on wearing Chinese dress'.[12]

Nellie Saunders sensed danger. 'I do assure you,' she wrote to two friends in Victoria, 'that I never in my life knew what it was to feel the force of the devil's power as I have known it since we came here.

> I could not put into words the awfulness of the force of temptations with which the devil assailed my soul after we came to China. It is not imagination – I am not an imaginative person – but real solid fact! and perhaps it is easy to understand after

all. This is truly the devil's own ground; here he reigns pretty well undisturbed, and anyone who dares to come and oppose him is not likely to be left in peace.[13]

Early on the morning of 1 August 1895 several thousand members of a newly formed sect called the *Tsaihui*, or Vegetarian Society, consisting of peasants, coolies, charcoal burners, cooks and most of the rabble of Kucheng, headed up the winding path towards 'The Sanatorium'. The society preached abstinence from opium, tobacco, meat and wine. It also saw the presence of Christians in the Chinese countryside as an affront to Confucianism and an attack on the national cult of ancestor worship.[14]

Many of the Vegetarians dropped out during the 16-kilometre uphill hike but a hard core of some 80 men arrived at 'The Sanatorium' and rounded up the missionaries. Lucy Codrington, a missionary from England, later revealed that the women pleaded with the mob to take their money and property, and leave them in peace. Some of the Vegetarians were inclined to do so and one old man, fearful of the consequences, begged for their lives. But the leader, a fanatical figure waving a red flag, shouted, 'You know your orders: kill outright.' The Vegetarians then set about their grisly task with bamboo spears and swords.[15] They attacked the Europeans, killing 11 of them, mostly women and children. Twenty minutes later, at the blast of a horn, the mob retreated down the hill, bearing armfuls of plunder.[16]

The Reverend Hugh Phillips of the English Church Mission Society, who was staying in a house five minutes' walk from the two main bungalows of 'The Sanatorium', overheard the departing Vegetarians say, 'Now are all the foreigners killed.' He found a scene of unutterable carnage. 'I rushed up to the back of the first house,' he said, 'and found the bodies of Miss Topsy Saunders, Miss Flora Stewart, Miss Annie Gordon and Miss Elsie Marshall, the latter being awfully cut and her head almost severed, but beyond the wounds given in the struggle the bodies were not mutilated.'[17]

Lucy Codrington had received a sword cut seven-inches long to the face; one deep cut on the head; one cut across the nose beneath the right eye five-inches long and another three-inches long on the right side of the neck. Her life was saved because she fell down and the mortally wounded Elsie Marshall collapsed on top of her.[18]

News of the massacre reached Australia on 5 August when the Church Missionary Association received a terse cable from Archdeacon John R. Wolfe at Foochow stating: 'Gordon, two Saunders, Stewart, wife, son and four others murdered. Inform relatives.'

At Shanghai, European residents held an urgent meeting at which they protested against the inadequate protection afforded to Westerners in the provinces by the Manchu authorities, and the lenient punishments meted out to Chinese found guilty of murdering foreigners. They demanded that Britain and France take action against the perpetrators of the Kucheng massacre.[19]

Foreign anger increased when it was learned there were 1000 Chinese soldiers at Kucheng at the time of the massacre, but none had been sent to protect the missionaries until it was too late. The Chinese Government ordered the Kucheng magistrate to take immediate steps to punish the Vegetarians.[20]

At her home, 'The Willows' in the Melbourne suburb of Kew, Nellie and Topsy's widowed mother, Mrs Eliza Saunders, spoke to a reporter from The Age on the night of 7 August. 'What,' she asked in a firm voice, 'have I to regret what God has seen fit to do? They went to death and they went to glory, and all I should say – all I desire to say – is "Hallelujah". I know that this is the act of God – God who can see the end. He knows the benefits to follow this martyrdom. Believe me, the grand work will go on; ten missionaries will arise for every one now gone, and the Christianising of this people will be expedited.'[21]

Within weeks, 26 members of the Vegetarian Society had been executed, 19 banished or imprisoned for life, 27 imprisoned for periods of ten to 15 years, and 20 others given minor punish-ments. But if Manchu justice was swift, change in the Celestial Empire was too slow for the gritty little physician-turned-revolu-tionary named Sun Yat-sen.

The future president of the Chinese Republic had been born Sun Wen at Hsiang-shan, a Cantonese village, on 12 November 1866. Sun's first political mentor was a Taiping veteran who spoke vividly about the rebels' revolutionary exploits and their policy of sharing land among the peasants. The impressionable youth grew up not far from the Taiping leader Hung Hsiu-ch'uan's birthplace and saw himself as his successor in the battle against the Manchu. Indeed, he revelled in the nickname 'Hung the Second'.[22]

At 13, Sun went to live with his elder brother Sun Mei in Honolulu, where he was taught English, mathematics and science. After his early exposure to the Taiping credo, he was now drawn towards Christianity. When he expressed an interest in converting, his brother became alarmed and sent him back to China. After a time at school in Canton, he moved to the Central School (later Queen's College) in Hong Kong, where he learned to play cricket and was baptised in the Christian faith. He was given the baptismal name Yat-sen. In 1884 he graduated as a doctor at the Hong Kong College of Medicine for Chinese after studying under its Scottish dean, Dr James Cantlie.[23]

Sun opened a practice in Macao, a Portuguese colony some 60 kilometres from Hong Kong. Cantlie made several trips from Hong Kong to assist him in major surgical operations. 'Why did I do this journey to Macao to help this man?' he later wrote. 'For the reason that others have fought for and died for him, because I loved and respected him.'[24] Meanwhile, Sun's parents arranged for him to marry a local Cantonese girl. Although frequently away from home, he became the father of three children.

Sun's views shifted irreversibly towards revolution when Li Hung-chang ignored a letter from him suggesting how China might be strengthened. Sun had only been partly trained in Chinese classicism, so his views were judged unworthy of consideration. From that point on, he campaigned for the violent overthrow of the Manchu. Returning to Honolulu in 1894, he founded the *Hsing-Chung hui*, or Revive China Society, to propagate his revolutionary ideas. One of his acolytes, Lu Hao-tung, designed the movement's flag, a white sun and blue sky against a red background.[25]

In October the following year Sun, then 29 years old, would attempt to launch an uprising in Canton involving commanders of some of the Chinese gunboats of the Pearl River squadron, high officials in the Canton arsenal and a considerable number of important mandarins.

In 1887 Tse Yet Chong moved his family from New South Wales to Hong Kong. His 17-year-old son Tse Tsan Tai enrolled in Sun Yat-sen's *alma mater* to prepare himself for a career as a clerk in the Public Works Department. One of his closest friends was Yang Chu-yun, a shipping clerk and fellow Christian, who had also received a Western education. In 1890 Tse and Yang founded the earliest revolutionary cell in China called the Chinese Patriotic Reform Association, with the motto *Ducit Amor Partiae* (The love of my country leads me on).[26]

'It was extremely difficult to gain recruits or even sympathisers,' Tse says. 'We always met the taunts and ridicule of our chicken-hearted "friends" in silence.' The celestial subversive chanced his luck by consorting with Manchu spies and *agents provocateurs* – 'persistently putting my head in the tiger's jaws', as he puts it – in order to get information about the enemy's strengths and weaknesses.[27]

Tse and Yang established their first revolutionary headquarters on 13 March 1892 on the first floor of 1 Pak Tze Lane, Hong Kong. In common with other Chinese clubs, the premises was visited by detectives of the Hong Kong Police Force, but all they found was a group of earnest young men talking excitedly over cups of green tea.

Tse also tried his hand as a propagandist, writing a series of newspaper articles opposing *feng shui*, foot-binding, opium-smoking and the *mui tsai* bonded female system.[28] His views attracted the ire of Hong Kong's colonial secretary, George O'Brien, who reprimanded him in May 1894 for 'dabbling in politics' while in government service.[29]

During the latter stages of the Sino-Japanese War in the spring of 1895, when the tremors of China's humiliating defeat were rippling through the Middle Kingdom, Tse's Reform Association merged with Sun Yat-sen's fledgling *Hsing-Chung hui* to form the Hong Kong branch of the latter society. A new revolutionary headquarters was established at 13 Staunton Street under the cover name 'the Kuen Hang Club'. The movement did not make an auspicious start. Tse relates that at his first meeting with Sun Yat-sen on 13 March 1895, '... his look and speech did not favourably impress me, and I had a *strange* feeling that it would be wise to keep away from him'.

Sun was angered when Yang, who had access to funds through a wealthy Hong Kong businessman, was elected the society's first leader 'because of his control of the movement's finances'. From the outset, Yang was committed to a republican form of government in the new China, whereas Sun was prepared to accept a Chinese emperor after the Manchu had been thrown out.

Despite this fundamental ideological difference, the group wasted no time in planning its first insurrection.[30] In the first two weeks of March 1895, Sun met secretly in Hong Kong with Yang, Tse and a wealthy new recruit to the *Hsing-Chung hui* named Huang Yung-shang. They concocted an extraordinary plot for a coalition of 3000 Triad members, bandits and mercenaries hired by the *Hsing-Chung hui* to make Canton the flashpoint of a widespread anti-Ching rebellion. Two Hong Kong newspaper editors, Thomas Reid of the *China Mail* and Chesney Duncan of the *Hong Kong Telegraph*, were persuaded by an intermediary, Dr Ho Kai, one of Sun Yat-sen's former teachers, to publish articles calling for reform of the Ching regime and pointing out the advantages to international trade if it were deposed in favour of a democratic Chinese government.

Reid, an Aberdonian with a well-developed faculty for making money,[31] had no compunction in rattling the Ching authorities. On 12 March, he hinted at the existence of the Canton plot – then in its most embryonic form – in discussing the unrest permeating the Cantonese provinces following the defeat in the Sino-Japanese War.

'When the rising does come, it will be on the part of a large section of the population in the provinces south of the Yangtze, although it may include the people of that locality,' Reid wrote in an editorial. 'Quietly, the inhabitants of South China have been fairly well organised, and all that is needed to kindle the flame of popular revolt is a leader of outstanding merit.'[32]

He outlined the benefits to the treaty ports and the free port of Hong Kong that might accrue if the 'Reform Party' (as the *Hsing-Chung hui* was euphemistically called) succeeded in creating 'a constitutional upheaval to rid their country of the iniquitous system of misrule which has shut out China from Western influence, Western trade and Western civilisation'.[33]

Tse Tsan Tai's unfavourable impression of Sun Yat-sen was confirmed on 5 May. 'Sun Yat-sen appears to be a rash and reckless fellow,' he wrote in his diary. 'He would risk his life to make a name for himself.' And a few weeks later on 23 June: 'Sun has got "revolution" on the brain, and is so "occupied" at times that he speaks and acts strangely! He will grow crazy yet. I for one could not trust him with the responsibility of the leadership of the Movement.'

While Yang Chu-yun and Tse Tsan Tai took care of the financial aspects of the rising, Sun Yat-sen and his confederate Lu Hao-tung headed up the Pearl River. 'Many lawless and desperate men had made their way from Hong Kong and other parts of China to Canton,' *The Times* later reported. 'For at least a month, Sun guided the movement from within the *yamen* of the *fantai*, or treasurer, of the province without his knowledge.'[34]

The Canton rising was due to begin at the city's arsenal on 26 October 1895 – a festival day – during a visit by the viceroy of Canton, Tan Chung-lin.[35] The gates at one of the arsenal's entrances would be closed on the visitor and he would be held captive while his *yamen*, or office, and the city's military head-quarters were seized. It was hoped the revolt would paralyse the two Cantonese provinces of Kwangtung and Kwangsi and trigger spontaneous revolts throughout the empire.

'There may be a few excesses at the outset,' Thomas Reid observed on 24 October, 'but that is probably inevitable, and it will be the duty of the Foreigners on the spot to guide the new impulse into the right channel. It will be a grievous mistake if Great Britain or any other Foreign Powers interfere to thrust China back into the arms of the gang of incompetents who at present rule ...'[36]

With so much advance publicity, it was also inevitable that word of the coup would leak out to Ching officials. When a ferry carrying some 500 coolies who had been promised HK$10 a month by Yang Chu-yun to join the revolt docked at Canton, the police pounced. A search of the ship revealed a large quantity of arms and ammunition hidden in barrels labelled 'Portland cement'. Most of the coolies escaped in the ensuing melee but some 50 arrests were made, including Lu Hao-tung, who was tried and executed. Imperial troops scoured the city looking for Sun Yat-sen, who escaped over the city walls at the end of a rope. With a price on his head, he made his way to the Portuguese colony of Macao and thence to Hong Kong.

The Manchu authorities insisted the British hand him over for trial and execution but he was allowed to flee to Japan where he changed his appearance. 'I cut off my queue, which had been growing all my life,' he says. 'For some days I had not shaved my head, and I allowed the hair to grow on my upper lip. Then I went out to a clothier's and bought a suit of modern Japanese garments.

When I was fully dressed I looked in the mirror, and was astonished – and a good deal reassured – by the transformation.'[37]

After lying low for several months Sun left Japan for
Honolulu to reinvigorate the Hawaiian branch of the *Hsing-
Chung hui*. Leaving his wife and daughters in the care of his
brother, he then travelled to San Francisco where he tapped
'overseas Chinese' for donations. He also posed for a newspaper
photograph, a foolish act that disclosed his new appearance
to the Chinese authorities. When he boarded the Liverpool-
bound SS *Majestic* in New York on 23 September 1896, news
of his departure was cabled ahead to the Chinese Legation
in London.

When Sun Yat-sen arrived at Liverpool on 1 October, a
private detective from Slater's Detective Agency picked up his
trail and followed him to London. Dr James Cantlie, who had
returned to London from Hong Kong, had arranged lodgings
for him at Gray's Inn Place. Over the next few days, Sun saw
the sights from the top of a London double-decker bus and
visited Cantlie's house at 46 Devonshire Street, Marylebone,
just around the corner from the Chinese Legation. There, he
bounced the Cantlies' baby son Kenneth on his knee.[38] The
agency reported all his movements to the Chinese minister
to London, Kung Chao-yuan, and his 63-year-old counsellor,
Sir Halliday Macartney, former scourge of the Taiping.[39]

On 11 October Sun Yat-sen entered the Chinese Legation,
an impressive six-storey building in Portland Place, without any
idea that he was about to become an international celebrity. He
was probably on a spying mission, although he later claimed two
Chinese men had hustled him inside as he passed the building.
What is not disputed is that they took him upstairs and locked
him in a room at the top of the legation. 'Immediately I got
into the room, a gentleman with a white beard, an Englishman,
came in,' Sun said in an interview with *The Times*. 'I think they
call him Macartney. He said, "Here is China for you." I did not
quite understand what he meant.'[40]

Macartney meant that the legation was Chinese territory and that Sun was therefore at the mercy of the Chinese minister. Sun protested that it would be legally impossible to send him back to China because no extradition treaty existed with Britain. 'Oh, we are not going to do that,' one of his captors told him. 'We are going to tie you up and block your mouth and carry you at night on board some ship.' He added, 'If we cannot smuggle you away, we can kill you here because this is China.'[41]

Sun tried to alert Dr Cantlie to his plight. 'I attempted to throw a note from the window to the next house,' he said. 'It appears it was picked up by one of the men at the embassy and the next day the window was screwed up.' The man who picked up the note was George Cole, the legation's English porter. He informed the housekeeper, a Mrs Howe, about Sun's efforts to get a message to Dr Cantlie. At 11.30 pm on 17 October, the physician was roused from his bed by the ringing of his doorbell. No one was there but a letter had been pushed under the door.

'There is a friend of yours imprisoned in the Chinese Legation here since last Sunday; they intend sending him out to China, where it is certain they will hang him,' the note said. 'It is very sad for the poor man, and unless something is done at once he will be taken away and no one will know it. I dare not sign my name, but this is the truth, so believe what I say. Whatever you do must be done at once, or it will be too late. His name is, I believe, Sin Yin Sen.'[42]

The author was Mrs Howe. 'Had this humble woman failed in her purpose,' Cantlie says, 'the regeneration of China would have been thrown back indefinitely.' He notified the Foreign Office that a Chinese doctor of his acquaintance was imprisoned in the Chinese Legation and gave the story to the *Globe* newspaper.[43] Little notes telling Sun that moves were being made to secure his freedom and a copy of the *Globe* carrying the story of his kidnapping were secreted among the coals taken up to his fireplace. Meanwhile, Scotland Yard detectives kept watch to ensure no attempt was made to smuggle him out of the premises.

At 3.30 pm on 23 October the Foreign Office summoned Sir Halliday Macartney to Whitehall where he was handed a statement from the Prime Minister, Lord Salisbury, 'requesting' the Chinese minister to release Sun Yat-sen. Macartney returned to Portland Place and later that afternoon Sun was taken down into the basement and released through a side door to avoid a crowd of reporters, well-wishers and demonstrators outside the Portland Place entrance.

Sun was overcome with gratitude. 'If anything were needed to convince me of the generous public spirit which pervades Great Britain, and the love of justice which distinguishes its people, the recent acts of the last few days have conclusively done so,' he wrote to *The Times* from Cantlie's home. 'Knowing and feeling more keenly than ever what a constitutional Government and an enlightened people mean, I am prompted still more actively to pursue the cause of advancement, education and civilisation in my own well-beloved but oppressed country.'[44]

Sun repaired to the Reading Room of the British Museum – the very place where Karl Marx had written *Das Kapital* – and began to study the principles of democracy and think about how they might be applied in the country whose rulers wanted him dead.

CHAPTER 4

Silk and Steel

George Morrison returned to China in the spring of 1897 as Peking correspondent of *The Times* after the newspaper's manager, the insightful, chain-smoking Moberly Bell, read his book, *An Australian in China*, and realised he had tremendous potential as a journalist. Morrison quickly established a formidable reputation through a series of scoops, including the revelation that the Russians intended to make Port Arthur the Chinese terminus of the Chinese Eastern Railway (later renamed the South Manchurian Railway by the Japanese), thus looping much of Manchuria on to the Russian Empire.

According to Russia's negotiator in the railway deal, Prince Esper Oukhtomsky, the crafty diplomat Li Hung-chang had accepted a bribe of three million roubles (US$1.9 million at the time) to be paid in three stages following the signing of the 'Mutual Defense Treaty' by China and Russia on 3 June 1896. Li's Faustian pact with the foreign devil stipulated that the first million roubles would be paid when the emperor announced approval of the Chinese Eastern Railway; the second when the contract to decide the route and build the railway was decided; the third when the railway was finished.

Li believed every man had his price. When George Morrison called at his Peking home soon after his arrival in the capital, he 'had the impudence to ask me if a money payment would induce me to write to *The Times* advocating a doubling of the import dues without compensation'.[1]

Following his narrow escape in London, Sun Yat-sen lived in exile in Europe, North America and Japan. As Yang Chu-yun and most of his *Hsing-Chung hui* colleagues had been forced to flee Hong Kong after the failure of the Canton coup, Tse Tsan Tai, whose role had remained undetected, was now the most senior revolutionary figure in the colony. Putting violence aside for the time being, he made overtures to Kang Youwei and Liang Chi-chao, the leading figures in a reform movement that was attempting to change the empire by peaceful means.

Kang Youwei, a brilliant 43-year-old Cantonese scholar, was stout and strong, with piercing black eyes. He was styled 'Kang Fu-tzu' (the New Confucius), although the Chinese *literati* denounced his use of Confucianism – hitherto a bulwark of the status quo – to promote reform. Appalled by Manchu inhumanity to its citizens, Kang sent a series of lively memorials about conditions in the Middle Kingdom to the young Emperor, Kuang-hsu, in which he urged a gradualist solution to China's ills through Confucian transformation from the top. Three of Kang's most ardent followers were his younger brother, Kang Guangren, and two brilliant scholars, Tan Sitong and Liang Chi-chao.

Kang Youwei had studied Japan's great leap forward in a single generation following a brief civil war in 1868, which had placed the Meiji Emperor on the Chrysanthemum Throne.[2] Progressive young statesmen, known collectively as the *Genro*, then took control of the 15-year-old emperor's domains and set about creating a new Japanese state capable of competing with Western countries on equal economic and military terms.

The Meiji Restoration reached its high point in 1890 with the opening of a new legislature, the Imperial Diet, in which members could help decide the great national issues. In just

30 years Japan had transformed herself from a feudal state ruled by a medieval shogunate into a constitutional monarchy. Kang firmly believed that China should take her first steps along the Japanese path.

Kuang-hsu, the 25-year-old Manchu Emperor, was despondent over the disintegration of the Chinese forces in the Sino-Japanese War, while the payment of the vast war indemnity represented one-third of the entire Ching treasury. He was receptive to new ideas. Taking up the vermilion pencil, he issued an edict in July 1895 outlining a program to modernise China through railway building, currency reform and the founding of a national university.[3]

The aspect of Kuang-hsu's program that most appealed to Western investors was his plan to build a railway line between Peking and Hankow in order to boost trade and provide jobs. Tenders were submitted and a Belgian consortium was chosen on the grounds that Belgium was a neutral country that had demanded few privileges from China. To the Court's consternation, it was then revealed that the Belgians were acting on behalf of the unpopular French, victors of the Sino-French War of 1883–84 that had deprived the empire of Annan (Vietnam), while the French were in collusion with the treacherous, grasping Russians.

Meanwhile, Tse Tsan Tai held meetings in Hong Kong with Kang Youwei and his brother Kang Guangren, and corresponded with their chief lieutenant Liang Chi-chao to see whether any common ground could be found between the *Hsing-Chung hui* and the reform movement. The future Chinese consul to Australia, Liang Lan-shun, attended the first meeting with Kang Guangren at the Bun Fong restaurant in Hong Kong on 21 February 1896. Seven months later Tse met Kang Youwei at the Wai Shing teahouse in Queen's Road Central. It was agreed in principle at both meetings that a measure of co-operation was desirable but a problem arose the following year when Kang Guangren questioned Sun Yat-sen's suitability as an ally.

Kang stressed that a peaceful revolution was essential to China's problems, rather than 'desperate attempts at reform'. 'Men like Sun Yat-sen frighten me – they spoil everything,' he said. 'My brother has numerous enemies and they would seize any opportunity to bring about his downfall. So you see we must be shrewd. No one must be able to say that ours is an anti-dynastic movement.'[4]

The reformers were anxious to meet Yang Chu-yun, who was seen as the acceptable face of the revolutionary faction. But Yang was living in exile with other Chinese revolutionaries in Japan. A short time later the emperor summoned Kang Youwei and his confederates to Peking and the opportunity for an alliance between reformers and revolutionaries was momentarily lost.[5]

The aggressive behaviour of Germany in Shantung and Russia in Manchuria filled the young emperor with shame and anger. At the suggestion of his former tutor Weng Tung-ho – who had been sacked by Kuang-hsu's formidable aunt Tzu Hsi for being too liberal – he read Kang Youwei's memorials and was galvanised into action. On 11 June 1898 he signed the first of 38 imperial decrees that would send a tornado of change sweeping throughout the empire.

Five days later he invited Kang and his young followers to an audience in the Summer Palace. They spoke for five hours.[6] Kang urged Kuang-hsu to shake off the bondage of the Manchu Court and replace his conservative advisers with bright young reformers. Expecting the existing officials to promote change, he said, would be 'like climbing a tree to catch fish'.

The Emperor duly abolished the cumbersome 'eight-legged essay' system of advancement within the mandarinate, converted ancient temples into modern schools and established bureaus to shake up agriculture, commerce and industry. He also appointed Kang Youwei as secretary to the *Tsungli Yamen* (the Chinese

Foreign Office) and made the 33-year-old philosopher Tan Sitong a member of the even more prestigious Grand Council.

Kang preached that China should not only follow Japan's path to modernity but should also become allied with her militarily. Chinese officers should be trained in Japan and the Chinese fleet reorganised under a Japanese admiral. Kuang-hsu wholeheartedly agreed. 'No one doubts the sincerity of the young Emperor,' George Morrison wrote in *Reminiscences*, his unpublished memoir, 'no one denies the wise tendency of the reforms. But the pace was too fast.'

Kuang-hsu had become emperor on 25 February 1875 following the death of the Dowager Empress Tzu Hsi's son. Although she had stepped down as regent when he reached the age of accession, she remained China's de facto ruler, a sinister figure behind a silk screen with a clique of eunuchs and Manchu bannermen at her beck and call. Tzu Hsi did nothing to restrain the reforming process until the Emperor abolished the stipends of the Manchu ruling caste and ordered the Eight Banners of the Manchu Army to be disbanded in favour of a modern fighting force. In retaliation, she banished Weng Tung-ho from Peking for having launched the emperor on his progressive path.

'The events of the week are important and significant,' Sir Robert Hart, the Inspector General of Customs who had spent his life trying to modernise China in co-operation with the European powers, wrote to George Morrison on 18 June 1898. 'I am sorry for poor old Weng who had many fine points, but he presumed on his position as tutor to interfere with the Emperor too much they say, or so thought the folk on duty. Pity the Emperor did not go about it more gently!'[7]

Sun Yat-sen ridiculed Kang Youwei and Liang Chi-chao for collaborating with the reactionary Ching Court. By September, it seemed he had a point. The Board of Rites expressed its outright opposition to the abolition of the 'eight-legged essay'; the *Tsungli Yamen* opposed the new administrative bureaus;

and most provincial governors either delayed or ignored the Emperor's edicts.[8]

Fearing that Tzu Hsi would depose him, the reformers plotted to strike first and exterminate her with the help of Yuan Shi-kai, the 39-year-old commander of the Newly Created Army, originally founded by Li Hung-chang to fight the Taiping and later renamed the Beiyang (or 'Northern Ocean') Army. Yuan was known to sympathise with the reform movement and it was hoped he would execute the Manchu commander Jung Lu, viceroy of Chihli (and supposedly Tzu Hsi's lover), and besiege the Summer Palace. The reformers would then move in and assassinate the Dowager Empress. Furthermore, Kang suggested the Emperor move to Shanghai, an 'open and untrammelled' city which would make an ideal capital for the reform movement.[9]

But the reformers had met their nemesis in Yuan Shi-kai, 'conceited, extravagant, lecherous, ruthless and treacherous', according to one of his colleagues. His army numbered only 7000 men, compared with Jung Lu's 100,000 troops in Tientsin and Peking. Prudence and loyalty to his Manchu masters seemed the wiser course. While pretending to co-operate with the conspirators, he travelled to Tientsin and betrayed them to Jung Lu, who rode to the Summer Palace and warned Tzu Hsi.

At daybreak on 21 September she had the emperor arrested and incarcerated on an island in the lake of the Forbidden City where, in the words of Sir Robert Hart, 'he was relegated to the nothingness of harem life'.[10] That same day, she proclaimed in the *Peking Gazette* that she had returned to rule China as regent after the Emperor had been struck down by a serious illness. The *Gazette* also published the first in a series of edicts annulling one by one all of the major reforms initiated by the Emperor until only the national university remained.

Six young reformers, including Tan Sitong and Kang Guangren and known collectively as 'The Six Gentlemen', were beheaded for treason. Kang Youwei received a warning from the Emperor that the Board of Punishments had charged him with conspiring against the Dowager Empress. He fled from Peking to Shanghai where the British consul, at the urging of J. O. P. Bland,[11] the municipal secretary who acted as *Times* correspondent, put him on the P&O steamer *Ballarat*, which took him to Hong Kong under naval escort.[12]

Before his departure, Kang told Bland that the backlash against the Reform Party was entirely a Manchu, and not a Chinese, affair. The Manchu had acted with the backing of the Russian minister who had pledged to preserve Manchuria as the Ching's ancestral seat, provided Russia received preferential treatment in future treaty negotiations.

Kang Youwei arrived in Hong Kong on 29 September 1898 and despite the hostility of Manchu officials in Canton was taken in by Tse's friend Robert Ho Tung, the Jardine Matheson comprador and the richest Chinese in the colony. Three weeks later he sailed for Japan where he denounced Tzu Hsi as a despot and accused Yuan Shi-kai of betraying his Emperor.[13]

Yuan Shi-kai was well rewarded for his treachery – within a week of the coup, he was named acting viceroy of Shantung and the following year took up the post of governor of that province. Similarly, Jung Lu was appointed to the Grand Council with the rank of generalissimo.

As the year 1898 closed, Morrison noted that the legacy of the 'Hundred Days' Reform' was a return to the most reactionary kind of Chinese conservatism. The six members of the *Tsungli Yamen* were Prince Ching, a placeman of the Dowager Empress, and 'five of the most incompetent old fossils that were ever entrusted with the foreign affairs of a country'. Their chief appeal to Tzu Hsi was their complete ignorance of anywhere outside the borders of the Celestial Empire.

The situation in Peking was so unstable that the diplomatic corps ordered troops from Tientsin to guard the legations. It was the first time since the notorious events of 1860 that foreign troops had entered Peking in military formation. Morrison had no doubt that 'the Old Buddha', as Tzu Hsi was nicknamed, was 'plotting schemes for the extermination of the foreigner'.

The failure of the reform movement, coupled with the 'Scramble of Concessions' which focused on China's railways and mining rights, had revitalised many of the country's secret societies. The sect which most effectively captured the mood of suppressed rage was the I-ho-ch'uan, or the 'Society of Righteous and Harmonious Fists'. Aware that Chinese peasants loathed and feared them above all other foreigners, missionaries watched the sect's emergence with growing concern. Noting its adherents' practice of shadow-boxing as part of an elaborate ritual to make themselves bullet-proof, they gave them a nickname: 'the Boxers'.

The Boxer Uprising of 1900 was initially directed against the Manchu regime but was cleverly diverted by Tzu Hsi and Prince Tuan, the Boxers' champion among her courtiers, into an insurgence against foreigners. The Boxers' slogan of 'Overthrow the Ching, wipe out the foreigners' was quietly changed to 'Support the Ching, wipe out the foreigners'.[14] The Boxers moved among the peasantry, propagating the belief that Catholics and Protestants 'have vilified our gods and sages, destroyed Buddhist images and seized our people's graveyards. This has angered Heaven.'[15]

The Boxer Uprising was China's third war against the West. Its express purpose was to end Western privileges – especially the right of extraterritoriality that granted foreigners immunity from Chinese law – and drive them out of the northern capital in defiance of the Treaty of Tientsin and the Convention of Peking. China had reached the unstable condition defined by Mao Tse-tung as 'semi-feudal and semi-colonial'.

The question that perplexed Western observers was: would she continue to disintegrate and become increasingly subservient to the West, or would she, through self-strengthening, reorganise her administration along modern lines and become increasingly independent? Given the checks and balances in the fabric of Chinese society to prevent change and promote harmony, few were prepared to gamble on the third way: revolution. Yet that is what the failure of the reform movement would achieve – the transference of power from Kang Youwei the moderate reformer to Sun Yat-sen the revolutionary.[16]

By 1897 – the 50th anniversary of its opening to Western trade – Shanghai had fulfilled Hugh Lindsay's prophecy of becoming 'the greatest emporium of commerce in the Far East and the commercial metropolis of China'.[17] The number of treaty ports wrested from the Ching Dynasty had increased from five in 1842 to 28 and now included the important cities of Nanking and Hankow on the Yangtze. The Manchu were outraged by the new concessions and privileges demanded by Westerners, yet they seemed powerless to resist. Similarly, the opium menace had spiralled out of control.

'Assuredly, it is not foreign intercourse that is ruining China,' the viceroy of Chihli and Hunan, Chang Chi-tung, the most anti-foreign of all China's viceroys,[18] wrote in a memorial, 'but this dreadful poison. Oh, the grief and desolation it has wrought to our people! Unless something is soon done to arrest this awful scourge in its devastating march, the Chinese people will be transformed into satyrs and devils!'[19]

Ironically, an interloper from the Indian sub-continent – the House of Sassoon – had descended on Shanghai and using its superior contacts with the opium producers pushed Jardines, Turners, Russells and the other traditional dealers out of the opium trade. Jardines continued to deal in tea, furs, skins, silks and oils and also became heavily involved in shipping, banking, insurance and even brewing.[20]

In the autumn of 1899 the *North-China Daily News* drew attention to the rise of the Boxer movement in Shantung and explained its dangerous aspirations. This and subsequent 'Cassandra-like' warnings in the press were laughed off and ignored. 'The cry of Wolf grew more and more meaningless,' Sir Robert Hart wrote, 'so it was not surprising that many supposed the Boxer scare would fizzle out with a minimum of danger to either Chinese Government or foreign interests.'[21]

On the last day of the century the body of the Reverend Sydney Brooks was found near a church run by the Society for the Propagation of the Gospel in Shantung. The young Anglican missionary had been decapitated. In his last letter, dated 19 November, Brooks reported on the rising of a sect that he called the Large Knife Society (*Ta-tao-hui*) which was attacking mainly Roman Catholic villages in the province. 'I glance uneasily round my room to see how much I have to lose,' he wrote. 'It is not much, but, naturally, I am not anxious to be deprived of what I have, and pray that the disturbance may pass over with no harm to ourselves.'[22]

Brooks was returning through flurries of falling snow to his mission station at Pingyin on the Yellow River when he was surrounded by a group of Chinese armed with swords. Instead of quietly handing over his money, Brooks fought back and was slashed on the head and arms. His assailants – who might have been Large Knives or Boxers – stripped him to his underwear, dragged him through the snow to a roadside tavern and tied him to a tree. While they celebrated their victory over the foreign devil inside the tavern, the innkeeper untied Brooks and he got away, although in his weakened state he did not get far. The Chinese caught up with him and cut him to pieces, throwing his head into a gully.[23]

The Court issued an imperial edict ordering Yuan Shi-kai, the Shantung governor, 'to arrest and immediately execute the perpetrators of the deed'.[24] However, Sydney Brooks had noted in an earlier letter that the Large Knife Society had become 'very powerful, being supported in an underhand way by the governor of the province'. Indeed, the Court informed Yuan

Shi-kai that there were many 'good and patriotic men' among anti-foreigner sects like the Large Knives and the Boxers, and 'to punish them indiscriminately would not be in accordance with the wishes of high heaven'.[25] More to the point, it would be contrary to the wishes of the Dowager Empress, who recognised the Boxers as a powerful weapon to be used against the foreign devil. Yuan lined several Boxers up and shot them to prove they weren't immune to the bullets of his guns and then left them alone.

George Morrison first noted the Boxers in his diary on 17 April 1900:

> The danger of the Boxers is increasing. The danger is scarcity
> of rain which is attributed to the disturbance of the feng shui by
> foreigners. If rains come, the Boxers will soon disappear.[26]

But there was no rain and famine gripped the land. Swathed in red bandanas and crimson sashes and slashing the air with their swords, the Boxers continued to reap a murderous harvest as they made their way north through Chihli, killing missionaries, burning down churches and destroying iron-dragon locomotives. One English missionary was reported to have been tied to a tree and skinned alive. His eyes were then gouged out with hot irons.[27]

By the end of May, Britain, Italy and the United States anchored warships off the Chinese forts at Taku on the Gulf of Chihli, the nearest port to Tientsin and Peking. In early June, a Western army, commanded by Admiral Sir Edward Seymour, left Tientsin for Peking by train but was forced to withdraw when imperial troops, sent by Tzu Hsi to support the Boxers, ripped up the railway track.

When the Boxers severed the telegraph lines, George Morrison had to smuggle his reports by messenger to Tientsin for relaying to Printing House Square. His last dispatch before the Foreign Quarter in Peking was besieged appeared in *The Times* on 18 June. It described the burning of some of the finest buildings in the eastern part of the city and the massacre of hundreds of Chinese Christians and servants employed by foreigners.

Morrison's house in the Foreign Quarter was connected to Sir Robert Hart's Customs Compound by a narrow laneway down which he managed to evacuate most of his precious library. When both buildings were burned down, Morrison and Hart withdrew to the British Legation. In the last telegram that Hart was able to send, he urged Li Hung-chang to use his influence with the Empress Dowager to prevent an attack on the foreign legations. Then he strapped a couple of Colt revolvers to his body and prepared to join the defenders in repulsing the Boxers.[28]

While barricades were hastily thrown up across Legation Street, Morrison, armed with a revolver, rode out of the Foreign Quarter with a band of volunteers to rescue Chinese converts abandoned to their fate in other parts of the city. In one operation, he admits to killing at least six Boxers himself while saving 'rice Christians', who were being used as human sacrifices in a Chinese temple. Hundreds of terrified converts were led to safety in the Fu, a walled palace next to the British Legation. The Sydney *Daily Telegraph* commented darkly, 'The whole revolt typifies a rising against Christianity and civilization.'[29]

Meanwhile, the Boxer Uprising had spread to many parts of the Middle Kingdom. On 9 July, 45 Christians were killed in the governor's compound at Shanshi. The American consul at Chinkiang, the treaty port at the junction of the Yangtze and the Grand Canal, ordered white people to evacuate by gunboat downstream to Shanghai. One of the refugees was the Nobel Prize-winning author Pearl Buck, then the eight-year-old daughter of American missionaries Absalom and Caroline Sydenstricker of the Southern Presbyterian Mission.

Absalom accompanied his family to Shanghai and while his wife and children moved into a boarding house in Bubbling

Well Road he returned to Chinkiang in search of martyrdom. Each steamer docking on the Whangpoo brought a fresh load of Westerners from the interior. 'The white people in Shanghai,' Pearl Buck recalled, 'seemed to be clinging to the edge of China, waiting to be shoved off.'[30]

Absalom refused to be 'shoved off'. After two of his chapels were burned down, he preached in the street, an unmissable figure in a crumpled white suit and pith helmet. Furious Chinese threw stones at him but he was protected by the Almighty's presence 'like a strong light shining, day and night'.[31]

But in Peking that light was being extinguished as the Boxers hacked Christian converts to pieces in the Chinese City and attacked the barricades in Legation Street. Tzu Hsi's plan to exterminate the foreign devils was on the brink of success.

CHAPTER 5

China Force

George Morrison took an active part in the celebrated defence of the Peking legations until 16 July 1900 when he was shot and badly wounded by a Chinese rifleman from a distance of just 30 metres. That same day a report headlined 'THE MASSACRE IN PEKING' appeared in later editions of *The Times*. It stated that Morrison, Sir Robert Hart, the British minister, Sir Claude MacDonald, and every other foreigner in the diplomatic quarter, including women and children, had been wiped out. The report was published 'by the courtesy of the Editor of the *Daily Mail*' who had received a telegram to that effect from his correspondent in Shanghai.

This telegram, dated 15 July, claimed that the defenders had held out against a frenzied attack by Boxers and imperial troops on the night of 6 July, but at five o'clock on the morning of the 7th the Muslim extremist General Tung Fu-hsiang had pitched his savage, white-turbaned Kansu warriors into the fray. The barricades were battered down and most of the British Legation's buildings destroyed by Chinese artillery fire.

Readers of the *Sydney Morning Herald* were horrified to learn that the defenders had bravely formed a hollow square to protect their women and children but had then shot them dead as the Kansu warriors swarmed towards them. 'The many guns of the Chinese force mowed down the foreigners,' the *SMH* claimed, taking its facts from the *Daily Mail*. 'The Boxers stabbed some of the victims. Others pursued the survivors into the burning buildings, whose fate they shared.'[1]

In Morrison's home town of Geelong, where he had been born on 4 February 1862, flags flew at half mast to mourn the loss of its most famous son. *The Times* printed a glowing two-column obituary paying tribute to his professionalism. But the *Daily Mail* report was fictitious: Morrison, Sir Robert Hart and all of the other 'victims' were still very much alive. The story had been filed by an American conman named Frederick Sutterlee, who was posing as a journalist in Shanghai after trying his hand at gun-running and fraud.[2] It took several days for the truth to emerge, by which time Queen Victoria had been 'greatly distressed', the Kaiser had vowed to avenge every drop of German blood and President McKinley was said to be hurrying 10,000 American troops to China.[3] The Sydney *Daily Telegraph* reminded its readers, 'Australia is perilously near to China and would be in a position of great danger if the mighty forces of empire, now dormant, could be awakened.'[4]

Meanwhile, a combined expeditionary force, commanded by General Sir Alfred Gaselee, had fought its way from Tientsin to the walls of Peking and after 55 days the Siege of the Legations was lifted at 3 am on 14 August. Morrison wrote a 30,000-word account of the siege for *The Times* in which he paid tribute to the 'excellent discipline, steadiness under fire, courage and eagerness' of the defenders and angrily castigated the Dowager Empress and her courtiers for their connivance with the Boxers. He also heaped scorn on some of the Western ministers, notably the highly strung French envoy Stephen Pichon, 'who, crying

"*Tout est perdu*", melodramatically burned the French archives in a ditch at the British Legation'.[5]

Sir Robert Hart understood Morrison's anger. 'I think his own sufferings,' he said, 'have made him take a more revengeful tone than he would otherwise have held.' To counteract the anti-Chinese hysteria which the siege had inevitably stirred up in the West, Hart published his own views in the *Fortnightly Review*, a serious magazine which was widely read in Europe and the United States.

In Hart's eyes the Boxers were embryonic nationalists and freedom fighters, while their movement was 'patriotic in origin, justifiable in its fundamental idea and in point of fact the outcome of either foreign advice or the study of foreign methods'.[6] The Boxers' primary aim, he said, was 'to terrify foreigners, frighten them out of the country and thus free China from foreign trespass, contamination and humiliation'.[7]

Hart, who had fathered several children with his Chinese mistress, blamed 'missionary propagandism' for much of the trouble: the Chinese, he said, saw the teaching of the Gospel as 'the corroding influence of a foreign cult'. In his experience, some Christians were far too high and mighty: for example, missionaries in Shantung insisted on being carried in green sedan chairs and recognised as the equals of governors and viceroys, while they interfered in legal matters on behalf of their Chinese converts to the dismay of local magistrates. Hart urged the occupying powers to reconsider their position in China, strip missionaries and merchants of their privileges and abandon extraterritoriality.[8]

Prophetically, he warned that the Boxer Uprising was merely 'the prelude to a century of change, the keynote of the future history of the Far East. The China of the year 2000 will be very different from the China of 1900.' The West should take note, he said, that 'twenty million or more of Boxers, armed, drilled, disciplined and animated by patriotic – if mistaken – motives, will make residence in China impossible for foreigners, will take back from foreigners everything foreigners have taken from China, will pay off old grudges with interest, and will carry the Chinese flag and Chinese arms into many a place that even fancy will not suggest today'.

He concluded, 'In 50 years' time there will be millions of Boxers in serried ranks and war's panoply at the call of the Chinese government: there is not the slightest doubt of that!'[9]

The powers were deaf to Hart's words. While stopping short of partitioning China, they nevertheless exacted a terrible revenge for the Ching's duplicity. Thousands of Chinese – some of them Boxers – were rounded up and executed and their villages destroyed in punitive expeditions into the countryside.

The Dowager Empress summoned Li Hung-chang from Shanghai to Peking to negotiate a peace settlement on the emperor's behalf. The talks ground on through August and the looting and reprisals continued unabated. One Chinese teacher told Morrison that his sister had been raped by Russian soldiers and as a result seven members of his family had committed suicide. 'This is a common story,' he noted. On 24 September he cabled *The Times*: 'The systematic denudation of the Summer Palace by the Russians has been completed. Every article of value is packed and labelled.'[10]

The siege had made Morrison an international celebrity, a role he found extremely irksome. Arthur Adams, a 28-year-old New Zealand writer, was staying in Morrison's new Peking house, the former residence of a Manchu prince, when he read his obituary in a copy of *The Times*.

'What do you think of this?' Morrison asked, handing his guest the newspaper.

'The only decent thing they can do,' Adams replied, 'is double your salary.'[11]

At the request of Britain's Colonial Secretary, Joe Chamberlain, a 'naval brigade' from New South Wales and Victoria sailed for China in the transport SS *Salamis* on 8 August 1900 to take part in the first Australian military action in Asia as members of the China Field Force consisting of troops from Britain, Germany, France, Russia and Japan. The Australian contingent numbered 500 men from NSW and Victoria, only 40 per cent of whom had been born in Australia. They had volunteered for service at the start of the siege but did not arrive in northern China until the end of August and early September. By then, there were nearly 75,000 foreign troops there and the Boxers and their imperial allies had been comprehensively defeated. The New South Welshmen were sent to Peking and the Victorians to Tientsin.[12]

According to Arthur Adams, who was covering the campaign for the *Sydney Morning Herald*, the Australian troops made a splendid impression.

> In build, they were the finest men out there and they were universally regarded as the handy men of the campaign. Wherever any special British corps was weak, a few Australians were drafted into it. It was somewhat strange to see them – naval men mounted on horseback – but whatever they undertook, they did well.[13]

The Russian soldiers were big, hulking fellows like the Australians, he said, but the comparison ended there: the Russians were in fact barbarians who committed some of the worst atrocities against the Chinese out of pure savagery. The French excused the brutality of their men with a Gallic shrug. 'You cannot restrain the gallantry of the French soldier,' an officer explained to Adams. The Germans and the Indian members of the British Expeditionary Force were also guilty of exploiting the chaos. Many Chinese women committed suicide by throwing themselves down wells rather than submit to the barbarities of the troops, Adams said, and in other cases, women were wantonly bayoneted.[14]

Adams was most impressed with the Japanese, although they too committed atrocities. 'The Chinese campaign went to show that Japan has the best soldiers in the world,' he wrote. 'I cannot say enough in admiration of them. If we have the Japs with us, we shall do very well.' Conversely, the American soldier was 'pampered, useless and absurd'.[15]

Adams accompanied 150 Victorians on a punitive expedition to the Boxer stronghold of Pao-ting Fu, the former provincial capital of Chihli. On the ten-day march from Tientsin, the heavily armed force of 7500 Australian, French, German and Indian troops were met at every village by peasants who kowtowed and offered them pears, chickens and eggs. Many of them were Boxers who had simply gone home and taken off their red garments.[16]

The Victorians arrived at Pao-ting Fu to discover the city fathers had already surrendered. Adams described the execution of the provincial treasurer, the military governor and the colonel who had commanded the Chinese cavalry:

> The chief executioner bowed low to the victims, then to the audience, after the manner of an acrobat about to perform a difficult feat. Another signal and the first victim was forced on his knees, two assistants held him firmly by the shoulders, a third seized his pigtail and hauled it taut, a fourth handed the axe to the executioner and he balanced it carefully, raised it slowly to the height of his shoulder, lowered it till the thin edge touched the bare neck and left a scarlet mark. Once, twice, thrice, and he swung it with all his might ...[17]

After 25 days in the field, the Victorians arrived back in Tientsin on 7 November. 'During that time,' Bob Nicholls writes in *Bluejackets and Boxers*, 'they had marched over 200 miles and taken part in innumerable sackings, looting, arson, pillage and executions without coming into contact with the enemy, let alone coming under his fire.'[18]

On 24 November George Morrison noted in his diary, 'German expeditions continue to harass the neighbourhood of Peking, mainly in search of loot. Such raids are incorrectly described in German official communications as important military operations.'[19]

On 31 December he launched a scathing attack in *The Times* on the Germans and their commanding officer, Field Marshal Count Alfred von Waldersee, who was also commander-in-chief of the entire China Field Force. He accused the Germans of punishing Chinese whether they were guilty or not and of 'systematically pillaging a people who had already been conquered when they arrived in China'.

'At present, though nominally at peace,' he wrote, 'German parties are harrying the country, sacrificing many innocent lives, levying fines on the quiet towns and villages, destroying the authority of the local officials, and fast provoking peaceful districts into anarchy.'[20] While his troops were out raping and pillaging, Waldersee was living in splendour at the Imperial Palace. Although 68 years of age, he was still virile enough to enjoy the services of a beautiful Chinese concubine.[21]

The German commander described Morrison as 'a wretched scamp' and threatened to have him court-martialled. Although he growled that he was 'no more impressed by press attacks than by the barking of a dog', he was clearly rattled. There was a noticeable improvement in the behaviour of German troops.[22]

Meanwhile, support for the Boxers came from an unexpected quarter. 'The Europeans, under the command of Field Marshal the Count von Waldersee, in their unprovoked and unpunished acts of murder, arson, robbery and rape, do not shine by contrast with the Boxers,' the *New York Times* editorialised. 'It is rather the Boxers who shine by contrast with them.'[23]

Such sympathy for the Chinese was anything but universal – it certainly did not apply to the correspondent of the Sydney *Daily Telegraph*. George Wynne, a thick-set bruiser with a walrus moustache, was embedded in the New South Wales contingent in Peking with the rank of assistant paymaster. Wynne had been born in Ballarat in 1872 and was keenly conscious of European hostility towards the Chinese on the Victorian goldfields. His dispatches to Sydney showed a pathological loathing of the Chinese that fitted the mood of many Australians at that time. 'The future of the Chinese offers a fearful problem,' he wrote in December 1900.

> Look on the frightful sights one sees in the streets of Peking, the pock-marked, the deformed, the blind, the hideous yellow faces, with their rows of blackened, broken teeth, the sickening blood-red eye-socket, telling of horrible disease. See the filthy tattered rags they wear around them. Smell them as they pass. Hear of their nameless immorality. Witness their shameless indecency, and picture them among your own people – ugh! It makes you shudder.[24]

The editor of the *Daily Telegraph* knew full well that the hottest political issue in the run-up to the federation of the Australian states on 1 January 1901 was immigration. He gave Wynne's xenophobia full rein:

> British interests compel some of us to live among them, we are told. British capital demands that some of them should give their pauper labour to our lands. British interests, British capital! Shut the Chinaman up in his own country and let him work out his own destruction. Let his unbridled lust, filth, famine and disease aid him in the world! Leave his country with its paltry trade that calls for human sacrifice to inhuman greed. See to it that he never leaves it. That is the only Chinese policy Australia can afford to entertain. That is the only way to keep back the yellow wave.[25]

The new Federal Parliament opened in Melbourne on 9 May 1901. The first substantive Act to be passed was the Immigration

Restriction Act, which put the White Australia policy into law. 'The doctrine of the equality of man,' the Prime Minister, Sir Edmund Barton, supposedly declared, 'was never intended to apply to the equality of the Englishman and the Chinaman.'

Ironically, the exiled scholar-reformer Liang Chi-chao, who was visiting Australia on a lecture tour, was one of the guests at a function at the Sydney Town Hall to celebrate federation in the company of the prime minister. The Act made it virtually impossible for Asians to be admitted to Australia for any purpose. A Chinese man or woman wishing to enter the country was required to write down 50 words dictated by an immigration officer in a European language, preferably one he or she would find unintelligible. 'It is not desirable that persons should be allowed to pass the test,' Atlee Hunt, secretary of the Department of External Affairs, wrote to the customs officer at Fremantle, 'and before putting it to anyone, the Officer should be satisfied that he will fail.'[26]

In September 1901 Li Hung-chang signed the Boxer Protocol, the last act in his astonishing career. He died two months later aged 78. China agreed to pay reparations of 450 million ounces of silver in varying amounts to Britain, Russia, Germany, France, the United States and Japan over 39 years. Russia would receive the biggest chunk – almost a third of the total.[27]

Ten days after the signing of the protocol, the author and poet A. B. 'Banjo' Paterson caught up with George Morrison at a hotel near the treaty port of Chefoo on the Shantung coast. 'In person, he was a tall ungainly man with a dour Scotch face and a curious drop at the corner of his mouth,' Paterson wrote. 'It was an education to listen to him, for he spoke with the self-confidence of genius. With Morrison it was not a case of "I think"; it was a case of "I know."'

Paterson claims Morrison told him the Boxers were 'just a rabble – washermen, and rickshaw coolies' and that Napoleon would have settled them before lunch with his whiff of grapeshot. 'The whole world,' he said, 'was waiting for England to declare a protectorate over the Yangtze Valley and stand for fair play and open the door for everybody. All the nations trusted England to give them fair play.' Morrison then commenced to sing:

> The English, the English,
> They don't amount to much;
> But anything is better
> Than the Goddamn Dutch
> or the Goddamn Russian or Turk, or Portugee either.[28]

Banjo Paterson left China with one abiding impression of the Chinese: 'Neither man nor beast in China has anything but hatred for the foreigner. The men scowl at us, the dogs snarl, the cattle snort and shiver if we pass near them. The people hate us with a cold intensity that surpasses any other hate that I have ever heard of.'

In time, the Chinese would deal with the Western barbarians, but first they had to free themselves from the Manchu yoke. The slow, painful process was recorded in the letters of Sir Robert Hart (whose diaries recording his extraordinary career had been destroyed by fire during the Boxer Rebellion). By 1894, he was writing, 'I am afraid we are tinkering with a cracked kettle.' The following year he had written, 'I fear that, as far as the dynasty is concerned, it is hopeless. In ten years' time, revolution will do the trick.' And then a year later, 'There must be a dynastic cataclysm before wholesome reform can operate.'[29]

When that happened, George Morrison would be in the thick of the action. On the second anniversary of the Boxer Uprising, he wrote:

> What hope is there for China? None at all. Is there any improvement? None at all. No attempt at reform. The officials in power now are as stiff-necked and reactionary as those that brought about the Boxer convulsion.

According to the historian C. P. FitzGerald, 'He, almost alone, could see beneath the dry bones of the dying Manchu Empire the stirring of fresh life, of a new, probably unintelligible and almost certainly disconcerting China, but yet a continuation of the life of that great nation into a new period of vigorous activity.'[30]

Morrison would not be alone – indeed, another adventurous Australian, as extraordinary in his own way as him, would be closer to the Chinese Revolution and its successes and failures than any other Westerner.

CHAPTER 6

Lithgow Express

At the time of the Boxer Uprising, William Henry Donald took the Zig Zag Railway over the Blue Mountains to join George Wynne's newspaper, the *Daily Telegraph*, in King Street, Sydney. Donald had been born at Lithgow, a robust coal-rich town on the western edge of the mountain range. He was the second surviving son of George McGarvie Donald, and his English-born wife, Mary Ann (known as Marion).[1]

The Donald family reached Australia from Dumfries in Scotland in the early 1800s when George Donald, a God-fearing Presbyterian builder who abhorred liquor, accepted an offer from his fellow Scot, Lachlan Macquarie, to emigrate to New South Wales. The 'Building Governor' wanted to develop a free economy in the colony and turn wild, ramshackle Sydney, so recently the scene of the Rum Rebellion, into a prosperous Georgian township.

Francis Greenway, the convict-architect, designed many of the buildings of colonial Sydney with a simple, dignified beauty, while George Donald had a hand in building some of them.[2] His son, also George, was born at Paddington in 1846. Six years later the Donald family moved to Yass where George Jr learned his father's trade as a stone mason and worked on the Great Western Railway from 1867 to 1876, including the massive sandstone viaducts of the Zig Zag Railway.[3] During this time he moved to Lithgow where, on 12 January 1870, he married Marion Wiles, daughter of a railway construction foreman. George Jr became a building contractor like his father.

Rich in coal, copper and iron, the town had made sturdy progress during the 1870s but its citizens had strict views on the sort of settlers who should share in its mineral bonanza. On a fine, warm night in May 1881, 200 people filled the local hall to make their voices heard at an anti-Chinese meeting. Resolutions demanding the restriction of Chinese immigration were passed and a committee set up to form an anti-Chinese league. One of the speakers put his objections succinctly, 'We don't like them, we don't want them, and we won't have them.'[4]

Indeed, on the very day of William Donald's birth – 22 June 1875 – debate was raging over the case of Quock Ping, a Chinese doctor who wished to register with the Medical Board in order to practise at Ballarat. The Medical Board turned up its nose at his diploma from the medical college of the district of Chung Low in China. His application was rejected.[5]

The chairman of the Medical Society of Victoria warned of 'the forced recognition of quackery and charlatanism' if Quock Ping were registered, while the editorial writer of the Brisbane Courier opined, 'How can we expect a learned body of men to admit an outside barbarian to a parity of practice with themselves?'[6]

William Donald was raised according to the Good Book in an abstemious household, with texts such as 'Honesty Is the Best Policy' and 'The Devil Finds Work for Idle Hands' hanging from the walls. From the age of five when the town's first library was opened, he was an avid reader. He would have been aware of the anti-Chinese feeling among some of his neighbours and he would also have followed the exploits of George Ernest

Morrison, son of the principal of Geelong College, who was making headlines in every Australian newspaper. Even in his wildest daydreams, he could never have conceived how China and Morrison would become entwined in his life.

At just 20, Morrison signed on for a South Seas cruise with a Queensland slaver and wrote an exposé of the iniquitous kanaka slave trade. His reports in the Melbourne *Age* led to a British Colonial Office inquiry. Then between Christmas 1882 and April 1883 he walked 3300 kilometres in 123 days from Normanton in North Queensland to Melbourne, tracing the route of the ill-fated Burke and Wills expedition of 1860 but in the opposite direction.[7] Later that year, he almost lost his life when he was speared in New Guinea while attempting to cross the island from south to north.

As the Donald brood grew to five sons and three daughters, George Donald entered politics as a leading figure in the campaign to have Lithgow declared a municipality. He was elected the town's first mayor in 1889, and from 1891 to 1894 served as one of two members representing the electorate of Hartley in the Legislative Assembly. Hartley's second MLA was the ex-miner and unionist Joseph Cook, a future prime minister of Australia, but whereas Cook was then a member of the Labor Party, George Donald was an independent freetrader who opposed government tariff policies which were preventing Lithgow's embryonic iron industry from creating another industrial crucible like Birmingham west of the Blue Mountains.[8]

William was known as Will to his siblings, Don to his friends and Bill to acquaintances. He was educated at Lithgow Public School and the all-male Cooerwull Academy, a Presbyterian training college built by Donald & Crowe at Bowenfels on the western outskirts of town. In fact, George Donald's company was largely instrumental in transforming Lithgow from an outback settlement into a bustling community with modern amenities.

One of his proudest achievements was St Mary's Presbyterian Church where Bill, always a boisterous boy, joined other young parishioners in jumping from a platform in the bell tower and swinging on the bell rope. One day he missed the rope and fell heavily, breaking his collarbone. Bill was due to follow the family tradition and join his father's firm as a builder but the fracture left him with a permanent weakness in his left arm.[9]

While accepting that the injury would prevent his son from an active life in the construction industry, George Donald insisted that he learn a trade. He arranged for him to be apprenticed as a printer at the Lithgow Mercury in which he was a shareholder. Once he had mastered typesetting and compositing skills, the paper's veteran editor James Ryan took him in hand and taught him the skills of journalism.

Ryan was a fine mentor. He had given the Mercury a sharp editorial edge, with campaigns demanding good housing and public amenities, education for all ages and government investment in local industries. He instilled a social conscience in his young charge. Given the influences at home and at work, it was inevitable that Bill Donald would take a great interest in the raw political movements that were leading the Australian colonies towards nationhood. In Donald's mind, politics came to mean republicanism, a united Australia freed from the bondage of empire.

At 23, Bill Donald moved further west to Bathurst, where the legendary Loong Hong Pung had preached revolution in his store on Howick Street. Donald became editor of the National Advocate, co-founded in 1889 by James Rutherford, the American owner of the great Cobb & Co coach service. Rutherford was a hard taskmaster: the previous editor, a young Englishman, complained he had to make do with just three and a half hours' sleep a night and had fled after a year in the job.[10] Donald stayed for two years and then headed for the big time of metropolitan journalism as a high-speed shorthand reporter on the Daily Telegraph, starting off on police rounds.

Sydney had become the hub of royalist Chinese support for the Emperor Kuang-hsu, who was still languishing in his island prison. At the urging of Kang Youwei and Liang Chi-chao, a group of merchants among Sydney's Chinese community had formed a branch of the Chinese Empire Reform Association in January 1900.[11] 'The object of this body is to get a satisfactory and modern form of government established in China,' one of the founders, Thomas Yee Hing of the firm of On Chong & Company, told the *Sydney Morning Herald*. 'We desire to abolish the old dynasty and <u>dethrone the Empress Dowager</u> and then adopt a kind of limited monarchy.'

Yee Hing said the reform association strongly objected to China being split up or divided among the powers. Its members believed that if the present government were replaced by the young emperor, with the aid of proper advisers 'things could gradually right themselves'.[12]

The association invited Liang Chi-chao to visit Australia for a lecture and fund-raising tour. Described in the Australian press as 'a distinguished Chinese nobleman' and 'ambassador of the Reform Party', Liang arrived in Fremantle in late October 1900. Addressing mass rallies in Perth, Geraldton, Adelaide, Sydney, Melbourne, Ballarat, Bendigo and the New England district of New South Wales, he impressed everyone with his vision for China of an equal society in which it was the duty of every citizen to be critical of its failings.

Liang's lectures were greeted with great enthusiasm by Chinese businessmen, British and Chinese clergymen and the lieutenant governor of Victoria. During his six-month visit, new branches of the Chinese Empire Reform Association were established in half a dozen cities and large sums contributed to a fighting fund. At a farewell function at the association's head-quarters in George Street, Sydney, Liang was presented with a gold medal studded with diamonds and rubies. He sailed for Yokohama to continue the liberation battle with other Chinese radicals living in exile in Japan.[13]

In 1902 fate intervened in the life of Bill Donald in the shape of William Petrie Watson, a young Scots journalist who had spent three years in Japan working for Alfred Curtis on the *Kobe Herald*.[14] He had gathered material for a book entitled *Japan: Aspects And Destinies* on Japan's sudden emergence on the world stage following the Boxer Protocol under which she gained the same rights as Western nations to station troops permanently in Peking and Shanghai to protect her diplomats and nationals.

On his way back to London via Australia and South Africa, Petrie Watson passed through Hong Kong where he learned from his fellow Aberdonian Thomas Reid that the *China Mail*'s proprietor was anxious to recruit a strictly teetotal shorthand writer with some knowledge of the printing trade.

Petrie Watson reached Sydney on Christmas Day, so the story goes, and called at the *Daily Telegraph* office looking for a loan to tide him over until the banks opened after the holiday period. He was referred to Donald, who had just been promoted to the sub-editors' desk. Donald took the stranger out for a meal. Both men ordered tea, Donald letting slip that he was a teetotaller who had never tasted alcohol in his life. He pumped the visitor for information about Japan. Petrie Watson, as he later wrote in the preface of his book, had been 'in close, daily, arduous association with its people, with its problems, with its politics'. He was happy to share his experiences.[15]

Donald was fascinated. As Petrie Watson spoke, he scribbled notes in shorthand. Back in the office, he asked the Scot to write down his thoughts in an article for the *Daily Telegraph* which Donald headlined 'The Hegemony of the Pacific'. As the cashier had gone off-duty for the night, he gave Petrie Watson all the money he had in his pocket – 17 shillings – and thought no more about it. Petrie Watson, though, made a mental note to mention Donald to his Aberdonian friend Thomas Reid in Hong Kong.[16]

During this time Tse Tsan Tai, the Australian revolutionary, had remained quietly in Hong Kong. He was now a married man and with his wife had joined the Hong Kong branch of the

Natural Foot Society, an organisation founded by Mrs Alicia Little, a crusading Englishwoman, to outlaw the medieval practice of foot-binding that virtually crippled millions of Chinese women.

Tse was a gifted illustrator and he found an outlet for his artistic talent – and political beliefs – in a cartoon strip thought to be the first drawn by a Chinese national. 'The Situation in the Far East' portrayed the conquest of China since 1842. It mocked the disgraceful behaviour of Ching collaborators and the general complacency of the Chinese people. Tse intended the cartoon to 'arouse the Chinese nation, and to warn the people of the impending danger of the partitioning of the Empire by the Foreign Powers'.[17] Predictably, 'The Situation in the Far East' was banned in China but a gleeful Japanese firm published it in 1899. When copies found their way into Hong Kong, its creator received a further reprimand from the colonial secretary for his 'extremist political views'.

In 1900, Tse's friend Yang Chu-yun, co-conspirator in the failed coup at Canton, returned to Hong Kong and, having lost his job in shipping, became an English teacher. On 17 June, the two men met Sun Yat-sen in a bobbing sampan tethered to Sun's ship, the SS *Indus*, in Hong Kong harbour. Sun was a marked man: there was a price on his head and he was banned from landing in Hong Kong for five years. The purpose of the meeting was to plan a joint enterprise between the *Hsing-chung hui* and the reformer Kang Youwei, who had gone into exile on the Malayan island of Penang.

The outbreak of the Boxer Rebellion a few days later disrupted the plan for concerted action and the two groups acted separately. Kang's insurrection centred on Hankow in the Middle Yangtze, but it ended farcically on 21 August when 30 rebels were arrested by Ching authorities without firing a shot. They were summarily executed.

Sun's uprising two months later was only marginally more successful, although the rebels at least had the satisfaction of putting their firearms to good use. For two weeks a Triad force financed by the *Hsing-chung hui* fought a series of battles against imperial forces at Huizhou in the Pearl River Delta, with casualties on both sides. When additional funds promised by Sun failed to arrive from Japan, the survivors ran out of food and ammunition and had to flee for their lives.[18]

Hearing that Yang Chu-yun had returned to Hong Kong, the Ching authorities took revenge. On 10 January 1901 a hired gunman tracked him down to his home and shot him in front of his students. He died in hospital the next day.[19] The assassination of his political soulmate was a grievous blow to Tse Tsan Tai. He cut all ties with the *Hsing-chung hui* and planned a new uprising completely independent of Sun Yat-sen whose schemes always ended in disaster.

While George Morrison's exploits in China have been well documented, his relationship with the Chinese revolutionaries, particularly his fellow Australian Tse Tsan Tai, is virtually unknown. He first met Tse at the Hong Kong Hotel on 22 November 1901. Tse describes him in his diary as 'tall and close-shaven, with a bold, broad and commanding brow, large eyes with a piercing look, straight eyebrows, long nose and firm mouth with thin lips. His hair is light and he is a fine looking type of Australian manhood.'

According to Tse's diary, 'We discussed the movement of Freedom and Independence and he assured me of his friendly sympathy and support.' He quotes Morrison as saying, 'I am quite willing to help you and shall do my best to further and support the movement. My support means the support of *The Times* and the support of *The Times* means the support of the British people.'[20]

Tse informed Morrison that he was planning another insurrection. As in 1895, the target would be Canton and the date – the Chinese New Year of 1903 – would coincide with a festival, which would give the fighters a legitimate reason for being in the city. Tse's idea was to throw out the monarchy and set up 'a commonwealth government under a protector'

– similar to Cromwell's England – rather than a republic, which Tse considered too advanced for China.[21]

On his return to Peking, Morrison kept in touch with Tse by mail. In a letter dated 25 June 1902 he expressed the opinion that the Chinese Government 'is the rottenest in existence with the possible exceptions of Persia and Turkey'. On 9 October, Tse replied, warning Morrison to be in readiness 'for the coming revolution'.

In the months leading up to the coup Tse wrote anti-Manchu articles for the English-language press in Hong Kong. He still had the support of Thomas Reid at the *China Mail* but Alfred Cunningham, editor of the *Hong Kong Daily Press*, was the more active participant in the new scheme. The 32-year-old Londoner even printed the revolutionaries' Proclamation of Independence on Christmas Eve 1902.[22]

One of the main conspirators was the bearded Taiping prince Hung Chun-fui, now a senior member of the Hung Men brotherhood. During his many years of exile, Hung had spent some time in Australia, where he had been in touch with Australian branches of that powerful secret society. On his return, he met up with Tse Yet Chong, the former Grafton grocer, who introduced him to his son Tse Tsan Tai.[23]

It was decided that Tse would raise awareness of the coup's aims among the foreign community, Li Jitang, a wealthy Hong Kong resident, would be responsible for finance, and Hung, who had led Taiping troops in battle, would take care of military matters. As his deputy, Tse chose his younger brother Tse Tsi Shau – Grafton-born and baptised Thomas See – who was recalled from his base in Singapore for the mission.[24]

On Christmas Day, while Bill Donald was meeting William Petrie Watson in Sydney, Tse Tsan Tai showed his brother the Proclamation of Independence and informed him that the coup would begin with an assault on the Temple of Longevity in Canton. When all of the leading Ching officials had gathered inside for the Chinese New Year festivities, the temple would be blown up. At the same time, one band of militia would destroy the provincial arsenal in Canton, while two other contingents attacked the provincial army and navy respectively. The three rebel groups would then converge on Canton and seize the city.[25]

On Boxing Day Morrison arrived in Hong Kong in the SS *Hoihao* and met Tse at the Hong Kong Hotel to discuss the coup. Two days later, Tse handed him a copy of the proclamation.[26] Morrison then sailed for Australia in the SS *Chingtu* on 29 December after extracting a promise from Tse that he would cable him with news of the uprising. 'Before parting,' Tse wrote, 'he assures me of his staunch support and promises to return to China immediately on receipt of my telegram.'

On 20 January 1903 Tse Tsan Tai, his father and brother completed their preparations at a meeting in Hong Kong. It must have been a tense moment: two brothers committing themselves to the cause that had been the subject of their father's obsession for the whole of their lives.

Two days later George Morrison stepped ashore at Sydney's Circular Quay. He checked into the Metropole Hotel where 'from an early hour he was besieged with friends anxious to welcome him back to Australia and have a few minutes' conversation with him'.[27]

He then retired to his bedroom to entertain a married German actress of his acquaintance, noting their couplings in his diary:

22 January X X X
9.30 am
11.30 am
6 pm
23 January X X
11.30 am
3 pm

Shortly after 3 pm on the 23rd, Morrison packed his bags and took the overnight express to Melbourne. He went on to Geelong where he was reunited with his family and driven to the town hall for a civic reception. Back in Hong Kong, Hung and Tse Tsi Shau left for Canton via Macau to direct operations for the capture of the city. They were still in Macau when a squad of Hong Kong police, acting on a tip-off, raided Hung's headquarters at 20 d'Aguilar Street and made a number of arrests. Hearing of the raid, Tse Tsan Tai sent an urgent message to a German missionary at Fong Chuen begging him to warn the revolutionary groups in Canton and Fong Chuen of the danger. Another messenger was sent to Macao to warn Hung and Tse Tsi Shau that they had been betrayed.

Tse Tsi Shau returned to Hong Kong but uniforms and equipment had been seized and more than 20 fighters rounded up and executed. Hung shaved off his beard and escaped into exile abroad. Tse Yet Chong, the young men's father, blamed the police raid on Hung for ignoring his advice and 'lacking in discretion'. He fell ill through anxiety and died on 11 March 1903 at the age of 72.[28]

Five days later Morrison reached Hong Kong on his way back to Peking from Australia. He met Tse Tsan Tai at their favourite location, the Hong Kong Hotel, and commiserated with him about the death of his father and the failure of the uprising. He assured the younger man of his unswerving support.

The Cantonese authorities investigating the uprising reported that a number of Chinese residents in Hong Kong, including Tse Tsan Tai, Tse Tsi Shau and Li Jitang, were involved in the plot. The list of suspects was sent to the Governor of Hong Kong, Sir Henry Blake, a great friend of George Morrison's. The 63-year-old Irishman had been appointed governor of Queensland in 1888 but had resigned before setting foot in the colony when the Queensland Premier, Sir Thomas McIlwraith, objected to his appointment on the grounds that 'his past career does not fit him for such an important position'.[29]

Queensland's loss was Hong Kong's gain: Blake was a gifted diplomat and able administrator. As he scanned the list of revolutionaries, he recognised Tse Tsan Tai's name. Tse and his wife were friendly with Blake's wife and daughter through their membership of the anti-foot-binding society. Furious over the breach of British sovereignty involved in Yang's assassination, the governor announced that he couldn't believe that any of the suspects could possibly be guilty and refused to take any action.

Back in Australia, Bill Donald quit the *Daily Telegraph* and accepted a job as political writer on *The Argus* in Melbourne, the political capital of Australia.[30] According to a reporter who 'pounded a typewriter on the same table in the old *Argus* building in Collins Street', Donald was 'bright as a new shilling. Small and wiry with the light of keen intelligence in sharp eyes that missed nothing.' He had been in his new post for only a matter of weeks when he was handed a letter by a copy boy.

'He read it and tossed it across,' the reporter relates. The letter was from Thomas Reid in Hong Kong offering him a job as sub-editor on the *China Mail*, with the promise of the editorship at a later date.

The reporter advised him, 'Adventure. Take it.'

Donald signalled his acceptance in a telegram to Reid and received one in reply: 'APPLY AT CHINA NAVIGATION COMPANY MELBOURNE FOR TICKET AND EXPENSE MONEY.' Donald did not hesitate. He was now 27 and this was his chance to see the mysterious Orient. His decision to change direction did not go down well with the *Argus* editor who tried to talk him out of leaving. But he had made up his mind. He sailed from Melbourne in May 1903.[31] Although he did not know it, he had accepted an invitation that would place him on the world stage at the most critical time in China's modern history.

'Small and wiry' did not do justice to Bill Donald. He was powerfully built, with a bold, purposeful stride which might have seemed like a swagger in a lesser man. He dressed in tweed jacket or navy-blue blazer, grey flannel pants, white shirt, tie often askew. According to his passport, he was five feet nine inches tall with a high forehead, blue eyes, a drooping left eyelid, straight nose and large mouth. His hair was brown, complexion fair. With his rugged Caledonian looks, he and George Morrison could have passed for brothers.

One fanciful version of Donald's arrival in China has him 'best described as ambitious but poor. When he ventured to China he was so poverty-stricken that he had to work his passage as the cook's helper aboard a ship that eventually docked in Hong Kong. There he got lucky and landed a job on the *China Mail* ...'[32] Nothing could be further from the truth. Donald travelled to Hong Kong in style with money in his pocket and the guarantee of a good job on arrival.

The *China Mail* had been founded in 1845 as a weekly newspaper published on Thursdays and was almost as old as the colony itself. Its proprietor since 1872 was George Murray Bain, a 61-year-old Montrose-born Scot, 'pious, temperate and acutely respectable', whose business partner and editor for the last nine years was the aforementioned Thomas Reid.[33] 'Its columns are never sullied by personalities,' the *China Mail*'s proprietors liked to boast, 'and, in general, the conduct of the journal is in line with the very best traditions of English journalism.'[34]

After suffering the vicissitudes of a succession of journalistic barflies, Bain had been anxious to recruit a teetotaller who could be relied on to get the paper to press in good order, while editor Reid was just as anxious to find a successor so he could retire 'back in Blighty'.

Donald moved into the Hong Kong Club and spent his first few weeks sleeping in a room with a commanding view of Victoria Harbour. He had taken an instant dislike to Chinese food – an aversion which would remain with him for life – and relished the British breakfasts of bacon and eggs, porridge, toast and Oxford marmalade. One of his colleagues later recalled,

'I once knew him to take a loaf of leavened bread to a presidential banquet and subsist on the loaf and the nut, fruit and other side dishes, while the rest of the company enjoyed the incomparable delicacies of Chinese cookery.'[35]

As for the colony's three newspapers, the China Mail, Daily Press and Hong Kong Telegraph, Donald later wrote that they 'were now with one accord moulded on high principles and thoroughly living down the evil reputation newspapers gained, some not undeservingly, in former years'.[36]

At the China Mail office, a three-storey building with cavernous arches, long overhanging verandas and shuttered windows at 5 Wyndham Street, he discovered that the newspaper's China coverage consisted mainly of strident editorials favouring the extension of trade with the West or anonymous articles calling for reform of the Chinese Government. A great deal of space was devoted to items from 'home': the deliberations at Westminster, snippets from the Court Circular and the latest cricket scores from Lord's. It all seemed a bit parochial to Donald, who wondered why no one was authorised to speak on behalf of China.

On 14 June 1903 Sir Henry Blake and his wife Edith entertained the new viceroy of Canton, Tsen Chun-hsuan, to Sunday lunch at Government House. 'He seems an energetic and determined man and is said to be very honest,' Lady Blake wrote to George Morrison. 'He is a strong anti-Opium smoker and anti-Foot Binder.'[37]

Tsen Chun-hsuan was the son of the former viceroy of Yunnan who had brutally suppressed a revolt by the emperor's Muslim subjects which had ravaged the province for 18 years from 1856 to 1873 and reduced the population from eight million to three million.[38]

Tsen had inherited many of his father's traits. According to Morrison, he was not only 'absolutely fearless and clean-handed' but also 'a man of violent character', so much so that several mandarins who were noted for 'squeezing' the citizens of Kwangtung and Kwangsi resigned their offices rather than answer to him.[39]

As the Manchu's representative in the two Kwangs, Tsen was the mortal enemy of Tse Tsan Tai and the revolutionaries, so it was probably just as well that the latter had withdrawn from the movement since the failure of the Canton coup and the death of his father. On 6 November 1903, Tse and Alfred Cunningham launched a new English-language broadsheet, the *South China Morning Post*, as 'the mouthpiece of China's reform movement'.[40] Tse wrote in his memoir that he decided to change tack to give 'Sun Yat-sen and his followers a free hand', while he pursued a pro-reform path through the Hong Kong press with the help of sympathetic financial backers.[41]

It was an uphill struggle. Within four years of the launch, Cunningham, an experienced foreign correspondent but a hopeless manager, was sacked and Tse was retrenched in a cost-cutting purge as the newspaper struggled for survival in the ultra-conservative Hong Kong market.[42]

The big issue in the first years of the new century was China's vain attempt to reclaim the three Manchurian provinces from the Russians who had made them the centrepiece of a vast new Eastern empire incorporating Siberia, northern China and Korea. The problem had arisen in November 1900 when the dissolute and corrupt Russian governor of the Liaotung Peninsula, Admiral Evgeni Ivanovich Alexeyev, forced the local Chinese authorities at the ancient Manchurian capital of Mukden to sign a secret agreement which allowed a virtual Russian takeover of the Manchu's homeland.

The Americans protested that such an encroachment posed a threat to the cornerstone of their foreign policy – the 'Open Door' under which countries trading with China were supposed to have equal access to all treaty ports. Tsar Nicholas II, however, having invested a large portion of his fortune in Manchuria, ignored Washington's protestations. By 1903, he had added 480,000 square kilometres of Manchuria to his empire and the great eastward trek of Russian immigrants, accompanied along the new Trans-Siberian Railway by thousands of political exiles in iron-barred carriages, had assumed gigantic proportions.[43]

Nicholas then appointed Alexeyev as viceroy of the Far East and commander-in-chief of Russia's fighting forces there with instructions to exploit the region's natural resources of timber and coal. 'The appointment was the height of absurdity,' Count Sergei Yulyevich Witte, the Russian finance minister responsible for building the Trans-Siberian Railway, noted. 'Alexeyev was not an army man. He could not even ride on horseback.'[44]

Indeed, Alexeyev had risen to the top of the Russian hierarchy thanks to his friendship with the Grand Duke Alexis, younger son of Nicholas's grandfather, Tsar Alexander II. As a young man, Alexis had gone on a drinking spree in a Marseilles bordello and been arrested for violent behaviour. Alexeyev, then a young naval officer, persuaded the French police that he was in fact the guilty party and took the punishment himself. During the reign of Alexander III, Alexis was appointed naval minister and his protégé rose to general-admiral and then governor of the Kwantung leased territory in Manchuria (not to be confused with Kwangtung province in South China).[45]

George Morrison exposed Alexeyev's secret treaty with the Chinese in The Times, with the result that it was never ratified. Under pressure from the other powers, Russia agreed to withdraw her troops from Manchuria in three stages over a period of 18 months. The first detachment pulled out in October 1902, but when Morrison visited Manchuria in April 1903 after his trip to Australia he discovered that Alexeyev had deferred further withdrawals while he tried to wring a new set of concessions out of the Chinese.[46]

Morrison promptly disclosed this latest act of Tsarist bullying. With the support of Britain and her new treaty partner Japan, China refused to comply with Russia's demands. Alexeyev then pushed Russian forces along the wide, meandering Yalu River, thus threatening Japanese interests in Korea.

At Britain's urging, Japan attempted to solve the matter peacefully through diplomatic channels. 'I am profoundly disappointed with Japan who, influenced by our Government, seems likely to throw away its last and only chance of grappling with Russia,' Morrison grumbled in a letter to J. O. P. Bland, the *Times* correspondent in Shanghai. 'Why did our Government make this alliance with Japan if the result of it was to be the strengthening of Russia's power in Eastern Asia? I still hope and pray there will be war.'[47]

To Morrison's delight, Japan's diplomatic efforts became bogged down in the slush of a St Petersburg winter. Valentine Chirol, the *Times* foreign editor, wrote to him, 'I think Japan would be justified in selecting the moment most convenient to herself [to go to war] without reference to our convenience and as far as I can judge Russia is likely to give her every opportunity of doing so.'[48]

Russia's obstinacy continued to frustrate the Japanese into the New Year. At a soiree at the Winter Palace in St Petersburg, the Japanese Ambassador, Shin'ichiro Kurino, begged Count Witte, who had been dismissed from office for opposing the Tsar's Far Eastern policy, to impress on the Foreign Minister, Count Lamsdorff, the necessity of replying to Japan's latest note without delay. Witte wrote in his memoirs, 'Japan was at the end of her patience, Kurino declared, and if within a few days no reply was given, hostilities would break out.'[49]

Lamsdorff could do nothing to break the deadlock – the Tsar had handed negotiations over to the man least likely to settle the border dispute with the Japanese: Admiral Alexeyev. By now, however, the Meiji Emperor and his advisers had realised just how beneficial it would be to the Japanese economy if Japan were to defeat Russia and claim Manchuria for herself.

With war imminent, Bill Donald sailed to Shanghai on 31 January 1904 on his way to Japan to cover the story for the *China Mail*, the Sydney *Daily Telegraph* and other Australian newspapers. At Shanghai, he read in the *North-China Daily News* that Kurino had quit St Petersburg on 3 February after issuing a final warning to the Russians. The sympathies of British Shanghailanders were with the Japanese, largely because of the Anglo-Japanese treaty, but also because they feared the Russian threat to British trade in East Asia.[50]

Donald landed at Kobe on the west coast of Japan on 5 February and made his way to Tokyo, where he checked into the Imperial Hotel. He soon had the company of a host of Western correspondents, photographers and war artists, all squabbling over who should be in the first press batch to go to the front with the Japanese Army.

War fever had electrified the Japanese. The prospect of fighting Russia had united the country behind the emperor, who believed his modern, foreign-trained forces would bring the arrogant Russian bear to its knees. Overlooking the immense logistical difficulties involved in fighting a war so far from Europe, the Russian public took victory for granted: a popular Muscovite illustration showed Cossacks crushing Japanese pygmies,[51] while Nicholas scoffed at the Japanese as *macaques*, a small species of East Asian monkey.[52]

At midnight on 7 February the First Pacific Squadron of the Russian Navy was at anchor in the roads outside the harbour walls at Port Arthur. Two destroyers were on routine patrol and searchlights played across the freezing waters. It was the lights that told Admiral Heihachiro Togo's striking force that it had found its target. Twenty minutes later, at 12.20 am on the 8th, blacked-out Japanese destroyers attacked with torpedoes, inflicting serious damage on the fleet's newest battleships *Retvizan* and *Tsarevitch* and incapacitating the cruiser *Pallada*.

The audacity of the attack caused great indignation in

indignation askew

St Petersburg, where the Japanese were stigmatised as 'traitors and aggressors' for launching an attack without first declaring war. The unenviable task of informing Tsar Nicholas about the disaster fell to Admiral Alexeyev. 'I most devotedly inform Your Majesty,' he cabled from his headquarters at Port Arthur, 'that about midnight on 8 and 9 February Japanese torpedo boats delivered a sudden mine attack on the squadron lying in the Chinese roads at Port Arthur, the battleships *Retvizan* and *Tsarevitch* and the cruiser *Pallada* being holed.'[53]

In Peking, George Morrison could 'hardly write with the excitement'. He yearned to cover the conflict as a war correspondent but Moberly Bell, the *Times* manager, had made other arrangements. He appointed Major-General Sir Alexander Tulloch, former military adviser to the Australian colonies, as the *Times* military expert on the spot and ordered Lionel James, a veteran of the Boer War, to charter a ship, equip it with advanced wireless technology and get as close as possible to the new theatre of operations. The idea was that James would visit the front then gallop back to the ship and radio his reports to another *Times* man, David Fraser, at a receiving station at Weihaiwei, now a British concession on the Shantung Peninsula.[54]

Prior to the attack at Port Arthur, the Russian Navy had boasted seven battleships in the Pacific to Japan's six. She had now lost her naval superiority and a second torpedo attack on 14 February and the sinking of four old stone-filled steamers partially blocking the harbour entrance kept the Russian fleet bottled up. The Japanese were able to land troops and supplies in Korea for the coming land battles without interference from the enemy.

At the Imperial Hotel in Tokyo, Bill Donald met up with Lionel Pratt, a former colleague from Sydney who was covering the war for Reuters, and two other Australian journalists, Alfred 'Smiler' Hales, representing the London *Daily News*, and Martin Donohoe of the *Daily Chronicle*. Hales, an Adelaide-born prospector, war correspondent and author of nine novels, had been serving in the Balkans with a band of Macedonian revolutionaries of which he had been made captain.

He was a big man, with a large moustache and a close-cropped head bearing the mark of a Mauser bullet that had creased his scalp in an earlier conflict. He had been with William Lambie of *The Age* in South Africa when he was shot dead by Boers in March 1901, making him the first Australian war correspondent to be killed in action.[55]

Hales and the excessively bright and lanky Donohoe[56] had sailed across the Pacific from San Francisco in the steamer *China*, arriving at Yokohama on 13 March with a contingent of Americans, including Richard Harding Davis and John Fox Jr. Davis was 'a big man of about 13-stone, high complexioned, dandified in dress, with a clean-shaven, round face', while Fox was 'a jolly little fellow, with a keen expression on a sharp face, underlooking a pair of pince-nez'. Both men had become successful novelists after covering Theodore Roosevelt's legendary charge up San Juan Hill with the Rough Riders in the Spanish–American War of 1898 (an episode that had lent itself to imaginative writing).[57]

Davis had brought his wife Cecil with him. 'I am almost hoping the Government won't let us go to the front,' he wrote in a letter to his mother, 'and that for a week at least Cecil and I can sit in tea houses with our shoes off while *nesans* bring us tea and the *geishas* rub their knees and make bows to us.'[58]

The Japanese did better than that: they registered all of the foreign newsmen in Tokyo, placed them in three columns which, they were told, would leave progressively for the front – and then left them sitting in their various watering holes. Things were so quiet that the Imperial Hotel was nicknamed 'the Imperial Tomb' and one reporter, to the envy of the others, dubbed himself 'the Cherry Blossom Correspondent'.[59] Davis regretted his desire for a holiday. 'In the day we shop and ride,' he wrote to his mother, 'but all day and all night we the correspondents plot and slave and intrigue over the places on the columns.'[60]

Then on April Fools' Day 1904 the first column of war corre-spondents packed their goatskin coats, rubber boots, cloaks, riding pants, caps, revolvers and cartridge belts and sailed from Yokohama for Chemulpo (now Inchon) on the Korean Penin-sula to join the First Japanese Army which hoped to storm across the Yalu and engage the Russian forces in Manchuria. Martin Donohoe was with them but Smiler Hales and Bill Donald had been left behind in Tokyo.

The Battle of the Yalu was fought just upstream from the Manchurian village of Antung through 26–30 April 1904. Although the newsmen got no closer than four kilometres to the fighting, they had their first war story 'from the front'.

As instructed, Lionel James had installed the latest trans-mitting equipment in the 1200-ton SS *Haimun*, which had been hired for £1500 per month, plus another £500 for crew and provisions. Unfortunately, the unsporting Japanese refused to allow the ship anywhere near the Manchurian coast. Even then, the on-board Japanese censor slashed James's reports so heavily that the vessel might as well have stayed in its Chinese port.

The Russians had also heard about Moberly Bell's secret project and Admiral Alexeyev warned that correspondents using ship's wireless to file news reports on the war 'shall be regarded as spies and the vessels provided with such apparatus shall be seized as lawful prizes'.[61] The jingoistic Sir Alexander Tulloch proposed that James mount a 12-pounder on the *Haimun*'s deck 'to sink any Russian torpedo boat that dared to interfere with us'.[62]

Morrison met up with Tulloch at Chefoo, where the 65-year-old Scottish warrior had come ashore 'fully armed against Chinese brigands and pirates', and fully intending to run the blockade of Port Arthur in a Chinese junk. 'I'm afraid he is older than he thinks,' Sir Claude MacDonald, now British minister to Japan, wrote to Morrison, '[and] a bowl of rice and one pickled plum will not hold the old warrior together for long.'[63]

Down in Shanghai, Russian agents bribed skippers to run the Japanese gauntlet and ferry supplies into the Russian forces at Port Arthur. The waters of the Yellow Sea between the Shantung coast and Manchuria were soon littered with the shattered remains of Chinese junks and their cargoes, destroyed by Japanese patrol boats.[64] Fortunately, Sir Alexander Tulloch had remained on dry land, where he regaled Morrison with stirring accounts of previous campaigns stretching back to the Crimea, where he had fought against the Russians as a 16-year-old boy soldier with the Royal Scots Regiment.

CHAPTER 7

War and Marriage

While the fighting grew ever fiercer in Manchuria, there was nothing for Bill Donald and Smiler Hales to do except hang around the bars of the Ginza, learn a little Japanese – *'Nippon banzai!'* – visit teahouses, watch sumo wrestling and write about one another. Some of the correspondents, notably Lionel Pratt, were heavy drinkers. Despite their urging, Donald drank nothing stronger than a barmaid's blush, a glass of soda water with a teaspoonful of port wine.[1]

Somehow Hales discovered that Sir Claude MacDonald had vetoed his pass to the front. 'Smiler had the British Legation working against him on account of his South African writings,' Donald informed his Australian readers. 'All men must be recommended by their respective legations, or else the Japanese will not recognise them. The British Legation would not recommend Smiler.'[2]

Hales was no longer smiling: his jowls wobbled, his eyes bulged and his jaw jutted. Arming himself with a revolver, he set off to shoot Claude MacDonald. Donald restrained him.[3] After that, Donald wrote, Hales 'wandered round Tokyo for some time, swearing great round oaths'.[4] Finally, he gave up and left Japan to try his luck with the Russian forces, which he hoped to join in Manchuria via Tientsin.[5]

By now, the Japanese had isolated Port Arthur and in June General Maresuke Nogi, commander of the Japanese Third Army, began to tighten the noose. Nogi had captured the same objective from the Chinese in 1894 with the loss of just 16 men. After breaching the two outer defensive lines in the hills to the east of Port Arthur, he was confident of another quick victory.

Admiral Alexeyev had fled to Mukden in May and command of the Russian garrison was now in the hands of an even bigger scoundrel, the corrupt and incompetent Baron Anatoli Mikhailovich Stoessel. Despite constant interference from Stoessel, two of his subordinates, Generals Smirnov and Kondratenko, built up a formidable array of defences, consisting of forts, miles of trenches and batteries containing many guns from the immobilised Pacific Squadron. Reaching the outskirts of the township, General Nogi threw wave after wave of Japanese troops into full-frontal assaults against these well-prepared Russian positions. The Russian line buckled but it did not break.[6]

On 18 July the second column – including such luminaries as Richard Harding Davis, John Fox Jr, George Lynch, an Irish writer, and Melton Prior, a famous war artist whose sketches had been appearing in the *Illustrated London News* since the Zulu War – embarked in the *Empress of China* for Moji on the route to Manchuria. They were promised they would witness the fall of Port Arthur. Landing on the Liaotung Peninsula, they set off mostly on horseback for the front, with George Lynch following on a bicycle. When he punctured a tyre, the ingenious Irishman mended the inner tube using 25-cent postage stamps.

At Port Arthur, however, the Russians were hanging on grimly and casualties on both sides were running into the thousands. General Nogi called in batteries of 11-inch howitzers, which hurled huge explosive shells into the town and blasted the blockaded Russian fleet at its moorings. Some of the ships were scuttled by their own officers who then retired ashore in the hope of avoiding further risk of annihilation.

The reporters could hear the cannons' roar and knew they were tantalisingly close to a tremendous story but the Russians were proving difficult to dislodge, so their Japanese guides diverted the newsmen away from Port Arthur and took them north where they met up with General Yasukata Oku's Second Army. At the Battle of Liaoyang on 26 August, the correspondents were kept at least 12 kilometres from the fighting. When a deputation protested that they might as well be back in Tokyo, General Oku replied that in future the distance would be cut to six kilometres.

After seven months of frustration and obstruction, Davis, Fox, Lynch and Prior knew they were beaten. They accepted defeat at the hands of the Japanese military establishment and quit the Second Army. John Fox recalled that his spoils of war consisted of 'post-mortem battlefields, wounded convalescents in hospitals, deserted trenches, a few graves and one Russian prisoner in a red shirt'.[7]

The two Americans made their way to Chefoo and then headed further south. 'Two days later we were threading a way through a wilderness of ships of all nations of the earth into Shanghai,' Fox wrote in his marvellous book, *Following the Sun-flag: A Vain Pursuit through Manchuria*.

> Shanghai – that 'Paris of the East' – with its stone buildings and hotels and floating flags; its beautiful Bund bordered with trees and paths, its streets thronged with a medley of modern equipages, rattling cabs, rattling rickshaws, and ancient Chinese wheelbarrows each with one big wooden wheel.[8]

Fox and Davis departed for San Francisco on 8 September without a backward glance at the war.[9] Nevertheless, the Emperor Meiji overlooked their desertion and duly awarded both men a medal: the Order of the Crown, Seventh Class.[10]

Bill Donald was grateful he had missed this fiasco – he had returned to Hong Kong to get married. By then, the Russians were losing the land battle and the Tsar staked everything on one final gamble. On 11 September, he dispatched 38 ships of his Baltic Fleet, including four brand new battleships which had barely completed their trials, on a voyage halfway around the world to relieve Port Arthur. Steaming at a mere seven knots per hour to keep older, slower vessels in touch, it would take several months for the fleet to reach the war zone.

On 17 September 1904 William Henry Donald married Mary Wall, a blue-eyed blonde known as 'Polly', in a quiet ceremony at the Wesleyan Methodist Church, Wanchai. The bride had been born to Robert and Mary Wall at Workington, Cumberland, on 14 January 1882. Five years earlier, her father had left his family in England and worked in Australia for two years before returning to collect them. Like George Donald, he had then founded his own building firm, Robert Wall & Sons of Crows Nest, which had the distinction of adding the first skyscraper – the 120-feet-high Culwulla Chambers in Castlereagh Street – to the Sydney skyline. Bride and groom both wrote 'contractor' next to their fathers' names on the marriage certificate.

'I was born in England and met Don on a visit to Australia,' Mary wrote to a friend many years later. The newlyweds didn't really know each other: they had conducted most of their courtship by mail and neither realised that the other possessed a fiery temper. In fact, they had little in common except a family background in the construction industry. As we shall see, they were incapable of building a happily married life together.

There was no time for a proper honeymoon. Thomas Reid had retired as editor of the *China Mail* and returned to 'Blighty' and Donald found himself responsible for getting the paper to press every afternoon. The newlyweds set up home at 'Goodwood',

5 Babington Path, Hong Kong. With the additional burden of his work for overseas newspapers, Bill often arrived home late in the evening. Mary was just 22 and the realisation that her husband's career came first did not augur well for their future happiness.

On 4 January 1905 General Stoessel surrendered Port Arthur after secretly accepting a Japanese bribe (and arranging safe passage for himself back to Moscow). 'It is not hard to die for one's country,' he said in his last proclamation, 'but I must be brave enough to surrender.'[11]

Mindful of George Morrison's role in initiating hostilities, the Japanese invited him to accompany General Nogi on his triumphal entry into the captured fortress. Morrison knew Port Arthur well – he had made four visits there the previous year – and he was astonished by what he found. 'No foreign officer can explain the reason for the capitulation,' he wrote in a report that stripped the Russian commander of all honour and dignity. 'All accounts praise the courage of the Russian rank and file, who were in too many cases shamefully commanded by their officers. All accounts agree that no man who ever held a responsible command less deserved the title of hero than General Stoessel.'[12]

The war, however, was far from over. The strategy of General Alexei Kuropatkin, commander of the Russian Army, had been to trade space for time in which to replenish his forces with thousands of reinforcements along the Trans-Siberian Railway. In March, the greatest land battle ever fought took place at Mukden when more than 600,000 troops were locked together in an horrendous 12-day struggle. Almost half the Russian force of 380,000 were either killed, wounded or captured and the rest were saved from annihilation only because Kuropatkin ordered yet another retreat.

Meanwhile, Britain had honoured her obligations under the 1902 Anglo-Japanese Alliance and closed the Suez Canal to the Baltic Fleet. The commander-in-chief, Vice-Admiral

Zinovy Petrovich Rozhdestvensky, was obliged to sail around the Cape of Good Hope. After passing Madagascar, the fleet supposedly disappeared. The Royal Navy, however, had kept the Russian ships under surveillance and knew exactly where they were.[13] Contrary to the laws of neutrality, the French had permitted Rozhdestvensky to shelter in Camranh Bay in French Indochina. Japan was notified that the fleet had been at anchor since 15 April and was filling its bunkers with coal and loading fresh provisions.[14]

As Britain was bound to prevent interference by a third party, the Foreign Office remonstrated with the French who, in the spirit of the new *entente cordiale* between the two countries, simply replied that nothing of the sort had occurred. 'The growing indignation felt by the Japanese respecting the use made by the Baltic Fleet of a neutral port is fully warranted,' the *Brisbane Courier* editorialised. 'It is only an historical accident that the Russian Armada is directed against Japan instead of Australia. If the precedent of Camranh Bay be tolerated, then it will be possible for any power to use Noumea or the German and Dutch coasts of New Guinea for the invasion of Australia.'[15]

Having failed to witness the land battles with the Japanese Army, Bill Donald decided to report the coming sea battle from the Russian side. He set off from Hong Kong for Camranh Bay. 'Donald did not discover the "lost" fleet, the movement of which was closely monitored as it arrived in the South China Sea,' wrote Professor Winston G. Lewis of Macquarie University who made an exhaustive study of Donald's life. 'He knew exactly where to find it and, in his own words, sailed south from Hong Kong "to endeavour to secure passage with it into action, if that be its ultimate destiny".'[16]

Donald and a correspondent from the French newspaper *Le Matin* found the Baltic Fleet at anchor in Camranh Bay on 5 May. The Australian was 'much struck with the imposing appearance of the vessels', but a closer inspection revealed that they included obsolete coastal ironclads and 25-year-old cruisers with antiquated armour which would be useless against the modern Japanese Navy. His admiration 'rapidly gave way to utter scepticism as to their capability to secure victory'.[17]

'We knew the officers were drunkards and the crews were untrained, undisciplined and unpatriotic men who had no shred of interest in their work and no concern as to the outcome of the battle,' Donald wrote. Admiral Rozhdestvensky was a harsh disciplinarian, who had hanged sailors and downgraded officers for trivial offences, but he could not keep his eye on the whole fleet and on many ships 'the utmost disorder and most incredible looseness prevailed'. Donald watched the ships at gunnery practice and noted that the gunners – many of them artillery men unused to naval ways – failed to hit their targets more than once in a dozen shots in calm waters. 'In the meantime, the officers drank merrily from large stocks of champagne, leaving the men to their carousals on vodka and other spirits.'[18]

The Russians declined to take Donald on board one of their ships as a war correspondent – just as well, considering the fate that lay in store for them. Rozhdestvensky knew that Port Arthur had fallen, so he set a course that would take his fleet west of Japan through the Tsushima Strait and then north across the Sea of Japan to Vladivostok. Togo's flagship *Mikasa*, a pre-dreadnought battleship of 15,000 tons, was directly in his path with the modern warships of the Imperial Fleet.

'Togo, the inscrutable, waited and watched, anticipating that Rozhdestvensky would act just as he did,' Donald wrote. 'Scouts posted well down south of Moji detected the advance of the Russians early on the evening of 26th May and were able to acquaint Togo by wireless telegraphy.'[19]

At 10 am on the 27th the Russians were approaching the island of Tsushima when the roar of guns told Rozhdestvensky that the land batteries were aware of his presence. He veered out of range, hoping that a heavy mist hanging low over the water would hide his ships from harm.

At two o'clock the Japanese naval war ensign – the blood-red disc of the Rising Sun with 16 sunrays – was hoisted in *Mikasa* to wild cheers. Admiral Togo had been raised on the Royal Navy principle of 'fight the enemy on sight' – *kenteki hissen* – and as the Russian ships appeared in view he signalled his fleet with a message reminiscent of Nelson at Trafalgar: 'ON THIS ONE BATTLE RESTS THE FATE OF OUR NATION. LET EVERY MAN DO HIS UTMOST.' 'The mists had now lifted and disclosed to the Russians the terrible trap into which they had run,' Donald wrote.

> On their port they saw indistinctly in the haze the first and second detachments of the Japanese fleet, while swinging round to starboard were the third and fourth. The fleets steamed alongside one another for a short time and when off Okinashima the Russians opened fire. The first shot from the Japanese was fired at 2.13 and soon an incessant and thunderous cannonade was proceeding. The marksmanship of the Russians was inaccurate, but most of the Japanese gunners found their marks and wrought havoc on the opposing ships, smashing the iron and woodwork and converting the decks into veritable shambles.

The battleship *Oslhabya* had armour-plating nine inches thick at the belt, eight inches at the barbettes, five inches around the casemates and six inches near the conning tower. The first straight shot from the Japanese wrecked the conning tower and killed several men. Peppered with huge ten-inch shells, *Oslhabya* was soon ablaze from stem to stern and became the first armoured battleship to be sunk by gunfire alone.

'The sight of the *Oslhabya* on fire no doubt disconcerted the Russians as much as it cheered the Japs for shortly afterwards the former changed their course again, this time to the west,' Donald wrote. 'The first Jap division steamed with all speed abreast of the enemy, pouring in severe fire, while the second division veered round to the flank, thus completely surrounding the armada. There was little hope of escape …'

The Russian fleet was almost annihilated: 21 ships out of 38 were sunk and seven captured for the loss of just three Japanese torpedo boats. Admiral Rozhdestvensky suffered a fractured skull and had the indignity of being taken prisoner after his flagship *Kniaz Suvorov* was sunk. Britain raised her hat to the 'plucky little Japs' for their success in what became known as the 'Trafalgar of the East'.

Donald's stirring account of the Battle of Tsushima was actually written at his desk in the *China Mail* office from news agency reports from Tokyo and St Petersburg. He also drew extensively on his first-hand knowledge of the Russian fleet from his visit to Camranh Bay. His articles were published under his byline – the *Brisbane Courier* prefaced each dispatch with this announcement: 'The following interesting particulars of the great naval battle of Tsushima are from the pen of the special correspondent of the Sydney *Daily Telegraph*, Mr W. H. Donald.'[20]

Tsushima decided the war in Japan's favour. It was the most popular victory of the period, not only in the East but in Britain and the United States. The American President Theodore Roosevelt, however, feared that Japan might become too powerful if Russia were completely crushed. '[W]e don't want the Japanese to come trailing their men-of-war right across *our* ocean,' he told *The Times* foreign editor, Valentine Chirol, during a meeting in Washington in October 1904.[21] The president suggested that peace talks should be held between the belligerent nations at Portsmouth, New Hampshire. Both sides agreed. The Japanese had lost 100,000 men and run up huge debts, while the Russians fervently hoped that Count Witte's superior diplomatic skills might save them from further humiliation.

Under the terms of the Treaty of Portsmouth of 5 September 1905, Russia agreed to recognise Japanese control of Korea and transferred to Japan the Kwantung Leased Territory in Manchuria, including Port Arthur and the South Manchurian Railway.

Japan also retained the sparsely populated southern half of Sakhalin Island off Siberia (later discovered to be rich in oil and natural gas). Both countries agreed to restore Manchuria to Chinese sovereignty and to evacuate their forces, although Japan was permitted to retain some troops to guard her rail network.[22]

The *Brisbane Courier* described Japan's triumph as 'a victory of outraged humanity against wanton aggression, despotism and that cruel bigotry which regards every land as the peculiar possession of white men'. The paper also recorded the fact that the Meiji Emperor had bestowed the Order of the Rising Sun, 6th class, on W. H. Donald in recognition of his services as a war correspondent during the hostilities.[23]

One of the unexpected consequences of the Russo-Japanese War was that thousands of Chinese students joined the growing clamour against the Manchu and thus provided the nucleus of a pan-Chinese nationalist movement. Angrily, Young China demanded to know why a relatively small Asiatic country like Japan could defeat one of the great powers, while China, with greater resources, greater manpower and a far greater land area, was controlled by Westerners. The long-standing anti-foreigner animus suddenly exploded and it was the Americans who provided the match.

PART II: 1905–1925

Conflict

'Little sympathy is expressed for the corrupt and effete Manchu
dynasty with its eunuchs and other barbaric surroundings.
The loyalty of the troops, even in Peking and Tientsin, is
doubtful, especially when they become aware of revolutionary
success elsewhere.'

GEORGE ERNEST MORRISON, THE TIMES, 14 OCTOBER 1911

CHAPTER 8

Mixed Emotions

In the summer of 1905 – the year designated by Sir Robert Hart for the outbreak of the Chinese Revolution – Shanghai witnessed the strange spectacle of the foreign-educated sons of the Chinese gentry leading violent demonstrations against the unequal treaties. 'The Boxer uprising was still livid in our minds,' says Anne Walter Fearn, an American physician who had arrived in Shanghai in 1893 to work in a hospital at nearby Soochow, the most beautiful of all Chinese cities. 'Only a small spark was needed to start a conflagration.'[1]

Young China's first target was the 1904 re-enactment of the Chinese Exclusion Act, which severely limited Chinese entry into the United States and denied all Chinese the right to naturalisation as American citizens.[2] Li Hung-chang had pleaded with President Roosevelt during a visit to Washington in 1896 to rescind the original Act but had been rebuffed. Since then, public hostility in China had been stirred up by lurid tales in the Chinese press about the murders of Chinese at the hands of racist Americans.

On 16 May 1905 one of Shanghai's commercial guilds, the Man Mirror Literary Society, called for a boycott of American goods in two months' time if the United States government refused to ease its restrictions. The American minister to Peking, William W. Rockhill, and the Shanghai consul, James L. Rodgers, assured the Chinese that their case would be considered during the next session of Congress. There was a brief lull in anti-American activity until the end of June when Edwin Conger, a pompous, self-regarding congressman who had been American minister in Peking during the Siege of the Legations, scoffed at the idea of the Chinese being able to organise anything like a boycott.[3]

Conger's comments were wired to Chinese newspapers and 'a storm of indignation' broke over Shanghai, coinciding with the news that three male students and their sister had been mistreated by immigration officials in Boston. Young Chinese men and women started a vigorous newspaper campaign insisting that strong measures be taken to force the United States to revise its immigration laws.[4]

On 16 July – the deadline for the boycott ultimatum – Feng Xiawei, an overseas Chinese who had come to Shanghai to join the protest, committed suicide by taking poison in front of the American Consulate in Shanghai. The Shanghai press published two suicide notes by the young man urging resistance to the Exclusion Act.[5] This emotional spark ignited the boycott. 'It is our earnest hope,' the Man Mirror Literary Society stated in a circular, 'that our purpose may be realised because upon this action our national power is based, upon it the rise and fall of our empire depends.'[6]

Other Chinese guilds took up the cry. The boycott started to bite deeply. On 29 July, Louis Getz, president of a big import–export house in San Francisco, received a telegram from his Shanghai agent: 'CANCEL ALL ORDERS STOP BOYCOTT OF AMERICAN TRADE EFFECTIVE AMONG CHINESE MERCHANTS STOP ALL BUSINESS ENTIRELY SUSPENDED.'[7] Rodgers confirmed the massive scale of the boycott and warned the State Department that foreign goods valued at US$25 million were likely to be affected.[8]

Activists returning Feng's body to his native Canton organised commemorative services at points along the route,
spreading the boycott to the treaty ports of Nanking, Hankow
and Canton. The exiled reformer Kang Youwei turned up at
a meeting in Los Angeles to add his support to the voices of
local Chinese protesters. Australian exporters took advantage
of the boycott and filled the gap in some products, especially
flour. 'The boycott gave stimulus to trade of the British Empire
and led to an important development of Australian trade with
China,' George Morrison commented. 'Personally I would
rejoice and so ought every patriotic Englishman if the Boycott
had become permanent.'[9]

In Japan, Sun Yat-sen chose this moment to found the
Tungmeng hui (the Revolutionary Alliance) 'to expel the Tartar
barbarians, to establish a republic and to distribute the land
equally among the people'. Having criticised Kang Youwei and
Liang Chi-chao for collaborating with the monarchy, Sun now
wanted to unite the various Chinese groups in Japan, ranging
from royalist reformers to revolutionaries and republicans, plus
the hundreds of Chinese service personnel who had been sent
to Japan for training.

At the inaugural meeting of the *Tungmeng hui*, Sun was duly
elected chairman by the 70 members present, with 31-year-old
Huang Hsing deputed to act for him in his absence abroad.
After each member had sworn an oath of loyalty, Sun revealed
a secret handshake and three passwords: 'Chinese', 'Chinese
things' and 'World affairs'.[10]

One of the most militant groups to join the new alliance was
the Restoration Society, whose anti-Manchu, anti-foreigner
sentiments were clearly expressed in their own blood oath,
'Restore the Chinese race, and recover our mountains and
rivers'. The society's members, mostly radical teachers and
intellectuals, planned to assassinate senior government officials
but were only too willing in the meantime to turn their wrath
on the Americans.[11]

By September, the Chinese Chamber of Commerce in Shanghai called for an end to the boycott when its members complained they were suffering as much as the Americans from the loss of trade. It made no difference. The movement had passed from the merchants to the students. 'The agitators are in power,' one correspondent wrote. 'The reports of murders and outrages in America have incensed the people.'[12]

China's sense of grievance was endorsed by that bastion of liberal America, the *New York Times*. 'We have been enacting barbarous laws to exclude Chinese and our execution of those laws has been even more barbarous than the laws themselves,' the newspaper editorialised. 'All that the people of Canton and Shanghai know about us is that their most dignified representatives who have ventured across the Pacific have been received with gross indignity.'

By the end of the month, the boycott had become 'an international phenomenon' and had spread to every Chinese community throughout Asia, inflicting enormous damage on American trade and prestige.[13] Washington caved in. It agreed to admit Chinese students, tourists and lecturers provided they did not settle or work in the United States, and promised to devote half of America's share of the Boxer indemnity to aid Chinese students studying abroad.[14]

Young China's second target was the Mixed Court, long a symbol of Western interference in Chinese affairs. On Friday 8 December, three Chinese women, one described as 'a lady from Szechuen', were accused in the court of kidnapping 15 young girls from that province and bringing them to Shanghai for unlawful purposes.

The trouble began when Bertie Twyman, the British consular official acting as court assessor, ordered the defendants to be remanded to the municipal jail rather than the Chinese-run detention wards attached to the courthouse. Twyman was doing no more than carrying out the wishes of the Municipal

Council, which considered the wards unsanitary and that women confined there were 'liable to constant extortion and ill-treatment by their custodians'.[15]

But the Shanghai *taotai*, Yuan Shu-hsun, objected to Chinese women being placed in foreign custody. When a British police inspector and his squad of Chinese constables placed the women in the back of a police van and attempted to drive out of the compound in Chekiang Road, court runners barred the gates. A 'disgraceful fracas' broke out between the runners and the policemen, with the assistant magistrate urging the Chinese constables 'to remember that they were Chinamen and not foreigners'. Meanwhile, the *taotai* used his powers to close the court, thereby throwing the matter into limbo.[16]

Over the weekend, thousands of Chinese residents abandoned the International Settlement after reading about the incident in the Chinese press. At noisy public meetings, speakers strongly advocated the maintenance of China's sovereign rights against 'foreign aggression'. J. O. P. Bland, now the *Times* full-time correspondent in Shanghai, saw the 'growing restlessness' among students and merchants as evidence of a policy of 'China for the Chinese' and a case of 'deliberate and organised resistance to all foreign influence'.

Some of the loudest voices in Shanghai were those of Chinese property owners to whom the Szechuen girls were being sold to join 'four or five thousand' women working in their brothels. The Municipal Council had been warned some months earlier that if any attempt were made to regulate the trade in young women from the provinces, their Chinese patrons 'would express their feelings in such an uncontrolled fashion as to cause great inconvenience to the foreign residents of the settlement'.[17] They protested that 'the lady from Szechuen' was simply trafficking in slave girls, which wasn't regarded as kidnapping under Chinese law.[18]

On 12 December the diplomat Tang Shao-yi informed Sir Ernest Satow, who had replaced Sir Claude MacDonald as

British minister in Peking, that the British had made a ghastly mistake. The women, Satow wrote in his diary that night, were the widow of a Szechuen official and her daughter who were returning to Canton with the latter's children 'and some girls (described in Chinese as serving maids, but really purchased) & that there can be no question of kidnapping'.[19]

The *taotai*, acting on behalf of the Chinese gentry who were insisting on taking a firm line with the British, refused to re-open the court unless Bertie Twyman was removed as court assessor and the police inspector discharged from his post.[20] The consular body representing 15 nationalities went into a huddle at the British Consulate on The Bund. They were shocked when Sir Pelham Warren, the British consul, informed them that his minister accepted the Chinese position in the dispute and there was no choice except to release the three defendants.[21]

Thus encouraged, the Chinese planned even more aggressive action. A general strike was declared, shops in Nanking Road and the Maloo leading to the Bubbling Well, the leafy, suburban extension of Nanking Road beyond the racecourse, were closed and thousands of Chinese took to the streets. The earliest outbreak of violence occurred at the giant Hongkew market, where country gardeners arriving with vegetables, fruit and poultry for the day's sales were attacked. Groups of rowdies overturned stalls and destroyed produce.[22]

Elsewhere, Chinese armed with clubs and knives turned on foreigners. James Rodgers, the American consul, was beaten up. In response, the Municipal Council declared martial law and the Volunteer Corps was mobilised, while landing parties disembarked from three British ships on the Whangpoo. Sir Ernest Satow warned the Wai-wu-pu (which had replaced the Tsungli Yamen as China's Foreign Office) that the riots 'must be firmly suppressed before the trouble attained such dimensions as to become a deplorable disaster'.

Inspector Eugene Lynch, a New South Welshman who had joined the Municipal Police Force in 1896, directed his constables in protecting private property. There were violent clashes with demonstrators when they surrounded Louza police station, just off Nanking Road.[23] The police had not been issued with live ammunition and were unable to defend themselves when the mob knocked down the surrounding wall and hurled bricks at them. Otto Rasmussen, a 17-year-old Melbourne youth, watched as the Chinese drove the police out of the station, released the prisoners from their cells and set the building ablaze.[24]

The mob then moved down Nanking Road and set fire to the annexe of the Metropole Hotel, half a block down Foochow Road from the American Club and overlooking the racecourse. Chairs and tables were thrown into the street and anything that escaped the flames was deliberately smashed. On The Bund, large crowds swarmed over the lawns of the public gardens and, in the words of one contemporary report, 'established themselves on the seats reserved for foreigners'. Lady Florence Boyle, daughter of the seventh Earl of Albemarle, complained that she and her maid could get no coolies to help with her luggage at the Custom Jetty and had to be escorted to the British Consulate by a couple of United States Marines in their blue woollen uniforms with the broad yellow stripe.[25]

At Soochow, Anne Walter Fearn and her husband John, an American missionary doctor, received the following telegram: 'ALL FOREIGNERS REQUESTED COME SHANGHAI AT ONCE STOP SERIOUS CONDITIONS EXISTING STOP RIOTS.' The Fearns made the 80-kilometre journey down Soochow Creek in their motorised houseboat and tied up at the Garden Bridge, where they were met by a squad of American Marines. The group marched down Nanking Road between a double line of bluejackets to a mission station. 'One could feel tension in the air,' Anne wrote. 'The crowds in the streets were not the usual joyous busy throng but an excited, threatening mob.'[26]

The following day the British vice consul's motor car was set on fire in the middle of Nanking Road and howling demonstrators roared down The Bund, dragging Europeans from rickshaws and ripping the clothing off their backs. Dr J. W. Jackson, a British physician, was attacked and had his watch stolen. The naval authorities summoned reinforcements from British, American, German, Austrian and Italian merchant ships moored in the Whangpoo and the mob was eventually dispersed.[27]

'A significant feature of the outbreak,' Bland reported in *The Times*, 'has been that the Japanese have been quite unmolested. In certain cases, they appeared to be actually fraternising with the mob.'[28] Bland deplored Sir Ernest Satow's weakness in releasing the women. So much flak was flying in Satow's direction that he thought it highly likely 'I shall get a scolding from the Foreign Office if not something worse'.[29]

On 22 December the viceroy of Nanking, Chou-fu, arrived in Shanghai with instructions from the Dowager Empress to investigate the riots and punish those responsible. He discussed the situation with the *taotai*, who judiciously decided to re-open the Mixed Court the following day. The issue was then resolved at a meeting between the *taotai* and members of the Municipal Council. To save face all round, it was decided that women prisoners should be housed at the Mixed Court but that suitable quarters would be provided for them and that these could be inspected by the municipal health officer.[30]

Nothing changed. When Henry Woodhead of the *North-China Daily News* made an unannounced visit to the women's quarters, he found great distress among the prisoners. Scores had been detained for years and some had no idea why they were there. In one section, he found mentally ill women confined in semi-darkness to filthy cages 'like wild beasts, but without the cleanliness or the space usually accorded even to animals in captivity'.[31]

Meanwhile, Bill and Mary Donald's marriage had run into a stormy patch. Mary wanted children, whereas Bill made it clear he regarded them as an impediment. He lived a journalist's life, he explained, and had to be free to travel. He also enjoyed the company of other journalists, notably the hard-drinking Lionel Pratt who had joined the staff of the *China Mail*. Despite his later protestations that he had never touched a drop of alcohol in his life, it seems clear from his correspondence that Donald had started drinking. There were arguments at 'Goodwood', exacerbated by the fiery tempers of both parties.

At times like this Donald retreated to the Royal Hong Kong Yacht Club on the Wanchai waterfront. He described himself as 'a humdinger of a sailor' and liked nothing better than taking his little yacht *Sprite* out on the bay. Professionally, his career was on an upward trajectory. His work in the Russo-Japanese War attracted the attention of the American newspaper magnate James Gordon Bennett, publisher of the *New York Herald*, who was looking for a China correspondent to match Morrison's dispatches from Peking. He cabled Donald in Hong Kong: 'YOU ARE THE ONLY MAN WHO CAN MAKE SENSE OUT OF CHINA STOP PLEASE ACCEPT APPOINTMENT AS SOUTH CHINA CORRESPONDENT FOR NY HERALD.'[32]

In his younger days Bennett had been described by his war correspondent Henry Morton Stanley as 'a tall, fierce-eyed, imperious-looking young man'.[33] He had taken over the *Herald* in 1866 from his Scots-born father James Gordon Bennett Sr, 'the most detested and hated man in America – and the most widely read'.[34] The *Herald* was a sensational and salacious newspaper and Bennett Jr remained faithful to his father's injunction, 'Make people talk about the *Herald* and they'll have to buy it.'[35] He turned Stanley into an explorer and sent him to find the Scots missionary David Livingstone in Africa. Livingstone wasn't really lost any more than the Baltic Fleet had been lost – he had just been incommunicado for a couple of years – but the exclusive story of his 'rescue', with its immortal catchphrase 'Dr Livingstone, I presume', sold many thousands of newspapers and made Stanley world famous.[36]

Bennett lived mainly in Paris where he had launched the *Paris Herald* (later the *International Herald Tribune*) but travelled widely in his yacht *Lysistrata* and was always on the lookout for new talent. Indeed, he was known to his staff as 'The Commodore' on account of his passion for yachting.

If Bennett knew Donald's reputation as a reporter, Donald also knew from the Hong Kong rumour mill that Bennett was an incorrigible eccentric. He had once asked the editor of the *Herald* for a list of staff men who were considered indispensable, then fired them all, with the comment, 'I will have no indispensable men in my employ.'

Donald accepted his offer to join the *Herald* as South China correspondent but retained his position as editor of the *China Mail*. It was the start of a long and productive relationship between the two men, one that would enable Donald to pursue a Chinese agenda outside the imperial confines of Wyndham Street.

One evening after work he took a steamer up the Pearl River to Canton to interview the new representative of the Ching Court, Chang Jen-chun.[37] On arriving in Canton the following morning, he was advised by the British commissioner of customs that it would take several days to see the viceroy: he would have to make an appointment. Donald refused to do so. While he grudgingly accepted that British imperialism had a place in colonial Hong Kong, it was intolerable to find the Chinese kowtowing to it in a Chinese city.[38]

Lighting one of his small cigars, he sat down on the steps outside the viceroy's *yamen* and waited. It was then 8.30 am. After several hours, surrounded by curious coolies and troubled by the hot sun, Donald was no closer to his objective. He had failed to appreciate that Chinese officials never started work until one o'clock in the afternoon.

Some time after midday a well-dressed young Chinese male stopped and asked him in perfect English what he was doing there. Donald explained he was a journalist on the *China Mail* and that he wanted to see the viceroy. The young man was Wen Shih-tsen, tutor to the viceroy's son. He advised Donald that he would have to see the British consul. 'You are a Chinese,' the Australian exploded, 'and you tell me to go through the British consul before I can see your viceroy? What's wrong with this blasted country?'[39]

Donald sat down and waited. Late that afternoon, his patience was rewarded when he was beckoned inside the *yamen*, where he was permitted to address Chang Jen-chun, 'a magnificent old man with a queue and the mandarin's button on his skull cap', through an interpreter. 'That was in the days of the elaborate tea-drinking ceremonial,' Donald later told Australian journalist Buzz Farmer in his first interview on the subject.

> When the Viceroy lifted his cup it was the signal to go. But I went on swallowing cups of tea until I nearly burst. The old aristocrat became interested in me. I suppose I was the first foreigner he'd met who did not come to ask him for something. I told him I was more useful to him than he was to me, and that if I trod on the corns of etiquette to take no notice.[40]

He explained that the purpose of his trip was to present China's viewpoint to the world. According to Donald's biographer, Earl Selle, the viceroy was so impressed that on his return to Hong Kong he received a letter appointing him viceregal adviser 'on all matters that pertained to government in South China'.

In his reply to the viceroy, Donald accepted the appointment but stipulated, 'As for your question about what compensation I require for my services, the answer is that I require none. I want no reward. If I may be of service at any time, that alone will be enough.'[41] It was an honourable but rash answer. Donald had a simple philosophy towards money, which he explained to his daughter Muriel in a letter some years hence. 'Be of good cheer and trust mostly to yourself,' he counselled.

If you are self-reliant and independent you can get along
well. Never depend on anyone. I never did, but I never got
on well, for I never did have any money sense. I was always
content to get enough to eat, and perhaps that is not wise.
Anyway on that score you can make up your own mind.[42]

Donald kept in touch with the viceroy through an English-
speaking member of his staff, Wen Tsung-yao, a talented young
man who had been educated in Hong Kong at Sun Yat-sen's
alma mater, the Central School, and in the United States. But
he did not confine himself to the Chinese establishment: he
also sought out members of the revolutionary movement in
the hope of meeting their mercurial leader Dr Sun Yat-sen.

The revolutionaries were astonished to receive a visit from
this important Westerner. They listened to his explanation that
he was interested in the regeneration of China and was willing
to help. They would, however, have to take it on trust that he
would not betray them to the authorities. Dr Hu Han-min, the
leader of the group, stepped forward, shook Donald's hand and
told him he was welcome.[43] 'From that time on, he was solidly a
part of the Revolutionary movement,' Earl Selle writes. 'He met
with them secretly, and day after day they found themselves
turning to him for explanations and advice.'[44]

On a summer's day in 1908 Gordon Bennett sailed his yacht
Lysistrata into Hong Kong harbour to meet his unorthodox
South China correspondent. Bennett suggested that Donald
attend a morning editorial conference on board the *Lysistrata*,
a £625,000 steam-driven vessel, with a crew of 100 and all the
amenities, including a Jersey cow to provide fresh milk for his
guests' breakfast Corn Flakes.

'We'll do no such thing,' the Australian snapped. 'I'm editor
of a paper. It's just as important to me as the *Herald* is to you.
You come and see me.' So each morning Bennett, then 67,

trekked up Wyndham Street to the *China Mail* offices to consult his correspondent on the news of the day. Peering through great horn-rimmed glasses and armed with a long blue pencil, he then cabled instructions to his staff in Paris and New York.[45]

Bennett had given Donald *carte blanche* to write anything he liked about Chinese affairs. He took full advantage of it. One day he suggested his story should be printed in Chinese characters on the front page of the *Herald*, with an English translation inside the paper. Bennett loved the idea and cabled his editor, who complied with Donald's suggestion, much to the bemusement of his non-Chinese readers.

To increase the flow of news from China to the American public, Donald suggested that Bennett establish a Peking bureau to report on the Ching Court and its dealings with foreign governments. He further suggested that the man for the job was J. K. Ohl, a respected American correspondent. Josiah Ohl had been plucked from his post in Washington the previous year and sent to Manila to report on America's performance as a colonial power after taking the Philippines from Spain in the Spanish–American War. He suddenly found himself in Peking, where he was given a roving commission to travel through China, Korea and Japan. According to the *New York Times*, he had 'a vision and grasp of the situation that gave him a reputation as the best informed on Far Eastern questions of journalists of his time'.[46]

Donald meanwhile had reached the pinnacle of his profession. He had been promoted to managing director of China Mail Limited after Murray Bain converted the business into a private company in 1906, with himself as chairman and members of his family as the other shareholders. Donald continued to edit the paper and at the same time founded *Who's Who in the Far East* on which he worked as co-editor with Lionel Pratt.

He also made time to promote pro-Chinese projects such as the founding of a university in Hong Kong which would be open to Chinese students. According to *The Times*, 'Donald first pressed the idea on Sir Matthew Nathan, the Governor from

1904 to 1907.'[47] He suggested in the columns of the *China Mail* that the nucleus of the university should be two existing establishments – the Medical College and the Technical Institute – that an endowment fund should be raised by the public and that the government should provide the land. The Colonial Office in Whitehall, however, was decidedly cool on the idea of introducing young Chinese to potentially dangerous learning. The project might have lapsed had the next governor, Sir Frederick Lugard (1907–11), not thrown his weight behind it.[48]

To attract local investors, Lugard published a fund-raising manifesto laying down the enlightened principle that although the students would be in a British colony, 'they do not separate themselves from all things Chinese and are in touch with Chinese public opinion. Thus they are preserved from the denationalising tendencies of a purely European education, and are enabled to take a lively and intelligent interest in the current events of both east and west.'[49]

Hormusjee Mody, a Bombay-born Parsee tycoon, made a grant of HK$150,000 to erect the main university building. The Hong Kong Government then provided a site on Pok Fu Lam Road on the slopes of Mt Victoria. On 16 March 1910, the foundation stone was laid at a viceregal ceremony during which Sir Frederick Lugard read out a telegram from King Edward VII bestowing a knighthood on Hormusjee Mody for his generosity.

By the time the university was opened in 1912 – with an appropriate Confucian motto *Sapientia et Virtus* (Wisdom and Virtue) on the escutcheon – a violent upheaval would have removed the Ching Dynasty from the Dragon Throne.

The docks and jetties dotted along the waterfront of the treaty ports, now numbering 48, not only provided a bridgehead for Western exploitation of the vast Chinese market but were also the point of entry through which revolutionary ideas reached the increasingly politicised Chinese workforce and student population. 'China has for years been hovering on the brink of revolution and South China, in particular, is the hotbed of the movement,' Thomas F. Millard reported from Shanghai in the *New York Times* in May 1908.

> During the last two years there has been a noticeable recrudes-
> cence of revolutionary sentiment in some parts of the empire.
> In several provinces a regular organisation has been formed,
> and preparations have been made to take advantage of any
> passing opportunity to begin an insurrection.[50]

The Ching Dynasty had good reason to believe that the Japanese were encouraging revolutionaries to incite disorder in China which might afford Japan an excuse for armed interven-tion. The Japanese monarchists, however, were ideologically opposed to republicanism and decided to keep Sun Yat-sen at arm's length. He was given a large sum of money and told to leave the country. Accompanied by a couple of Japanese minders to report his movements back to Tokyo, Sun sailed to Hanoi in Cochin China (Vietnam). French officials weren't taking any chances and moved him on; Britain also refused to grant him political asylum in Singapore and Hong Kong.[51] Then in early 1908 Bill Donald received a tip that Sun had slipped into Macao.

The indefatigable doctor was planning his most audacious coup of all. Through his Japanese connections, he had arranged for a large quantity of arms and ammunition to be smuggled into Chinese waters on board the Japanese freighter *Tatsu Maru II*. The ship had been hired by the British firm of Holme, Ringer and Company to take 3000 tons of coal to Hong Kong.

On 5 February, ten days after the *Tatsu Maru* sailed from Moji, she was spotted by Chinese Customs launches at anchor near Macao with a number of Chinese junks alongside. On her decks were 94 cases of rifles and 50 cases of ammunition. The senior Chinese officer had no hesitation in detaining the freighter on a charge of smuggling arms into China and arresting her officers and crew.[52] He also ordered the Japanese flag to be hauled down.

Baron Hayashi, the Japanese minister to Peking, presented an ultimatum to the Wai-wu-pu that unless the freighter was handed over to Japan with the payment of a suitable indemnity and an apology for insulting the Japanese flag, his country would 'take immediate action'.[53] After some haggling over terms, the Chinese agreed to comply with the Japanese demands.

Donald sailed up the Pearl River to Canton to report this latest crisis for the *China Mail* and *New York Herald*. He found his viceregal friend, Chang Jen-chun, in a distressed state. Chang had opposed the punishment of the Chinese commander who had lowered the Japanese flag on the *Tatsu Maru* and had been ordered by Peking to kowtow to it, while the citizens of Canton were told to pay an indemnity of US$15,000 to Japan. Donald saw an opportunity to strike a blow at both the Manchu administration and the Japanese. As China was Japan's largest export market, a boycott of Japanese products similar to the one that had proved effective against American goods in Shanghai in 1905 would cause enormous losses.

Over the next 48 hours, according to his biographer, he visited many of the Cantonese guilds, including the powerful Bankers and Merchants' Guild, to drum up support for an anti-Japanese boycott. He was given a good hearing. The Self-Government Society of Canton organised a series of mass rallies and the National Disgrace Society placed speakers aboard the Pearl River steamers to harangue Chinese passengers about their country's humiliation at the hands of the Japanese. Cantonese buildings were draped in black banners as a sign of mourning.

At one meeting a 12-year-old boy galvanised a crowd of 50,000 people with his fervent pleas in favour of the boycott. People in the crowd were reduced to tears and some tore off Japanese garments and made a bonfire of them in the street.[54]

Donald wrote in the *New York Herald* on 10 April that the

boycott had almost unanimous support among the Cantonese. A total of 157 merchants had agreed to ban Japanese goods and would not lift the ban until the Japanese had suffered losses of US$150 million – 10,000 times the amount of the *Tatsu Maru* indemnity.[55] Faced with a massive popular protest, Peking backed down from provoking a full-scale confrontation. It was the Chinese Government that apologised for the affront to the Japanese flag and paid the indemnity.[56]

Donald worked tirelessly to place positive stories about China on international news schedules. One of his brain-waves was to suggest to Gordon Bennett an alliance between China and the United States, 'linking the oldest country in the Eastern World with the youngest and most vigorous in the West'. Bennett liked the idea so much he ordered the *Herald* to run stories about it day after day at the expense of coverage for that year's presidential election.

'The advocacy of an alliance between the United States and China by the *Herald* has sent a thrill through the backbone of the old Celestial Empire and has perhaps done more toward a genuine awakening than any movement that has gone before,' Donald cabled on 8 October 1908.

> The suggested linking of the oldest country in the Eastern World with the youngest and most vigorous in the West has fired the Chinese imagination and those who realise the vast possibilities in such a union are spreading the tidings and incidentally laying the foundation for a sound commercial connection with America, if not for a political bond, which will undoubtedly tie down for all times the erstwhile irrepress-ible turbulence that has ever made the Far East a source of concern to the Great Powers of the world.

Shortly afterwards, just as he appeared unassailable, Donald resigned from the *China Mail* over a dispute with one of his fellow directors, a self-important member of the Yacht Club with whom he had previously clashed. Anyway, he was fed up with publishing stories from Westminster and Lord's; from now on, he intended to concentrate on China's revolutionary struggle, clearly the most important story of the new century.

Donald opened an office in Queen's Road Central, where his neighbours included two Australian-inspired department stores, the Sincere and the Wing On. The Sincere's founder was Ma Ying-piu, whose father had returned home to Kwangtung after joining the Victorian gold rush of the 1850s. Ma arrived in Sydney as a 19-year-old in 1883 and went to work among the Chinese enterprises in Sydney's Haymarket. Seven years later he founded the Wing Sang import–export company with several partners, including Choy Hing and George Kwok Bew.[57]

In 1893 Ma Ying-piu, a devout Christian, sold his shares in Wing Sang and sailed to Hong Kong with his wife to spread the Gospel. For several years, they travelled around South China in a horse-drawn cart, towing a piano and lantern slide-show. Ma Ying-piu eventually settled in Hong Kong and, in January 1900, he and his Sydney partners opened the Sincere department store. Everything from its window displays to company policy was modelled on Anthony Horderns in Sydney. It was Sincere's proud boast that within its doors the grandest Englishman, the highest mandarin and the most humble housewife received the same courteous service. Hong Kong had never seen anything like it.[58]

Seven years later the Wing On department store was founded in the same street on exactly the same model by the brothers Kwok Lok (James Gocklock) and Kwok Chuen (Philip Gockchin), who had started the Wing On fruit company in Haymarket in 1897. With two other stores, the Sun Sun and the Sun Company, the Sincere and Wing On would become known in China as 'The Four Great Companies'. It was an astonishing feat: a group of Australian Chinese entrepreneurs had used their experiences of Sydney's retailing methods to revolutionise China's commercial life.

CHAPTER 9

Battle Stations

Freed from the constraints of the *China Mail*, Bill Donald sat in his office at Queen's Road Central in November 1908 and while one of his small cigars smouldered on the edge of his desk pounded out long stories – diatribes, really – on the state of the country for the *New York Herald* and his Australian newspaper clients. The theme was always the same: China was a vast country with immense riches in undeveloped resources that the European nations coveted. Only their jealousy of one another was saving her from partition. And while they bickered China remained one of the poorest countries on earth.

The United States had declared its 'Open Door for all' policy in September 1899 when it became apparent that American commercial interests in China had fallen behind those of Britain, Russia and Germany. The 26th American President, Theodore Roosevelt, was a militant advocate of Manifest Destiny, the belief that his country had a God-given right to impose Anglo-Saxon leadership on the Asian races of the Pacific. Having brokered the peace between Russia and Japan in 1905, he now agitated for his country to wrest the lion's share of the China trade from the British.

The prevailing jingoist attitude was perfectly expressed by the British conqueror of Tibet, Colonel Francis Younghusband, who declared in a letter to *The Times* during the Boxer Uprising, 'The earth is too small; the portion of it they occupy too big and too rich; and the intercourse of nations is now too intimate to permit the Chinese keeping China to themselves while at the same time they freely invade all the corners of the earth.'[1]

The very decrepitude of the Ching Court in Peking, where the 73-year-old regent Tzu Hsi was slowly dying following a stroke, seemed to prove that only a revolution could save China from being broken into pieces and shared among Westerners. George Morrison, however, discerned 'a sensible improvement' in the conduct of China's foreign affairs, dating from Yuan Shi-kai's appointment to a seat in the Wai-wu-pu and the promotion of Liang Tun-yen, a Yale graduate, to the vice-presidency on that body. Yuan, he wrote in *The Times*, had added 'the requisite strength of character, prestige and influence among his contemporaries, while Liang Tun-yen has supported [him] with a knowledge, rarely equalled among his countrymen'. Never had China's foreign affairs been more ably conducted, but it was only a reprieve from the usual chaos.[2]

Morrison's newspaper had just been acquired by Britain's own version of Gordon Bennett, Lord Northcliffe. The self-made press baron greatly admired Morrison's work and was keen for him to remain in Peking. Morrison's crown slipped, however, when he made the mistake of going on a five-day hunting trip on the Yellow River on 10 November 1908, leaving J. O. P. Bland to cover for him.

On 13 November 1908 Tzu Hsi struggled from her bed and named Pu Yi (pronounced 'poo yee'), the infant son of her nephew Prince Chun II, as crown prince. Simultaneously, the 38-year-old Emperor Kuang-hsu was struck down by a sudden illness just as he was hoping to regain his throne. Confined to bed in the lethal care of the Dowager's eunuchs, he joined his ancestors the following day. Although it was said he died of natural causes, Morrison suspected he had been poisoned on the orders of his malevolent aunt to prevent him from resuming his interrupted rule. Others blamed Yuan Shi-kai on the grounds that if Kuang-hsu had assumed the throne again one of his first acts would have been to execute Yuan for betraying the reform movement in 1898.

At 3 pm that same day – 14 November – Tzu Hsi turned her face west and expired. According to legend, her last words were, 'Never again allow any woman to hold the supreme power in the state. It is against the house-law of our dynasty and should be strictly forbidden. Be careful not to permit eunuchs to meddle in government matters.'[3]

Morrison arrived back in Peking the following day feeling 'mighty sick' at having missed this huge news story. He threw himself into his work 'trying to retrieve my blunder'. Prince Chun, he reported, would now rule as regent until his three-year-old son turned 18, while Kuang-hsu's widow, Empress Lung-yu, who was Tzu Hsi's niece, became the new Dowager Empress. One of Prince Chun's first acts was to punish Yuan Shi-kai for his role in betraying Kuang-hsu.

On 4 January 1909 Morrison was handed a copy of an imperial decree that stripped Yuan of all power on the grounds that he was suffering a foot infection which made it difficult to walk. As it was 'hardly possible for him to discharge his duties adequately', he was ordered to resign his offices at once and return 'to his native place to treat and to convalesce from the ailment'.[4]

Yuan's fall from grace was loudly applauded among the membership of the Chinese Empire Reform Association in Sydney. 'His behaviour towards the cause of reform proved him to be a renegade,' Ping Nam, the association's president, said. 'His duplicity showed him to be a reformer only on certain lines, namely personal gain and aggrandisement.'

Ping was devastated by the emperor's sudden demise and strongly suspected he had been poisoned.[5] It wasn't until 2008 that scientists confirmed that the Emperor had indeed been killed by arsenic after finding lethal levels of the poison in his hair, stomach and burial clothes. The identity of the person who administered the fatal dose remains unknown, although Kang Youwei always believed Yuan Shi-kai was responsible. Donald told his biographer that Kang said during a meeting at his hideout at Penang, 'I know that he paid a doctor $55,000 to poison the Emperor.'[6]

The Australian Chinese were delighted when Prince Chun appointed China's first consul-general to Australia. The man chosen for the post was Liang Lan-shun, who had attended meetings between Tse Tsan Tai and the scholar-reformers in Hong Kong. His arrival at Perth in the SS *Mongolia* on 16 March 1909 on his way to Melbourne was described in the *Sydney Morning Herald* as 'a diplomatic event of some significance. It shows for one thing that the name of Australia is being recognised in China as standing for great potentialities.' The paper saw Liang as 'an accomplished and able man to stand between us and the uncomplimentary legends that must be afloat concerning us in the Flowery Land'.[7]

Liang Lan-shun told a reporter that trade between the two countries 'should attain much greater dimensions than it has up to the present'.

> We have now a Government in power which is liberal and which is doing great work in moulding the Empire into one progressive whole. With our new Emperor and our new Government, China is forging ahead steadily, but much has to be done. We are building railways and opening up large districts. We are, in fact, rejuvenating the nation.[8]

Asked whether there was any truth in the belief that the Chinese coveted the wide open spaces of northern Australia, Liang replied that China had plenty of wide open spaces of her own in Manchuria and Mongolia. 'Some of our cities are certainly overcrowded, but this is being remedied, and people are being encouraged to improve other parts of the Empire,' he said. 'China has to take her internal arrangements into consideration before she seeks for outside affairs. To my mind, there is no surplus population in the Empire, and there is no need for us to have designs on Northern Australia.'

The *Sydney Morning Herald* welcomed the opportunities to increase trade between the two nations, and then created another 'uncomplimentary legend' by adding, 'it must be confessed that the Chinaman is unpopular in Australia. We not only do not welcome him as an immigrant, but we take special pains to prevent him reaching our shores.'[9]

On 20 April 1910 Halley's Comet made its appearance in the heavens, arousing intense excitement among the Chinese, who took it to portend a grave national crisis. To allay Chinese fears, the Christian Literature Society issued posters reproducing the comet as depicted in the Bayeux Tapestry. The posters and literature giving details of the astronomical phenomenon were given to the Wai-we-pu, schools and newspapers.[10]

On 18 May, Planet Earth actually passed through the comet's fiery tail, creating a sales opportunity for entrepreneurs who sold anti-comet gasmasks, anti-comet umbrellas and even anti-comet pills – not in China but to the gullible in Western capitals.

Despite Bill Donald's objections to children, Mary had fallen pregnant in late 1908 and their only child, a daughter christened Muriel Mary, was born in Hong Kong on 22 July 1909. Donald celebrated with one of his friends from Sydney, an American impresario named Hugh Ward who was visiting the colony with his theatrical troupe.

Donald invited Ward to accompany him to the opening of a new port at Hankow on the north bank of the Yangtze. 'We were royally entertained,' Ward says, 'and met the Chinese Commander-in-Chief and the Admiral of the Fleet.'[11]

Despite his exalted status, Donald was restless. Hong Kong was simply too colonial, too British, too claustrophobic. It was time to move on. With Gordon Bennett's blessing, he packed his bags and took Mary and Muriel up the China coast to Shanghai.

The steamer anchored at the Woosung bar in early 1911 and the family proceeded the 25 kilometres up the Whangpoo by tugboat to the Customs jetty. The river was packed with fast tea clippers, slow-moving ferries and junks with huge eyes painted on their bows. Sampans poled by semi-naked coolies slid past foreign gunboats bobbing at anchor in midstream. Closer inshore were the hulks of two ancient sailing vessels that had been converted into storehouses for imported opium.[12]

The building boom that would give The Bund its distinctive European character was just getting under way. The tallest buildings were still no more than four or five storeys high, solid, provincial structures with columns and porticos that contrasted vividly with the Chinese-styled *hongs* of yesteryear.

At the southern end of The Bund[13] was the brand new premises of the Shanghai Club, where members downed chota pegs[14] and pink gins at a bar stretching 110-feet seven-inches along one wall of the clubhouse.[15] At one end of the Long Bar – proudly but wrongly claimed to be 'the longest in the world' – the high-powered *taipans* who ran the Shanghai business world held court, while the pecking order moved progressively down the bar to the most newly arrived *griffin* barely discernible in the deeper recesses of the saloon through a haze of blue smoke.

The British satirist Jay Denby defined a *griffin* as 'a person who has not had time to have his constitution destroyed by the climate, his stomach ruined by the food and his good temper utterly spoiled by Chinese servants'. Shanghailanders, he said, affected to despise the *griffin*, but he could see that they had 'a sneaking regard for one as yet so free from the awful disabilities under which they themselves suffer'.[16]

The Donald family was transported along The Bund in a couple of rickshaws, with baggage coolies following behind.

They passed the exclusively white 'public' gardens[17] opposite the cast-iron fence and little apron of lawn fronting the British Consulate and crossed Garden Bridge to the Astor House Hotel on the northern bank of Soochow Creek. The hotel had just re-opened after being extensively rebuilt and was billed as 'the Waldorf-Astoria of the East'.

One of Donald's friends, the British diplomat Berkeley Gage – known as 'Through a Glass Berkeley' on account of his love of malt whisky – once memorably described Shanghai as the place 'where East and West met on the worst possible terms'. As he took in the five-storey hotel standing in gardens that stretched down to the waterfront, Donald's first impressions were much more favourable.

On the ground floor he found a spacious lobby with cane and leather easy chairs, a barroom and buffet, a large billiard room and a reading room containing the latest newspapers and magazines. On the first floor there was a magnificent two-storey dining room beneath an arched glass ceiling. From the second floor up, there were 211 bedrooms and seven suites.[18]

Around the block on Astor Road, a colony of journalists occupied rooms in the slightly older northern section of the hotel where rooms could be rented for as little as US$60 a month. Its first long-term guest Edwin Pickwoad was dead but the *North-China Daily News* was still in his family. His widow Janet had sold the paper to their son-in-law, Henry Morriss, a real estate tycoon who was married to their daughter Una. Morriss, a British Catholic of Jewish descent, built a large house in Frenchtown for his wife and three sons, Harry, Gordon and Hayley,[19] and kept a stable of racehorses, which he named after American Indians. He was known among the turf fraternity as 'Mohawk' Morriss.

For many years the *North-China Daily News* had enjoyed a virtual monopoly of Shanghai's advertising market, while presenting a stolidly imperial point of view in its editorial columns. Since 1906, it had been edited by Thurburn Montague Bell, nephew of the great *Times* manager Moberly Bell and a distinguished war correspondent for that newspaper. Its predominance in the affairs of the foreign concessions so annoyed another long-term Astor House guest, Thomas Millard of the *New York Times*, that he was in the process of founding the *China Press*, which would give the city its first American-style paper.[20]

Millard's business partners in the venture were Wu Ting-fang, a former Chinese minister to the United States (who was also a secret member of the revolutionary faction), and Charles R. Crane, a Chicago manufacturer.[21] Editorial offices were acquired close to The Bund, and Millard travelled to the United States to purchase type and mechanical equipment.[22] The paper's star recruit was Carl Crow, a 28-year-old graduate of his old college, the Missouri University's School of Journalism. Crow, who had like Bill Donald started his working life as a printer's apprentice, was a fine writer and sub-editor whose name would later become synonymous with the Shanghai advertising industry of which he was a founding member.

To counteract the threat of the new journal, Mohawk Morriss dispensed with Montague Bell's services and imported Owen M. Green, a rabid 34-year-old right-winger from England, with a brief to defend Britain's rights under the unequal treaties.[23] Millard took the opposing, pro-Chinese view. As he explained to Carl Crow, the *China Press* would pioneer the novel concept of treating Chinese news with the same respect as news from the United States, Britain or anywhere else.[24]

Bill Donald enjoyed his nightly discussions with Millard in the hotel's spacious lobby, especially stories about his proprietor Gordon Bennett whom the dapper 42-year-old American knew well. He had been a drama critic on Broadway when Bennett sent him off to war. He had covered the Boxer Uprising in 1900 for the *New York Herald* and had returned to China four years later for the Russo-Japanese War.

It was an opportune time for the launch of a newspaper with a pro-Chinese stance. The Chinese land-owning and merchant classes had forced the Ching Government to cancel several railway contracts with foreigners and had taken over the rights to build those lines themselves. At the same time, the country was taking its first tentative steps towards a constitutional monarchy with the setting up by imperial decree of assemblies in all provinces. Prince Chun had promised that a partially elected National Assembly, the *Tsuehen Yeun*, would be convened in Peking in 1910 but that was a step too far for the conservatives, who insisted it should be delayed until 1916. As a sign of the new militancy, a delegation of provincial assemblymen descended on Peking with a petition calling for the assembly's immediate convocation. 'That the authorities realise that something must be done to meet the changing conditions is evident from the concession already made in the direction of representative government,' Donald reported in the Adelaide *Advertiser*, 'but they do not go far enough to satisfy the modernists, who want an elective Parliament without delay.'[25]

The Hong Kong Revolutionary Party had supplied Donald with a contact in Shanghai, an American-educated Methodist minister named Charlie Soong. Donald visited him at his print shop on Shantung Road, where Bibles came out the front door and revolutionary pamphlets out the back.

Charlie Soong had been born Han Chiao-shun on the island of Hainan off the South China coast in 1861. As a youth, he had spent eight years in the United States, where he studied theology at Vanderbilt University. Returning to China as a Methodist preacher, he changed direction in 1896 with the founding of Commercial Press, which published Bibles, religious tracts and later Western-style textbooks.[26]

By 1911, Charlie Soong's Methodist work ethic had made him a rich man and his wife, Ni Guizhen, whom he called 'Mamie', had borne him three daughters – Ayling, Chingling and Mayling* – and three sons – Tse-ven (T. V.), Tse-liang (T. L.)

---

*   Mayling Soong's first name is spelled in various ways. This author has seen her signature on letters after her marriage to Chiang Kai-shek which are rendered 'Mayling Soong Chiang (Madame Chiang Kai-shek)'.

and Tse-an (T. A.) – all of whom would become indelibly linked with the Revolution. Charlie built a huge American-style house at Hongkew and sent all six children one after another to be educated in the United States.

Soong introduced Donald to Ayling, a spirited 20-year-old who was assisting her father in his revolutionary activities. Ayling had always been a bit of a rebel: she was credited with being the first Chinese girl to ride a bicycle in Shanghai (although it's difficult to see how such a claim could be substantiated). Her political education began in 1904 when she was travelling from Shanghai to Wesleyan College for Women at Macon, Georgia. She had been detained for three weeks by immigration officials at San Francisco under the Chinese Exclusion Act and was permitted to enter the country only after the intervention of the Board of Missions of the Methodist Church.

Two years later she was introduced to President Theodore Roosevelt by one of her influential relatives. 'Why should a Chinese girl be kept out of a country if it is so free?' she demanded, speaking English with a pronounced Southern accent. 'We would never treat visitors to China like that. America is supposed to be the Land of Liberty!' Roosevelt was taken by surprise and found himself apologising for one of his favourite laws. He would have been even more surprised had he known about the activities of Ayling's father in Shanghai.

Charlie Soong had met his fellow Christian Sun Yat-sen in 1894 just as the doctor was planning his first coup at the Canton arsenal. When Sun moved to Japan and formed the *Tungmeng hui*, Soong had become one of his chief financial backers.[27]

The first thing Donald and Soong discussed was the latest disaster to befall the revolutionary movement. In April, Sun had launched yet another coup – his tenth since 1895 – and once again the target had been Canton. Like all of his other attempts, success depended on the initial attack triggering risings in other cities and setting off mutinies in the armed forces. This time, Huang Hsing, Sun's chief lieutenant, led one hundred revolutionaries in an attack on the residence of the viceroy of Canton, Chang Ming-chi, with the intention of holding him hostage.

One revolutionary carried grenades in a box concealed beneath biblical tracts, possibly printed by Charlie Soong. The coup was foiled when imperial troops were rushed to the viceroy's compound to reinforce the guard. Most of the revolutionaries were killed in the fighting; one of Huang's fingers was blown off by a bullet but he escaped.[28]

Fearing the revolution had finally broken out, panic-stricken members of the Cantonese gentry transferred large parts of their fortune to Shanghai banks. 'The flight of wealthy Cantonese has already caused something like a "boom" in house property in Hong Kong,' *The Times* reported, 'and has called down the wrath of the Viceroy Chang Ming-chi on timorous officials.'[29]

Only 72 of the 86 bodies found at the scene of the battle could be identified, mainly those of young Chinese radicals who had returned from Japan. The martyrs, as they were called, were buried together at Yellow Flower Mound in the city's northern suburbs. Their grave became a place of veneration for generations of republicans.[30]

Donald told Charlie Soong the latest failure simply illustrated the revolutionaries' lack of cohesion and planning. Even if the coup had succeeded and the Manchu had been deposed, how would Sun have responded to the challenge of running the country? 'You people have dodged the matter of government,' Donald said. 'You must have men trained and capable who will fill it with democracy.'[31]

Soong nodded glumly. The movement had a long way to go before it would be able to seize power, let alone unite the country. Yet for all its flaws and the windiness of its ideology, the revolution was a lot closer than either of them would have believed possible.

Despite Shanghai's global reputation as an entrepot, it lagged behind Hong Kong in some basic respects. Even in the International Settlement (which had now expanded from its original plot to 5583 acres), there were no paved streets, no fly screens, no electric fans and sanitation was poor: flush toilets were considered 'unhealthy', so night-soil carts made their rounds at dawn.

At the same time, a municipal cart picked up the bodies of Chinese refugees who had died of starvation, disease or the cold during the night. Malarial mosquitoes bred in every available patch of stagnant water, even laying their eggs in the fire buckets in the corridors of the British Supreme Court.[32]

By night, sailors roistered among the fleshpots of Blood Alley and then had to fight their way out, while the bon ton dined and danced at the Astor House or the Palace Hotel at the corner of The Bund and Nanking Road. As the night owls headed home, wheelbarrows loaded with vegetables trundled along the narrow paths into Shanghai, passing the vile-smelling 'honey carts' bearing the night soil used to fertilise the fields in which they had been grown.

Poverty abounded in the walled Chinese city of Nantao and the industrialised Chinese boroughs of Chapei and Yangtzepoo. Thousands of workers had flocked to the city's factories and textile mills where they laboured for 12 hours a day seven days a week. Wages were often below subsistence level and the chronic housing shortage meant that many workers slept in shifts in the same beds.[33]

For Western businessmen, there had been commercial opportunities galore as the Ching Government pawned the country's assets in exchange for huge loans from foreign combines and banks. The British and Chinese Corporation signed a contract with Peking in July 1903 to build the railway line between Shanghai and Nanking. As surveyors moved into the Yangtze countryside, the theodolite became 'an object of unfailing interest and terror to the Chinese'.[34]

The pyramidal grave mounds of ancestors were violated during construction and when the line opened carters and boatmen were thrown out of work.[35] Other lines stretched from Peking to Hankow and would soon run down to Canton and Hong Kong, and as far west as Szechuen. Far from knitting the provinces together, as the Emperor Kuang-Hsu had envisaged, one Chinese statesman compared the rail network to a pair of scissors which imperialist powers were using to cut up the country.[36]

Proving Tocqueville's axiom 'that the most perilous moment for a bad government is that in which it begins to reform itself', Sheng Hsuan-huai, a notorious hustler who headed the Ministry of Communications, decided to nationalise the main railway system. Confrontation between Peking and the provinces became inevitable when an imperial decree announced on 9 May 1911 that Peking had taken over the Canton–Hankow and Szechuen–Hankow lines. This was simply a ploy to hand these lucrative projects to a British-American-French-German consortium, which was offering a huge loan to replenish the depleted Ching treasury.[37]

'Railway protection clubs' were formed in four provinces to defend local interests, mainly those of the scholar-gentry, rich landlords and wealthy merchants. Resistance was strongest in Szechuen, where the provincial assembly was dominated by rights recoverists whose main objective was personal enrichment. Its leaders organised a mass movement of outraged citizens who demanded that the nationalisation program be scrapped and Sheng impeached for corruption. Although the vast majority of the population had no financial stake in the railways, local pride had been injured and the gulf between Peking and the people widened perceptibly.[38]

On 22 June, in honour of the Coronation of King George V at Westminster Abbey, the Chinese population of Shanghai was given permission to enter the hallowed turf of the 'public' gardens for just one day. The band played 'Rule Britannia',

Union flags fluttered along The Bund and British buildings were bathed in patriotic red, white and blue electric light. The royal celebrations emphasised the lowly position that the Chinese occupied in their own country. By one of the quirks of history, they also saw the start of a catalogue of disasters that would strike the length and breadth of the Yangtze Valley.

Over centuries, silting had raised the river level several metres above the surrounding countryside. Levees had been built up, but there was nothing to hold back the floodwaters if these were breached. While large sums had been allocated towards flood control, much of the money had gone into the pockets of corrupt officials. The *taotai* of Shanghai, Tsai Nai-huang, had squandered 160,000 taels[39] from the Whangpoo conservancy fund, with the result that dredging of the river system had ceased at a critical time. Donald's friend Chang Jen-chun, who now occupied the viceregal seat of Liang-Kiang, a region comprising the central provinces of Anhwei, Kiangsi and Kiangsu, was ordered by Peking to investigate the charges against the *taotai*. Incredibly, Tsai Nai-huang had used the funds to buy up anti-government Chinese newspapers in order to close them down. He was politely asked to repay the money from his share of the Customs duties.[40]

Just a few days after the King's coronation, the engorged Yangtze broke its banks during the monsoon. Floods spread over the valley until it resembled a turbulent inland sea. At one popular crossing point near Shanghai, the river was 70 kilometres wide; upstream as far as Hankow, the scenes of desolation were described as 'pitiable in the extreme'. The racing tide washed away crops and threatened to breach the Hankow Bund and engulf the city. Groups of starving *banditti* roamed the valley, pillaging and burning farms and villages.[41]

Amos P. Wilder, the American consul in Shanghai (and father of the playwright Thornton Wilder), launched a famine relief committee to raise funds among foreign firms although, according to *The Times*, 'local officials, prominent gentry and men of wealth would rather see their people starve by thousands than have them fed by foreign aid'. When aid was distributed, it was regarded as 'legitimate prey' and invariably disappeared into the pockets of Chinese officials. 'It debauches the employees, it demoralises the community generally,' *The Times* said. 'It is almost impossible to have anyone punished for graft because all think they are entitled to all they can grab.'[42]

The chronic food shortages were exacerbated by speculators who hoarded grain in the good times in order to make a killing during the floods. Unable to afford the inflated prices, thousands of peasants died of hunger. 'The crime of cornering the people's food is, theoretically, one of the most heinous in the Chinese code, but it is practised constantly with impunity,' *The Times* noted.[43]

Meanwhile, Thomas Millard had published a prospectus to attract readers and advertisers to his new newspaper. 'Promoters of the enterprise have acted on the assumption that Shanghai has become a modern city, and that it will be a focus of the wonderful development just beginning in the Far East,' he wrote.

> As an up-to-date city, Shanghai affords a field for an up-to-date newspaper, provided at an up-to-date price. Such a newspaper at such a price the *China Press* is designed to be ... The enterprise is sustained by no special interest or Government, and will present the news of China and the world without restraint or partiality.[44]

There was certainly no shortage of newsworthy events in Shanghai. A few days after the first edition of the *China Press* hit the streets, bubonic plague broke out in Chapei, killing 14 Chinese and filling the beds of the Chinese Public Isolation Hospital with plague patients. At a meeting between the *taotai* and representatives of the hospital and the Chapei Chinese police force, it was decided that the infected quarter should be fenced off from the International Settlement to prevent the plague virus spreading to Europeans. *The Times* correspondent reported, 'The conditions under which the people live generally are such as to make plague in all probability endemic, not to speak of such diseases as smallpox, diphtheria and other infectious illnesses.'[45]

Bill Donald travelled upstream to report on the twin calamities of flood and famine. Entering Nanking in a sampan, he found Chang Jen-chun in the viceregal *yamen* that had once been a Taiping palace. Chang was carrying out a survey of conservancy requirements within his jurisdiction. Such schemes were always being attempted and then postponed for lack of funds. It was clear to Donald that nothing less than a comprehensive program of canalisation, dredging and embanking would stop the floods from recurring.

At the Custom House he watched in bewilderment as a coolie whose job was to clean up the courtyard swept the top of the swirling floodwaters. To the Australian, the sight seemed to symbolise the impossibility of uprooting old customs and changing traditional methods. With a heavy heart, Donald returned to Shanghai.

By mid-September, mass protests were paralysing many parts of Szechuen. In the provincial capital of Chengtu, wailing crowds demonstrated in front of a placard in memory of the Emperor Kuang-hsu who had granted them the right to build their own railway. The governor-general ordered the arrest of agitators and fighting broke out between troops and demonstrators, with the loss of 32 lives. The Szechuen Railway Protecting Society joined the fray with its battle cry, 'Drive out the foreign invaders and overthrow the Ching Dynasty.' Branches of the railway society were organised by guilds and trades; even beggars had their own branch. The authorities rushed troops of the New Army in Hupeh to Chengtu, unaware that a revolutionary student group calling itself the 'Literary Society' had infiltrated the Hupeh garrison and converted many of its officers and men to the anti-Manchu cause.[46]

Meanwhile, Sun Yat-sen had set up a Central China Bureau of the *Tungmeng hui* in Shanghai under his deputy Huang Hsing and one of his protégés, Sung Chiao-jen. He had then left on a fund-raising trip in the United States. Huang and Sung were invited by the dissident students in Wuchang, provincial capital of Hupeh and Hunan, to travel up the Yangtze to foment disturbances.[47]

Huang planned to strike at the end of October. He had no way of knowing that the 'dynastic cataclysm' predicted by Sir Robert Hart and to which Sun Yat-sen had devoted his life was about to happen in the most unexpected way.

CHAPTER 10

Revolution

White was the colour of the Revolution. And like the spectral white mist that rose from the flooded creeks and canals of the Yangtze Delta, it drifted slowly up the great river until it settled like a shroud over Wuhan, the tri-city area comprising Hankow, Hanyang and Wuchang at the junction of the Yangtze and Han rivers.

On the night of 9 October 1911 an explosion ripped apart revolutionary headquarters in the Russian concession of Hankow, the first tremor of an earthquake that would bring the 267-year-old Ching Dynasty crashing down. Police who searched the wreckage discovered that the house was a bomb-making factory and that a bomb had gone off prematurely. They also uncovered a cache of arms and a list naming conspirators who were planning to stage an uprising the following week. Some of them were officers of the New Army serving in the local garrison.[1]

In another part of Hankow that night, Chinese police raided a radical meeting and arrested 32 people, three of whom were publicly executed at dawn on 10 October – the Double Tenth. Anger spread among the soldiers, two of whom shot an officer when he questioned them about the weapons they were carrying.[2] Later that morning, the engineering unit of the New Army seized the government munitions depot at Wuchang and artillery units joined in a combined attack on the *yamen* of the governor-general, who fled down the Yangtze in a Japanese gunboat. By midday, the New Army had complete control of the city. The Double Tenth Revolution was under way.[3]

Fierce fighting broke out between some 3600 revolutionaries and a 3000-strong loyal Ching force. A British reporter described 'the streets deserted and the corpses of Manchus lying in all directions, 50 bodies being heaped together outside one gate alone. The Rebel troops are still hunting for Manchus, of whom 800 are reported to have been killed.'[4]

By 12 October, rebels from the 8th Division and a mixed brigade of the 21st Division had captured Wuchang and Hanyang and seized China's chief arsenal and the government mint containing two million taels.[5] At Hankow, the mixed brigade took the historic step of establishing a provisional republican government. As none of the revolutionary leaders was anywhere near Wuhan, the Ching commander, Lieutenant-Colonel Li Yuan-hung, was drafted in as military governor of Hupeh.

The reluctant Li's main qualifications for the post were that he was the most senior officer available and that he was a Han, not a Manchu. He proclaimed Hupeh part of the 'Chinese Republic' and assured the city's foreign consuls that he would respect all treaty obligations provided the powers stayed neutral during the struggle. The consuls cabled this message to their legations in Peking and, as mutinies and uprisings broke out sporadically throughout China, the powers heeded the warning and did nothing.[6]

The causes of the Revolution were quickly linked to the railways. 'Undoubtedly it is a striking manifestation of the general hatred of the Manchu regime, but it was precipitated by the Government's nationalisation object,' *The West Australian* reported from Hong Kong.

Under the original scheme many thousands of the plebeian population of China had a financial interest in the railways, very small, perhaps, but nevertheless actual. The Imperial authorities formed the opinion that better results could be obtained by nationalisation and with this end in view they sought the famous Four Power Loan. The project excited the bitter opposition of the people, who in all parts organised angry demonstrations in condemnation of the scheme. Meanwhile, the more daring agitators and the secret societies were sowing the seeds of insurrection and carefully nurturing them.[7]

George Morrison and Bill Donald were in their element with the big breaking news story, firing off tightly worded cables to *The Times* and the *New York Herald*. 'The rebellion gains increasing force and its well-organised appearances indicate that the Government is confronted with the most formidable danger since the Taiping rebellion,' Morrison cabled on 12 October. 'At any moment a message may arrive announcing a sympathetic outbreak at Canton, where revolutionary agitation has been simmering for a long time.'

China, he said, was learning the folly of stationing troops in the province of their birth where they were likely to sympathise with the local population. The Minister of War, Yin Chang, had been ordered to take two of the Northern divisions to Hankow to suppress the rebellion. The following day he reported that the immense mass of educated Chinese in Peking were unreservedly backing the revolutionaries. 'Little sympathy is expressed for the corrupt and effete Manchu dynasty with its eunuchs and other barbaric surroundings,' he said. 'The loyalty of the troops, even in Peking and Tientsin, is doubtful, especially when they become aware of revolutionary success elsewhere.'[8]

Dudley Braham, the *Times*' former Russian correspondent (and later editor of the Sydney *Daily Telegraph*), was standing in as foreign editor at Printing House Square. He congratulated Morrison on his 'most excellent' news coverage. 'We have left every other paper standing,' he said. 'So far I have only ventured to change one word in your messages – the word revolution. Our stylistic experts assure me that it can only be applied to a successful rebellion and then only after it has been successful.'[9]

Bill Donald decided to pay a call on Dr Wu Ting-fang, who had returned from a stint as China's minister to Washington and joined the rebels. He found Wu's home in Avenue Road in the International Settlement in a state of chaos. The Double Tenth coup had apparently caught the revolutionary leaders unprepared. Donald told his biographer that Wu 'was striding up and down his living room, hands behind back, muttering. Other than the general idea that the Manchu must be ousted, there were no workable plans.' According to Earl Selle, 'The revolution had been born in a dream. Until now it had remained beautiful and visionary, undisturbed by practical matters. Worst of all, no one had heard from Dr Sun Yat-sen.'[10]

Contrary to this account, the revolutionaries knew that Sun was in the United States and had cabled him with the news. Although he hadn't replied to those cables, he had in fact given members of the *Tungmeng hui* a clear, three-phase plan on how post-Manchu China should be governed.

During the first phase of three years, a military government would control all military and civil affairs at district level in the areas liberated by the revolutionary forces.[11] The second phase would involve a period of political tutelage, lasting not more than six years. The military would retain control of the central government but a form of local self-government would be introduced in the districts and popular elections held for local assemblies and administrative positions. During this period, a provisional constitution stipulating the rights of the people and the duties of the military government would be approved. In the third and final phase, the military government would be dissolved and the country would be governed by the new constitution.[12]

Indeed, Li Yuan-hung, promoted to general, was already implementing the first phase of Sun's plan as military governor in charge of the provisional government at Hankow. One of its members, T'ang Hua-lung, the former chairman of Hupeh Provincial Assembly, sent telegrams to other provinces urging them to declare independence of the Ching Court.

Donald visited Everard Fraser at the British Consulate in Shanghai to enlist his support. 'Well, Mr Donald,' Fraser said, 'I suppose you have come about the revolution.' Donald's republican sympathies were an open secret among members of the British community. He told Fraser that the revolutionaries were not asking for recognition of their fledgling republic at this point but were willing to provide 'exclusive information' in the hope that British banks would provide them with loans once the republic became a reality.

Fraser agreed to listen. The following day Donald brought Dr Wu, Wen Tsung-yao and other members of the Revolutionary Party to the consulate. 'Mr Fraser,' Donald said, 'there's one thing I didn't tell you yesterday – in case the Japanese attempt to jump into this arena, we expect the British to pull them out.'

Fraser laughed. He was in no position to commit his country to armed intervention against her Asian ally. However, in the days that followed, Donald briefed him on important developments which the consul reported to Sir John Jordan, who had replaced Sir Ernest Satow as British minister at Peking. Morrison described Donald as Fraser's 'chief source of information with regard to the Revolutionary Party'. And once he had learned to trust the Australian, Fraser became the revolutionaries' chief advocate and protector.[13]

Despite the hesitancy of the *Times* stylists, a full-scale revolution was in progress. The minister of war's attempts at suppression having failed, the government had little choice but to appeal to China's most effective and fearsome commander, Yuan Shi-kai, to retrieve the situation. Since his banishment from the Ching Court for betraying his emperor,

Yuan had bided his time with numerous wives and concubines at his home, the Garden for Cultivating Longevity at Tientsin. Considering the dire state of affairs in the Forbidden City, he was not surprised to receive an urgent summons from the regent, Prince Chun, informing him that he had been appointed viceroy of Hunan and Hupeh, with orders to suppress the rebellion in Wuhan.

While Yuan was deciding whether to obey this command, the revolutionaries approached him with an even more enticing proposal: they would, they said, make him president of the Chinese Republic if the revolution succeeded. Once again, a benevolent fate had placed Yuan in a pivotal position. He thanked the rebels for their offer and went back to his garden.[14]

On 17 October Morrison wrote, 'The Government is scared out of its wits but is acting with considerable resolution. But I cannot meet anyone, Chinese or foreign associates of the Chinese, who will not tell me the same thing privately – that they wish for the success of the revolution.'

Seven days later financial panic threatened to engulf the capital. 'The Treasury has less than one million taels, and it is certain that it will not be able to pay the official salaries,' he wrote. 'Failure will increase the panic. Chinese are leaving in large numbers, or sending away their families, because they fear Manchu reprisals. Manchus are leaving because they fear the future. Treasure of all kinds is being sent out of Peking to places of safety.'

Braham responded, 'Your telegrams have been excellent and are exciting much comment. You must feel like old times again writing the telegrams that are "the" news of the day.'

Morrison interviewed the Japanese military attaché, General Shuzo Aoki, who told him, 'This revolution is the end of the dynasty. Every hour the power of Yuan Shi-kai is increasing. He will end up with dictatorial powers.' Indeed, Yuan had given Prince Chun a list of demands. He would come out of retirement, he said, if the government made him supreme commander of the armed forces, with adequate funds and supplies to crush the rebellion. Furthermore, the existing cabinet of princes must be replaced with a more representative body and a national assembly set up within a year. Finally, the revolutionaries must be pardoned after he had suppressed their rebellion.

With more army units joining the revolution almost daily, Prince Chun agreed to make Yuan imperial commissioner in charge of the army and navy. Yuan rejected the offer and stayed at home. To demonstrate his power, he ordered General Tuan Chi-jui to recapture Hankow from the revolutionaries. As the Chinese city burned and the population fled in panic, the rebels retreated across the river to Wuchang and Hanyang, leaving behind many casualties. On Yuan's orders the foreign concessions were left untouched.[15]

At the same time the Ching Court received a demand from the 20th Division in North China that a constitutional monarchy should be set up within a year.[16] Faced with the prospect of a large armed force descending on Peking, the government surrendered. Prince Chun announced on 1 November that Yuan Shi-kai had been appointed prime minister in place of the wily and corrupt Prince Ching.

The following day the revolution spread to Shanghai. Everard Fraser received a letter from the 'Military Government of the Chinese people' announcing it was taking over the Chinese districts to preserve order and restore the confidence of the business community. Right on cue, the Chinese police force in Chapei mutinied and the police station was burned down. The taotai sought sanctuary in the International Settlement.

Bands of revolutionaries wearing white badges stormed into Kiangnan on the Whangpoo and seized the arsenal and the dockyards. 'The people who attacked Kiangnan were not soldiers but men of the labouring class armed with rifles,' The Times' Shanghai correspondent O. M. Green, the John Bullish editor of the North-China Daily News, reported.[17] White flags fluttered from the houses of Chapei and Chinese police wore white armbands bearing the words 'restoration of the Han people'. The revolution had finally reached the masses.

Shanghai's provisional government ordered men to cut off their queues. Police armed with scissors enforced the order. 'Many a poor innocent farmer, who had never heard of the revolution, found himself rudely nabbed and clipped as he came into the market,' one eye witness was quoted as saying. Even more liberating, the wall surrounding Nantao was torn down brick by brick and its slums exposed to daylight.[18]

On 11 November *The Times* carried startling allegations that the troops of the Manchu commander, General Chang Hsun – who had once served as the groom, or *mafoo*, to the Dowager Empress Tzu Hsi and was therefore known as 'the Mafoo General' – had run amok in Nanking and massacred Chinese men, women and children. Students who had cut off their queues were butchered on sight and anyone wearing a white badge or even white clothing – such as the white raiment worn in mourning – was in danger of decapitation. People had fled south along the Nanking–Shanghai railway line in desperate efforts to get away from the marauding soldiers. The *North-China Daily News*, whose editor had filed the story to London, appealed to the powers to protest against the massacre.[19]

Five days later *The Times* reported that Everard Fraser, on the instructions of Sir John Jordan, had given permission to the revolutionaries to transport troops and ammunition by railway to Nanking to stop the killing. The revolutionaries had put a price of $5000 on General Chang's head and promised revenge.[20]

Morrison was furious when he discovered that Green's source for these two sensational stories was Charles R. Maguire, an inebriated contractor whom he described as 'the champion liar of Nanking'.[21] Morrison remonstrated with Green, who admitted he was in the wrong. There had been no massacre in Nanking: the killings had been in Hankow. 'I expressed regret that he had not seen his way to correct the false stories he had been the chief means of disseminating,' Morrison wrote to

Braham. 'Of course I know he did so in good faith, but he had taken no adequate steps to have them verified.'[22]

Meanwhile, it was a fact that the railway authorities had withdrawn their staff and telegraphic equipment from Nanking down the line to the river port of Chinkiang. The evacuation was carried out under the surly gaze of a strong imperial detachment, which was waiting at the station to attack the revolutionaries. General Chang placed 35 guns on the city walls to cover any revolutionary advance from the north. Nanking, the key strategic city of the Yangtze, was completely cut off. If it fell to the revolution, further resistance by imperial forces would be futile.[23]

On 13 November Li Yuan-hung sent a notice to the consular body at Hankow stating that at the request of the revolutionary armies he was acting temporarily as the representative of the 'Central Government of the Republic' at Wuchang. He added that all treaties and loan agreements concluded by the Ching Government prior to the outbreak of the revolution would be honoured.[24]

Donald's associates Wu Ting-fang and Wen Tsung-yao were nominated by the Revolutionary Party in Shanghai to run foreign affairs. The party's domestic program was clearly defined as provincial self-government, with central military control at Wuchang, although the eventual capital would probably be Nanking. The unequivocal choice for president was Sun Yat-sen, who was still incommunicado abroad.[25]

On 14 November George Morrison watched Yuan Shi-kai arrive in Peking by special train from Tientsin protected by 'wild-looking halberdiers carrying long two-handled swords'. Yuan formed a new central government of ten Han and one Manchu with the aim of creating a constitutional monarchy. Morrison was pleased about his intervention as a counterweight to some of the Yangtze republicans whom he regarded as hot-headed. He was also in good spirits for another reason: he was having an affair.

Throwing caution to the wind, he had fallen for a girl named Bessie, an Australian visitor who dyed her hair and flirted with the diplomatic young bucks. 'So bright, attractive, winning, kind and sympathetic,' he told his diary, 'so sweet to look upon, so exquisitely formed, so natural . . . all day in a haze that fair image was ever before me, that beautiful voice ringing in my ear.' The following day he asked himself, 'What have I done to deserve such happiness and how horribly I will suffer when such happiness is taken from me.'

On 16 November Morrison discussed the civil war with Captain Tsai Ting-kan, a member of the Navy Board who was acting as Yuan Shi-kai's representative in talks with the revolutionaries at Wuchang. Tsai had known General Li Yuan-hung in a previous life when Li had served as third engineer in a torpedo boat in the flotilla of which Tsai was commander. Morrison suspected Tsai had thrown his lot in with the revolutionaries. 'While defending constitutional monarchy in theory, he is as strongly anti-Manchu as the men with whom he was sent to parley,' he noted.[26]

Several days later Tsai informed Morrison that Yuan Shi-kai wanted to meet him. He drove in a carriage to Yuan's residence, where he found that the general, always stout, had become quite rotund during his retirement. He was 'very cordial and complimentary', however. Speaking in a harsh bronchial whisper, Yuan said: 'If there were more pressure, perhaps the Court would leave for Jehol.' Morrison left the meeting convinced that the court was planning to leave Peking and that Yuan was conspiring to achieve that end. If they fled to the imperial hunting lodge at Jehol, 200 kilometres north of the capital, it would be only a matter of time before the Peking government collapsed.

On 21 November delegates from 11 of the 22 provinces arrived in Shanghai for the first national convention in China's history. As Dr Wu pointed out, with a provisional government at Wuchang and a National Assembly at Shanghai, a constitution was urgently needed to sort things out. Delegates declared that troops had been enlisted in sufficient number to overpower Nanking within a week. Donald decided to accompany them up the Yangtze to report the battle. It was the right decision but one that would transform him from journalist into participant.

The revolutionary armies gathered in great numbers at Chinkiang, where they pitched camp and waited. Although it was vital to take Nanking as soon as possible, intense rivalry between two of their leaders had created an impasse. When Donald arrived at Chinkiang station, a tall man with a clipped moustache and an impressively large girth was stalking the platform. This was Roy Scott Anderson, the local Standard Oil manager, who had been born into an American missionary family in Soochow in 1879. According to the *New York Times*, Anderson 'took an active part in the first Chinese revolution, serving as a General in the revolutionary army'.[27]

Anderson had heard that Donald was on his way and wanted to meet him. He told the Australian that the military governor of Chinkiang, General Ling, insisted on being the senior general in the forthcoming battle in order to claim the honour of victory. To this end, he had obstructed the advance of the other Chinese commander, General Hsu Ko-ching.[28]

Together, Donald and Anderson visited General Ling's headquarters where they found him drowsy from smoking opium. Donald told Ling he was speaking on behalf of the National Assembly. He then informed him that Nanking was to be the new capital of China and ordered him to resolve his differences with Hsu and permit the advance to go ahead. Ling agreed to do so, but even then Hsu refused to budge. The track between Chinkiang and Nanking had been mined, he said, and his trains would be blown up.

Donald and Anderson decided to call his bluff. Borrowing a locomotive from Arthur Pope, manager of the Shanghai–Nanking Railway, they made the 120-kilometre round trip to Nanking and back without incident.[29] Having reconnoitred the area, Donald informed General Hsu that the most vital strategic feature was Purple Mountain which overlooked the walls of Nanking. It was essential, he said, that the slopes of this shrub-covered peak be captured prior to attacking the Ching defences.

General Hsu's army proceeded by rail to Yao-hua-men on the outskirts of Nanking, pitched camp and waited. As the shadows lengthened and cooking fires glowed in the gathering darkness, Donald visited Hsu's headquarters and demanded to know the reason for the delay. The general informed him that there were guns on top of Purple Mountain, which would blast his men when they attacked the city walls. For the second time, Donald crossed the line between journalist and participant. Leaving Anderson at the camp the following morning, he climbed Purple Mountain, had tea with some monks at a monastery on the summit, and returned unscathed. There were no guns up there, he told Hsu, and ordered him to get on with it.

On 30 November Donald reported that the revolutionary army had captured Purple Mountain outside the Taiping gate on the east side of the city. The revolutionaries made a combined infantry attack in three columns and rushed the strongly fortified position in the face of heavy fire. Having secured the command of the adjacent hills, they placed their artillery in position with the help of their two European comrades and called on the imperialists to surrender. General Chang and his cohorts fled from the battlefield, abandoning Nanking to its fate.[30] The republican force then swarmed into the Tartar city, sacked its buildings and burned many to the ground.

According to the Hobart *Mercury*, it appeared that the revolutionary generals could not make up their minds to attack until a mysterious, unnamed foreigner suggested that a flanking movement might be added to the frontal attack. Once again, Donald had crossed the line. There were reports that he and Anderson had even been seen manoeuvring a republican field gun into position.[31]

On 4 December Prince Chun abdicated as regent of the Ching Government. The Dowager Empress instructed Yuan Shi-kai to negotiate a peace settlement with the revolutionaries. One of Yuan's first moves was to invite Morrison to visit Hankow in a complimentary railway carriage in which he was 'fed and wined with sybaritic luxury'. Looking at the burned buildings and wretched citizens, he concluded that 'China is indifferent whether Yuan Shi-kai makes himself President or Emperor; the Manchus must go. There seems absolute unanimity about this.'[32]

By 18 December, Donald was back in Shanghai. From the Palace Hotel on The Bund, he watched Yuan Shi-kai's peace emissary Tang Shao-yi and his entourage arrive by steamer at one of the Whangpoo jetties. Like his republican hosts, Tang Shao-yi had lopped off his queue as a sign of defiance to the Manchu. At their meeting, Dr Wu Ting-fang proposed a four-point peace plan: the abdication of the Manchu, the establishment of a republic, a generous pension for the Emperor, and relief for aged and poor Manchus. Tang Shao-yi informed him that he was in sympathy with their aims and agreed to hammer out the details of a settlement.

Morrison was reporting the conference first hand and was greatly helped by Bill Donald whom he had first met in Hong Kong. Donald, he noted, 'knows more about the inside of the revolutionary movement than any other foreigner'.

The American reporter Carl Crow had made the trip to Hankow to report on the revolution for the China Press. He was now covering the political developments in Shanghai and turned to Donald for enlightenment. 'Donald,' he said later, 'was the only foreigner in Shanghai who had the remotest idea of what the revolt in China was all about.'[33]

The supreme irony of the Double Tenth Revolution was that Sun Yat-sen, who had risked his life for this moment many times, was nowhere to be seen – he was on a fund-raising trip abroad and played no part in the early stages of the revolution. Although telegrams were sent to him at the hotels on his itinerary, he had inadvertently left his codebook behind and was unable to decipher them. One morning over breakfast at Denver, Colorado, he read the news in a local paper.

Sun's first instinct was to dash back to Shanghai to take control of matters as the senior revolutionary. But on reflection he decided his wisest course would be to visit Washington, London and Paris to seek assurances from ministers that their governments wouldn't prolong the life of the Ching Dynasty with an injection of arms and loans. Success in this mission would enhance his reputation as an international figure and enable him to return to China triumphant.

He travelled to Capitol Hill where Frank Knox, the United States secretary of state, refused to see him, even though he had been named in American newspapers as frontrunner for the presidency of the future republic.[34] It was much the same story in London. When the Foreign Secretary Sir Edward Grey declined to meet him, Sun sent assurances of his goodwill towards Britain through a third party, the arms dealer Sir Trevor Dawson of Vickers, Sons & Maxim. Dawson, who hoped to secure large orders from the Chinese armed forces, informed Grey that Britain would receive preferential treatment if Sun's party came to power and he were appointed president. He would place the navy under the command of British officers and accept British advice on China's relations with Japan.

The Foreign Office, however, had described Sun in a memorandum to the British cabinet as 'an armchair politician and windbag'. Grey ordered Dawson to tell him that Britain would remain neutral in the conflict, adding the biting comment that 'there seemed to be one good man on the side opposed to the revolutionaries, Yuan Shi-kai'.[35]

Further disappointment awaited in Paris. Although 'warmly greeted' by Premier Georges Clemenceau, Sun's efforts to secure the support of the French Government and a loan from French bankers fell on stony ground. For the time being, he accepted defeat. Before sailing from Marseilles for Hong Kong on 24 November, he cabled the revolutionary leaders in Shanghai and Nanking that either Yuan Shi-kai or Li Yuan-hung would be acceptable to him as presidential candidates.[36]

Sun arrived in Shanghai via Hong Kong on Christmas Day to great jubilation among his supporters. His reception became more muted when he confessed he had returned home without desperately needed funds for the revolutionary treasury. And it turned to bewilderment when he introduced Homer Lea, a so-called 'general' who had been recruited in the United States to train legions of Chinese revolutionaries to defeat the Manchu armies.

Lea was a dwarf and an amateur strategist whose main military accomplishment had been teaching the goosestep to Chinese laundrymen in Los Angeles.[37] Morrison and Donald must have feared the worst. Fortunately, Lea did not remain in Sun's employ for long but the damage had been done to Sun's reputation and Donald began to question his sanity.[38]

Since mid-December, republican delegates in Nanking had been squabbling over the leadership issue, with one faction favouring Huang Hsing and another Li Yuan-hung. Sun's arrival seemed providential: he would be the perfect compromise candidate. On 29 December, delegates from 16 of the 17 provinces represented in Nanking elected him provisional president of the Chinese Republic.[39]

Li Yuan-hung disliked Sun Yat-sen, claiming he had nothing to do with the overthrow of the monarchy and that his reputation was largely founded on fiction. 'The Revolution was finished when he reached China,' he said.[40] Sun had no illusions about his position: he knew his appointment as president was a matter of convenience and merely a temporary measure. The republican leaders had taken heed of Morrison's advice that Yuan Shi-kai was the only man who could persuade the foreign powers to recognise the republic. They assured him that Yuan would be offered the presidency once things had settled down. Indeed, Sun was as anxious as anybody to avoid armed conflict between the Northern and Southern arms of the revolution. He notified Yuan Shi-kai that he could take over as president if he declared allegiance to the republic. But there was a problem. 'Now the question is, will Yuan Shi-kai accept this appointment?' Morrison wrote to Braham on 29 December. 'He said that he and his ancestors have served the Manchu dynasty faithfully, and he could not go down to the future as a usurper. But suppose the Manchus themselves should desire his appointment?'

Two days later Morrison met Yuan Shi-kai's aide Tsai Ting-kan and outlined a plan under which the Manchu themselves would support Yuan's appointment, thus ensuring the abdication of the Emperor. Tsai passed the scheme to Yuan and reported back that he would not only act on it but would be 'tickled to death' to do so. Like Bill Donald, Morrison had crossed the line and was now an active participant in the events shaping China's destiny.

Meanwhile, the Double Tenth Revolution had created uproar in Australia's Chinese communities. The editors of the royalist *Tung Wah Times* in Sydney, who favoured retaining the monarchy under the child Emperor Pu Yi, at first minimised the extent of the uprising and predicted it would fail like all of the other attempts. In Melbourne, the republican *Chinese Times* rejoiced that the Ching Dynasty was fast approaching its end and that the Han race would soon rule China once again.[41]

As events moved towards a dramatic climax, Tsai Ting-kan suggested George Morrison should be styled 'The Australian Hero of the Chinese Reform Movement'. The Australian reporter just smiled.

CHAPTER 11

The Sinking Sun

On 1 January 1912 Sun Yat-sen left his house behind a white picket fence at 63 Route Vallon,[1] Frenchtown, and took the train to Nanking with his political confreres. 'Oh! Such a rag-tag and bobtail lot!' said Arthur Pope, who watched their departure from North Station. 'It is impossible to recognise a cabinet of scallywags, like the one put up by Dr Sun Yat-sen.'[2]

At 11 o'clock that night Sun was sworn in as provisional president of the Republic of China. He took the oath in a ceremony of considerable pomp:

> I will faithfully obey the wishes of the citizens, be loyal to the nation and perform my duty in the interest of the public, until the downfall of the despotic government . . . then I shall relinquish the office of provisional president. I hereby swear this before the citizens.

At the same time the Ching Dynasty issued an imperial proclamation accepting the creation of the republic. Commemorative vases, kettles and teapots flooded the market stalls and the republican battle flag – a white sun in a blue sky on a red background – fluttered from flagpoles and buildings. After the ceremony, the new president telegraphed Yuan Shi-kai to confirm his promise to stand down once Yuan announced his support for the republic. It was now Yuan's task to secure the abdication of the Ching Dynasty.[3]

Bill Donald attended the Nanking ceremony, filed his story to the *New York Herald* and then returned to Shanghai. Twenty-four hours later he received an urgent plea from Sun Yat-sen. He was being pressured to publish a manifesto. Would Donald write it? Despite his reservations about Sun, the Australian needed no persuading. The republicans needed to explain their aims to the Chinese people and the wider world. Sitting down at his battered typewriter, he started to type.

Donald's writing tended to be verbose but he wanted this document to be simplicity itself: in clear, crisp, unambiguous language, it had to crystallise the aspirations of every Chinese idealist for a better, fairer, more equal way of life. 'We will remodel our laws,' he wrote, 'revise our civil, criminal and commercial and mining codes, reform our finances; abolish restrictions to trade and commerce, and ensure religious toleration.' Donald spent most of the night drafting the manifesto with, it is said, the aid of a bottle of bourbon – quite possibly true, because despite his later denials it seems he had tasted Kentucky mountain dew and found that he liked it. In the morning, he cabled the manifesto to Nanking and on 5 January it went out under the signature of Provisional President Sun Yat-sen.

All that remained was the formal reading of the last rites over the supine form of the Ching Dynasty. On 10 January, Morrison got the scoop of the revolution when he predicted the abdication of the Manchu after Yuan Shi-kai supplied him with a copy of an edict in the name of the Dowager Empress ending the dynasty's rule. Morrison showed it to Sir John Jordan, who exclaimed that Britain 'cared not a damn whether there was a republic or a monarchy'.[4]

Six days later extremists in the Revolutionary Party tried to assassinate Yuan Shi-kai as he travelled to the Winter Palace to make arrangements with the Dowager Empress for her exodus. Four party members were stationed along the route and at 11.15 am, as Yuan returned from his audience, they threw bombs at his carriage. At least two bombs exploded, killing 12 guards.

Morrison had just escorted his young New Zealand-born secretary Jennie Robin to the gate of his house to watch Yuan pass by. As the carriage reached the corner, 'there was a loud explosion and a burst of smoke,' Morrison wrote. 'At once I knew a bomb had been thrown. A riderless horse dashed past, other men riding after it, and then after a moment of suspense the carriage was seen coming round the corner. It paced quickly past giving us a glimpse of Yuan seated. Nothing had happened to him, thank God.'[5]

Three of the bomb throwers were apprehended at the scene and admitted they were revolutionaries whose intention was to kill Yuan Shi-kai 'for continuing hostilities against his fellow-countrymen'. All three were strangled by the official executioner in the iron collar of the official Manchu garroting machine.[6] Yuan accused Dr Wu and his Shanghai colleagues of masterminding the attempt on his life. He retired for several weeks to his Peking residence, the Temple of Worthies, to await the royal summons.

On 12 February the Dowager Empress and the boy Emperor Pu Yi, the Son of Heaven, ascended their thrones in the Yang-hsin Hall, the ceremonial inner sanctum of the Forbidden City, for the final act in the abdication drama. In the presence of Yuan Shi-kai and his cabinet, Her Majesty read the abdication edict with tears streaming down her face, while her courtiers wailed and prostrated themselves on the floor:

Yuan Shi-kai, having been elected Prime Minister some time ago by the Political Consultative Council, is able at this time of change to unite the north and the south. Let him then, with the full power so to do, organise a provisional republican government ... that peace may be assured to the people and that the complete integrity of the territories of the five races – Han, Manchu, Mongol, Muslim and Tibetan – is at the same time maintained in a great state under the title of the Republic of China.

The Ching Dynasty had been swept away and the great republican vision had become a reality. It was a unique situation: two Australians had helped to topple a 2000-year-old empire and replace it with what would become the world's biggest and most diverse republic.

On 10 March Sun Yat-sen handed over the reins of power to Yuan Shi-kai, the world's most unlikely democrat. It came as no surprise to discover he had inherited a fragile, bankrupt government. The revolution had been starved of funds because the revenues of the British-run Chinese Maritime Customs Service were being handed over to British banks to repay previous British loans to the Manchu.[7] 'The Chinese Republic is a very young baby,' Yuan said. 'It must be nursed and kept from taking strong meat or potent medicines like those prescribed by foreign doctors.'[8]

Yuan was speaking figuratively but there was one 'foreign doctor' he urgently wanted to recruit into his team to guide the Chinese Government through the political minefields abroad: Dr George Morrison.

From Morrison's point of view, the timing couldn't have been better. Bessie's nagging and jealousy had driven him into what he described as 'a fiery rage'. On 28 February he had finally snapped. 'Before it was delightful having you here,' he told her, 'now you are a regular damned nuisance!' 'What a virago!' he wrote in his diary. 'It will be an immense burden lifted from my shoulders when Bessie departs for other clients.' His former love was now 'a champion sponger' and, worst of all, 'She was unclean in mouth and body. I could not get her to wash!'[9]

Morrison was now 50 and, according to his middle son Alastair, had had 'hundreds of lovers'.[10] It seemed he would never find the woman of his dreams. J. K. Ohl hosted a ball and pointedly snubbed him. 'I am a social failure,' he moaned. His ostracism might well have had something to do with his opinion of Ohl: in his diary, the American's name appears on a list of reporters 'who may write well and will write to order but have no standing and no personality'. Also on the list – unfairly, as we shall see – was a 41-year-old Australian journalist, Major Albert Wearne of Liverpool, New South Wales. Wearne had been wounded in the Boer War while serving with the New South Wales Mounted Rifles (and later won the Military Cross in World War I). He had come to China to work for the *North-China Daily News* and had since been appointed to run Reuters' Peking bureau.[11]

In early April, there was a complete reversal of fortune in Morrison's romantic life when he realised he had fallen in love with his 23-year-old secretary Jennie Robin. 'I long to take her in my arms and tell her I love her,' he wrote in his diary. 'But there is an awful disparity in our ages.' Then he asked himself, 'I wonder does she care for me?'

One spring morning, as they walked along a section of the Great Wall, he plucked up the courage to declare his love. To his relief, it was reciprocated. The joy of it sent him into raptures: 'My God, how I do love her – better than anything on this earth.' She was 'a refined, pure-minded English girl, highly educated . . . secretive and trustworthy . . . sings prettily and plays nicely . . . one of the best mimics I have ever known'.

Morrison made plans to leave *The Times* – it had never paid him well and he was fed up with the day-to-day grind of reporting Chinese politics. He and Jennie would get married and live on the sale of his library. It contained 20,000 books, 4000 pamphlets and 2000 maps and engravings, and would fetch £40,000. 'I am tired of the incessant strain,' he said, 'the late hours, the irregular work, the difficulty of sifting truth from falsehood, the difficulty of understanding Chinese springs of action. I want to settle down quietly in a country village in Australia.'[12]

When Donald visited Peking the following month, Morrison arranged for him to meet Sir John Jordan. He also suggested the younger man might replace him as the *Times* Peking correspondent. Donald was deeply touched. 'Now, Doctor, when you were flattering enough to mention this subject to me I did not say much,' he wrote on 25 May. 'You know that I would but indifferently follow in your footsteps. However, I appreciate to the bottom of my heart the kindly feeling embodied in your suggestion and I will not forget it.'[13]

Then Yuan Shi-kai approached Morrison through his confidential secretary Tsai Ting-kan with the offer of a five-year contract, all travelling expenses, a £250 annual housing allowance and a salary of no less than £3500, almost triple his *Times* pay. The offer changed Morrison's mind about leaving Peking. He would now be able to offer his young wife-to-be a good life in the Chinese capital as the well-paid political adviser to the Chinese Government. Jennie was sent ahead to London to stay with her family in Surrey while she prepared for the wedding. Morrison would join her there in August after his appointment had been announced.

Meanwhile, Bill Donald had developed serious misgivings about Sun Yat-sen. The Australian's typewriter fairly crackled with anger as he listed Sun's shortcomings in a letter to Morrison on 4 July. Things were in 'as great a muddle as they could possibly get this side of open anarchy', he said. Although Sun assured him he was out of politics for good, Donald doubted it: when his Chinese followers came to see him, they addressed him as 'President' and virtually prostrated themselves in the despised kowtow. 'He, I am convinced, has come to imagine himself to be the Moses of China who is destined to lead the hordes into the promised land,' Donald wrote.

A few days earlier Sun had produced a large map of China showing his plans for a new Chinese rail network. The map took in Tibet and Mongolia and the western extremities of China. From time to time, Sun had taken his brush and a stick of ink and filled in every province and dependency with as many lines as he could cram in. There were double lines to indicate trunk lines sweeping round the coast from Shanghai to Canton, then leading across precipitous mountains to Lhasa, the Tibetan capital.

The map was 'nothing but a grotesque Chinese puzzle', Donald said. 'Sun sat down on the floor to explain things to me, and as he sat there I thought that never could such a scene be drawn to depict the ineptitude of this, the first President of the Chinese Republic. He is mad!

'Sun is not only as mad as a hatter, but he is madder. He is absolutely unpractical, without common sense and devoid of the most elementary ideas of the subject he professes to be now fathering.'

Donald signed off with a postscript which removed any doubts that he had turned to liquor to deal with the pressures of the time. 'Now I'll go and get drunk under old Glory, and see stars and stripes,' he scribbled in a bold hand, 'for this is the 4th [of July] and I'll jubilate because the Lord so worked it that we are not responsible for Americans!'[14]

Donald's drinking career seems to have been short-lived; friends recalled him throughout the 1920s and '30s as a committed teetotaller. In later life his drinking completely slipped his mind. 'I never imbibe,' he wrote to a friend in 1945, just a year before his death, 'so do not understand the effects.'[15]

Morrison's appointment as political adviser to Yuan Shi-kai was greeted with enormous enthusiasm in the United States. 'Here is a unique man in a unique job, and his success or failure may affect the whole future of the Far East, and, incidentally, of the other nations of the world,' James M. Macpherson wrote in the *New York Times*.[16]

While Morrison was travelling to London, Yuan Shi-kai laid a clever trap to remove his opponent, who, he believed, was still a political threat. He invited Sun Yat-sen to Peking where rooms were made available for him at the Wai-wu-pu building and a meeting arranged with the Dowager Empress. Having flattered his ego, Yuan then offered him the post of 'Director for the Construction of All Railways in China'. The grandiose title (plus a salary of $30,000 Chinese a month) was irresistible: proclaiming the new president a great man whose opinions 'embodied very largely my own views', Sun gleefully accepted.

Commandeering Tzu Hsi's personal rail carriages, he embarked on an inspection tour of the existing rail system with Bill Donald acting as adviser. The entourage included Sun's wife Nee Lu and his personal secretary, Charlie Soong's eldest daughter, Ayling. It was Sun's secret ambition to divorce his wife and marry the beautiful, much younger Ayling.

Pride of place in his luxurious Pullman coach was given to 'The Map' which, Sun explained to Donald, would be shown to reporters as proof of his commitment to railway-building. To Donald, this was sheer madness – it would expose Sun as a hopeless dreamer and embarrass the young republic. When reporters from Western newspapers and news agencies filed on board the train at the big railway junction of Fengtai, Sun discovered to his consternation that 'The Map' had mysteriously disappeared. One newsman asked Sun whether he was a Socialist. He turned inquiringly to Donald, 'Am I?' The Australian answered, 'You are everything that is required as a Nationalist.' Donald then contrived a security alert so that he could throw the pressmen off the train. Once Sun was tootling through the countryside again, 'The Map' magically reappeared.

Despite Sun's apparent aversion to politics, Donald learned from his Shanghai revolutionary friends that the *Tungmeng hui* was secretly preparing to put him up against Yuan Shi-kai for the presidency in China's first democratic elections to be held under the new constitution. 'While Sun Yat-sen gives it out to the world that he is done with politics and is devoting his energies to the development of the natural resources, he is conspiring here with his bottle-washer coterie to become the President,' he wrote to Morrison from Shanghai on 4 August.[17]

Donald claimed he bore no animus towards Sun – 'I must hasten to add, we are good friends' – but in his opinion Sun was a 'pseudo-patriot', 'a pitiful, uneducated, incapable charlatan', 'an imposter' and a 'willing instrument in the hands of a crowd of wirepullers'. Sun and Huang Hsing had tried to persuade Wen Tsung-yao to dissolve the Revolutionary Party and join the *Tungmeng hui* in founding a new political entity. Wen sought Donald's advice and was warned to 'give the *Tungmeng hui* a wide berth'. Since then, Donald had been working in the background to undermine the *Tungmeng hui*'s credibility in order to support Yuan Shi-kai, whom he regarded as China's best hope of stability.

'I thirsted to have a public whack at the *Tungmeng hui*,' he wrote, 'and chance came my way when O'Shea, the proprietor of the *Shanghai Times*, fell ill. He asked [Lionel] Pratt to take over the editorial writing and you can judge that I soon had heaps of subjects for Pratt. I set him after the *Tungmeng hui*'s scalp hot and strong, and we have been after it ever since.'

Even more furiously, Donald wrote to Morrison on the same subject a week later. 'Everyone is sick of the way things are going,' he said, 'and the sooner you can get back and advice [sic] Yuan to lop the heads off all obstructionists the better. What Yuan ought to do is to seize a big stick and wipe [sic] the *Tungmeng hui* and all its members on the head.'[18]

Donald's efforts to destabilise Sun Yat-sen's 'bottle-washer coterie' failed to have the desired effect. On 25 August the *Tungmeng hui* combined with other revolutionary groups to form the *Kuomintang* – the National People's Party. The new party's manifesto pledged 'to adopt the principles of social service to prepare the way for the introduction of socialism in order to facilitate and better the standard of living, and to employ the powers and strength of the Government quickly and evenly to develop the resources of our country'. It was a major victory for Sun Yat-sen; Donald had seriously underestimated his influence.

The following day in faraway London, George Morrison and Jennie Robin were married at the Emmanuel Church, South Croydon, in front of friends and family, including Morrison's mother Rebecca, Jennie's parents and his old friend, the diplomat Sir John McLeavy Brown.[19] Morrison was on honeymoon when Yuan Shi-kai reacted to the *Kuomintang*'s manifesto and the provocation of the pro-Sun lobby in his cabinet. The first victim was his former ally Tang Shao-yi, whom he had appointed prime minister even though he knew his sympathies were with the Southern revolutionaries. Tang was dismissed in August, ending a friendship that stretched back to their service in Korea in the 1890s.

As he left office, he sadly noted: '[Yuan Shi-kai] is the only man who can unify the country, provided he co-operates sincerely with the Revolutionary Party. But judging from what has happened in the past three months, I fear that disillusionment may come in the end.'

In Moscow, Lenin had no intention of leaving the development of the new republic up to President Yuan. 'China is seething,' he said, 'it is our duty to keep the pot boiling.'[20]

As things turned out, the purpose of Josiah Ohl's ball from which Morrison had been excluded was to celebrate the American's departure from Peking. His replacement was Bill Donald. As well as serving the *New York Herald* in Shanghai, Donald had become editor of the monthly *Far Eastern Review* in partnership with a controversial American right-winger, George Bronson Rea. The *Review* was regarded as the best edited and best informed magazine on Chinese affairs in Asia. Donald was determined to maintain its pro-Chinese, pro-American stance.

In 1913 Bill and Mary Donald bought a two-storey redbrick house with a roof garden at 24 Tsung Pu Hutung, one of the cobbled lanes that crisscrossed the eastern part of Peking. Most of the purchase price came from money that Mary's family had left to her. The house was one of two in a large compound, surrounded by the smoking chimneys and tiled roofs of modest Chinese dwellings. The occupant of the second house was Roy Anderson, who had left Standard Oil and was making a living as an interpreter for the American Legation and an intermediary for American businessmen trying to enter the Chinese market.

The Donalds employed three Chinese servants: an amah to take care of Muriel, a cook, and a coolie who looked after Donald's two horses. With Rodney Gilbert, the 24-year-old Peking correspondent of the *North-China Daily News*, Donald set up a press bureau in a dusty little office in the old Russo-Asiatic Bank building. He would travel down to Shanghai once a month by ship or train to put the *Review* to bed. Gilbert was a Pennsylvanian who had seen much of China as a medicine salesman. He would later become an arch-conservative and, to Donald's disgust, one of China's harshest critics in books such as *What's Wrong with China*.[21]

Although Peking lagged behind Shanghai as a world city, it had great charm. The twisting *hutung* echoed to the chants of hawkers and peddlers, and there was a wide variety of nightspots, theatres, teahouses and restaurants. Living in this fascinating place, however, failed to bring Bill and Mary Donald closer together. Donald later drew a veil over his marriage, claiming to his biographer it had ended in 1912 after Mary told him, 'Don, you are married more to China than to me.' But he wasn't being truthful about what really happened between them, possibly because the truth hurt too much.[22]

Mary later chastised Earl Selle for publishing her husband's version of events. The marriage broke up in 1919, not 1912, she said, which meant she had been with him in Peking during the early years of the republic and right through the turbulent times of World War I. Selle wrote back to her, 'I am sorry if you felt any annoyance over what I wrote concerning your separation from Mr Donald. The words are his and I am sure that that is the way he liked to remember it.'[23]

Donald's daughter Muriel also contacted Selle. Her letter is lost but he replied, 'If there were errors concerning your mother and yourself this was due to the fact that this seemed to be a sealed chapter in his life. I am sorry to say that he felt very strongly about your mother to the end. For you, however, he had an intense devotion. I am sure that you were his one big love.'[24]

While Sun Yat-sen was happily occupied playing trains, the main threat to Yuan Shi-kai's authority came from Sung Chiao-jen, who led the *Kuomintang* to victory in the national elections for the new American-style Senate (*Tsan Cheng Yuan*) and House of Representatives (*Li Fan Yuan*). On 20 March 1913 Sung was setting off from Shanghai's North Station for Peking to become prime minister when he was shot by an assassin, described as 'a short man in black'.[25] He was rushed to hospital, where doctors were forbidden to operate until they received permission from the capital. By then, it was too late; Sung was dead. A Western doctor testified he could have been saved if she had operated immediately.[26]

Yuan's administration claimed Sung's rivals in Shanghai were behind the assassination but incontrovertible evidence in the form of telegrams sent from Peking to the assassin – a provincial police chief named Ying Kwei-shing – linked the murder to Yuan Shi-kai's regime.[27] Yuan denied complicity in the crime but having survived a bomb attack himself it seemed clear to the republicans that he was prepared to use the same ruthless methods to silence his opponents.

On 31 May 1913 Jennie Morrison gave birth to the first of Morrison's three sons, Ian Ernest McLeavy Morrison. 'I hope the little chap will thrive heartily,' Bill Donald wrote to Jennie, showing that he appreciated the compensations of fatherhood. 'He will be a great comfort to you and will surely be a credit to you and his distinguished father.'[28] The Donalds were invited to the christening party. Bill was, however, 'very depressing' in his comments about China's immediate future. Morrison's diary notes read: 'Outlook very bad. Country on the rocks. Recrimination. Distrust of the Kuomintang.'

Lionel Pratt moved from Hong Kong to Shanghai to work under Donald on the *Review*. He wrote to Morrison that he hoped to see China recover from her 'Republican delirium'. The feeling among the Chinese in Shanghai was decidedly pessimistic, he added, and the incapacity of 'the scum that came to the top during the turmoil' became more evident with every day.[29] Morrison found Pratt's views even more depressing and put them down to his consumption of liquor; he also despaired over the views expressed in a letter from the Australian revolutionary Tse Tsan Tai, who was now living in retirement in Hong Kong.

Since being laid off by the *South China Morning Post*, Tse had devoted his time to writing a book based on his Bible studies. *The Creation, the Real Situation of Eden, and the Origin of the Chinese* was an extraordinary work which located the Garden of Eden in Sinkiang, China's north-western province. On 14 April 1913 Tse received a letter from Dr Hiram Maxim, inventor of the automatic machine-gun which had doomed the Gatling gun to obsolescence, offering his services to China.

Switching from Genesis to Apocalypse, Tse suggested to Morrison that Maxim be appointed military adviser to the Chinese government. Maxim was offering his 'weapons of destruction' to China, Tse said, and his 'great Capitalist' friends the Rothschilds would be only too happy to help with a loan.

In his reply to Tse, the upright Presbyterian in Morrison overcame the imperialist. More in sorrow than in anger, he asked Tse, 'Do you really think such a man is needed in China at the present time?' China had been a dumping ground for weapons for the past 25 years, he said, and what it needed now was industrial development and an end to the appalling destruction of life.[30]

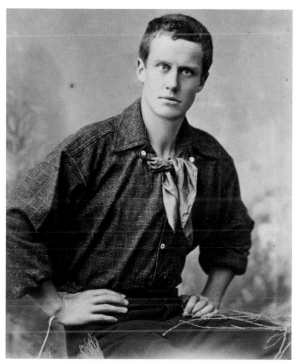

DARING: Young George Ernest Morrison caught the imagination of the Australian public with his exploits in the South Seas and New Guinea before heading for China in 1897 as the *Times* correspondent in Peking. His reputation as a great lover ended when he married the beautiful New Zealand-born Jennie Robin in 1912. *Mitchell Library, State Library of NSW, a742002*

ADORABLE: Mrs George Morrison, the former Jennie Robin. *Mitchell Library, State Library of NSW, a1012001*

ADORING: Dr George Morrison with his three sons, (from left) Ian, Colin and Alastair. *Mitchell Library, State Library of NSW, a1012005*

CHINA FORCE: Four members of the Australian Naval Brigade who served in China following the Boxer Rebellion of 1900. George Wynne, who wrote violently anti-Chinese articles for the *Daily Telegraph*, is on the right of the front row. *Australian War Memorial Negative Number P00417.035*

WRECKED: The bullet-ridden British Legation after the Boxer siege in which George Morrison was badly wounded helping Chinese refugees. *Australian War Memorial Negative Number P00417.009*

ANGRY: A crudely armed Boxer with imperial soldiers, as depicted by a Western artist. The Boxers murdered Chinese Christians and besieged the Foreign Quarter of Peking during the rebellion. *The Granger Collection/Topfoto*

LEGEND: William Henry Donald of Lithgow, NSW, was closely involved with China's affairs for four decades, serving as adviser of Sun Yat-sen, Chiang Kai-shek and Madame Mayling Soong Chiang. *Mitchell Library, State Library of New South Wales*

WEDDING: In 1904, Bill Donald married English-born Mary Wall in Hong Kong. *Mitchell Library, State Library of New South Wales*

DAUGHTER: Muriel Donald, born in Hong Kong on 22 July 1909, was the Donalds' only child. *Mitchell Library, State Library of New South Wales*

UNITED: William Henry Donald, hat in hand and tie askew, with Madame Chiang Kai-shek in Shanghai circa 1937. According to the American spy James McHugh, Donald was bound to the former Mayling Soong by blind faith and devotion, but she ultimately betrayed him. *Associated Press*

BEFORE AND AFTER: The city of
Hankow on the Yangtze prior to the
revolution of 1911 and blazing fiercely
during fighting between revolutionaries
and Manchu troops. *Press Association*

MAJESTIC: Warlord Yuan Shi-kai is borne aloft at his inauguration as second president of
the Republic of China in 1913. *Press Association*

REVERED: A bronze sculpture of Sun Yat-sen, first president of the Chinese Republic and known today as 'the Great Forerunner of the Chinese democratic revolution', sits outside a museum devoted to his life in the former Frenchtown, Shanghai. *Author's collection*

POWER PAIR: Sun Yat-sen's protégé, Chiang Kai-shek, pictured with his wife, Mayling Soong Chiang, in Cairo during a summit meeting with British Prime Minister Winston Churchill and American President Franklin D. Roosevelt in November 1943. Australia's Prime Minister John Curtin was not invited, even though the meeting discussed vital strategic and political matters relating to the Pacific War. *Australian War Memorial Negative Number MED2043.* ABOVE RIGHT: Chiang Kai-shek with Sun Yat-sen at the Whampoa Military Academy in 1924. *Press Association*

MORTAL ENEMIES: Communist leader Mao Tse-tung drinks a toast with his Nationalist rival Chiang Kai-shek in Chungking to celebrate Japan's defeat in World War II. Mao, pictured right as a young Communist firebrand, then drove Chiang out of China and declared the People's Republic of China on 1 October 1949. *Australian War Memorial Negative Number P02018.416, Press Association*

COLD WAR THAW: Australia's Prime Minister Gough Whitlam meets an aging Chairman Mao Tse-tung of the People's Republic of China in Peking during his historic 1973 visit behind the Bamboo Curtain. *National Archives of Australia: M2153, 18/5*

HEROINE: Eleanor Mary Hinder, the Australian who tackled child labour in Shanghai's sweatshops and the enforced prostitution of young Chinese women. Eleanor fell in love with American consul Viola Smith, who fought to liberate her after she was trapped by the Japanese invasion of Shanghai in World War II.

WITNESS: Colin Malcolm McDonald, who followed George Morrison as *Times* correspondent, was on board the gunboat USS *Panay* when it was bombed by the Japanese in December 1937. He also reported the Rape of Nanking. *University of Western Australia*

FREED: William Henry Donald poses under a Manila palm tree for his friend Carl Mydans of *Life* magazine, following his release from the Los Banos internment camp in February 1945. The Japanese had Donald in their clutches but failed to recognise him. *Carl Mydans/ Time & Life Pictures/Getty Images*

RAGING: The Bull on the Bund sculpture in front of the former Hong Kong and Shanghai Bank building (now the Bank of China) and the former Shanghai Custom House. The Bull was designed especially for Shanghai by Arturo Ugo Di Modica, the Italian–American creator of Wall Street's famous Charging Bull. *Author's collection*

ROARING: Stitt and Stephen, the two bronze lions outside the former Hong Kong and Shanghai Bank building, named after two of the bank's former managers. *Author's collection*

WAITING FOR WAR: Shanghai police and British troops man a barricade in Nanking Road during the First Battle of Shanghai in January 1932. *Thomas Macauley Collection*

VOLUNTEERS: Westerners prepare barricades in Shanghai to withstand the Japanese assault. These men are probably members of the Shanghai Volunteer Force. *Thomas Macauley Collection*

HUMILIATION: Chinese civilians are searched by a Japanese marine while one of the Japanese civilian ruffians known as *ronin* (wearing the hat) looks on. ABOVE RIGHT AND BELOW: Japanese troops in action in Shanghai during the 1932 campaign against China. *Thomas Macauley Collection*

ARMOUR: Two Japanese tankettes, armed with machine guns, rumble up to reinforce the Japanese frontline. BELOW: Steel-helmeted Japanese marines and soldiers prepare to repel a Chinese assault with fixed bayonets. *Thomas Macauley Collection*

SILHOUETTE: Japanese soldiers attack a Chinese position during the Battle of Shanghai. *Thomas Macauley Collection*

SHADE: Heavily armed Japanese troops move stealthily through a bamboo thicket. *Thomas Macauley Collection*

CROSSING: Japanese troops use improvised rafts to cross a canal outside Shanghai. *Thomas Macauley Collection*

BANZAI: Cheering Japanese troops pose for a propaganda photograph during the Battle of Shanghai, but they could not beat the 19th Route Army and were forced to negotiate a ceasefire with the Chinese. *Thomas Macauley Collection*

CARNAGE: Rescuers carry a mutilated body from the scene of the bomb blast in August 1937 outside the Cathay Hotel on the corner of The Bund and Nanking Road. *Pictures Inc./Time & Life Pictures/Getty Images*

DEATH SHIP: The Japanese cruiser *Idzuma* moored beside 'Little Tokyo' in the Whangpoo River and acted as a floating battery to destroy large parts of Chinese Shanghai in 1932 and 1937. *Thomas Macauley Collection*

HEROIC: Gordon Bowden (third from left), the Australian Trade Commissioner brutally murdered by the Japanese, relaxes with friends and members of his family at a St George's night dance at the French Club in pre-war Shanghai. *Courtesy of Ivor Bowden*

HISTORIC: The offices of the *North-China Daily News* (left) where Ivor Bowden watched the Battle of Chapei with his father, Gordon Bowden, in 1932 and, on the right, the art-deco Palace Hotel on the corner of Nanking Road and The Bund, scene of the devastating bomb blast in August 1937. *Author's collection*

TRAITOR: Alan Willoughby Raymond, photographed during World War II, collaborated with the Japanese in Shanghai during the war but escaped being tried for treason.

PROGRESS: With the futuristic Pearl TV Tower taking centre stage, the modern skyline of Pudong (formerly Pootung) on the Huangpu (Whangpoo) River houses Shanghai's new financial district. *Author's collection*

EXHIBITION: Detail from the façade of the Australian Pavilion at the 2010 Shanghai Expo, and Nanjing Road today. *Author's collection*

It was a forlorn hope. On 12 July 1913 the 'Second Revolution' broke out when the uneasy armistice between Northern and Southern troops ended in Kiangsi. Two days later, Huang Hsing threw down the gauntlet to Yuan Shi-kai. He declared Nanking 'independent' and issued a proclamation calling for a 'punitive expedition' against the president. Four provinces joined the revolt – Kiangsu, Kiangsi, Anhwei and Kwangtung – and on 20 July the insurrectionists tried to seize the telegraph station in Shanghai. This threatened foreign interests and the British threw a military cordon around the International Settlement, barring entry to likely dissidents.

On 23 July 1913 Yuan dismissed Sun Yat-sen from his post as railways supremo and accused him of using railway funds to finance the rebellion. He branded the republicans 'outlaws' and prescribed 'military pacification' as the only possible course. Sun was forced to flee to Japan, where he was joined by several supporters including Huang Hsing and one of his new protégés, Chiang Kai-shek, a former Shanghai commodity and currency dealer who had led a Japanese-sponsored regiment in the Chinese Revolution. Chiang had been born on 31 October 1887 in the village of Chikow near the south-east coast and was raised mainly by his widowed mother before travelling to Japan to study at a military academy.

Also in Japan at that time were the revolutionary publisher Charlie Soong and most of his family, including his daughters Ayling and Chingling. His third daughter, Mayling, the future Madame Chiang Kai-shek, was still at college in the United States. This little group of exiles included many of the names that would make Chinese history over the next 35 years.

Yuan Shi-kai dispatched three Northern armies, many of the troops still wearing the traditional Manchu pigtails, to besiege Nanking. He promised General Chang Hsun the honour of retaking the republican stronghold as compensation for having had to forfeit it in 1911. The city was captured and ruthlessly sacked in early September. Many republicans and their supporters were executed. Yuan's troops pursued the rebels into the adjoining province of Honan, and in the year following the collapse of the Second Revolution the number of executions there was estimated at 21,000.[31]

On 6 October Yuan Shi-kai pressured parliament into electing him lifetime president, the position he had been holding on a provisional basis ever since Sun Yat-sen had stood down the previous year. The next day the major powers officially recognised the republic. The new American minister to China, Paul S. Reinsch, journeyed to Nanking to see the devastation of the city for himself. 'They had sacked the town, ostensibly suppressing the last vestiges of the "Revolution",' he reported on 4 November. 'Everywhere charred walls without roofs, the contents of houses broken and cast on the street, fragments of shrapnel on the walls – withal a depressing picture of misery.'

That same day Yuan Shi-kai outlawed the *Kuomintang* and expelled its representatives from parliament. Murder squads roamed Peking's streets looking for *Kuomintangists*. The party's panic-stricken leader in the National Assembly, C. T. Wang, telephoned Bill Donald to say that gunmen were outside his house and he was in fear of his life. Donald suggested he dress up as an old woman and tell a servant to drive him to the Methodist Mission. Donald then enlisted the aid of the American Legation to smuggle him on to a train to the foreign concession in Tientsin.[32]

Meanwhile, to Morrison's embarrassment, Albert Wearne had written a laudatory piece about him in the *Sydney Morning Herald*. 'Dr G. E. Morrison has more than justified the hopes of his many friends and admirers since his appointment in the post of political adviser to President Yuan Shi-kai,' he wrote.

Australians in the Far East hoped and expected that when Dr Morrison's work for the London *Times* came to an end he would be knighted by the British Government. His 17 years of magnificent service, during which he neglected no opportunity to further British interests in the Far East, surely entitled him to high reward. But Dr Morrison is an Australian, and the British Government is not likely to move in the matter unless it is taken up by the Commonwealth. In his case it appears to be a matter of 'out of sight, out of mind'.[33]

Few Australians, Wearne said, had had a more distinguished career than Morrison and fewer still had worked so brilliantly and faithfully in imperial interests. 'A distinct obligation rests upon his country and his countrymen, whom he holds so dear, to see that he get a fair measure of reward.'[34]

By June 1914, Morrison was on leave in London with Jennie and baby Ian. Denying he was merely a paid advocate of the Chinese Government, he beat the drum for the new China in a series of interviews and speeches. 'There is peace and quiet in every important city throughout all China, north and south, east and west,' he told his old newspaper. 'Many of the leaders of the first revolution are now working quietly in the Government.' He refuted suggestions that Yuan Shi-kai had cut himself off from Young China, or that he aimed to set up a family dynasty. Instead, Morrison added, the president had endeavoured to draw his advisers and helpers from every party in the State.[35]

Six days later *The Times* published an article from Bill Donald – standing in for Morrison's successor David Fraser – which completely contradicted this rosy view. Under the heading 'Dictator of China', Donald revealed that Yuan Shi-kai, having promulgated a new provisional constitution, had lost no time in making use of his extended powers by nominating men who would make the Senate 'solely a Presidential organ'. 'There are 70 of them, their names all savouring of the past, a regular mobilisation of the old brigade,' Donald wrote. 'There are no Young Chinese among them.'[36]

The contradiction between the two reports mattered little. Almost immediately, China was swept off the news pages by the assassination of the Austrian archduke at Sarajevo. The Great War began on 1 August with Germany's declaration of war on Russia, who had rallied to the defence of her troublesome Serbian ally. In Morrison's absence, Donald urged Yuan Shi-kai to seize Tsingtao, the holiday resort that the Germans had built on the Shantung Peninsula, and occupy the rest of Germany's leased territory in that province. Indeed, Yuan offered Sir John Jordan 50,000 troops for the campaign but Jordan turned down the offer and, mystifyingly, advised Yuan to keep quiet about it.

His purpose was revealed when the Japanese declared war on Germany on 23 August. The Anglo-Japanese Treaty, renewed in 1905 and 1911, enabled Britain to withdraw five battleships based on China Station at Hong Kong, while Japanese cruisers and destroyers took their place to defend the colony against German raiders. With British help, Japan then seized Germany's leased territory in Shantung, while the Japanese Navy implemented its 'southward advance' strategy for the first time when it occupied Germany's colonies in Micronesia: the Marshall, Mariana, Caroline and Palau islands.

By the time George Morrison arrived back in Peking, the Japanese Army had occupied half of Shantung, and China, far from joining the Allied cause, had 'gone mad about neutrality'. The following months would see the beginning of Japan's offensive against China which would ultimately claim the lives of more than 20 million Chinese.

CHAPTER 12

Perfidious Albion

Having violated Chinese sovereignty in Shantung, Japan turned up the heat in her campaign to reduce China to a vassal state. To Britain's shame, she aided and abetted this heinous enterprise in which the British minister Sir John Jordan, while posing as a trusted friend of the Chinese president, secretly conspired with the Japanese.

On 18 January 1915 the Japanese minister Eki Hioki issued President Yuan Shi-kai with '21 Demands' whose purpose was to bend China to his country's will. There were five groups of demands, the most controversial of which were in Group Five. These gave the Japanese virtual control over China's finances, armed forces and law enforcement agencies, as well as granting themselves an extensive list of new railway and mining concessions.

Bill Donald knew from republican sources that the demands had been made but was unable to confirm his information with the Chinese, the Japanese or Sir John Jordan. Once again, Yuan had been warned to keep quiet – this time by Hioki, who threatened dire consequences if he spoke out. Publicly, the Japanese claimed they had made just 11 demands, all of which were in line with other treaty arrangements between China and the powers. In the face of this denial, *The Times* was reluctant to publish Donald's story. 'Verify carefully,' the foreign editor admonished him. 'Reason believe reports from Peking wilfully exaggerated.'

At the same time Donald's home life was thrown into turmoil when Mary was taken seriously ill. 'I was at the hospital when the flowers which you kindly sent to Mrs Donald arrived but the coolie flew without waiting acknowledgement,' Donald wrote to Morrison. 'Mrs Donald desires me to express her appreciation of your kind thought. She is at present suffering great pain, mainly because the doctors are loath to give her morphia.'[1]

Shortly afterwards Donald visited Morrison at his house close to the Legation Quarter and raised the question of the 21 Demands. As the government's political adviser, Morrison was unable to say anything officially but he indicated a document on his desk and then left the room for a few minutes. Donald took the hint and slipped the document into his jacket. It was an English translation of the 21 Demands. Donald was now able to write an authoritative story about the true extent of Japan's attempted takeover of China. He also tipped off other reporters. Published in Australia, Britain and the United States, their stories exposed the Japanese Government's mendacity. Such was the embarrassment in Tokyo that the *genro* intervened and, despite the objections of the militarists who were taking control of the government, deleted the swingeing terms of Group Five from the Japanese demands.

Surprisingly, Sir John Jordan did not congratulate Yuan Shi-kai on his narrow escape. He and Yuan had been friends since the 1890s when they had served in Korea. Instead, he informed the Chinese president that he had no alternative but to accept the remaining Japanese demands, which had been resubmitted with an ultimatum that rejection would mean war between Japan and China. Yuan's compliance triggered a rash of strikes, demonstrations and boycotts throughout the country.

asinine – stupid.

Jordan's role throughout the 21 Demands affair appeared to be so blindly asinine that Morrison attributed it to senility, but there was a much more sinister reason. The British minister was adhering to the terms of a secret treaty between Britain and Japan that would enable the Japanese to retain the German concessions after the Great War in defiance of China's moral and legal right to regain her territory.[2] For her part of the secret deal, Japan would support the Allied war effort in the East (and escort Anzac troopships to the Mediterranean).

Sun Yat-sen followed the drama from his political haven in Japan. George Bronson Rea later claimed in the *Japan Times* that Sun had branded the 21 Demands a put-up job, invited and even drafted by Yuan Shi-kai himself as the price he was prepared to pay for Japanese support.[3] Ludicrous as this claim might sound, it was indeed Sun's view that China should co-operate with Japan in developing into a modern nation – 'without Japan, there is no China; without China there is no Japan,' he had once said.

Having failed to win the hand of Ayling Soong, who had married the Chinese banker H. H. Kung the previous year, Sun proposed to Charlie Soong's 23-year-old daughter Chingling. Charlie was furious with him but Chingling, even more beautiful than her sister and devoted to the republican cause, was determined to marry the 48-year-old 'Father of the Republic'.

The wedding took place in Japan on 25 October 1915. As Sun had failed to divorce Nee Lu, he was shunned by Charlie Soong and his strictly Methodist wife who considered his behaviour an affront to Christianity. H. H. Kung wrote to Donald that his new brother-in-law could perhaps be excused because 'his dangers and anxieties have affected his nervous system'.[4] Donald must have smiled. He knew all about Sun's womanising. 'That was the trouble with the old boy,' he said. 'Couldn't keep him off the women.'[5]

Sun might have quietly faded into obscurity had Yuan Shi-kai not made a fatal error of judgment in his efforts to unify the country and centralise the government. Against Morrison's advice, he abolished the military governors in the provinces, dissolved parliament and in a lavish ceremony at the Temple of Heaven on 23 December 1915 proclaimed himself emperor. The great mass of the Chinese people did not respond to the restoration of the monarchy as he had expected: Yuan had no ancestral right to the Dragon Throne and was seen as an interloper. Riots broke out in many places and a new revolution was threatened to depose him.

The agitation spread to Australia's Chinese communities. In Melbourne, the republican *Chinese Times* campaigned for a 'Third Revolution' to remove the new emperor, while in Sydney a new publication, the *Chinese Republic News*, edited by two Chinese revolutionaries, Chiu Kwok-chun and Ng Hung-pui, stirred up anti-Yuan feelings with skilful propaganda. As a result, many conservatives and royalists were converted to the republican cause, sparking a revival in Sun Yat-sen's fortunes.[6] Instead of being written off as a spent force, he was suddenly on the brink of a dramatic comeback.

On 18 March 1916 Bill Donald and his American comrade-in-arms Roy Anderson made the journey from their walled compound to visit the emperor at his gilded palace inside the Forbidden City. With Anderson translating, Donald – whom Yuan always addressed as 'Old Southern Republican' – spelled out the dire state of the nation. The provinces were in open revolt, he said, and China was in danger of breaking up.

Yuan Shi-kai stroked his walrus moustache. Only seven provinces were dissatisfied, he said. Seventeen, Donald countered. 'You must abdicate,' he bluntly told him. 'You must stop this make-believe.' Yuan could have had Donald's head chopped off for such insolence but instead he murmured, 'Old Southern Republican, I am tired,' and shuffled out of the room.[7]

Three days later he issued a proclamation ending his three-month reign and restoring the republic. 'Truly,' he declared, 'my lack of virtue is to be blamed for the compliance to the wishes of others which has brought this discord on the country.' It was his intention to resign as president and go into retirement in the Garden for Cultivating Longevity at Tientsin.

Yuan asked Donald to confer with the revolutionaries in Shanghai to see whether they would grant him safe conduct for the journey from the capital to Tientsin. Donald made the trip and was surprised to find that Sun Yat-sen had slipped back into the country under one of his aliases to join the anti-Yuan chorus.

The *Kuomintangists* gave Donald a good hearing; some, like C. T. Wang, probably owed their lives to him. They also realised that Yuan's capitulation gave them a great opportunity to become undisputed rulers of China and readily agreed to his request for safe conduct. But Yuan never made the trip. He had been ailing with 'fever of the belly' and on the morning of 6 June 1916 he was found dead in his bed at the age of 56. His family said he had died of a broken heart. His French physicians listed the cause of death as blood-poisoning and said Yuan might have survived had his family permitted them to treat him with Western methods.[8]

Plagued by political problems and ill-health, Yuan had lost control of his once-obedient Beiyang Army during the latter stages of his reign. His commanders were now at each other's throats and the army had split into factions, each vying for the right to set up the government in Peking and thus gain control over the customs revenue and raise foreign loans to finance their military adventures. The main contenders in this power struggle were the Anhwei Clique's Tuan Chi-jui, known as 'Mr Democracy' for opposing Yuan's elevation to the throne, and Feng Kuo-chang and Wu Pei-fu of the Chihli Clique. A third force belonged to 'the Old Marshal' Chang Tso-lin, a former bandit chieftain and staunch monarchist whose Fengtien Clique included some Beiyang troops, though the majority hailed from his native Manchuria. With a number of other aspirants who lived by the sword in different parts of China's vast domains, these four commanders would usher in the blood-soaked Warlord Era that created havoc from 1916 to 1926.

The most immediate issue to be resolved, however, was China's neutrality in the European war. Morrison and Donald joined forces with Paul Reinsch in an effort to persuade Li Yuan-hung, who had been appointed temporary president, that China must unite with the Allies against the Central Powers. Otherwise, they said, China would have no voice at the peace talks to demand the return of Shantung from the Japanese. Li, however, believed German propaganda that the Allies were being defeated and opted to remain neutral.

As a result, German citizens enjoyed complete freedom to come and go as they pleased, even in Shanghai, despite the predominant position of Britain and France. Every day at midday, British, French and German businessmen passed one another on The Bund on the way to their respective clubs without any sign of recognition or hostility. Not even warfare was allowed to interfere with Yangtze trade.[9]

Despite President Li's reluctance, the Chinese Government bowed to Morrison's persistent 'advice' and in January 1917 dispatched the first contingent in a labour force that would total 100,000 to France to dig trenches and carry out other vital, non-combatant duties for the British Army on the Western Front. At the beginning of February, Germany announced her submarines would sink on sight all ships in the vicinity of the British Isles irrespective of nationality. The United States immediately broke off diplomatic relations and urged other neutral countries to do the same. Donald wrote to Morrison:

Now that America has severed diplomatic relations with Germany, China should follow suit within 48 hours. I am doing my best with the Chinese I know to stir the government up.

Reinsch went to the Wai-wu-pu a few minutes ago on the same mission. Could you not get at the President tonight?[10]

Morrison saw Li Yuan-hung but came away disappointed with his 'weak, vacillating and tremulous' attitude. The mood changed after news reached Peking that 543 Chinese labourers had been killed when the French ship *Athos* was torpedoed in the Mediterranean. On 13 March China broke off diplomatic relations with Germany and seized all German shipping off Shanghai.[11]

Li Yuan-hung, however, was still embroiled in a power struggle with Southern insurgents who were demanding his resignation over his removal of the prime minister, Tuan Chi-jui, in May for negotiating secret loans with Japan and for trying to push China into World War I. He invited General Chang Hsun, the former *mafoo* in the imperial stables, into Peking to mediate with Tuan on his behalf.

The republicans had made a serious tactical error in permitting the imperial family to remain in the Forbidden City and Chang, a fanatical Manchu loyalist, decided to take this opportunity to restore them to the Dragon Throne. His head full of rice wine at the end of a rowdy banquet, Chang sent his pigtailed troops to force President Li to sign an edict authorising the immediate restoration of Pu Yi. Armed with this presidential decree, he then turned up at the Forbidden City in the early hours, prostrated himself before the startled, sleepy-eyed 11-year-old, and informed him that he was emperor once again.[12]

As the first pale shafts of dawn light illuminated the capital, Chang's soldiers hoisted the Manchu's dragon flag. Kang Youwei, who had discussed the coup with Chang after arriving in Peking a few days earlier, hot-footed it to the palace to offer Emperor Pu Yi advice on a new set of much-needed reforms.

Morrison was enjoying a bird-watching holiday in Chihli with a party including the new premier, Wu Ting-fang, while

Jennie rested at their seaside house at Pei-tai-po following the birth of their third son, Colin George Mervyn. He was just completing a letter to her when he received a telegram from Bill Donald, who had been one of the guests at Chang's banquet and had followed the imperial restoration at a discreet distance: 'EMPEROR RESTORED TWO OCLOCK.' Morrison scribbled a post-script to Jennie, 'I have shown this to Wu Ting-fang. He cannot believe it. I have wired Donald asking him for confirmation.'

Real though it was, the restoration lasted but a couple of weeks. General Tuan Chi-jui arrived from Tientsin with his troops and on 13 July clashed with Chang Hsun's army. 'You never heard such a terrific banging,' Morrison wrote. 'In my district several thousand fought and one was slightly wounded.' Chang fled from the battlefield and sought asylum in the German Legation, while Pu Yi returned to his schoolbooks in the Forbidden City. Kang Youwei, his imperial ambitions once again thwarted, retired to Shanghai where he died of natural causes in 1927.

Tuan Chi-jui was hailed as the saviour of the republic and, much empowered, returned to office. After all these shenanigans, he finally declared war on Germany on 14 August 1917. Shortly afterwards Li stepped down as president and was replaced by the Chihli strongman Feng Kuo-chang.

The declaration of war meant that Germany's extrality privileges were automatically cancelled, making her citizens subject to Chinese law. In response to French pressure, Peking ordered the deportation of all Germans and Austrians living in the International Settlement and the French Concession. Hundreds of enemy aliens simply moved to Chinese sections of the city where Peking's orders were ignored on principle; nothing, however, could be done to prevent the confiscation of their property. The German Club on The Bund was occupied by the Bank of China and an American company took over the leading German drugstore on Nanking Road (although its German staff were retained in their jobs).[13]

All of these events failed to solve the complex problems of China's disunity. When a national council was summoned at Peking, the *Kuomintang* refused to attend and established a rival parliament at Nanking, which took the provocative step of electing Sun Yat-sen as president of the Chinese Republic. China now had two capitals, two parliaments and two presidents. The revolution had gone into reverse gear.

Sun set up his headquarters in a Nanking cement factory. With a soldier's cap on his head and a gold-encrusted sword at his side, he was sworn in as Generalissimo of the Chinese Army and Navy. 'His emergence as a Generalissimo provokes derisive laughter,' Morrison wrote from Shanghai in November as he prepared to set sail for Australia on six months' leave with Jennie and his children, 'but it is one of the most serious indications of the trend of Chinese politics.'

The failure to unite North and South had brought nothing but turmoil to Peking as the warlords jostled for power through alliances with the gentry, the intelligentsia and the *Kuomintang*. In February 1918 Chang Tso-lin, the 'Mukden Tiger', surrounded Peking and ousted Feng Kuo-chang from the presidential palace. His replacement, Hsu Shih-ch'ang, known as 'Susie' and one of the few survivors of the Manchu administration, was chosen in a compromise deal between Northerners and Southerners.

Morrison journeyed to Shanghai to join his ship and at the same time bury the hatchet with Sun Yat-sen over his role in Sun's bitter feud with Yuan Shi-kai. There had been many changes since he had first seen the city in the horse-and-buggy days of 1894: the buildings on The Bund were much taller and grander now, trams powered by the British-owned Shanghai Electric Construction Company clanged down Nanking Road and the internal combustion engine added a new hazard to life and limb. Across the river, settlements and businesses had sprung up on the thumb-shaped peninsula of Pootung, while in Nanking Road the Sincere department store had driven consumers into raptures with its Australian-inspired approach to merchandising.

Some things hadn't changed. Rickshaws hauled by skeletal, barefoot pullers dodged coolies staggering beneath huge weights; beggars swarmed around him demanding alms; red-turbaned Sikh policemen sweated to impose order; and the filthy brown waters of the Whangpoo added a foul stench to the pervading aroma of hot oil and spices from the street vendors' stalls.

Shanghai had developed a reputation as the wickedest, most decadent city in the East, 'the whore of Asia', peopled by an astonishing array of tycoons, spies, gamblers, gangsters, revolutionaries, refugees and prostitutes. Its reputation for wickedness owed much to thousands of penniless White Russian women who had been driven out of their homeland by the Bolsheviks after the 1917 Revolution.

Morrison drove into Frenchtown, where Russian women disported themselves as hostesses, cabaret artistes, 'taxi dancers' (metered for time spent on the dance-floor) and prostitutes, consorting with Occidentals and Orientals alike. In the words of the left-wing American journalist Agnes Smedley, 'The French Concession smells to high heaven of gangsters and opium and prostitution and White Russian thugs and whores!'

It took Morrison some time to find 29 Rue de Moliere,[14] the neat two-storey pebble-dash house that Sun Yat-sen shared with his wife Chingling in a quiet tree-lined street. The shelves of books, the tidy desk with its sheaf of papers and the Western-style furnishings spoke of a life of study and quiet domesticity; it was the home of a professor or a poet. Only the brooding presence of Sun's bodyguard reminded the visitor he was calling on a violent revolutionary.

Sun had abandoned his Japanese suit and was dressed in flowing Chinese robes. He was 'very cordial and sincere', Morrison noted, and possessed of 'a certain magnetism which I did not previously notice'. Nor did he appear to have aged – his young wife had given him a new lease of life and was keeping the years at bay. Expressing himself forcibly, Sun reminded Morrison that at their previous meeting the Australian had argued in favour of China entering the war on the side of the Allies and repeated that he was opposed to China's participation. 'Powers always support the wrong side,' he said, 'as they did with the Taipings and now the Northern Party.'

break/vacation

Morrison was back in Peking following his Australian sojourn when the Armistice was declared in Europe on 11 November 1918, generating widespread joy throughout China. The Chinese had high hopes that the Peace Conference at Versailles would abolish extraterritoriality and return Shantung to the republic, thus removing the stain of the Japanese violation. The decision would be in the hands of the 'Big Four' among the peacemakers – Woodrow Wilson of the United States, Lloyd George of Britain, Georges Clemenceau of France and Vittorio Orlando of Italy. Morrison and Donald also hoped President Wilson's Fourteen Points enshrining the principle of justice and equality for all peoples, 'whether they be strong or weak', would be accepted.[15]

Morrison reached Paris at the end of January 1919 just as the conference was discussing these vital questions. China's brilliant 32-year-old minister to Washington, Wellington Koo, made an impassioned speech for the return of Chinese territory and everything seemed to be going China's way. Surely the peacemakers would recognise the fact that whereas Japan had done none of the fighting against Germany, China's labour battalions had suffered almost 2000 deaths on the Western Front while carrying out vital work for the Allies.

Woodrow Wilson's first priority, however, was the founding of the League of Nations and that meant dealing with a Japanese proposal for a clause in the league's charter ensuring racial equality. 'Now is the time,' the Japanese delegation leader, Prince Saionji, told delegates, 'to confront international racial discrimination.'[16]

Wilson knew that many of the white nations would never agree to such a proposal and his search for a compromise put him on a collision course with Australia's increasingly deaf prime minister, William Morris 'Billy' Hughes, who saw racial equality as a threat to the sacred White Australia Policy. He violently rejected any compromise. 'It may be all right,' he scribbled across the draft of one proposal, 'but sooner than agree to it I would walk into the Seine – or the *Folies Bergeres* – with my clothes off.' Wilson shook his head. 'What can you do with a man who won't read and can't hear?' The official Australian historian, Ernest Scott, saw Hughes's role differently. 'By characteristic methods,' he wrote, 'he had gained single handed at least the points that were vital to his country's existence.'[17]

The political infighting at Paris became so fractious that at one point Wilson had to step between Lloyd George and Clemenceau to prevent a fist fight. By the time the China question came up for resolution, the Japanese had placed Wilson in an impossible position. They would drop their demand for equality and join his League of Nations, Prince Saionji said, only if they were allowed to retain Shantung and the German islands in Micronesia. The Big Four caved in.

On 4 May word flashed across the world that China had been sold out: Japan would retain her hold on Chinese territory, as well as the German islands in Micronesia. Three thousand student demonstrators stormed through the Legation Quarter of Peking screaming in anger at this rank betrayal by their wartime allies. One of them was a young library assistant at Peking University named Mao Tse-tung.

When police moved the mob on, they attacked the residence of the Chinese minister of communications. The occupants were pelted with eggs and a Japanese visitor was bashed with the legs of an old iron bedstead. Rodney Gilbert, who covered the riots for the *North-China Herald*, wrote in sardonic vein that whatever their motives the rioters 'deserve full credit for being the first in China to substitute talk for action'.[18]

The riots gave birth to the 'May Fourth' movement symbolising Young China's frustration, rage and shame over the unequal treaties. Hostility was so vehement that China never ratified the Versailles Peace Treaty. Paul Reinsch was shocked at the betrayal. 'Probably nowhere else in the world have expectations of America's leadership in Paris been raised so high as in China,' he wrote.

> The Chinese trusted America. They trusted the frequent declarations of principle uttered by President Wilson, whose words had reached China in its remotest parts. It sickened and disillusioned me to think how the Chinese people would receive this blow which meant the blasting of their hopes and the destruction of their confidence in the equity of nations.[19]

Chinese anger reached a new pitch when Thomas Millard exposed the secret treaty arrangements between Britain, France and Japan that had settled the fate of Shantung.

Millard had been forced to sell his interest in the *China Press* in 1915 over his refusal to back Britain at the outbreak of the war. Its new owner was Edward I. Ezra, a Levantine Jew who had made his fortune in the opium trade like so many of Shanghai's *haute bourgeoisie*.[20] Millard was covering the peace talks for his own weekly publication, *Millard's Review of the Far East*. He revealed that at the very time Paul Reinsch, George Morrison and Bill Donald were attempting to induce China to break with Germany in 1917, the British, French, Russian and Italian governments had secretly entered into agreements with Japan 'by which China's rights were traded off'.[21]

Millard claimed – correctly – that the sellout had been determined some time before the decision was made by the Big Four at Versailles. It would be 'utter folly to presume that the British and French Governments are not fully informed as to the true character of Japan's actions and policy in China, or that they have any illusions as to its future import and tendency'. He added that the Anglo-French entente with Japan was 'conclusive evidence that those powers have decided to accept a Japanese suzerainty over certain [Asian] regions as a *fait accompli*'.

Billy Hughes's press liaison officer in Paris was Henry Gullett, a Melbourne journalist who had served as official Australian war correspondent with the British and French armies on the Western Front and later with the AIF in Palestine. He was shocked by 'the lust of territory', which defined the peace conference. Gullett saw territorial issues as 'the sinister and dominating note of the proceedings' and later wrote a pamphlet, *Unguarded Australia*, in which he argued that it would be folly for Australia to rely on an untried League of Nations for its defence. 'We must face the fact that of all nations in the world Australia is at present the most unprotected,' he wrote.

> With its three million square miles of territory and its garrison of five million souls, it is in the eyes of overcrowded Europe and Asia, a wide, rich, undeveloped squattage. Our only effective and permanent safety lies in greater population and this can only be attained by immigration.
>
> We do not necessarily need great standing arsenals. But we do need huge manufacturing plants capable of quick adaptation for war purposes. And we shall not have these plants until we have great local markets, or, in other words, a population many times larger than that which we have now.[22]

Billy Hughes took the initiative to increase Australia's market share in China. He appointed 56-year-old Edward S. Little as Australia's first trade commissioner, based in Shanghai. Little spoke fluent Mandarin and had been in business in China for many years. He was visiting Melbourne on his way to start a new life in New Zealand in January 1921 when he was introduced to Hughes. He was as startled as the prime ministerial advisers when Hughes suddenly offered him a salary of £2000 a year to spearhead Australia's export drive in the republic.

There was just one problem that the London-born prime minister seems to have overlooked: Little was an Englishman. The lack of consultation enraged Australia's business community, which had campaigned for years for the right to recommend a suitable candidate for such a post. 'The appointment of an unknown Englishman with no first-hand knowledge of Australia was a slap in the face,' the official history of the Australian Trade Commissioner Service says.[23] Perversely, the British also objected to the fact that Australia was seeking her own trade representation, thus superseding the authority of the British Consulate in such matters.

Little, a proud, upstanding former missionary, returned to Shanghai loaded down with a vast array of samples of Australian produce and a one-year contract, with the possibility of a four-year extension. For the next two years, he fought valiantly to do his job while the city's expatriate Australian businessmen subjected him to what he described as 'malicious and groundless agitation', *The Age* mercilessly attacked him in its columns and the British Consulate refused to recognise him.

The pressure for his dismissal was such that while on an official visit to Manchuria in mid-July 1923 he received a telegram from Melbourne: 'GOVERNMENT HAVE DECIDED ON TERMINATION OF YOUR ENGAGEMENT COMMISSIONER OCTOBER 18. NOBODY WILL BE APPOINTED VACANCY. CONFIRMATION AND INSTRUCTIONS FOR WINDING UP FOLLOWING BY FIRST MAIL.'[24] Little hurried back to Shanghai, where he wrote to Austin Chapman, the minister for trade and customs, begging for the chance to return to Australia to state his case in person.

While awaiting a reply, he assisted two Sydney women, Rose Venn Brown and Jean Armstrong, in organising an Australian exhibition for a trade fair to be held at Shanghai Racecourse. For the next two months, Little was left in limbo while Rose Venn Brown, who had come to China in 1920 as agent for a group of Australian manufacturers, and Jean Armstrong, social editor of the *Ladies' Companion* magazine, sought support for the trade fair from Australian manufacturers.

Austin Chapman ignored Little's role in this worthy endeavour but heartily commended the women's efforts. He said it was hoped the fair would be the largest of its kind ever held in Shanghai.[25] At the same time, he denied Little the basic right of a hearing and refused to enter into correspondence with him. The Englishman had no alternative but to close down his office and dismiss his staff. The office furniture was sold at auction. When the last lot had gone under the hammer, Farmer Whyte, an Australian reporter who was visiting Shanghai from Sydney, asked Little's typist Mrs Wrench for her opinion. 'I think it is a very foolish thing and that is the opinion of everybody here,' she said. 'As for Mr Little, I can say without any hesitation that he has done a great deal of valuable work for Australia. He put his heart and soul into it.'[26]

The only reason Little could extract from the tight-lipped Melbourne bureaucrats for his dismissal was a vague comment that his appointment had not achieved its objective. 'Australian trade profited not one whit by the stupid Trade Commissioner stunt,' *The Age* gloated. 'No Australian businessman ever seriously expected it would.' It added with calculated malice, 'It would be a mistake to regard Mr Little with anger. The most obvious reflection is that the position of Trade Commissioner seems to deprive any temporary holder of his sense of humour.'[27]

However, the Little affair rebounded badly on Australia's good name in East Asia. In Shanghai and Hong Kong, where he was a respected figure, there was almost universal condemnation of his treatment. The *North-China Daily News* thought the manner in which he had been 'thrown to the wolves does not impress one favourably with Dominion politics'.[28]

Edward Little resumed his interrupted journey to New Zealand but later made frequent trips to China. For the next ten years, he bombarded successive Australian prime ministers with letters and cables seeking justice and compensation. At the time of his death in February 1939 he had been completely unsuccessful in achieving either objective.

Defence had been the paramount issue in Australian politics ever since the Anglo-Japanese military alliance was scrapped at the Washington Naval Conference of 1921–22 to enable Britain to form closer links with the United States. Australia and New Zealand had seen the treaty as a guarantee of stability in the Pacific and, although they welcomed closer ties with America, protested in vain against its abrogation. The blow to Japan's self-esteem was enormous. In the words of a former Japanese foreign minister, the treaty had been discarded 'like an old pair of sandals'.

Billy Hughes warned his countrymen about the dangers of an expansionist Japan, which he described as 'a nation of nearly 70 million people crowded together on the margin of subsistence'. 'She wants both room for her increasing millions of population and markets for her manufactured goods,' he said.

> And she wants these very badly indeed. America and Australia say to her millions, 'Ye cannot enter in.' Japan, then, is faced with the great problem which has bred wars since time began. For when the tribes and nations of the past outgrew the resources of their own territory they moved on and on, hacking their way to the fertile pastures of their neighbours.

In August 1920 Marxist-Leninist students returning from Paris formed the Chinese Communist Party in Shanghai. The following year Mao Tse-tung attended the party's first convention in a deserted girls' boarding school in Frenchtown as the Moscow-sponsored representative of his home province of Hunan.[29] The delegates demanded the establishment of 'a militant and disciplined Party of the proletariat' and although they criticised the teachings of Sun Yat-sen as rabidly militarist, it was agreed to support 'his various practical and progressive actions', opening the way for collaboration between the Chinese Communist Party and the *Kuomintang*.[30]

In London, the British and Soviet governments signed an agreement under which the Russians pledged to 'refrain from any attempt by military or diplomatic or any other form of action or propaganda to encourage any of the peoples of Asia in any form of hostile action against British interests or the British Empire'. This didn't stop Lenin sending agents from the Third International of the Communist Party (the Comintern) to China with orders to fight Chinese feudalism and foreign imperialism. 'In the last analysis,' he said, 'the outcome of the struggle will be determined by the fact that Russia, India, China etc., account for the overwhelming majority of the population of the globe . . . so that in this respect there cannot be the slightest doubt what the final outcome of the world struggle will be . . . The complete victory of socialism is fully and absolutely assured.'[31]

Mao Tse-tung agitated for a break with China's Confucian past and prophesied that the humiliation in Paris would lead to 'an anti-feudal and anti-imperialistic culture of the masses'. As a sign of goodwill, the Soviets issued the 'Karakhan Manifesto', named after the vice-commissar for foreign affairs, Lev Karakhan, which renounced 'without any compensation and for ever' all of Russia's treaty rights in China that 'had been predatorily seized from her by the Tsar's Government and the Russian bourgeoisie'. Suspecting a Russian plot to spread Bolshevism in the republic, Peking declined the offer and the Soviets later wriggled out of it.

Chinese society had rarely been so fractured. The Reverend Burgoyne Chapman, the Australian headmaster of a Christian school in Wuchang, had witnessed the revolution and its aftermath at close quarters. In 1920, he painted the dismal picture of a China steadily growing weaker through famine, flood and civil war. 'Not only is there no republic, but there is no real national government,' he said on arriving back in Sydney on leave. 'There have been various parliaments and assemblies since 1911, but all constituted by purchase of seats or by the nomination of place-hunting factions and interested parties or military cliques.'[32]

These representatives had proved at least as corrupt, selfish and inefficient as their imperial predecessors. As a result, power had fallen into the hands of two of the Northern *tuchuns*, or warlords, the Old Marshal Chang Tso-lin and General Wu Pei-fu, one of the most capable commanders of the Chihli Clique. The civil war between North and South was as ferocious as ever and Sun Yat-sen's plans for a united China seemed an impossible dream.

CHAPTER 13

Bitter Endings

During the sweltering summer months of 1919, the marriage of Bill and Mary Donald reached breaking point. After what she described as 'a couple of attempts to leave him', Mary finally walked out for good. Donald took the break-up of his marriage badly. He was left to explain to his circle of friends that his wife had abandoned him. To be a deserted husband was just one step away from being a cuckold and it is possible he was both.

His colleague Rodney Gilbert claimed in a letter to his friend Grey Martel Hall, manager of the Peking branch of the National City Bank of New York (predecessor of Citibank), to know the intimate details behind the break-up. He insisted that fault was to be found on both sides, and that the possession of a fiery temper by husband and wife exacerbated their problems. Hall himself described Mary Donald as a rather 'frigid' woman, although many years later Donald suggested to his Chinese secretary Ansie Lee that the real reason for the separation was Mary's infidelity.[1]

Mary herself blamed 'the women who spoiled D by their adoration'. It seems the temptations of life in Peking were just too great and the opportunities for extramarital liaisons just too many for the union to survive.

Mary returned to Shanghai with Muriel and then moved to Hong Kong, where she had made several friends, including Noel Croucher, founder of the Hong Kong Stock Exchange and one of the colony's wealthiest men.[2] According to Mary in a letter to Croucher, Donald 'made a fuss to his lady friends saying I had robbed him of his child so I sent her back with a white nurse knowing full well he would not keep her very long; in three weeks she was back – said he couldn't stand her fussing for her mother'.[3]

Mary took Muriel to England and Australia and then, on 27 June 1927, just one week after the death of her father, the builder Robert Wall, they sailed from Sydney in the SS *Ventura* for the United States. Donald never divorced his wife, nor did he forgive her. He continued to live in their house in Tsung Pu Hutung, although he made no effort to buy out her share.

At 44, he was ruggedly handsome and could have had his pick of the single women at diplomatic soirees in the Legation Quarter but he detested such frivolities. Instead, his social life revolved around his American friends Roy Anderson and Rodney Gilbert and a random group of people who would meet at his home for drinks. According to one anonymous guest, Donald's house was 'perhaps the most sumptuous home in Peking'. It was furnished with Chinese antiques and among the knick-knacks were historical paraphernalia for smoking opium. For his guests, there were French wines, Scotch whisky and Cuban cigars – 'astounding for a man who himself never took a puff or a drop'.[4] Donald also had an extensive collection of classical records and during his parties Caruso's rendition of 'O Sole Mio' would soar over the Peking rooftops.

One of Donald's party guests in 1919 was Harry F. Payne, head of the American Bank Note Company, which engraved China's national currency and postage stamps. To the accompaniment of castanets and soaring strings, Payne started flirting with Eleanora Cox, an employee of the United States Secret Service who was visiting the capital from Shanghai. According to Eleanora, he 'made ardent love from the very beginning'.[5]

Eleanora's job included handling the confidential correspondence of American officers working for the United States
Army and Navy departments. She also had dealings with the
British and Danish consulates at Shanghai. Over the next
few days, Payne bombarded her with dozens of love letters.
When she acquiesced to the desires of her hot-blooded suitor,
he promised to give her some shares in his banknote company
but neglected to tell her that he had a wife and daughter
in Chicago. The relationship broke up after she discovered
this fact and she successfully sued him in the United States
Supreme Court for ownership of the shares. Such were the
perils of taking strong drink and listening to Italian love
songs *chez* Donald.

At the Versailles peace conference, George Morrison had been
struck down by a mysterious illness. Instead of returning to
China, he sought treatment in Britain from a variety of doctors
ranging from Harley Street specialists to Caledonian quacks.
No one could arrest his dramatic loss of weight. In May 1920
he took Jennie and his three sons, Ian, Alastair and Colin,
to the Devon seaside resort of Sidmouth in the hope that the
bracing sea air might restore his vitality.

But Morrison was suffering from undiagnosed pancreatic
cancer and his life was slipping away. With Jennie at his side, he
died on Sunday 30 May at the age of 58. Peking's greatest foreign
correspondent during the most turbulent of times was laid to
rest in a cemetery overlooking a placid English river. A wreath
of orchids was placed on the coffin. It bore the inscription:
'In sorrow and gratitude, from the President of the Republic
of China.' There was no wreath from the Commonwealth of
Australia, although Major A. W. Arkill represented the Australian high commissioner. As Albert Wearne had wisely observed,
'out of sight out of mind'.

Morrison had sold his library containing his vast collection of books on Chinese life and history for £35,000 to a Japanese aristocrat, Baron Iwasaki Hisaya, who promised to house it in Tokyo and make it available to all scholars who sought access. The lease on his Peking house, his furniture and other belongings remained to be sold. Bill Donald put himself at Jennie's service to arrange the transfer of the lease to a Russian diplomat, Ignatius Yourin, head of the Russian Far Eastern Mission which was intent on bringing the dubious benefits of Bolshevism to the young republic. Yourin was anxious to move into the house and gave Donald a cheque for 15,000 silver dollars.

The Japanese Government, however, had no intention of allowing Yourin to set up a nest of Comintern spies in the Chinese capital. On 26 October, Donald warned Jennie, 'Dear Mrs M, Get ready to shed tears . . .' It was his sad duty to inform her that the police would not agree to the Russians taking up residence in the capital. The matter had been referred to the cabinet and although some members were in favour, the Japanese had objected so strongly to the Wai-wu-pu that 'the matter assumed a purely political aspect and the Government hasn't backbone enough to go against the influence of Japan, America and France'.[6]

Donald had tiffin with the minister of foreign affairs, Dr Yen, in an effort to have the decision overturned but was unsuccessful. There was nothing for him to do, he said, except hand back the cheque and 'continue to try to help you out, which I will do with great pleasure'. Donald suggested that an auction might be the best way to dispose of the assets and Jennie agreed. Just three years later, however, she died unexpectedly in London at the young age of 34. The raising of her three orphaned sons was left in the hands of an elderly and distant English cousin.[7]

Meanwhile, Donald had run into serious trouble in his work. During the Versailles peace talks, he moved to Shanghai to take over all duties relating to the publication of the *Far Eastern Review*. His partner, George Bronson Rea, was in Paris, where he began filing strongly pro-Japanese articles just as the Chinese delegation was fighting to regain sovereignty of Shantung. Donald spiked the first article because it clearly conflicted with the magazine's pro-Chinese policy. When other articles in a similar vein followed, he discovered that Rea was actually in the pay of the Japanese. As Rea was the majority shareholder in the *Review*, Donald published these articles under his byline and added a disclaimer, 'The Editor does not necessarily personally accord with or support opinions expressed in signed articles appearing in the *Far Eastern Review*.'

The United States Consulate in Shanghai was so disturbed by the articles that it prepared a document for the American State Department on Rea's character and activities in China. The source of the information – described as 'reliable' – was probably Carl Crow. The document stated that the December 1919 and January/February 1920 editions of the *Far Eastern Review* contained articles written by Rea attacking Paul Reinsch and criticising United States' policy in East Asia. The articles, with such headlines as 'Another view of the Shantung issue', 'Democratic dollar diplomacy', 'America's Far Eastern muddle' and 'Minding our own business', were 'thoroughly pro-Japanese in every way'. The document continued, 'Positive information is at hand that Rea is actually in the pay of the Japanese Government to further Japanese interests. The editor of the *Far Eastern Review*, an Australian by the name of Mr W. H. Donald, a very highly thought of man in the Far East, has cabled Rea that he will resign his position if Rea insists on publishing, in the future, articles of the character referred to above.'[8]

When Rea returned to Shanghai in early 1920, Donald resigned as editor, having announced on page one of the magazine's next issue that the *Review*'s publisher was now unacceptably pro-Japanese. Rea replied it was his intention for the *Review* 'to combat a conspiracy hatched in Peking during the World War to pit the United States against Japan in the Pacific'. While it was in order for Americans to work with the Chinese Government, he complained that anyone who did the same work for Japan was characterised as 'a notorious Japanese propagandist'.[9]

Donald returned to Peking, where he continued to file stories for *The Times* but after receiving a curt telegram saying, 'Why attack an ally?' in response to an article about Japanese aggression, he switched his allegiance to the more liberal *Manchester Guardian*. Without the stimulus of George Morrison, Peking had lost much of its appeal. He was preparing to sell his house and move back to Shanghai when the Chinese Government approached him with a project dear to his heart.

Donald had always complained about the lack of facts and figures relating to Chinese life. The Chinese offered him 2000 Mexican silver dollars per month to set up a Bureau of Economic Information whose primary function would be to assemble statistical data on the Chinese people and Chinese industry. Donald accepted the challenge and started work with a handpicked staff, including the American writer George E. Sokolsky.

The son of a Russian-speaking rabbi, Sokolsky had travelled to St Petersburg in 1917 to join the Russian Revolution. As editor of the English-language *Russian Daily News*, he had supported the moderate regime of Alexander Kerensky against the Bolsheviks and fled to China when the latter were victorious. Such was the bitterness of those memories that he acquired the title of 'the high priest of anti-Communism'.[10]

Donald also hired Herbert B. Elliston, a 24-year-old Yorkshireman and former officer in the British Army who had arrived in China in 1919 to work as a reporter on the *Shanghai Times*, but quit after discovering it was funded by Japanese money. He went to Peking when he heard Donald was looking for an editor and joined the Bureau of Economic Information in the winter of 1920–21. The bureau supplied statistical supplements, memoranda, bulletins, booklets, books, and published a journal, the *Chinese Economic Monthly*, which Elliston edited intermittently over the next seven years.

As an echo of his Lithgow childhood, Donald put up a slogan on the wall, 'Get the facts.' He also added several attractive European women to his staff. As winter gripped the capital in its icy embrace, friends noted that the boss had become intensely possessive of one of the women. One evening when she left a party at his house in the company of a young man, he followed them. Apparently distraught at seeing them enter the woman's house next to the city wall, he climbed the steps to the top of the wall and, despite the freezing wind whipping in from Mongolia, paced anxiously up and down until the young man left an hour later. The woman had noted Donald's presence and it was probably just as well that she left Peking before matters got out of hand.

'Don was a man of the highest moral and intellectual integrity, delightful humour and natural charm,' says Harold K. Hochschild, an American businessman who arrived in Peking in 1921. Through the American Legation he met Roy Anderson, who introduced him to the Donald milieu. 'Although Don wasn't interested in money as such, and was sometimes without any, he used his income as a journalist to live well,' he wrote to Professor Winston Lewis in 1969–70.

> He had a comfortable, well-staffed house and liked to entertain. He ran a good table. Although a teetotaller he provided plenty of good drink – wines and spirits – for his guests. There was sometimes dancing in his home to the music of a record player.
>
> He had a host of friends among Chinese officialdom, the Peking diplomatic corps, foreign businessmen and Chinese and foreign journalists. There were always interesting people at his parties, including attractive women. He was at least as susceptible to women as the average man.

Hochschild, a 28-year-old Yale graduate, was the son of Berthold Hochschild, one of the founders of the immensely wealthy

American Metal Company. His mission in Peking was to collect payment from the Chinese Government for bar silver shipped to the Canton Mint on which the latter had defaulted. He expected to be there for two months but stayed two years during which time he got to know Donald well.

> My recollection of the men I used to meet at Donald's house was that they were there because of his and their mutual political or journalistic interests; my impression of the women was that Donald cultivated them because of their good looks and charm. His predilection for social intercourse, at least with attractive women, was one of his outstanding characteristics.[11]

One of the male guests was Hochschild's colleague at American Metal, Chester Fritz, an economist from Buxton, North Dakota. Fritz had been sent to China by the Fisher Flour Mills of Seattle in 1914 but after three years resigned in order to travel around China. When he arrived in Peking, he was hired by American Metal as its China representative to trade in precious metals, mainly silver bullion. Donald enjoyed talking to the economist about his travels and ways in which China's mineral resources might be harnessed.

In November 1921 George Morrison's old employer Lord Northcliffe arrived in Peking on an around-the-world tour. David Fraser was retiring as *Times* correspondent and over dinner Northcliffe offered Donald the job. Donald explained his difficulties with the paper's pro-Japanese stance and related the 'why attack an ally?' incident. Northcliffe immediately cabled London ordering the *Times* editor, Wickham Steed, to sack the man responsible. He then asked Donald to write the paper's editorials on East Asia and cable them to London; once again, Donald declined but agreed to write occasional pieces for *The Times* as a special correspondent.[12]

Meanwhile, a 17-year-old Australian named John Pal pitched up in Shanghai looking for a job in the Maritime Customs

Service. The Commissioner of Customs in Shanghai, Leonard A. Lyall, took a shine to the young man who had worked his passage from Sydney to London in the hope of joining the service only to be told there that all recruiting was done on the spot in Shanghai. Lyall was impressed with Pal's initiative in making the long trip back to the East and offered him a post as the service's youngest-ever recruit.[13]

Commissioner Lyall was known to hold a low opinion of expatriate Britons and their privileges. 'The British residents in Shanghai are the spoilt children of the Empire,' he once famously said. 'Judges and consuls are provided for them; they are protected by the British fleet, and for several years they have had in addition a British army to defend them; and for all this expenditure the British taxpayer pays.'[14]

John Pal was given a uniform with brass buttons and a room in the customs' spacious and well-run quarters at Quinsan Gardens, Hongkew. 'It is generally reckoned,' his training officer at the Custom House told him, 'that each brass button has the value of a machine-gun in the eyes of the Chinese. Your authority on the waterfront is supreme, and don't ever forget it.'[15]

Pal also learned the service had two classes of employee: one class dressed in civilian clothes, worked inside the Custom House, socialised with the business and consular communities and never got their feet wet, while the inspectorate of which he was a member fought an endless battle against crime and corruption on Shanghai's waterways. With the semi-crippled Lyall egging him on, Pal patrolled wharfs and searched ships in the hunt for contraband, smugglers and tariff-dodgers. Whenever shippers failed to declare goods, the goods were seized and sold at auction, with the customs officer being paid 10 per cent of the sale price.

The biggest prizes were illegal shipments of opium. Shanghai was China's biggest opium market by virtue of its geographic position and enormous population. Bales of opium came down the Yangtze from the poppy-fields of Szechuen or up the river from India, Turkey and Persia, or through the network of canals from Anhwei and Fukien, the two closest opium-producing provinces.[16]

Nothing was more important to the warlords in financing their armies or paying off Japanese loans than opium. Indeed, the Anti-Opium Association identified opium as the very life-blood of warlordism. Peasants were forced under pain of death to grow poppies which were processed into sticky balls of the drug. At the wharfs, armed guards escorted the bales – worth around 10,000 taels each – to the opium cartel in the French Concession. Large bonuses were paid to customs officers who intercepted these shipments. The bales were then consigned to the bonfire.[17]

The poppy was the warlords' leitmotif. They fought and killed one another for dominance of the opium crop in particular provinces in order to fund their armies. Armoured trains loaded with guns transported large bodies of troops to the various fronts; campaigns were planned to finish around harvest time; alliances were made and broken because of it. And with every year of that dreadful decade China slipped further into the abyss.[18]

The forces of righteousness fought back. The British-born, American-educated missionary Frank Rawlinson was chairman of the Moral Welfare Society and a member of the vice commission of the Municipal Council. He had come to China as editor of the *Chinese Recorder* in 1914 and turned it into the most popular Protestant magazine of the period.

Rawlinson was affronted by the power of American madams who ran a series of bordellos in the foreign concessions. Nothing had changed since the 1890s when they first paraded their success down Bubbling Well Road in 'crest-emblazoned carriages'. They 'had their fingers in all the concerns of the city', an American journalist reported, and 'were on terms of closest intimacy with Shanghai's men of affairs, foreign as well as native'.[19]

Rawlinson's first victory was a 'moral welfare crusade' in the early 1920s that forced the council to withdraw licences from brothels in the International Settlement. The most famous of these was The Line, an exotic bordello in a row of neat houses in Kiangsi Road within easy walking distance of The Bund. The madam was a San Franciscan named Gracie Gale, who served French champagne to her Western clientele and offered them beautiful British, French and American girls in a cosy club-house atmosphere. She invited Frank Rawlinson around for tea but her argument that she was providing a vital public service fell on deaf ears.[20]

One by one, the police closed down all of these establish-ments, with the result that they took their business to the less stringent climes of Frenchtown, while on the street corners of the British Concession large numbers of dispossessed prostitutes openly propositioned potential male clients.

No one was more aware of the prostitutes than Dr Anne Walter Fearn. 'I knew them all,' she says. 'I delivered their babies, applied the stomach pump when they took an overdose. I closed their eyes in death, officiated at their weddings and for almost a quarter of a century listened to their heart-breaking stories.'[21]

As well as working as a hospital clinician, Dr Fearn was drafted in to work at the Door of Hope, a refuge for runaway prostitutes and *mui tsai* girls that had grown from a single room on Hankow Road into a well-run institution after the Mixed Court ruled in the early 1900s that any girl who could escape from a brothel and find her way to the Door of Hope would be safe in the eyes of the law. Thus the doorway represented an escape route from a life of misery and degradation for many women, although some died at the hands of pimps while trying to reach it.[22]

The most dangerous part of the demimonde was the district known as 'the Trenches', which was to be found across Garden Bridge in the back alleys of Hongkew. 'By knocking down walls to join ground-floor rooms, draping a few coloured streamers around and economising on the candle-power, Chinese owners and Russian entrepreneurs went into the night-club business with the help of half a dozen scattered Filipino bands,' John Pal wrote in his memoir.

> These dim dives hung so close together that if the bouncer knocked a man out of one, he fell into another; and though the flesh-hungry Oriental customers spoke no Russian, the language of the banknote overcame all difficulties. Shrewdly the refugee Russian girls, many of them blonde, beautiful and bewitching in the eyes of young and exiled Englishmen and Americans, sensed their power, and it was because of the nightly brawls for their affections, the clash of tempers, fits of jealousy and never-ending hostilities, that the district became known as the Trenches.[23]

Edna Lee Booker had just arrived from California as a reporter on the *China Press* when Dr Rawlinson launched a 'Clean up the Trenches' campaign. One night Edna drove with him along North Szechuen Road where the maze of brothels and opium dens extended into Chinese territory. The killing of an American sailor and a Chinese singing girl in a brawl had given him the necessary leverage to force General Ho Feng-ling, military governor of the Chinese Municipality, to take action.

Edna saw lines of rickshaws delivering foreign sailors to the brothels and clip joints. 'The girls were a seasoned lot,' she wrote in her memoir. 'It was play for them to lure a seaman into a dive, ply him with liquor or dope, perhaps prepare him a pipe, and later rob him.'[24]

Edna's newspaper created such a storm of protest that General Ho was forced to issue an edict: 'In response to agitation on the part of the foreign community, the Chinese authorities have resolved that the Trenches be closed within a month.' The

Russian entrepreneurs merely shut down their establishments and joined the exodus of American madams to Frenchtown.

In early April 1922 Edna Lee Booker arrived in Peking seeking an interview with President Hsu Shih-ch'ang. Inevitably, she found herself knocking on Donald's door. He invited her to a four-day picnic at his holiday home – a temple in the Western Hills. 'Mr Donald was famous as a host and organised his picnics in a grand way,' she wrote in her memoir.

> His 'temple', in reality a one-time Imperial hunting lodge, was perched high in the mountains far away from all things foreign and modern yet life moved on in a sophisticated way. We dined by candlelight, enjoyed beautifully served dishes with appropriate wines, and wore evening dress. During the day we rode on donkeys over hills which through the ages have given shelter to holy men seeking to solve the mystery of life. It was an unforgettable experience.[25]

Back in Peking, Edna Booker caught a train from the capital's silver-domed station to Mukden to interview the Old Marshal Chang Tso-lin. The 'Mukden Tiger' turned out to be a slim little man with a kindly smile and gentle manner. He was dressed in a short black velvet jacket over a long satin robe. Looking at Edna through shining brown eyes beneath a black satin hat studded with an enormous pearl, he explained why he wanted to remove the Chihli Clique from Peking. 'China is sick,' he said, 'and like a sick man may need an operation. The operation will be painful, but I hope it will be justified by results.' General Wu Pei-fu was 'an obstacle preventing reunification' and would therefore have to be removed. 'I have no presidential ambitions,' he added. 'I am working only for the good of China.'[26]

Later that month, Chang Tso-lin marched on Peking again but suffered a comprehensive defeat at the hands of General

Wu. 'The Fengtien forces have been rolled back and are trying to make their way to Tientsin and Kalgan,' *The Times* reported. 'Chang Tso-lin is himself in flight to Mukden.'[27]

Sun Yat-sen also suffered a serious reverse in his own province of Kwangtung, where General Chen Chiung-ming, the commander-in-chief of his army, rose in revolt and expelled him from Canton. Sun fled to Shanghai but returned to Canton the following February and re-established himself in power, largely by playing off one group of mercenaries against another.[28]

He sought help for the struggling republic in the United States and Europe. Every Western country refused to take him seriously, so in 1923 he ended up in Moscow. At the Hotel Lux, so the legend goes, he met an unemployed revolutionary named Mikhail Markovich Gruzenberg, the 39-year-old son of a Latvian blacksmith who spoke English with a Chicago accent, having lived in the Windy City as a tsarist exile for 11 years, during which he acquired an American wife named Fanya.[29]

Lenin was close to death and Stalin was locked in his winner-take-all struggle for the succession with Leon Trotsky over the latter's plans to foment world revolution through the Comintern rather than consolidate the revolution at home. Someone at the Kremlin, however, found time to speak to the Chinese visitor. Mikhail Gruzenberg, taking the *nom de guerre* Mikhail M. Borodin after his favourite Russian composer, was sent to Canton in October as the Politburo's special adviser to Sun Yat-sen, with orders to bring China into the Soviet orbit.

It was an inspired move: the beefy Bolshevik got along incredibly well with the little doctor. He was an impressive figure: more than six-feet tall, with a full head of dark, glossy hair, a walrus moustache and a proud leonine head set firmly on a pair of weightlifter's shoulders.[30]

At the same time, Lev Karakhan, author of the pro-Chinese 'Karakhan Manifesto', was sent to Peking as the Soviet minister. He was given substantial funds, which were secretly distributed to Borodin and his comrades in Canton, as well as the Chinese Communist Party, union activists and various fellow travellers, including at least one senior American newspaperman in Peking.

Striding from one meeting to another in his khaki commissar's uniform, Borodin hammered the *Kuomintang* into a formidable political and military weapon. He drafted a new constitution for the party and with General Galen, the *nom de guerre* of Vasily Konstantinovich Blucher, a former corporal in the Tsar's army, established the Whampoa Military Academy on an island near Canton. Sun's protégé Chiang Kai-shek, who had trained in the Soviet Union, was installed as commander. Chinese Communists were planted in key positions within the party hierarchy: Mao Tse-tung was head of the press and propaganda department, while Chou En-lai, a brilliant young Marxist recently returned from Paris, instructed Whampoa cadets in political theory. One of Chou's protégés was Lin Piao, the future commander of the People's Liberation Army.[31]

Within a year Borodin and his Soviet comrades had penetrated the top echelon of the *Kuomintang* and were tackling their main task of converting the rank and file to Communism. Sun, however, was all too aware of their intentions. While he was happy to take Soviet money, he insisted that Communists could join the *Kuomintang* only as individuals with no loyalty to any other party.[32] Nevertheless, the Nationalist movement now consisted of two overlapping but distinct groups: conservative members of the *Kuomintang* on the Right and Communists on the Left. It was only in deference to Sun Yat-sen that they united in an uneasy coalition to take on the warlords who were causing mayhem in the provinces.[33]

At 2.30 am on 6 May 1923 a band of 1000 renegade soldiers derailed the Blue Express from Nanking to Tientsin at Lincheng in Shantung. As the locomotive ploughed to a standstill, they attacked the carriages with blood-curdling yells, smashing windows and firing their guns in the air. A Romanian passenger threw a teapot at one of the bandits who took aim and shot him dead.[34]

At bayonet point, 26 Westerners and 100 Chinese were taken hostage and marched out of the railway cutting into the foothills. The hostages included Lucy Aldrich, sister-in-law of John D. Rockefeller Jr of the Standard Oil dynasty, and the American journalist John Powell, editor of the *China Weekly Review* (formerly *Millard's Review of the Far East*).

Stumbling in the dark, the captives were forced along a rough trail to a crude fort. In the morning, the bandits examined their loot: evening gowns, feathered hats, watches, wallets stuffed with paper money, bed-clothing, portable typewriters, toiletries, briefcases. One young bandit ate a tube of toothpaste, while another danced around in a pink satin corset.[35]

Fortunately, the rebels had no idea of Lucy Aldrich's true identity and, scratched and bruised but otherwise unhurt, she was released along with the rest of the female passengers. The male prisoners, however, were marched further up the mountain to the Temple of the Clouds at a place called Pao-tzu-ku high above Roy Anderson's home city of Soochow. When he heard what had happened, Anderson made the trip south from Peking and was carried uninvited into the bandits' camp in a sedan chair to assume the role of peacemaker.[36]

Meanwhile, John Powell's friend Carl Crow talked the American Red Cross into sending him to the bandit area to establish contact with the foreign captives. 'One day we saw in the distance across the valley a long caravan of carrier coolies approaching our stronghold,' Powell wrote in his memoir.

After a wait of what seemed to be hours the head of the caravan appeared at the gate of the temple courtyard. The sweating coolies were carrying several large boxes, each bearing the insignia of the Red Cross. We tore into the boxes in short order.

They were filled with food: bread, cans of bully-beef, vegetables and fruit, and even several boxes of California raisins. That night we staged a never-to-be-forgotten banquet.[37]

Having succeeded in setting up a regular supply chain for the Europeans, Carl Crow was then approached by one of the local warlords and paid US$3000 to do the same for the Chinese captives, who had been existing on whatever scanty rations they could scrounge from the bandits.[38]

Anderson spoke the local dialect and in accordance with local custom asked the bandit chief Sven Mao-yao to nominate 'an elder brother' with the power to negotiate on their behalf. Over the next four weeks, he reasoned with and cajoled the bandits, warning them of the severe reprisals that would be inflicted on their people by foreign armies unless they released the hostages. But the bandits remained intransigent in the hope of receiving better terms. They wanted to be granted an amnesty by the Nanking government and to be recruited into the Nationalist Army with uniforms and proper rates of pay.

Meanwhile, Chinese troops had thrown a cordon around the bandit camp, cutting off their supplies. The Chinese Government commissioned Carl Crow to feed 2000 bandits and their dependants so they would not confiscate supplies intended for their captives. Finally, Roy Anderson brokered a 'win-win' deal under which the prisoners would be released and the bandits recruited into the Chinese Army. Scruffy and unshaven, the hostages were brought down from the mountain in sedan chairs and on the backs of donkeys.

Chinese newspapers hailed Anderson as the hero of the stand-off and compared him with the legendary Frederick Townsend Ward, organiser of the Ever Victorious Army in the Taiping Rebellion.[39] Carl Crow rated the six weeks he spent in Shantung 'one of the most interesting holidays it is possible to imagine. I learned a lot about the techniques and ethics of banditry and also a good deal about the cost of living in China.'

In the winter of 1923–24 Bill Donald took time off from his duties as director of the Economic Bureau to see an old friend, Farmer Whyte, who was visiting China. Writing in the Sydney *Daily Telegraph*, Whyte said that when his train pulled into Peking station, 'an old *Daily Telegraph* colleague of mine was there to meet me. We had not seen each other for 22 years. Today he is one of the big men of China, an adviser to the Government of China on foreign affairs – another Dr Morrison. I am speaking of W. H. Donald, head of the Bureau of Information.'

In trench coat and rakish fedora hat, Donald posed for a photograph for Whyte and wrote a caption: 'Greetings from the Yellow Temple, Peking, W. H. Donald.'[40]

Despite his high spirits, Donald's eyesight was giving him serious trouble and he took a long holiday to visit the United States by way of Europe to consult specialists. He spent six weeks in New York with Harold Hochschild.[41] Donald had acquired a British passport from the British Embassy in Peking in 1918 which had been renewed in 1924 (and again in 1931 – as shown in the photographic section). While he was away, Herbie Elliston lived in his house in Tsung Pu Hutung, spent weekends at his temple in the hills and did his job at the bureau. He later used his knowledge of the Donald persona to write a definitive profile of him in the mass-selling American magazine, the *Saturday Evening Post*.

Donald had just returned to Peking when the Old Marshal, Chang Tso-lin, made another attempt to capture the capital and take over the Central Government while most of the Northern armies were down on the Yangtze fighting the Nationalists. Rose Venn Brown was now working for Asiatic Petroleum, the East Asian arm of Royal Dutch-Shell. She happened to be visiting Shanhaiguan, the town in North China where the Great Wall runs down to the sea. 'I walked along the Great Wall looking over Manchuria on one side and Chihli* on the other,' she said.

---

* The Nationalist Government dissolved Chihli in 1928 and formed the province of Hopeh (Hebei).

'Little did we think that in less than two weeks a modern war would break out at the exact spot on which we were walking. We just got through before Marshal Chang Tso-lin mobilised his troops.'[42]

In late September Donald visited Chang's great opponent General Wu Pei-fu at his camp. Wu had once been described in *The Times* as 'an attractive personality, and his smile and beaming eyes warm one to friendliness'. As well as being an able commander who drilled his own troops, he was also an accomplished poet 'with a healthy appreciation of spirituous liquor'. Compared with his autocratic contemporaries, his nickname was 'the Liberal General'.[43] Donald noted that Wu's eyes were clear, skin fresh and he looked fit – 'no evidence of Shaoshing wine'.[44]

However, the campaign did not go as the Old Marshal planned. Despite equipping his Fengtien Army with modern radios to aid communication and machine-guns to cut down large numbers of the enemy, he was being roundly defeated by General Wu until Wu's main ally, Feng Yu-hsiang, dubbed 'the Christian General' after baptising thousands of his troops with a garden hose, suddenly betrayed him. 'General Feng,' Donald wrote, 'mistaking Judas for Christ, turned on his patron and erstwhile friend, Wu Pei-fu, while the latter was being jammed in a nasty corner fighting Chang Tso-lin at Shanhaiguan.'[45]

Having taken over Russia's interests in Manchuria, the Japanese were anxious to extend their influence on its ruling warlord. As Wu moved his forces along the Peking–Mukden railway line, Japanese spies in Tientsin radioed his movements ahead to a receiver on the Old Marshal's train. Japanese field guns manned by Japanese gunners in the vanguard of the Manchurian Army laid down a barrage around Wu's railway terminus at the Shanhaiguan border crossing point, inflicting 10,000 casualties in a few hours.[46]

With the whiff of cordite in the autumn air, the telegraph wires cut and food in short supply, it seemed like old times. Donald drove his large American-made Locomobile roadster from Peking to Feng Yu-hsiang's headquarters to the north of the city. The Christian General had made headlines when he invited the Melbourne-born Sinologist, the Reverend Robert Henry Mathews, to conduct Bible classes among his men. The China Inland Mission, believing Feng would introduce a new moral code into China, was only too willing to send the clergy-man up from Shanghai to take care of the spiritual well-being of his army.[47]

Feng assured Donald he was a true Chinese patriot and promised to restore peace and stability to the people. His political henchman C. T. Wang added that Feng was bound to defeat General Wu; in a matter of days Wu would kill himself or flee from the battlefield. Indeed, Feng's defection embold-ened another warlord, General Chang Tsung-chang – known as 'the Dogmeat General of Shantung'* – to join forces with Chang Tso-lin. General Wu's army was routed and driven south to the Yangtze.

Fired with crusading zeal, Feng then seized Peking and tossed the pro-Chihli head of state, General Tsao Kun, into prison. He also evicted Pu Yi and the Manchu Royal Family from the Forbidden City and placed them under armed guard. Burgoyne Chapman sounded a note of caution. 'As for General Feng, apart from his incorruptible sincerity, I hope that the Church abroad will not expect any specially "Christian" action from this Christian General,' he warned.

> To do this would be as dangerous an error as when certain enthusiasts advertised Dr Sun as a Christian patriot years ago. In the dearth of great men, Dr Sun stood out as an idealist of unselfish sincerity, who would, however, use any means and any men to attain his object. He everywhere encouraged Russian agents and Bolshevist propaganda against the 'wicked capitalist powers' and the 'unequal treaties'.[48]

---

*   The Dogmeat General got his nickname because of his fondness for the Chinese gambling game of *Pai Gow*, which Northern Chinese call 'eating dog meat'.

Sadly for the evangelical movement, Feng was funded largely by Soviet money and the code of his forces, the *Kuominchun*, or National People's Army, was actually Matthew, Marx, Luke and John. Marching into battle, his troops sang 'Onward Christian Soldiers' with suitably altered Marxist lyrics.

Rose Venn Brown was as accustomed to war as many of the Chinese generals. The former assistant registrar at Sydney's Royal Hospital for Women was in London when World War I broke out and volunteered for service with the British Expeditionary Force. Three months later, she was in war-torn France as assistant accountant of the YMCA. Over the next four years she organised Red Cross centres as far north as Abbeville on the Somme near the Dutch border and supervised entertainment for the troops in YMCA canteens. After the war, Rose stayed behind to locate and photograph hundreds of previously unrecorded graves of the Australian fallen at the Abbeville cemetery and then contacted their relatives back in Australia.[49]

One of her AIF friends in Peking was Harold John Timperley, a 26-year-old West Australian who had joined Reuters' staff in the capital. For the past three years, 'Timp' had been working on Donald's old paper, the *China Mail*, with his boyhood friend from Perth, Colin Malcolm McDonald. He was soon enmeshed in the Peking news scene and became a member of Donald's group. With his bright blue eyes, wavy blond hair and refined tastes, he reminded one visiting European woman of 'a marquis from the court of Louis XV'.[50]

Born at Bunbury in 1898, Timperley had served with the AIF in France during World War I, starting as an 18-year-old recruit with the famous 11th Battalion, the first infantry unit to leave Western Australia. Transferring to the Pay Corps, he didn't forget his mates in the 11th. He wrote to the *West Australian* two months before the end of the war criticising 'smug stay-at-homes' and demanding that Australian servicemen should get their old jobs back.[51]

Meanwhile, Rose Venn Brown had just made it to Shanghai when war broke out between the provinces of Kiangsu and Chekiang for control of Shanghai's narcotics trade. The military governor of Chekiang, General Lu Yuang-hsiang, had jurisdiction over Shanghai, a post which entitled him to $6 million a month in protection money from the city's hundreds of illegal opium houses. 'The Kiangsu troops have come to take Shanghai from Chekiang and it looks as if they will win,' Rose wrote to a friend in Australia. 'They are advancing rapidly and if they get to the arsenal and the forts at Woosung, the Chekiang troops will be defeated. The fighting is only about four miles outside the settlement, so we can hear the guns quite plainly. It is like being in France again.'[52]

The Shanghai Municipal Council declared a state of emergency and mobilised the Volunteer Corps. This latest version of the 'opium war' ended when General Sun Chuan-fang, the military governor of Fukien, joined forces with the Kiangsu commander, General Chi Shi-yuan. Sun's Eastern troops reached North Station in Chapei and occupied the Kiangnan Arsenal, thus ensuring General Lu's defeat. At 3 pm on 12 October, Lu boarded a steamer with his chief of staff and the chief of police and fled to Japan with his ill-gotten gains.

Towards the end of 1924 the treacherous Feng Yu-hsiang invited his fellow pro-Russian Christian Sun Yat-sen to Peking to resurrect the Republican Government and unify the country. Perhaps wisely, his spiritual mentor Robert Mathews had moved to Szechuen in the far west to spread the Gospel and supervise the work of young Chinese seminarians.[53] Sun left Canton in November and made his way to Peking. To his immense pleasure, a cheering crowd of 100,000 people took to the streets to welcome him. But Sun's hopes of reconciliation were dashed almost immediately when he was struck down by a serious illness. An exploratory operation disclosed he was suffering from cancer of the liver.

Bill Donald took Lieutenant James M. McHugh, a young officer of the Marine Detachment at the American Legation (where his father-in-law Jacob Gould Schurman was now the American minister), to see him at the Rockefeller Hospital in Peking. 'He was a gaunt little man with very large, brilliant eyes,' McHugh recalls.

When medical science could do nothing further for 'The Father of the Republic', he was moved to Wellington Koo's home, where he died on 12 March 1925 without ever having achieved the national harmony he desperately desired. On his deathbed, it is said, he spoke of his love for Mikhail Borodin and his faith in his advice. He urged his wife Chingling and Chiang Kai-shek to take counsel from him at all times.

'The *Kuomintang* loses its titular head and has no outstanding figure with which to replace him,' *The Times* noted. 'The Party, moreover, has lately been much divided, largely owing to Sun Yat-sen's coquetting with the Bolsheviks. The moderate elements had already drifted away from him, and it remains to be seen whether the extremist or the moderate group will control the party in future.'[54]

It seemed tragic to many Westerners who had followed the vacillating fortunes of the Chinese Revolution that his long struggle should end in so pitiful a failure.

Just an hour before Sun Yat-sen breathed his last, Roy Anderson died of pneumonia in the French Hospital at the age of just 46. Donald stood beside his bed with tears running down his cheeks. 'We failed, Don,' the intrepid, big-hearted American had said to him. 'We were never able to do what we tried in this country.'[55]

PART III (1925–1938)

Conflagration

'Strikes of workmen go on at Shanghai, Hankow and Hong Kong.
War is wanted with Great Britain. The curious thing is that the
Chinese believe they could fight anyone and defeat them.
The valour of ignorance, of course.'

– W. H. DONALD IN A LETTER TO FRIENDS IN 1925

CHAPTER 14

Shanghai Fury

Through these desperate, extravagant years, Shanghai outshone all other Chinese cities. The Bund symbolised British dominion over the Yangtze Valley, its semi-skyscrapers anchored to rafts of concrete that floated on pilings of Oregon pine like 'a long line of poisonous toadstools sprung up from the mud'.[1]

To the city's three million Chinese residents, these buildings, heavily ornamented with art deco symbols, were *motian dalou* – literally, the magical edifices that reach the skies. In the words of one Chinese commentator, they saw the foreign concessions as 'an exotic world of glitter and vice dominated by Western capitalism'.[2]

The flashing neon lights of Nanking Road illuminated the soaring spires of the Australian-styled Sincere, Wing On, Sun Sun and Sun Company department stores, each one of the 'Four Great Companies' offering an astonishing array of hotels, restaurants, theatres, amusement arcades, skating rinks and roof gardens, as well as counters piled high with merchandise from Europe and the United States.[3]

In the middle of these retail temples, the Sweetmeat Castle, long the favourite spot for tea and cakes, had become the more modern Bakerite Chocolate Shop dispensing American-style waffles, ice cream and sodas. On Avenue Edward VII, the borderline between the British and French concessions, the Great World amusement centre presented a galaxy of attractions. Climbing the stairs from one floor to the next, Josef von Sternberg, director of the Marlene Dietrich film *Shanghai Express*, goggled at 'gambling tables, singing girls, magicians, pickpockets, slot machines, fireworks, birdcages, fans, stick incense, acrobats and ginger'. And that was before he reached the 'shooting galleries, fan-tan tables, revolving wheels, massage benches, acupuncture, hot-towel counters, dried fish and intestines, and dance platforms serviced by hordes of music makers competing with each other to see who could drown out the others . . .'4

'Shanghai has always been different,' says the former Australian diplomat Ivor Bowden, who was born in Frenchtown on 19 August 1925. 'It regarded itself as a world city and saw Peking as provincial.'5

The city's street names provided tangible evidence of its cosmopolitan nature. In the Central District, roads bearing the names of provinces – Chekiang, Honan, Shantung, Szechuen – ran north and south, while the cross streets running east and west were named after cities: Nanking, Peking, Ningpo, Foochow. Elsewhere, they were named after the outposts of empire – Penang, Rangoon and Singapore – or were reminders of 'home', such as Edinburgh Road for the British and Broadway for the Americans. Even Lord Elgin, 'Chinese' Gordon and the opium dealer Thomas Dent were commemorated in street names; you had to go to Frenchtown to find the arts honoured in Rue Moliere and Rue Wagner.6

Marshal Joffre, the World War I hero, visited the French Concession, where one of the grand boulevards had been renamed in his honour (although owing to the prevalence of White Russians it was known to the locals as 'Little Moscow').

Albert Einstein and Bertrand Russell came to Shanghai to give lectures, while Aldous Huxley thought the spectacle of Shanghai life 'inspired something like terror'. And in the dance studio of the Russian émigré George Goncharov eight-year-old Margaret Hookham took her first steps as a ballerina. She would find fame at Sadlers Wells as Dame Margot Fonteyn.

Australians came from far and wide to add colour and dash to the Shanghai panorama as well as performing important civic duties. Indeed, they had an influence far beyond their relatively small numbers. Les Lawrance visited Shanghai and thrilled the crowds with his daring as a Queensland speedway star but stayed to run the transport section of the Shanghai Telephone System. Melburnian Dr Bill O'Hara, a member of the 7th Light Horse at Gallipoli, arrived in Shanghai in 1929 and built up a successful medical practice in the China United Building just off Nanking Road. He also earned a reputation as one of the city's biggest gamblers.

Otto Rasmussen, the Melbourne teenager who had witnessed the 1905 riots, was now an eye doctor treating glaucoma and other eye diseases among the Chinese workforce. And the Reverend Robert Mathews, on his return to Shanghai from Szechuen, compiled the monumental, 1200-page *Mathews' Chinese–English Dictionary* containing 7785 Chinese characters and more than 100,000 phrases including modern and technical terms.

For the vast majority of Chinese, life in Shanghai was a desperate struggle against starvation. Indeed, the bright lights and fluttering red banners masked the misery of back-lane sweatshops and oppressive Hongkew factories in which children as young as five or six stood for 12 hours a day over boiling kettles in the silk filatures. Their tiny fingers were red and swollen from brushing the cocoons into silk strands for female workers to unwind. The children's eyes were inflamed from the heat; some were crying from a beating at the hands of the foreman who walked up and down behind their long rows swinging a piece of no. 8 gauge wire like a whip. If they passed a thread incorrectly, their arms were scalded in boiling water.[7]

There was no distinction between boys and girls – all were treated with the same impersonal cruelty. In the workshops, young boys laboured over open chromium vats whose fumes created 'chrome holes' – incurable sores – in their hands, arms and feet. Others making batteries died of lead poisoning. All of the children were denied even the most basic of human rights in order to make profits for their Chinese, Japanese and European masters.[8]

In 1923 the Municipal Council, at the urging of female members of the National Christian Council and the Young Women's Christian Association of China, appointed a Commission on Child Labour to study the conditions under which children worked in Shanghai's factories. One of the commission's members was the Australian-born crusader Dame Adelaide Anderson and another was Charlie Soong's youngest daughter Mayling, who had returned to Shanghai after graduating in English literature from Wellesley College in the United States.

Like a pocket battleship, Dame Adelaide steamed up the Whangpoo clutching an umbrella and a bag bulging with documents to apply her expertise as Britain's former 'principal lady inspector of factories' to Shanghai's horrendous labour problems.

In one of the silk filatures, she met 'a little old man' who told her he was five and a half years old, that his name was 'Little Tiger', and that he was working 'to be able to eat rice'. 'He earned his rice,' she says, 'for he worked like a little tiger and came and went daily alone to and from the filature.' To her question of what became of these tiny workers, she was told, 'When they go to work so early, they mostly die young.'[9]

Adelaide Mary Anderson was born on 8 April 1863 in Melbourne, the eldest child in the large family of an immigrant Scottish shipbroker. She was educated in London and then sent to France and Germany before going up to Girton College,

Cambridge, where she obtained a second-class honours degree in the moral sciences. She was introduced to the harshness of working women's lives in late Victorian England as a lecturer in philosophy and economics at the Women's Co-operative Guild.[10]

In 1894 she was appointed one of the first female factory inspectors in Britain and three years later was made principal lady inspector, with the responsibility of enforcing legislation protecting women and children in factories and workshops. Her small stature and fragile looks belied a steely resolve, coupled with great powers of endurance.[11] Her reports combined literary skill with shrewd observation and reflected her profound belief in the future of women in industry.[12]

In Shanghai, she had had no hesitation in plunging into the Chinese districts to gather information. Walking along a street, she was attracted by a brightly-lit building which she supposed to be a temple. She went in and was welcomed by the owner of a private house who was celebrating the approaching nuptials of his daughter. The uninvited guest was taken to see the decorations, introduced to the bride and her relatives, and pressed to remain for the festivities. Dame Adelaide came away impressed with the happy family life of many Chinese.

She found the same commitment in the hot, dusty atmosphere of the factories, where tiny children laboured and younger ones slept or played under the roaring machines. One important effect of the factory system, she said, was that it had brought Chinese women out of their isolation into an organised world. She was delighted when a group of female workers asked to speak to her. Their first priority was that their children should be well cared for, they said, and the second was a 'mild limitation' of working hours to give them more time with their families. When she asked whether they would like the heat reduced in the workplace, they replied they did not want anything done that would hamper production and thus reduce their earnings.

While in Shanghai, Dame Adelaide met Eleanor Hinder, an Australian feminist who was responsible for the health and welfare of female employees at Farmer's department store in Sydney. In a remarkably enlightened move, the store had sent her on a one-year trip abroad to study work practices and trade union activities. Mary Dingman, the American international industrial secretary of the YWCA, who thought Eleanor 'the most intelligent and ablest young woman I met in Australia', suggested she visited the cotton mills, silk filatures and match factories that had appalled Dame Adelaide. Eleanor did so and wrote to her mother, 'It seems as if this is a laboratory of things directly concerned with my own education – it is a wonderful thing that I should have come.'[13]

Dame Adelaide was still in Shanghai on May Day 1924 and appeared in front of 80,000 workers at a Shanghai Labour Federation rally on the same platform as a handsome *Kuomintang* apparatchik named Wang Ching-wei.[14] 'I had never spoken at a Labour meeting before,' she said later. 'It was an extraordinary experience to begin in China.'[15]

Born into a poor family in Kwangtung, Wang had joined Sun Yat-sen's revolutionary movement after graduating from Tokyo Law College in 1906. Four years later he threw a bomb at the Manchu regent, Prince Chun. The prince survived and Wang was thrown into prison but the attempt made him a national hero. He was released during the 1911 Revolution.

Ten resolutions were passed at the rally including demands for children under 14 to be banned from factories, for an eight-hour working day and for a national labour conference to address workers' concerns. The final resolution read, 'Unite with the workers of the whole country, and of the whole world, organise a great united front, and clear away obstacles to humanity.'

Dame Adelaide returned to London convinced of the solidarity of Chinese family life. 'My belief is that Chinese women have it largely in their power to re-make the country if they get the chance,' she said. 'They have character, dignity and a beautiful suppleness of mind, with an affinity for things of the imagination. The responsibility that is thrust upon the mother or the grandmother at the head of the household has its effects on the whole family.'[16]

In July 1924 the commission released its report highlighting the scandalous conditions of Shanghai's Chinese workforce. One member of parliament described it as 'one of the most melancholy social documents of recent years'. The commission suggested new regulations to eliminate the major abuses, including a bye-law making it illegal for children to start work before the age of 10, rising at a later date to 12. The following year, however, the reformers failed to get a quorum at two special meetings of Shanghai ratepayers – the first step in introducing any change in the workings of the British Concession – to set a minimum working age.

Reactionary members of the Municipal Council pointed to the existing Land Regulations, which prevented them taking action against Chinese mill owners employing child labour. To alter the regulations would require a three-quarters majority of ratepayers, the unanimous decision of the consuls of every nationality in Shanghai and the concurrence of every minister in the Peking legations.[17] One of the chief obstacles was Sterling Fessenden, the Municipal Council's short, plump American chairman, who was described in a British Legation assessment as 'a feeble creature, one of those who have gone to pieces in the East, and conspicuously unfit for his position'.[18]

To exacerbate the hardship among Shanghai's Chinese citizens, the cost of living had risen sharply since the First World War. Rice was up to 135 per cent more expensive, whereas wages had risen only 80 per cent.[19] Nationalists agitated among the growing labour class for higher wages and protested against medieval work practices. Strikes, protests and boycotts escalated but the strikers' demands were rarely met and the authorities cracked down on all public demonstrations.

In February 1925 Chinese workers went on strike in protest against low wages at the Naiga Wata cotton-weaving mill, one of 32 Japanese textile mills in Shanghai. The Chinese Chamber of Commerce was asked to mediate in the dispute and succeeded in reaching a preliminary settlement, which the Japanese owner then ignored.

Sun Yat-sen's death the following month, however, gave Chinese workers a focal point in the wider issues at stake. His Three Principles swept the city and his photograph was printed on flags, posters and banners. In death, Sun's rallying cry had become far more powerful than it had ever been during his lifetime.[20]

At dawn on Anzac Day 40 Australian and New Zealand members of the Anzac Society gathered on The Bund as Dr Bill O'Hara, a captain-surgeon at Gallipoli, laid a wreath at the war memorial, a bronze statue of Winged Victory on a spare stone pillar. 'As the mixed river traffic and the queer medley of rushing vehicles passed closely alongside the monument,' the Reuters correspondent reported, 'they slowed down while the little band paid homage to the dead.'[21]

The following week the Naiga Wata mill workers started a second strike and on 15 May sent an eight-man delegation to negotiate with the Japanese management. The confrontation ended in a violent clash in which Japanese guards opened fire, mortally wounding one worker, Ku Cheng-hung, and injuring the other seven.[22]

The Municipal Council declined to prosecute the guards, but municipal police arrested a number of Chinese workers on charges of disturbing the peace. On 22 May students and workers held a memorial service for Ku Cheng-hung in the International Settlement. He was a popular figure at the Workers' Club, a quiet chess player who was also interested in furthering his education. Union leaders made impassioned speeches attacking the Japanese factory owner. The police made more arrests.[23]

At 12.40 pm on Saturday 30 May Inspector Edward Everson,

the officer in charge of Louza police station, received a telephone message from the chief of police, Commissioner Kenneth McEuen, that students were holding anti-Japanese protests in the Chinese districts and that steps should be taken to prevent them spreading to the International Settlement.[24]

Saturday was McEuen's day off and he had several social commitments in his diary, including lunch at the Shanghai Club and a visit to the Shanghai Race Club. As a captain-superintendent at the time of the 1905 riot, he had witnessed the destructive power of the Shanghai mob and had been present when the Louza police station was burned down.[25] But McEuen was a 'notoriously incompetent loafer', according to a report by the British Consulate, and there is some doubt he issued any orders at all. In the morning, he left the settlement for a couple of hours, returned for a leisurely lunch at the Shanghai Club and then, dressed in blazer and panama hat, drove to the racecourse at the western end of Nanking Road without contacting any of his subordinates.[26]

Meanwhile, large numbers of chanting, banner-carrying students had entered the settlement and started to demonstrate outside the Japanese Consulate and the Mixed Court, while another large group gathered in the Nanking Road shopping precinct. The police arrested hundreds of demonstrators, mostly students, although all were released before two o'clock. By then, the gathering in Nanking Road had turned into a mass rally, with a large crowd concentrated in the Louza district.

Around two o'clock Inspector Everson and three European officers broke up a small meeting near the station. Through an interpreter, he asked one of the students who was making a speech, 'What is the nature of your speech?' The student replied it was anti-Japanese. Everson asked him if he knew it was illegal to hold political demonstrations in the British Concession. The student replied he was simply carrying out the instructions of the students' union. 'I then picked out three of the ringleaders,' Everson related, 'and said, "Very well, I am going to lock you up."'[27]

Fifteen demonstrators followed the officers and their three prisoners back to the station, entered the charge room and demanded to be arrested as well. Everson locked them all in the cells. This should have been a warning that matters were getting out of hand. Instead of securing the station, Everson decided to show a firm hand. Taking a small detachment of constables a few blocks down Nanking Road, he arrested another man carrying an anti-Japanese banner. This time, a 'huge crowd of hundreds' followed the police squad back to the station. On the way one of Everson's constables was knocked to the ground and his six assailants were taken into custody.

Back at the station, protesters forced their way into the charge room and a violent struggle broke out in which students struck at police with the poles of their banners and Everson lashed out with his Malacca cane, while his comrades rushed the mob with wooden stools and forced them out into the street. Several students had been injured in the melee and the sight of their bloodied comrades enraged the crowd. Fearing a repeat of the 1905 incident, Everson ordered his officers to force the demonstrators east along Nanking Road. He locked the back gate of the police compound and placed an armed guard at the front of the building.

The Chinese were pushed back on to Nanking Road and up to the Wing On department store. Just as Everson thought the police were getting the upper hand, students assaulted two constables and attempted to take their pistols. The police fought back with sticks and batons but were gradually driven back against the wall of the police station. As the crowd surged forward, the traffic was brought to a halt and there were shouts of 'Kill the foreigners' in Chinese and English.

Everson, a quietly spoken Welshman, pulled out his pistol and shouted a verbal warning, 'Ding, veh ding-ts-meh iau tang-sah.' ('Stop, if you do not stop I will shoot.') 'I knew it was useless,' he said, 'and pointed [the pistol] here and there in the crowd.' Everson's words were lost in the uproar but the sight of the pistol provoked the crowd into making 'one blind rush to the station gate'.

At precisely 3.37 pm Everson gave the order to open fire. None of his squad of 23 armed Sikhs and Chinese heard him, so he snatched a rifle from one of his men and fired the first shot himself. His men then fired two volleys into the crowd, killing four men and wounding many others, five of whom later died. The police report simply stated, 'The shooting had the immediate effect of dispersing the crowd and traffic became normal shortly afterwards.'

It was now just after 3.30 pm. At the races, Commissioner McEuen learned of the shootings – he was close enough to have heard the gunfire – and immediately turned out the emergency squad.[28] He also communicated with Sterling Fessenden, who was commandant of the Shanghai Volunteer Corps. It was later claimed that had McEuen showed up at the Louza Police Station even as late as 3.15 pm and taken control of his force, the tragedy could have been averted.

While the bodies of the dead were being laid out, student leaders and unionists met at *Kuomintang* headquarters at 44 Route Vallon in Frenchtown. The Communist-led General Labour Union decided to call a strike in all areas of commerce, education and labour over the next few days. Telegrams were also sent enlisting the support of peasants, workers, merchants and students throughout the country. There was an instant public outcry against foreign privilege and the unequal treaties. In the street, Westerners were called 'foreign pigs' and spat on.

Agitators led by Li Li-san, a Paris-educated Communist, stirred up trouble among Chinese workers and bosses alike. At one point, Li convinced the Chinese Chamber of Commerce to underwrite the strikers' pay until the Municipal Council ordered engineers to throw a switch at the Shanghai Power Company and shut down the electricity supply to Chinese-owned factories. The Chinese manufacturers suddenly saw the error of their ways and withdrew their support from the unions.

In this hostile atmosphere, the issue of factory reform was thrown into limbo. Sterling Fessenden mobilised the Volunteer Corps, which patrolled the streets for weeks, severely disrupting the business and social life of the city. 'Strikes of workmen go on at Shanghai, Hankow and Hong Kong,' Bill Donald wrote to friends. 'War is wanted with Great Britain. The curious thing is that the Chinese believe they could fight anyone and defeat them. The valour of ignorance, of course.'[29]

Unfortunately for Fessenden and the municipal reactionaries, Dame Adelaide Anderson roared back into Shanghai a short time later as a member of the Foreign Office's powerful advisory committee on the Boxer Indemnity Fund. Alarmed at the prospect of a Bolshevik China, the British Government had set up the fund as part of its policy to assist her faltering republican government in Nanking along a progressive, democratic path. Millions of pounds paid to Britain since 22 December 1922 under the terms of the Boxer Protocol would be devoted to 'purposes which are beneficial to the mutual interests of his Majesty King George and of the Republic of China'.[30]

Dame Adelaide knew exactly what was required to solve the child labour problem in Shanghai – an inspectorate with powers similar to those in Britain setting minimum working ages for children and forcing mill owners to address health and safety issues. It would take her another five years of hard work to accomplish her objective. And in that time Shanghai would have drastically changed.

In the middle of the 'Red wave' of strikes, the Dogmeat General Chang Tsung-chang descended on Shanghai from Shantung and attacked the areas controlled by General Chi Shi-yuan with 60,000 troops. Having lost the support of his former ally General Sun Chuan-fang, Chi left his troops to fend for themselves and, like his predecessor, escaped down the Whangpoo in a ship bound for Japan.

With Chi's leaderless troops looting, burning and raping among the population of the Chinese districts, Dogmeat Chang and Sun Chuan-fang decided it would be foolish to fight one another, so they arrived at a truce under which the Chinese districts were partitioned between them.[31] The remnants of Chi's army were pacified by the simple expedient of beheading a few and recruiting the rest into the ranks of the other two armies. The warlords then invited leading Chinese and foreign business-men to a celebration at the Chinese Chamber of Commerce.

Chang's Manchurian ally, the Old Marshal, sent his eldest son, 26-year-old Chang Hsueh-liang, down from Peking as his representative. The party was a lavish affair, but as soon as the foreigners had departed, the bandit chiefs presented the Chinese merchants with a bill for their costs in 'liberating' the city and as a guarantee of future peace and prosperity. According to John Pal, who had left the Customs Service to become a freelance reporter for Australian newspapers, the Chinese paid up.[32]

Dogmeat Chang moved his military headquarters into the handsome new administrative building at North Station in Chapei and claimed the opium bounty from the city's drug traf-fickers for himself. He had no sympathy for the May Thirtieth political movement, which had grown up around the massacre of that date, and strongly opposed the abolition of child labour, describing the reformers as 'crazy'.

According to the president of Peking University, Chang had 'the physique of an elephant, the brain of a pig and the temper-ament of a tiger'. His nickname among his troops was 'Old Sixty-three' because someone had taken the trouble to estab-lish that his erect member equalled a stack of 63 silver dollars. Indeed, he and the Young Marshal partied with such inordinate excess that even hardened Shanghailanders were amazed at the stories of their wild, drug-fuelled orgies.[33]

Despite Dogmeat Chang's sordid reputation, the American Chamber of Commerce in Shanghai supported the warlords because they posed no threat to Westerners; however, they advocated armed foreign intervention to deal with the Communists, who were determined to end the unequal treaties and expel all foreigners. The chamber appointed the pro-Japanese propagandist George Bronson Rea as its Washington representative to lobby the Federal Government. It also held a special meeting to expel the journalist John Powell from its ranks because of his support for Chiang Kai-shek and outspoken opposition to its interventionist policies.[34]

Wallis Warfield Spencer, the American social climber who became Duchess of Windsor, chose this moment to make her entrance on the Shanghai stage. She sailed up the China coast from Hong Kong in the *Empress of Russia* in late November 1924 after her first husband Earl Winfield 'Win' Spencer, a cross-dressing, bisexual naval officer, moved in with a handsome painter.

The 28-year-old Wallis immersed herself in the party scene with gay abandon; according to Wellington Koo's second wife Hui-lan, the only Mandarin phrase she ever mastered was, 'Boy, pass me the champagne.' Her favourite nightspot was the Summer Garden at the new Majestic Hotel on Bubbling Well Road. One night she heard the band there playing 'Tea for Two', the signature tune from the 1925 Broadway musical *No, No Nanette*. 'The combination of the melody, the moonlight, the perfume of jasmine, not to mention the Shangri-la illusion of the courtyard, made me feel that I had really entered the Celestial Kingdom,' she wrote. 'No doubt about it, life in Shanghai was good, very good, and in fact, almost too good for a woman.'[35]

Wallis's exploits in Hong Kong, Shanghai and Peking in 1924–25 became the subject of official scrutiny after King George V exclaimed, 'Who is this woman?' when she later became the mistress of his son David, the Prince of Wales. According to the China Report, compiled by the British Secret Service at that time, she indulged in 'perverse practices' in one of Hong Kong's singing houses; engaged in rigged games of roulette in Shanghai in exchange for sex, and entered into a bizarre *ménage a trois* with an American diplomat and his wife in Peking.[36]

However, a claim by the wife of Vice-Admiral Milton E. Miles, chief of United States Naval Intelligence operations in China, that Wallis was impregnated by the dashing Italian philanderer Count Galeazzo Ciano is impossible to substantiate. She certainly met Mussolini's future son-in-law while he was on a brief visit to Peking in 1925 but her subsequent pregnancy and abortion, which supposedly left her unable to conceive children, remain unproven. She did, however, find time in Peking to have an affair with the naval attaché at the Italian Embassy, Alberto da Zara, who read Italian poetry to her, took her horse-riding and called her 'Wally'.[37]

In the autumn of 1925 General Sun Chuan-fang decided Shanghai would be better off without the self-indulgent, barbaric Dogmeat Chang. Breaking the terms of their truce, he launched a surprise attack with his troops that ousted Chang from the railway station and drove his army back across the Yangtze. Sun then united all of the Chinese areas in a new Municipality of Greater Shanghai under a Chinese mayor.[38] Having established things to his liking (and taken custody of the opium bounty), he moved up the Yangtze and on 25 November 1925 took control of Nanking.

Meanwhile, protests and strikes over the 'May Thirtieth Martyrs' had spread to neighbouring provinces until 28 cities were embroiled in what was described as 'an amount of hostility that astonished even the most experienced observers'.[39] The Chinese attitude came as no surprise to Milly Bennett, the *nom de plume* of the radical San Francisco-born journalist Mildred Jacqueline Bremler. She arrived in Shanghai in October 1926 and checked into Mrs Kathleen Daniels's moderately priced American Boarding House.

At 29, Milly was escaping from a broken marriage and was almost penniless. While looking for work, she clashed with a number of British residents. 'I was finding out,' she wrote,

> that practically all of the British in Shanghai were diehard reac-
> tionaries, and the only way to gain access to the business and
> social circles that they controlled was to echo their hidebound
> dogma that the Chinese were a dirty, low, mongrel race, that
> they should be everlastingly grateful for being booted round
> by the extremely superior British, and how what the Chinese
> really needed was the firm British government to guide them.
> The backbone, so to speak, of these British arbiters were small
> fry, cashiers in banks, vice-consuls, traders, newspapermen,
> folk who would be lucky at home to have a charwoman in once
> a week, but here could staff their flats as a princely ménage –
> every $300 a month employee had cook, helper, amah, table
> boy, six or eight fulltime, well-trained servants.[40]

To Milly's dismay, her own countrywomen were as bad as the British. 'It is appalling what can happen to the average American housewife when she gets within hailing distance of what she thinks is high society, especially if it happens to have a British accent,' she wrote. 'It makes my flesh crawl to hear American women go around imitating the *la-de-da* manners of the British.'

While Milly Bennett's criticisms were undoubtedly true of some foreign residents, they were only part of the story. There was no better example of someone who had made the most of his chances than Inspector Roy Fernandez of the Shanghai Municipal Police. Roy was born in Coonamble, New South Wales, but following the break-up of his parents' marriage and the death of his father, he was made a ward of the state and raised in an orphanage. 'My father worked as a jackeroo from the age of 14,' his son Roy Jr, a retired Australian diplomat, says. 'He didn't drink or smoke and sustained that despite a lot of chiacking from his mates. He'd saved £50 to go on holiday in Sydney but he met a bullocky who had been to China and he ended up in Shanghai.'[41]

Roy took a job in the Maritime Customs Service and then switched to the Municipal Police Force. He married Sybil Morgan, the eldest of Robert and Mary Ann Morgan's five children, and rose through the ranks, starting as a constable in the police traffic office. He learned Chinese and was promoted to sergeant with the right to interrogate suspects. He was then promoted to the CID counterfeit squad which specialised in tracking down forged stamps and banknotes. He and Sybil raised two children, Roy Jr and Stephanie, in a modern flat in the horseshoe-shaped Cosmopolitan Apartments block and took their holidays in the United States and Europe.[42]

Firearms were an everyday feature of life in Shanghai and Roy Fernandez became a self-taught expert in detecting whether a suspect had fired a gun. His skill with the so-called 'nitrate test' saved more than one citizen from the executioner.

In an article written for the *Sydney Morning Herald* in 1954, Fernandez cites the case of a Chinese merchant he calls Wong, who was suspected of murdering his concubine. After an argument, Wong had left his revolver under the woman's pillow when he walked out of her apartment. Half an hour later, a shot was heard and the landlord found her lying on the floor with a bullet through the heart. Instead of calling the police, he telephoned Wong who dashed back to the apartment, picked up his mistress, put her on the bed and retrieved his gun. He then went to a police station and reported that his concubine had committed suicide.

It seemed an unlikely story, so Fernandez tested Wong's hands and the sleeves of his shirt, jacket and overcoat for the tiny particles of nitrate that escape with great force from the breech of a gun when it is fired and become embedded in the skin of the person firing the weapon. He covered the back of Wong's hand and the sleeves of his clothing with wax, which was then peeled off and treated with a chemical called diphenylamine. The test proved negative except for the sleeve of Wong's overcoat.

In the morgue, the policeman then tested the dead woman's hand and the material of her dress around the gunshot wound. The hand was positive to the nitrate test and there was a quantity of unburned gunpowder on the dress. Fernandez says, 'My findings were: Wong had not fired the gun. The two spots of nitrate found on the sleeve of his overcoat got there when he picked his mistress up off the floor.' Thanks to Fernandez's forensic skills, Wong walked free.[43]

One of Roy Fernandez's closest friends was Gordon Bowden, a leading light among the expatriate Australian business community. Vivian Gordon Bowden, a brown-eyed, slimly built, energetic man with a clipped moustache, was born in the Sydney suburb of Stanmore on 28 May 1884. He was educated at Sydney Church of England Grammar School (known as Shore) and Bedford School in England. He learned the silk trade in Europe and at the age of 21 became a silk inspector in Canton on behalf of European purchasers.

Three years later in 1908 Bowden joined a branch of Bowden Gomei Kaisha, the family firm in Japan. He was looking after its interests in a salmon fishery at Kamchatka on the north-east Russian coast when he heard about the outbreak of World War I from a passing Russian sailor. Taking ship to England, he served with the Royal Engineers in France, earned a mention in dispatches and was demobilised with the rank of major. In 1917, he married an English girl, Dorothy Dennis, while on leave. He spoke fluent French, German and Japanese and had some Italian and Russian.[44]

In 1919 he was in the Caucasus with 'The Black Sea Venture', a bold attempt to resurrect the Anglo-Caucasian Oil Company. The company was registered on the London Stock Exchange and had been one of the star performers of Tsarist Russia's booming petroleum industry. Indeed, George Morrison had attended a banquet in its honour at the Russian Legation in Peking as far back as December 1898. Anglo-Caucasian had been shut down following the Russian Revolution. When the Bolsheviks sabotaged any chance of restarting it, Gordon Bowden left Russia and rejoined the family firm in Japan.

Dorothy and Gordon's first child, a daughter named Doreen, was born in Japan in August 1919. Towards the end of 1921, the family moved to China when Gordon was appointed managing director of the import–export house A. Cameron & Company (China) Limited of Shanghai. Bowden, a practical man with a literary bent – he had published two novels under the *nom de plume* Vivian Gordon – was prominent in the affairs of Shanghai's expatriate community.

One of Dorothy's closest friends was the former Laura Bullmore, wife of Frederick Maze, future inspector-general of the Chinese Maritime Customs Service at Shanghai. Laura had been raised and educated in Ipswich, Queensland, and met her husband, the Belfast-born nephew of Sir Robert Hart, in Colombo at the beginning of World War I. She was returning to Australia from England and he was on his way to China. They corresponded for a couple of years and then in 1917 Laura travelled to Shanghai for their wedding.[45]

Dorothy and Gordon's second daughter, June, was born in Shanghai in 1921 and their son Ivor four years later. Ivor started his education in the kindergarten at the Cathedral Girls' School and then moved to the Public School, an international, non-denominational school in Yu Yuen Road. 'I learned enough Shanghai dialect to count a little, swear a little and call a rickshaw,' he says. He was taught to swim at the Country Club by Billy Tingle, the popular Australian boxing champion and gym teacher.

'The favourite weekend event was the paper chase when riders with saddlebags filled with red, white and green paper laid the trail for the hunt to follow,' he says. 'The Boxing Day paper chase was a particularly festive event. Those who had hunting pinks wore them, with holly in their hats and lots of Christmas cheer under their belts.'

For the school holidays, Gordon Bowden took his family to the former German resort of Tsingtao or the Repulse Bay Hotel in Hong Kong. Life was good. Now, with Communist-inspired strikes breaking out all over Shanghai and wall posters denouncing Britain and the unequal treaties, it seemed the Bolsheviks had come back into his life and that of his adopted city.

Public anger over the May Thirtieth killings did not subside until December 1925 when Commissioner McEuen and Inspector Everson were dismissed from the force and the Municipal Council paid compensation to the families of the deceased and wounded. McEuen, described by Maurice Tinkler, one of his officers, as 'easygoing but otherwise of little use', retired to Japan on a large pension, while Everson lived out his days in Gloucestershire. 'There is no suggestion,' he was reassured in an official letter from his superiors, 'that you failed in or exceeded your duty as a responsible police officer in any respect whatsoever.'[46]

The International Settlement settled down to its normal routine of business and pleasure. Octavia Down, a young Australian who worked for a British trading house, enjoyed an active social life. It could scarcely be otherwise, Miss Down told The Argus during a holiday in Melbourne, 'because there is nothing for the women to do except enjoy themselves'.

> When the Chinese are trained by the foreigners [the paper reported], they make such perfect servants that there is no need for the women to do anything in their homes, quite apart from the fact that they would 'lose face' if they did so. There is plenty of sport, golf, tennis, riding and dancing, with swimming in the summer. It was interesting to learn that many of the better class Chinese take their wives to dance at cafes and hotels like the Majestic and the Carlton, though they are never seen at the American or the French Club. Both the men and women dance very well.[47]

Such condescension towards the Chinese infuriated Otto Rasmussen, who had got to know many Chinese families through his medical work. Born in 1888, he was the eldest child of Danish settler Christian Rasmussen and his Australian wife Mary, née Jennings, who raised him with a firm belief in human rights. He was outraged by Rodney Gilbert's anti-Chinese tirade *What's Wrong with China*, which was published as a series of articles in the *North-China Daily News* and then released in 1925 as a book. Gilbert concluded, 'We have therefore to be grateful to the fire-brand element in China which is driving furiously on towards the complete ruin of China as a nation, the utter collapse of foreign trade with this bad-boy people, and very possibly the martyrdom of those of us who are foolish enough to live in China.'

As Gilbert's prophecy seemed like coming true, Rasmussen sat down to write his own book, *What's Right with China: an answer to foreign criticisms*. He dedicated it to 'the young men and women of China whose exalted idealism is leading their country from the stagnant marshes of an alien-imposed regression to the hard highway of progress'.[48]

Meanwhile, thousands of newcomers of all political shades continued to stream through Shanghai's porous borders. Among them was the sinister Trebitsch Lincoln, a Hungarian-born Jewish émigré who had served as a Liberal member of parliament at Westminster after changing his name and converting to Christianity. During World War I, he worked as a German agent spying on British shipping and later served three years in prison for fraud.[49]

Stripped of his British citizenship, Trebitsch Lincoln came to China in the early 1920s and earned a living as an arms dealer and political adviser to several warlords, including General Wu Pei-fu, who had become the dominant militarist of the Middle Yangtze following his defeat at the hands of the Old Marshal and the Dogmeat General in North China.

In 1925, Lincoln appeared to put his dark past behind him when he converted to Buddhism, taking the Chinese name Chao Kung. After six years of religious study, he was ordained a monk with the rank of Bodhisattva. Supported by a small group of European Buddhist monks and nuns, he established the Trebitsch Lincoln Buddhist Monastery in Shanghai. As we shall see, the spiritual life had done little to reform him.

CHAPTER 15

Yangtze Thunder

The May Thirtieth killings at Shanghai strengthened the hand of the Nationalists in their avowed aim of ending foreign imperialism and establishing Sun Yat-sen's Three Principles of the People. Conservative elements of the *Kuomintang* threw their weight behind Sun's protégé Chiang Kai-shek, who had spent three months in Moscow but had singularly failed to embrace the Communist system. It was inevitable he would clash with Mikhail Borodin and his nominee for party leader, Wang Ching-wei, the handsome demagogue who had risen to acting chairman.[1]

Long before Mao Tse-tung emerged as a contender, the battle between the neurotic, ambitious Chiang and his charismatic rival Wang for the hearts and minds of China would become one of the dominant features of Chinese politics. Chiang seemed a stiff, militaristic figure compared with the silky-smooth Wang, although the radical journalist Milly Bennett detected a slippery quality in the latter which she put down to 'a shallow and treacherous nature'.[2]

Ho Chi Minh, a young Vietnamese who had graduated in Marxist agitation at the University of the Toilers of the East in Moscow, was dispatched to Canton as an interpreter to help Borodin tighten his grip on the party. The Communists were intent on agrarian reform and redistributing the land among the peasants, whereas Chiang had no intention of empowering the masses. Despite their conflicting aims, Chiang and Borodin joined forces in the spring of 1926 to achieve Sun Yat-sen's cherished dream of a united China. Once power had been wrested from the Northern warlords, they could argue over the ideological spoils.

All eyes were turned to Red Canton in May when the legions of the National Revolutionary Army, trained by Communist advisers and armed with Russian weapons, marched smartly out of their barracks. The destination of the long-awaited Northern Expedition was Peking via Britain's sphere of influence, the Yangtze Valley. But whereas the Communist-led section headed for Hankow, Hanyang and Wuchang – the three cities that constituted Wuhan – Chiang Kai-shek set off with his forces in a more north-easterly direction for the walled city of Nanchang in Kiangsi.[3]

Prior to each engagement with Northern forces, Borodin's *agents provocateurs* were sent ahead to undermine enemy morale and create chaos in factories and schools. Large agricultural estates were broken up and the land distributed among the peasants; many landlords and governors were tortured and beheaded.[4] One of the most enthusiastic party officials involved in the bloodletting was Mao Tse-tung. The former librarian seemed to get a visceral thrill from watching the humiliation of Chinese officials and their gory executions.[5]

At the beginning of September, Borodin's troops besieged Wuchang.[6] Burgoyne Chapman, the Australian education-ist, described living in 'an atmosphere of strikes and demands, placards and speeches of denunciation' after Communist *provocateurs* targeted his Central China Teachers' College.

During the siege, the college formed part of the southern boundary and teachers and students were ordered to evacuate the premises. 'When we returned, the fighting had moved to the north and we thought our troubles were over,' he said.

> However, six students from Hunan immediately started to cause a disturbance. Certain demands were made, and a student strike was organised. When our reply to their demands proved unsatisfactory, the vice-principal was imprisoned, beaten and driven away. The other students were terrorised.[7]

The gang of six remained in control of the school for two weeks but left after Chapman agreed to their demands. Two days later they returned, destroyed books, posted menacing notices and threatened to beat certain students. The college had to close down.

Chapman said high officials in the Nationalist Government had declared that the party was not anti-Christian or anti-foreign, but revolutionary elements had been let loose and were beyond control. An unfortunate feature of the situation was the predominance of Russian advisers and the complete accept-ance of Soviet methods. 'The only hope,' he said, 'is in the more moderate section of the party asserting itself and ending the terrorist methods now so widely practised.'[8]

Hanyang, the second of Wuhan's three cities and site of a huge Japanese ironworks, an arsenal and an important Buddhist monastery, collapsed without a fight in early September after the disloyal Northern commander accepted a bribe. On 6 September, Hankow's Chinese defenders withdrew when the Nationalists warned General Wu Pei-fu that he should evacuate the city before daylight the following day. Wu took the hint and during the night evacuated his troops in 294 railway wagons after promising the foreign consuls that he would return to liberate Hankow from the Nationalists as soon as he received reinforcements. When Wuchang threw open its gates to the Nationalists on the symbolic date of 10 October, Wu realised that further resistance was futile and headed north to Honan.[9]

All of Hankow's foreign enclaves lay along the riverbank of the Yangtze and could be protected from the front by destroyers and gunboats, but were vulnerable to attack from open countryside at the rear if the Nationalists chose to do so. Moreover, the British, French and Japanese concessions were separated by the former Russian and German concessions, which were now under Chinese control. 'It is not Hankow alone that is in danger,' The Times warned, 'but the whole range of British interests throughout China.'[10]

By December, the Nationalist armies controlled five provinces in South and Central China and it was time for the Nationalist Government and its Soviet allies to move from Canton to Hankow. The group included the Harvard-educated Finance Minister T. V. Soong and two of his sisters, Ayling (Madame H. H. Kung) and Chingling (Madame Sun Yat-sen), the tubby, short-sighted Industry Minister H. H. Kung, and the Trinidad-born Foreign Minister, Eugene Chen.

Their most pressing task was to orchestrate the advance across the Yangtze for the march to the north, where the Old Marshal Chang Tso-lin, having declared he would not tolerate Feng Yu-hsiang's efforts to 'bolshevise' North China, had finally succeeded in deposing the Christian General and fulfilling his dream of ruling Peking.[11]

Chiang Kai-shek, meanwhile, set up his winter headquarters 320 kilometres south of Hankow at Nanchang. Although protesting his loyalty to the Nationalist Government, his intention was to let the Communist-led armies fight their way to Peking while he made a two-pronged attack on the old Ming capital of Nanking and the richest prize of all: Shanghai.[12]

Borodin suspected that the united front was dead but, as instructed by his Comintern masters, concentrated on taking the fight to Britain, the biggest and most powerful nation on the Yangtze. His walrus moustache bristling with righteous Leninist indignation, he urged his agents to stir up anti-British feeling among the industrial proletariat of the three Wuhan cities.

'Seemingly the impresario of insurrection, master of every move and every situation,' the Sinologist Nicholas R. Clifford wrote, 'Borodin was never too busy to receive the throng of foreign writers and journalists who made the pilgrimage that winter and spring to the new Jerusalem on the Yangtze.'[13]

By the New Year, anti-British feeling had reached fever pitch after it was learned that British police at Tientsin had arrested seven *Kuomintang* activists and handed them over to the Old Marshal's Fengtien commanders, who had promptly executed them. Borodin denounced the British Concession at Hankow – a mini-Shanghai, with its own bund, custom house, consulate, police force and banks – as a nest of counter-revolutionary activity. He demanded it be seized.

For several days, farm labourers and coolies were given free passes on Hankow-bound trains until large numbers had gathered in the Chinese city on the banks of the Han River.[14] As agitators inflamed passions with anti-imperialist speeches at mass rallies, a British destroyer anchored off the British Concession alongside the 645-ton gunboat HMS *Bee*, flagship of the Yangtze patrol.

On Monday, 3 January 1927, the British consul Herbert Goffe asked the British naval commander Rear-Admiral J. S. Cameron for a naval landing party to reinforce the small contingent of Royal Marines who were defending the concession with a group of special constables and some firemen armed with hoses. A detachment of naval ratings commanded by Lieutenant T. Ellis came ashore and joined the Marines, who were building a barricade of sandbags and barbed wire entanglements. The sight of the bluejackets enraged the Chinese who shouted insults and pelted the troops with stones. Meanwhile, Herbert Goffe called in vain on the Nationalist authorities to restore order.

Between four and five o'clock that afternoon a mob estimated at 50,000 stampeded towards the concession and succeeded in capturing the first line of barbed-wire defences. The rush was stemmed by the defenders, but not before a naval officer and two special constables had been seriously injured.[15]

Burgoyne Chapman, who had escaped across the river from Wuchang and was sheltering in the British Concession at Hankow, paid tribute to the Marines' valour. For hour after hour, they stood guard with fixed bayonets and Lewis guns at the ready, while small children standing a few paces in front of the mob hurled mud and stones at them. After the slaughter in Shanghai on 30 May 1925, no amount of provocation could induce them to shoot.[16] 'Time after time I expected to hear the order given to open fire, in spite of the odds against the men,' *The Times* correspondent reported. 'Discipline prevailed.'[17]

The mob then turned in mindless fury on the nearest available building which happened to be a shelter for rickshaw pullers on the foreshore. The shed was torn to pieces and set ablaze. One of the Marines guarding the foreshore was set upon by rioters, who seized his rifle and bayoneted him in the leg.[18]

'Everywhere was a dense human mass, with thousands of waving lanterns,' *The Times* man reported. 'The uproar caused by the shouting and yelling, the banging of drums, the crashing of cymbals, and the blowing of all kinds of noise-producing instruments was at times deafening.'[19]

At 5.30 pm, a large detachment of Nationalist soldiers finally forced their way through the besieging mob and were admitted to the British Concession. However, the Nationalist commander refused to take any action unless he was placed in complete charge of the area. Goffe and Cameron knew that their small force of 240 men could easily be overwhelmed and reluctantly agreed to the naval unit returning to its ship.

On Tuesday morning the mob was permitted to tear down the barricades and occupy the concession, where they plastered the war memorial with *Kuomintang* posters and held rowdy meetings.[20] That afternoon, the demonstrators were driven out by Nationalist troops and, with Goffe's permission, the British flag was hauled down from the municipal building and replaced with the Nationalist flag, the white-rayed sun on a navy blue field. All was in readiness for the arrival that evening of a provisional committee, including such luminaries as Eugene Chen, T. V. Soong and Sun Yat-sen's 36-year-old son Sun Fo, who would take charge of the concession. The Communist labour organiser Liu Shaoqi took great delight in establishing the headquarters of the Hupeh General Labour Union in the British Consulate.

The following day the mob attacked the concession's police station and occupied the Union Jack Club. British women and children were herded on to the Hankow Bund and loaded on to steamers bound for Shanghai. As dark clouds blanketed the sun and an icy rain pelted down, the mortification of British arms was complete. One of the most galling aspects of the shameful episode was that the French and Japanese concessions had been left untouched.

Eugene Chen professed to regret the mob's unruly behaviour, apologised for the defacement of the war memorial and promised that government forces would maintain order. *The Times*, however, blamed Chen and his comrades for the debacle: 'First by intimidation, then by keeping the harassed local authorities in play with negotiations and smooth promises, the Chinese Nationalists have succeeded in their immediate aim of seizing control of an important concession secured to Great Britain by treaty.'[21]

The events at Hankow were a crushing setback to Britain's diplomatic efforts to achieve a detente with the Nationalists. The British minister Sir Miles Lampson, a great bear of a man six-feet five-inches tall with the girth of an oak tree, had visited the treaty port three weeks earlier. At a meeting with the diminutive Eugene Chen, he explained that His Majesty's Government no longer believed that China needed the guiding hand of foreign powers in her development as a modern nation. He also promised to co-operate with the Nationalist Government in negotiating a revision of the unequal treaties.[22]

After 3 January, however, Lampson had done a complete about-face. 'The Hankow capitulation,' he raged, 'is the worst blow to British prestige that has occurred in the last 35 years.' He sent the British chargé d'affaires Owen O'Malley to Hankow to try to retrieve something from the wreckage.

Despite an attack of malarial fever that rattled his teeth like dice,[23] Borodin hailed the takeover of the British Concession as a major political victory. He had previously ridden around town on a humble Chinese pony but switched to a more grandiose conveyance: General Wu Pei-fu's French-made, bullet-proof limousine. His children, aged nine and 11, were said to be receiving a bourgeois education at the American School in Shanghai under the name Ginzburg.[24]

The turn of events at Hankow surprised the Nationalist leaders. They had expected the British soldiers to inflict casualties on the demonstrators, thus presenting a further opportunity for anti-British agitation. Now, they waited in trepidation for Britain's time-honoured response: a bombardment by a fleet of British gunboats. The Nationalist cabinet was debating what to do when Borodin entered the room. 'Do nothing,' he advised, 'and the British will do nothing either.' He was right. A few weeks later, in the first major victory over the unequal treaties, Lampson signed an agreement surrendering the British Concession to Chinese control.[25]

Despite the apparent camaraderie among the members of the Nationalist Government in Hankow, the united front was in danger of disintegrating, seemingly placing them at odds with Chiang Kai-shek and his right-wing supporters. Curiously, only Chingling Soong and Eugene Chen could be described as genuine left-wingers, whereas Ayling Soong and her husband H. H. Kung – who claimed to be a direct descendant of Confucius – were conservatives, and Wang Ching-wei and T. V. Soong were becoming increasingly right-wing.[26]

The distinction between the two factions was lost on diehard Shanghailanders, who had been shocked by Britain's capitulation in Hankow. They saw all Nationalist forces as a 'Red army' and feared being slaughtered in a full-scale Communist insurrection. 'There is an increasing menace to Shanghai, where emissaries from Canton are now doing their utmost to foment strikes and disorders in preparation for the advance of the *Kuomintang* troops,' *The Times* reported. 'The Peking Government has finally thrown up the pretence of being the Government of China, and has resigned for lack of funds.'[27]

O. M. Green in the *North-China Daily News* described Chiang Kai-shek and the *Kuomintang* as 'the new Boxer movement' and demanded that Britain suppress it.[28] The thundering presses in the basement of the paper's new seven-storey, twin-towered building at 17 The Bund spewed out a stream of news and features on the crisis. Among a *pot pourri* of scare-mongering articles in a supplement devoted to the Red menace was one that became a classic of its kind. It was headlined, 'How to Spot Communists at Moving Picture Shows and Other Public Gatherings'.

The 'Boxerism/Red menace' view was most strongly expressed among members of the Shanghai Club. The *Manchester Guardian* writer Arthur Ransome coined the phrase 'Shanghai Mind' to describe the outdated, imperialist and bellicose mindset he encountered there. 'They look on their magnificent buildings,' he wrote, 'and are surprised that China is not grateful to them for these gifts, forgetting that the money to build them came out of China.'[29]

Otto Rasmussen, who mixed with Chinese patients and their families every day, understood that the basic problem in Shanghai wasn't Communism but the soaring prices of rice and other staple foods. 'The local English press saw "the hand of Moscow" in every abnormality from robberies to the laundry bill,' he wrote. 'In this way, they arrived at a state of high nervous tension, from which their only release was golf and race-meetings.'[30]

On 17 February the Nationalists' Eastern Route Army, commanded by Chiang's chief of staff Pai Chung-hsi, defeated

General Sun Chuan-fang's forces at Hangchow, 150 kilometres south of Shanghai, creating panic in the International Settlement. Coolies were employed day and night in freezing winter weather digging trenches, putting up barbed-wire entanglements and building concrete blockhouses. Within a matter of weeks 25,000 soldiers from Britain, the United States, France, Italy and Japan had rushed to Shanghai.

'The demand for barracks, food, hotel accommodation, entertainment, was unprecedented,' Otto Rasmussen wrote. 'Reluctant landlords, hotel managers, cabaret owners were obliged to charge their saviour defenders double the previous price.'[31] Most commanders had orders to avoid conflict with Nationalist forces but to protect the city's 75,000 foreign citizens from mob violence.[32] Wildly impractical plans from an earlier crisis for the establishment of a *cordon sanitaire* 80 kilometres wide along the Yangtze from Shanghai to Hankow were dusted down.

On 19 February the Communist-dominated General Labour Union paralysed the city with a general strike with the intention of setting up a fully fledged Soviet commune. The union leaders issued a statement calling for the withdrawal of all foreign forces from the city, the return of the concessions to Chinese rule and the establishment of a popular municipal government under their leaders in Red Hankow 'to build a new Shanghai, free and independent, and wash away 80 years of shame and insult'.[33]

Factory production lines ground to a standstill, the docks fell silent and thousands of power workers, tram drivers and even rickshaw pullers refused to work. The defiant mood rapidly changed when murder squads, led by black-clad executioners, moved through the Chinese districts. General Sun Chuan-fang, who had returned to Shanghai from Nanking, ordered his soldiers to accompany the executioners. Dozens of strikers and protesters – often students just handing out leaflets – were beheaded with broadswords and their heads placed in bamboo cages which were hung from telephone poles.[34]

On 20 February the Chinese Communist Party escalated the strike into an armed insurrection with the intention of toppling Sun Chuan-fang. The future Chinese premier Chou En-lai ordered his militia, a forerunner of the Red Guards, to raid police stations for arms and occupy buildings at Chapei, Hongkew, Nantao and Pootung. But all these efforts ended in fiasco. That night Communist sailors aboard two Chinese gunboats fired several shells to signal the start of the uprising. Unfortunately, the missiles rained down on the French Concession, one shell passing through the French Club in Rue Cardinal Mercier while a female member was delivering a lecture on Chinese culture. One of the guests, Bishop Graves, thought the intrusion 'rather a rude commentary' on the learned treatise.[35]

It quickly transpired that right-wing unionists had no stomach for a fight and failed to order their units into battle, leaving scattered bands of left-wingers to take on Sun's troops and the Chinese police through the wet winter's night. Two days later the General Labour Union admitted defeat and called off all industrial action. It was a bitter setback for the Communist Party but one that provided a blueprint for future action.

Meanwhile, the Nationalists had advanced up the Hang-chow–Shanghai railway line to within 60 kilometres of Shanghai. General Sun abandoned the defence of the city and was seen crossing the Yangtze to the safety of the north bank. The departure of his commanders created a vacuum which the dreaded 'Dogmeat General', Chang Tsung-chang, who had ended up in Shantung again, was only too happy to fill. On 25 February he and his troops headed south into Kiangsu in an armoured train known as 'the Great Wall', manned by a squadron of White Russian mercenaries.

The following day Major-General Sir John Duncan and his chief of staff, Viscount Gort, sailed up the Whangpoo in the troopship *Megantic*, with two more British battalions on board. While the troops marched out to their camp at Jessfield Park, near St John's University on the western outskirts of the International

Settlement, the two senior officers found agreeable quarters at the Astor House Hotel and sat back to await developments.

By now, the Nationalists had broken through the last defensive line south of Shanghai. Hundreds of General Sun's troops tried to join refugees streaming into the foreign concessions but were kept at bay by British infantrymen manning all points of entry. Deserters were reduced to offering their rifles and pistols for sale at 10 cents apiece in order to eat.

On 21 March the Nationalist vanguard, clutching Soviet weapons and with large straw sunhats strapped to their backs, reached Lunghwa on the southern outskirts of Shanghai. In the intervening weeks, Chou En-lai had secretly drilled 5000 union pickets, many of them armed with stolen police weapons, and placed them in makeshift redoubts at strategic points in the Chinese districts. When Dogmeat Chang's train pulled into North Station, he found himself surrounded by a force of hostile, well-entrenched workers.

At midday on the 21st the Nationalist flag was broken out from a mast on the cupola of the Chinese Post Office in Soochow Road and the General Labour Union called another strike of all Chinese workers. Once again, the mills and factories fell silent, the trams stopped running and there was a riot among the staff of the big department stores in Nanking Road. Ostensibly, the purpose of the strike was to welcome the Nationalist liberation of Shanghai, but while wall posters and banners hailed the triumph of the *Kuomintang*, the Chinese Communist Party secretly planned to pull off its greatest coup by creating a 'Red Shanghai' during the change-over in power.

Chou En-lai's pickets moved through the Chinese districts disarming police and remnants of General Sun's army; the Municipal Council declared a state of emergency and mobilised the Volunteer Corps; White Russians were brought in as scab labour to run water and power plants.[36]

Dogmeat Chang's usual method of dealing with industrial trouble in Shantung was to execute the strikers' leaders. When a burst of gunfire heralded the start of a full-scale workers' uprising, Chang responded with characteristic violence. Houses bordering the station were set ablaze and the workers' positions shelled with a three-inch artillery piece mounted on his armoured train.

Hongkew and Nantao fell to the revolutionaries without much of a struggle and Pootung and west Shanghai soon followed. But in Chapei, Chang's troops in the vast Commercial Press building fought back doggedly with machine-guns and the White Russian mercenaries kept up a barrage from 'the Great Wall' as it chugged up and down the railway line crossing Honan Road. The uprising's leaders took over a police station in Baoshan Road to direct their ragged battalions.

By now, fires were burning out of control around North Station. Whole blocks of houses, godowns and factories were destroyed in the conflagration and thousands of inhabitants joined the long line of refugees flocking into the International Settlement. The battle continued all through the night but in the morning, with ammunition running low and no sign of Dogmeat Chang to be found, the forces holding the Commercial Press building surrendered.

At North Station, Chang's troops began to vacate the battlefield and late that afternoon made a fighting retreat to the British barricades at Elgin Road. Only 'the Great Wall', a monstrous war machine painted yellow, black and brown, kept up its bombardment until it too ran out of ammunition and hoisted a white flag.[37]

Lord Gort sallied forth from the Astor House Hotel to assist a group of French nuns who had been cut off in Hongkew. He was taken prisoner by Nationalist troops and it took the intervention of the British consul Sir Sidney Barton to set him free.[38]

Chou En-lai congratulated his men on their victory. They had, he said, 'taken the leadership of the expedition against the warlords'. A provisional citizens' government was set up, while armed pickets policed the streets to await the arrival of the *Kuomintang*'s main force.[39]

Chiang Kai-shek's original plan was to isolate Nanking to prevent reinforcements being sent up the Yangtze, but the collapse of the warlord armies in Shanghai had left Nanking in desperate straits. At the first sign of trouble, General Sun's garrison there began to retreat, burning and looting buildings in the Chinese city on the way to the North Gate. Although foreign property was left untouched, the American consul, John K. Davis, advised American women and children to evacuate the city. Every train from Pukow, the southern terminus of the Pukow–Tientsin line on the north bank of the Yangtze opposite Nanking, was loaded with soldiers, many clinging to the sides of carriages or riding on the roof, while south-bound steamers were packed with refugees.

At seven o'clock on the morning of the 24th, the Nationalists' Sixth Army, commanded by General Chang Chien, stormed into the undefended Foreign Quarter. The soldiers' first target was the Japanese Consulate, which was looted and burned, and the staff savagely beaten. Next in order came the United States Consulate, which was invaded at 8 am. John Davis was expecting trouble and had set off with his family and consular staff across country for Socony House, a secure building on Standard Oil Hill,* one of a series of low mounds inside the city walls overlooking the Yangtze. This small group was escorted by 12 United States Marines who were under orders not to shoot, even though Nationalist soldiers repeatedly fired at them, wounding one of the Marines.[40]

At 9.30 am the 53-year-old British consul, Bertram Giles, was shot and wounded on the lawn of the British Consulate after challenging a couple of Nationalist soldiers who were looking for loot. The port medical officer, Dr Satchwell Smith, went to Giles's assistance and was shot dead because he resisted a soldier who attempted to cut off his finger in order to steal his wedding ring. The consulate's intelligence officer, Captain

---

*   Standard Oil Company of New York

Spear of the Indian Army, was shot twice when he tried to intervene but managed to carry the stricken Giles to the consulate office, where the consul's wife Violet and other consular staff were sheltering in the strong-room.

The soldiers forced them to come out by threatening to shoot through the wooden door. Violet Giles, who had been married for 24 years, described what happened next. 'Three soldiers at once seized me, tore rings off my fingers, inflicting considerable pain, and snatched the broach in my dress and the chain from my neck and also my watch and a bracelet from my wrist,' she said. 'They took the shoes from my feet and felt to see if there was anything in my stocking. They treated me with great brutality.'[41]

After the consul's house had been comprehensively looted, an auction was held on the blood-flecked lawn. Violet Giles's sable coat fetched $3. Dr Smith's Australian wife, the former May Williams, daughter of a Thursday Island ship's captain, escaped in one of the steamers heading for Shanghai.[42]

Elsewhere, the soldiers murdered Dr Jack Williams, the American president emeritus of Nanking University and a warm friend of the Nationalist movement, the British harbourmaster of Nanking and two Catholic priests, while missionaries were chased through the streets, beaten, robbed and in some cases stripped down to their underwear.[43]

There were surprisingly few deaths, thanks to the besieged American Marines who signalled for assistance with flags from the roof of Socony House. Their messages were received on board warships on the Yangtze and 100 Royal Marines from HMS *Emerald* and 100 bluejackets from the United States destroyers *Peston* and *Noa* came ashore and advanced towards the city walls under the cover of a thundering naval bombardment.[44]

The barrage had a salutary effect on the marauding Southern troops who suddenly came to their senses. The killing and looting ceased and Nationalist officers were able to regain control of their men. The Americans escaped down Standard Oil Hill and lowered themselves over the city wall to safety.

Potentially, the 'Nanking Incident' was a public relations disaster for Chiang Kai-shek just as he was attempting to sell himself to the world as the strongman who could save China from Communism. His minions claimed the crimes had been committed by 'bad characters from the North dressed in Southern uniforms, and what might be called an anti-missionary movement'. As proof, several dozen soldiers were held culpable for the disorder and executed.

Blinking through thick lenses and with his bushy white hair awry, Sterling Fessenden made a fighting speech at a British dinner party. 'According to the legend, St George achieved fame slaying a dragon,' he said. 'If necessary, another dragon will be slain here, the head of which is in Hankow, the tail at Canton. There is an army and navy here, which means that the white race will not be ousted from China. These forces are not here for war, but to maintain the prestige of their own races.'[45]

Alarmed at the power of the unions, the Chinese business community sent emissaries from Shanghai to see Chiang at his winter headquarters after Fessenden invited the Chinese Chamber of Commerce to discuss ways of curbing the labour movement. The Chinese capitalists were as anxious as their Western counterparts about the threat to public order and trade. 'It is no exaggeration to say that spontaneous combustion is apt to take place at the slightest provocation which may lead to a worse conflagration than that of last year,' the Chinese leader Yu Hsia-ching told the municipal councillors. 'For our respective and common interests we must by all means prevent it.'[46]

Chiang knew better than anyone that he needed the recognition of the foreign powers and the loans available from Shanghai's banks and corporations to fund his campaign; he no longer needed fanatical supporters bent on ousting the imperialists and smashing the power of the corporate bourgeoisie.

Chiang's strategy was to build support among the rural gentry and urban financiers in his quest to become undisputed ruler of the *Kuomintang*. He understood that the faction which controlled Shanghai's revenues would have the resources to master the whole country. It would be the utmost folly, the former commodities broker reasoned, to strangle the geese that laid these golden eggs.[47] The emissaries returned to Shanghai confident he was willing to contend with the Red menace.

Chiang's commander in Shanghai, General Pai Chung-hsi, was a fiercely anti-Communist Muslim from Kwangsi. He ordered the workers to put down their weapons and instructed his troops to take severe measures against anyone who dissented. The workers, however, refused to surrender. They executed 'running dog' employees of foreigners, attacked strike-breakers and turned 25 union buildings into armed fortresses.[48]

On the afternoon of 26 March, Chiang Kai-shek arrived in Shanghai in a Chinese gunboat and moored at The Bund. As news of the events at Nanking flooded into the foreign concessions, Patrick Givens, the Irish head of the Special Branch and a staunch anti-Communist, stepped on board to present Chiang with a pass entitling him to go ashore in the International Settlement with his bodyguard. Only a few weeks earlier, Givens had launched a propaganda campaign to portray Chiang as 'an unscrupulous, avaricious and blood-thirsty traitor'; now he was welcomed as the city's saviour.[49]

Wang Ching-wei, who reached Shanghai on 5 April, pleaded with Chiang for time to bring the unions into line. Chiang, however, had conceived a plan to deal a mortal blow to the Communists and all other left-wingers in Shanghai through the city's notorious Green Gang, of which he had been a member since his days as a commodities broker.[50]

The Green Gang's boss, 'Big-Eared' Tu Yueh-sheng, not only controlled Shanghai's gambling, narcotics and prostitution rackets but also hired out thugs to intimidate strikers. He had no love of Communists, who would dearly liked to have put him out of business. Chiang summoned Tu's chief lieutenant, Huang Jinrong, known as 'Pockmarked Huang', to his gunboat and explained that he wanted his boss to act as executioner-in-chief in a massive purge of their Communist enemies. Tu responded favourably to the suggestion. His first move was to order the French police chief, Captain Etienne Fiori, to invite Sterling Fessenden to a meeting at his home in Frenchtown.[51]

At the meeting Fiori told Fessenden that all foreigners faced a grave threat from Communist extremists, whereupon Tu volunteered to take care of the problem. He would need 5000 rifles and ammunition from the French, he said, and permission from Fessenden for his men to drive through the International Settlement to reach the Chinese areas. When Chiang heard that Tu had been given assurances on both counts, he moved all but his most reliable troops out of the city and then sailed for Nanking to set up his new capital.[52]

Just before dawn on 12 April 1927, 2000 armed gangsters posing as members of the 'China Mutual Progress Association' moved through the deserted streets of the International Settlement. They wore blue denim overalls and white armbands bearing the Chinese character for 'worker' – in fact, Owen Green described them as '*Kuomintang* labourers' in his dispatch to *The Times*. During the night, General Pai Chung-hsi had posted Nationalist soldiers in key positions in Nantao, Chapei and Hongkew, the western suburb of Jessfield and across the river in Pootung. He also warned the foreign authorities to close all barriers.

As early morning light crept over the Whangpoo, a gunboat siren signalled the attack. Tu's thugs then launched vicious raids on dozens of union branches and Chiang's troops shot anyone who tried to escape. 'Members of the General Labour Union barricaded themselves in the Huchow Guild house,' Green reported, 'while 300 Communists with machine-guns stood at bay in the Commercial Press building.' The workers resisted heroically but were overwhelmed when Nationalist artillery pieces were brought into play. Those who surrendered were mostly shot or beheaded.[53] 'It is too much perhaps to say that the Communist power is broken,' Green concluded, 'but certainly the Communists have had a heavy setback.'

The following day a huge procession of Chinese citizens marched down Paoshan Road with the intention of presenting a petition protesting about the slaughter of their husbands, fathers, sons and brothers to the Nationalist military commander, General Pai Chung-hsi. Sentries and nests of hidden machine-gunners opened fire, killing 66 people and wounding 316. While soldiers with fixed bayonets murdered civilians who had been chased into alleys and back streets, the bodies of the dead and wounded were thrown into trucks and driven away.[54]

Over the next few weeks the Nationalists' military camp at Lunghwa on the outskirts of the city became a death camp where hundreds were executed. Among those who escaped the carnage was Chou En-lai, who moved into room 311 at the Astor House Hotel with his wife. To avoid detection, he reverted to his thoroughly middle-class upbringing, donned a three-piece suit and passed himself off as a successful businessman.

The hostility among the surviving workers towards Europeans was palpable. One Chinese docker spat in the face of Rewi Alley, a young New Zealand ex-serviceman who had just stepped ashore 'to have a look' at the city. 'That's a strange thing to do,' he thought. 'What an extraordinary country!'[55] Alley found lodgings in a White Russian boarding house and went looking for work. 'I saw five lads being carried naked and hanging from poles,' he said. 'Right in front of me they were dumped on the ground and an officer got down from a horse and pumped a bullet into the head of each of them. Next day I read in the papers that they were young "agitators", trying to organise a trade union among the silk filature workers.'[56]

British engineer Albert Howkins had hoped to create a new life for his wife Winifred and six-year-old daughter Freda. 'We lived in Birkenhead and my father worked in Liverpool but he hated going to work in the dark and getting home in the dark,' Freda says.

When a job with the Shanghai Power Company was advertised, he applied and got it. We arrived in the middle of the emergency. We were supposed to stay at the Palace Hotel but the British Army had taken it over, so we were put in a hotel in a back road. My mother didn't like it at all – there was a lot of shooting going on during the night. We got to know the wife of a pilot who had a spare bedroom in a safe district and we stayed there.[57]

The exact number of deaths in what became known as the 'White Terror' is unknown but it ran into many thousands when similar acts of repression followed in the provinces. The Chinese Communist Party's hopes of a Marxist revolution had been brutally dashed. 'It was not Communists that Chiang was suppressing,' Wang Ching-wei charged after returning to the safety of Hankow, 'but all the members of the *Kuomintang* who oppose the dictatorship of Chiang Kai-shek.'[58]

On 17 April, five days after the slaughter had commenced, Wang's faction in Hankow accused Chiang of 'the massacre of the people' and expelled him from the *Kuomintang*. Chiang, however, was also tough on the Chinese bourgeoisie. He demanded that the chairman of the Chinese Chamber of Commerce provide the bulk of a $10 million loan to help finance the Northern Expedition. When the man refused, his property was confiscated and he was driven into exile. Millions were extorted from Chinese industrialists with similar threats, or their children were kidnapped and accused of Communist sympathies to force them to pay up.[59]

'Red Hankow' acted like a magnet to Milly Bennett, who took a steamer up the Yangtze to work with her American friends Rhayna and Bill Prohme on the *People's Tribune*, the Hankow clique's revolutionary newspaper. A week after arriving, she was interviewing Tom Mann, the roly-poly 70-year-old English firebrand who had played a key role in the 1909 miners strike at Broken Hill. He turned up in the newspaper office with Earl Browder, the timid, shabby-looking American Communist leader, and M. N. Roy, a tall, slender Comintern agent from a Hindu Brahmin family.

'Setbacks? Maybe,' Tom Mann thundered. 'But the real revolution, deep in the Chinese people, will not be stopped again. Revolution has become the material of their lives. It is doing its work thoroughly.' The white-haired old rabble-rouser then invited Milly out for a drink in an unashamedly bourgeois German beer garden.

CHAPTER 16

Donald's Dilemma

Having lost his close friend Roy Anderson, Bill Donald peopled his Peking house with an ever more eclectic bunch of visitors. According to Lieutenant Jimmy McHugh, a frequent visitor, Donald's little amah 'bossed him around in a fierce manner and he always obeyed orders'. For exercise, Donald drove his Locomobile roadster to the Western Hills Golf and Country Club when he played golf. According to McHugh, Donald's agricultural swing suggested passion rather than finesse.[1]

One of Donald's closest female friends was a beautiful young Russian woman named Irina, whom he met in 1925. The Bolsheviks had shot her father and brother and confiscated the family estate on the banks of the Volga. With thousands of other White Russian refugees, she and her mother travelled to Manchuria on the Trans-Siberian Railway and then made their way to Shanghai.

'We drifted finally to Peking, where I learned French in a convent,' Irina says. 'We were very poor and lived on the sale of some of our family jewellery.'[2] Donald and Irina grew close in

Peking and she would later accompany him on a well-publicised trip to Europe.

Although he enjoyed female company, Donald resisted all efforts to recruit him on to the diplomatic social circuit. When Lady Lampson, wife of the British ambassador, invited him to dinner, he replied, 'Dear Lady, I will not go to an ordinary social dinner because it is a waste of time. I have no time to waste. But if you want me to come to dinner and there is somebody who wants to talk about China, then you tell me and I'll come. Otherwise, please don't ask because I won't.'[3]

Henry Gullett, Billy Hughes's former press officer and future Australian cabinet minister, arrived in Peking in 1925 at the height of the warlords' struggle for control of the capital. Donald was on good terms with the victor, the Old Marshal Chang Tso-lin, whom he described as 'almost feminine in physique and a moderate opium smoker'. He took Gullett with him on a trip to Manchuria and West China.[4]

The purpose of the trip is unknown but Donald was involved in a number of business ventures at that time, usually with men who wanted him to use his influence with the powers-that-be to secure contracts for them, although there is no suggestion that Gullett fell into that category. According to his son, the Australian war hero and parliamentarian Jo Gullett, they became firm friends and conducted a 'fairly continuous' correspondence thereafter.[5]

Donald also befriended President Theodore Roosevelt's son Kermit Roosevelt and his brother Theodore Roosevelt Jr, who arrived in Peking via the Silk Road after undertaking a hunting expedition across the Himalayas. During the trip, they shot the legendary big horn wild sheep called *Ovis Poli*, mentioned in the writings of Marco Polo and one of the most coveted of all game trophies.

Mrs Theodore Roosevelt Jr, who had been shooting tigers in India, met up with her husband on his travels. She enjoyed

Donald's stories of revolutionary China 'told with a delightfully humorous slant'.

On a later trip the Roosevelt brothers bagged a giant panda. 'It took three hours to track the panda to its lair in a hollow tree,' the *New York Times* breathlessly reported. 'The big bear-like animal came out of its hiding place, and when he was fully in view the Roosevelts fired simultaneously. The animal came rolling down.'[6]

Donald was also happy to take in the Baroness von Ungern-Sternberg, described as 'a charming woman and talented pianist' from an old German family of Baltic Russia. She was related to Baron Roman von Ungern-Sternberg, a White Russian military leader who was executed after fighting the Bolsheviks in Siberia in 1919–21.[7]

Jimmy McHugh returned to the United States in May 1926 but was back in Peking six months later as one of the United States Navy's Chinese language students. He reported to the American naval attaché, a former destroyer captain named George Pettengill. 'Donald was in his office at the time selling some information on Chinese politics for a few dollars,' McHugh recalls.

Money was tight. For running the Economic Bureau, he was supposed to receive $2000 Mexican a month plus expenses, half from Maritime Customs and half from the Ministry of Finance. 'The latter never paid him and was $36,000 in arrears,' McHugh says. 'He had to pay all expenses including salaries of the editor and Chinese staff. He was hard up except when he sold a news column or two.'

One guest, identified only as 'AM', claimed that Donald some-times suffered fits of depression. At such times, he took a few grains of calomel, a tasteless powder consisting chiefly of mercurous chloride and used medicinally as a cathartic. 'He said it was the surest of all remedies against the blues,' AM wrote in *Smiths Weekly*.

Despite his role as the champion of China's economic devel-opment, Donald abhorred the greed of Western speculators.

He wrote to Harold Hochschild in New York in July 1927 that 'a few silly fools want to try and do business in this part of the world and a group is trying to make some deal for the operation of gold mines in north Manchuria'. This was probably a reference to Manchuria Goldfields Limited with which Donald's name was associated in the 1927 British Foreign Office Index.

According to Professor Lewis, Donald found himself 'in something of a bind' at this time. Financially, it was clear things could not go on as they were. Donald's dilemma was: what did he do now? He could have charged large fees as a business consultant but refused to do so. He had nothing but loathing for, as he described them in a letter to his friend Colonel Kenneth Cantlie, 'big men with bigger ideas and still bigger brass bands who were going to make millions out of the natural resources of this country; how they festooned the lobbies of the old Wagons-Lits Hotel, and later the Hotel de Pekin at Peking; how they overflowed the reception rooms of Legations, Embassies and Chinese Yamens, and how they swelled with hopes one day and flattened with disappointment the next, till, at last, they collapsed like busted bladders, and crept off as quietly as possible to the railway station . . .'

As an economy measure, Donald rented his 'sumptuous' house to Chang Tso-lin's younger son. The young man proved to be a tearaway who threw wild parties that caused considerable damage on the property. When Donald complained, the Old Marshal sent his eldest son Chang Hsueh-liang, no mean party animal himself, down to Peking to sort things out. The matter must have been resolved to Donald's satisfaction because he and 'the Young Marshal', as Hsueh-liang was called, became friends.

In Sydney, the memories of women and children labouring in Dickensian conditions in Shanghai factories lingered in the mind of the Australian feminist Eleanor Hinder. After she returned to her duties at Farmer's department store, she kept in touch with a group of YWCA activists, including Gertrude Owen and Constance Duncan from Australia and Ella MacNeil from New Zealand. Everything in her background spurred her into going back to China and doing something about it.

Eleanor Mary Hinder was born at East Maitland, NSW, on 19 January 1893, third daughter of headmaster John Hinder and his wife Sarah, née Mills. She was educated at Maitland West Girls' High School, Teachers' College and the University of Sydney. Having graduated in science, she taught biology at North Sydney Girls' High School and was active in schemes to improve workers' education.

In 1919 she joined Farmer & Company as superintendent of women's welfare in an age when an enlightened and benevolent employer clearly cared for its staff. With Jean Stevenson of the YWCA, she founded the City Girls Amateur Sports Association for competition in seven sports. For Farmer's girls, many of these activities were conducted from a company cottage in the seaside suburb of Dee Why. Eleanor also campaigned with the National Council for Women to oppose an employers' move to reduce the basic wage for female workers below the present two pounds one shilling, successfully arguing that any reduction would raise 'moral and spiritual issues in the lives of women'.

Then in 1926 she took two years' leave of absence from Farmer's and returned to Shanghai on a Rockefeller fellowship to work with Lily K. Haas, the YWCA's industrial secretary. She persuaded the organisation to set up a small house in an alleyway in the silk district of Chapei where she lived with Lily Haas and two Chinese colleagues. 'She absolutely insisted that they should get near to the factory women and children whose conditions they hoped to better,' her biographer, Frances Wheelhouse, writes.[8]

Eleanor took Professor Griffith Taylor, a visiting geographer from the University of Sydney, on a tour of the factories. 'The first was a large cotton mill, which was probably as well run as any in China,' he related.

The manager was careful to tell us that no children under 12 years of age were employed. The mill worked in 12-hour shifts day and night, and one wondered how long it would be before modern industrial hours would be enforced in China. There were apparently no safeguards against accidents and no fans to clear the air of the fluff, which soon covered our clothes and is so dangerous to breathe.[9]

Later the same day Eleanor escorted the professor into a typical silk filature. 'We ascended a narrow stairway and entered a room so filled with steam that at first nothing was visible,' he wrote.

As we stumbled along a narrow gangway, babies crawled from beneath our feet towards their mothers. In the centre of the room, the air was clearer and we saw two rows of children, many of them only five or six years old, standing in front of bowls of boiling water in which they were stirring masses of cocoons. From six to six in that atmosphere of steam these youngsters toiled to produce the silk of the world.[10]

Professor Taylor left Shanghai shocked at what he had seen and full of praise for Eleanor Hinder.

In March of that year Lily Haas took Eleanor to the Yellow Jacket Tearoom and introduced her to a fellow American, Viola Smith, a 33-year-old Californian who was an assistant trade commissioner in Shanghai, the first woman to be given such a post in the United States Foreign Service. Addie Viola Smith, known as 'Vee', had graduated from the Washington College of Law in 1920 and had come to China that year and worked her way up from humble clerk in the US Department of Commerce.

Viola Smith was a member of the Shanghai Women's Organisation comprising representatives from a whole range of European and Asian bodies: the American Women's Club, the British Women's Association, the Japanese Women's Society, the Shanghai Women's Club and the Shanghai Chinese YWCA.

Over the teacups, the two women realised that these groups would have considerable political power within the foreign concessions if they could be marshalled into a pressure group. Viola Smith speculated that it might even be possible for one of them to storm the all-male bastion of the Shanghai Municipal Council.

Chiang Kai-shek responded to his expulsion from the *Kuomintang* by forming his own Nationalist Government at Nanking on 18 April 1927 in opposition to the Wang Ching-wei government at Hankow. Reporting the civil war for *The Times* as a special correspondent was Basil Riley, a 34-year-old Australian who was sympathetic towards the Chinese democratic cause. 'I want to travel in order to get some idea of what Australia ought to develop into before plunging into Australian politics,' he had written to a friend before setting off on a series of foreign adventures that took him from Baghdad to New York to Shanghai.[11]

Frank Basil Riley was one of the three sons of the Reverend Charles Riley, the Archbishop of Perth. Born on 20 September 1893, Basil was educated at Perth High School (renamed Hale School in 1929) and was school head for two years until 1912 when he went up to New College, Oxford, as a 19-year-old Rhodes Scholar. He had a sturdy confidence in himself and proved to be a young man of ability, grit and potential leadership.

Riley arrived at Shanghai in May with 'a roving commission from *The Times* to observe in various provinces the rapidly changing conditions'. At meetings with Shanghailanders, he scandalised his hosts by suggesting greater Chinese representation on the Municipal Council, opening the parks to the Chinese, tackling the child labour problem 'and generally trying to treat the Chinese as equals, not as inferiors'.

The Times later admitted that some of Riley's conversations had been extremely controversial 'for he loved argument and was fond of assuming an attitude merely for the sake of getting at the facts'. 'I discovered,' Riley wrote in one letter to a colleague in London, 'that many, if not most [business leaders in Shanghai] are not free agents. They have to take account of the opinions and decisions of their head offices in London or New York.' This meant making unpopular decisions to protect their investments in the International Settlement, which resulted in the boycott of British goods and agitation against foreign 'imperialists'.[12]

Riley took a particular interest in the activities of General Feng Yu-hsiang, the Christian General who had betrayed his fellow Northerners in 1924 and then fled to Moscow after being kicked out of Peking the following year.[13] Feng returned to China in 1926 and in April 1927 his revitalised National People's Army intervened in a battle between the two warring factions of the *Kuomintang*. The battle was indecisive until Feng occupied the Lunghai sector of the Honan railway system, putting himself in a position to decide the outcome.[14]

Mikhail Borodin, Wang Ching-wei and Eugene Chen travelled from Hankow to Chengchow, at the junction of the Peking–Hankow and Lunghai railways, in an endeavour to persuade the renegade commander to join forces with them against Chiang Kai-shek. Riley reported from Shanghai that 'the Hankow faction is expected to propose that it should confine itself to the provinces of Hunan and Hupeh and hand over Honan to Feng Yu-hsiang – provided Wu Pei-fu (to whom, as War Lord, the province nominally belongs) does not interfere'. Riley added that Hankow had dispatched its entire propaganda department to Honan with large stocks of silver dollars to open up the route to Peking.[15]

Milly Bennett agreed this was indeed the Hankow delegation's plan. 'The side that could buy General Feng for a partner was likely to get to Peking first,' she wrote. 'It looked as simple as that.'[16] The Hankow delegation's spirits rose when Feng described Chiang as a 'wolf-hearted, dog-lunged, inhuman thing' and pledged his loyalty to the Hankow Government. The *People's*

Tribune hailed the three-day meeting as 'a victory for the united front'. Secretly, though, Feng had also turned on his Moscow masters. He told Wang Ching-wei that Borodin and the rest of the Soviet advisers should be sent back to Russia and all Chinese Communists purged from their positions in the *Kuomintang*. Wang was inclined to agree. For economic as well as political reasons, he favoured a rapprochement with Nanking, which was impossible while Borodin remained active in China.[17]

Feng then turned his attention to Chiang Kai-shek. He knew he had been high up on Chiang's death list in his campaign against the warlords but all that was forgotten when they met in the railway station at the key rail junction of Hsuchow on 19 June. Chiang proposed that Feng encourage the pro-Hankow armies to fight their way to the very gates of Peking. At the last minute, Chiang and Feng would show up with fresh troops, brush aside the Communists and enter the city as victors. Betrayal was second nature to Feng and the idea of two-timing the Communists greatly appealed to him. He agreed to throw in his lot with Chiang.[18]

Meanwhile, Basil Riley had taken a steamer up the Yangtze to Nanking and Hankow. He found both factions of the *Kuomintang* 'honeycombed with friends of the other regime'. Nanking had the money that Wang Ching-wei desired, but Hankow had an arsenal turning out 200 rifles and nearly 200,000 rounds of ammunition daily, as well as pistols, bombs, machine-guns and even field pieces. 'During a visit to the arsenal, I saw some 4000 men working 16 and 17 hours daily on behalf of the revolution with apparently adequate supplies of steel, brass, chemicals and powder,' he wrote. 'Little more than personal quarrels keep the regimes apart. Intelligent leaders fear Chiang Kai-shek's domination; they fail to appreciate that it is an enormous asset in the present conditions of the country.

The only apparent beneficiaries [of the dispute between Hankow and Nanking] will be the Northerners, either

Chang Tso-lin, who will secure a longer lease of life at Peking, or Feng Yu-hsiang. The latter sits astride the Lunghai Railway . . . carefully placing supporters both at Nanking and Hankow.[19]

In the capital on 3 July 1927, the reigning warlord Chang Tso-lin issued the manifesto of his new government, which shrewdly denounced the evils of Bolshevism and at the same time advocated peaceful revision of the unequal treaties. 'We in North China are just as Nationalist as our Southern fellow-countrymen,' he said, 'in fact, more so, for our policy is China for the Chinese, not for the "Reds".'[20]

On 21 July Basil Riley left Hankow and headed north by rail towards Chengchow. According to a report in The West Australian, he joined the Belgian vice-consul with the idea of visiting Feng's headquarters. Two days later he vanished. Despite the presence of dozens of witnesses in the Chengchow area, all attempts by the British diplomatic staff in Peking to find any trace of Riley drew a blank. The editor of The Times, Geoffrey Dawson, authorised the hiring of a confidential Chinese agent to make a secret investigation into the disappearance of his special correspondent.[21]

According to the investigator, Riley reached Chengchow on 22 July and the following morning decided to visit a nearby Christian village. He was to have been accompanied by Chen Tzu-shen, manager of the YMCA at Chengchow, but Chen, who was known to be hostile towards foreigners, claimed to be unwell. Riley set off alone along the railway line and stopped to question some villagers. They were unable to understand him and a small crowd gathered. Some of General Feng's soldiers came up to see what was happening.

The Chinese troops became aggressive at the sight of a foreigner in their midst. Excitement and noise ensued and the villagers ran away to avoid being implicated in any trouble. They watched from a distance as the soldiers attacked Riley with swords. Struck on the head, neck and body, he fell mortally wounded. His killers dragged his body into a field and buried it. 'Other accounts filtering from Chengchow vary considerably in regard to details,' *The Times* said, 'but are unanimous on the point that the culprits were soldiers.'[22]

Vivian Chow, the Lismore-born journalist, wrote a short story entitled 'What Happened to Riley?' which was published in his magazine, *United China*, in 1932. Although a work of fiction, the story professes to tell the real story behind Riley's violent demise. Chow states that Riley had been sent to China on a mission for the British Secret Service. 'But at Shanghai, he was warned both by the Chinese authorities and by the foreigners not to proceed inland,' Chow wrote.

> He was urged to make Shanghai his base, but all entreaties were unavailing. It seemed to the foreigners that he had set his heart upon going to the war zone, and knowing the tenacity of Australians, none were surprised, weeks later, to be notified by Hankow people that Riley was missing. Then the news flashed around the world, and Riley's newspaper came out with an urgent reward of ten thousand pounds for information leading to the discovery of Riley, dead or alive.[23]

According to Chow's version, 'Captain Riley' was caught spying on Feng Yu-hsiang's troops. He was taken to the soldiers' camp, interrogated by an officer and then executed. While this version of events might have been the product of Chow's fertile imagination, it is true that Riley had served as an officer in the British Army in World War I. It was also true that the British Secret Service sometimes used *The Times* as a cover for agents involved in the Great Game against Britannia's enemies in Asia. And the newspaper itself admitted that Riley 'went northward on his own initiative to find out the truth about Feng Yu-hsiang', leaving little doubt that he would have been regarded as a spy if caught by Feng's troops.[24]

Given Riley's earlier conversations with British businessmen, the paper added, 'it is not altogether surprising, perhaps,
that some of those with whom he came in contact in Shanghai
should have regarded him at the time as a dangerous newcomer
with revolutionary notions'.[25]

There were in fact plenty of revolutionaries roaming the
countryside, many of them spying on Chiang Kai-shek. Moscow
had set up a military advisory group in the Soviet Union
to deliver intelligence to Mao's poorly armed Communists
through a network of agents operating in Nationalist offices
near the Red Army. Nationalists, Communists and warlords
were now locked in a disastrous pattern of ideological conflict
and military confrontation that would weaken all sides and
leave the field open to Japan.

The previous year Borodin's paymaster Lev Karakhan had
invited Bill Donald to the Soviet Legation to discuss the
Russian presence in China. 'At that time Borodin and the Cantonese element were in Kiangsi province pushing towards
Hankow,' Donald said.

> My brief prophecy to Karakhan was this: Soviet propaganda
> would fail in China and the Soviet crowd would be kicked
> out for the simple reason that to consummate their plans
> they would have to dictate to the Chinese what they must
> do. When that time did come, Borodin would make the great
> discovery that the Chinese would refuse to be ordered about
> and the whole dream would burst and Borodin would be forced
> out. That is what happened.[26]

Karakhan was recalled to Moscow soon after speaking to
Donald and missed seeing his prediction come true. Borodin
was expelled from China in July 1927, just a few weeks after his
meeting with General Feng, when Chang Tso-lin ordered his
men to raid the Soviet military attaché's office in Peking. Documents were found which proved conclusively that the Soviet

adviser was not a freelance revolutionary, as he had claimed, but a fully-fledged Comintern agent committed to turning China into a Communist country.

General Galen, the Soviet commander who had played a major role in the Nationalists' early victories, was also expelled from China and later executed on Stalin's orders. Karakhan did not escape, either – he was shot during a Stalinist purge a few years hence.[27]

The military council at Nanking now sought to make peace with the three Wuhan cities in order to unify the entire Yangtze Valley under a single Nationalist government. Wang Ching-wei hoped the expulsion of the Russians from his ranks would satisfy Chiang Kai-shek but the latter was determined to extinguish the flame of Red Hankow for all time. To break the deadlock, the council asked Chiang to step down as commander of the Revolutionary Army and accept the lesser post of commander of the Eastern Army. Instead, the wily Chiang resigned his command altogether and returned to his home village to allow events to play into his hands.[28]

Ten days later General Sun Chuan-fang, the warlord who had formerly ruled Shanghai and Nanking, crossed the Yangtze with 30,000 troops in an attempt to overthrow the Nationalist regime. The ferocious Kwangsi Clique – which hailed from the same province as the Taiping rebels of the previous century – included General Li Tsung-jen, commander of the Nationalists' Seventh Army, and General Pai Chung-hsi, the Nationalist 'liberator' of Shanghai. They fought Sun off in a six-day battle. General Li then marched on Wuhan and deposed Wang Ching-wei and his supporters.

With Nanking in disarray, Chiang Kai-shek moved to Shanghai and met a crestfallen Wang, who agreed to serve with him in a new government. Triumphant, Chiang then moved to consolidate his relationship with the powerful Soong family. First, he sent his wife Chen Chieh-ju, known as Jennie Chen, off to the United States with a promise that their marriage would be resumed in five years' time. Then on 1 December he climbed into a cutaway coat with flowery buttonhole and married the third Soong sister, Mayling, in a civil ceremony in front of more than one thousand guests at the Majestic Hotel in Bubbling Well Road.

The matchmaker of this long, difficult and apparently sexless union had been Ayling Soong, who seized the chance to enhance her family's position politically and financially, if not socially, with 'China's man of destiny'.[29] Chingling Soong, however, vehemently opposed the marriage. She had turned down a proposal from Chiang shortly after the death of Sun Yat-sen and branded him a traitor to the revolution over the 'White Terror' slaughter of the Communists.

At 30, Mayling Soong was a slim, elegant woman with a striking, porcelain beauty and boyishly bobbed hair. Charlie Soong hadn't lived to see his daughters rise to positions of eminence in the new China. He died on 3 May 1918 and was buried in Shanghai's International Cemetery.

As newsreel cameras whirred inside the nuptial ballroom, Chiang issued a statement that his wedding would greatly benefit the *Kuomintang* 'because I can henceforth bear the tremendous responsibility of the revolution with peace of heart'. The Nationalist regime at Nanking responded favourably. On 1 January 1928 Chiang was returned to power. Under his deal with Wang Ching-wei, he became commander-in-chief of the armed forces, with Wang as head of the Nationalist Government.

When Chiang's armies fought their way into Peking six months later, Chang Tso-lin made a diplomatic withdrawal back to his Manchurian homeland. As his train was passing under a bridge on the outskirts of Mukden, an officer of the Kwantung Army, the Japanese force stationed in the Manchurian railway zone, detonated a bomb. Tons of bricks and mortar rained down on Chang's sky-blue carriage, fatally injuring him. He died in a Japanese hospital four hours later at the age of 54. Chiang

Kai-shek's capture of Peking and the Old Marshal's assassination effectively ended the Warlord Era, although there would be sporadic outbreaks from time to time for years to come.

On 10 October 1928 – the 17th anniversary of the Chinese Revolution – Bill Donald quit as director of the Bureau of Economic Information in protest against the financial pressure of Chiang's government and its clumsy attempts to turn the bureau into a propaganda vehicle. The minister of finance expected a bribe of $5000 Mexican a month, which he reduced to $1000 when Donald declined to pay up. 'I refused all overtures and eventually got away with it,' he wrote to Herbie Elliston, who was working for the United States Government in Washington.

In the end, Donald was spending his own money to keep the bureau going. 'He resigned under circumstances that enhanced his reputation in responsible quarters,' the *Sydney Morning Herald* reported.[30] 'He is the only adviser of China I know who never felt he had to sing for his supper,' Elliston said. 'More, he was incorruptible – also a rare feat in China.'

When Donald's first resignation failed to take effect, he planned a more dramatic exit. 'I am going to do what the average Chinese official does when things get beyond endurance – flee,' he wrote to Elliston from Shanghai on 7 December 1928. 'I shall go to Mukden. They want me to work for them.'

Donald took a steamer down the Yangtze and across to Dairen on the Liaotung Peninsula and then caught a train to Mukden. His new employer was Chang Hsueh-liang, the Young Marshal, who had turned 27 on 3 June, the day before his father was murdered.[31]

It was no secret that since they had last met Chang had turned into a full-blown opium addict. Hallett Abend of the *New York Times* revealed as much back in October when he wrote how he was met on a visit to Mukden by an anxious, broken man, with sunken cheeks, furtive eyes and a cold, unresponsive handshake. 'And today Chang Hsueh-liang may be considered a confirmed opium smoker,' he wrote. 'Mental clarity and balance and physical vigour and endurance would be a great asset just now to the little General. Unfortunately, he has none of these.'[32]

Donald met the young man in the Tiger Room – so-called because of the presence of two huge stuffed Manchurian tigers – in his palace in the old walled city. The man he had known in Peking as a fine sportsman and dashing Romeo had indeed turned into a trembling drug addict. 'The Young Fellow', as Donald called him, had taken to smoking vast amounts of opium two years earlier while commanding his father's troops. Prescribed morphine as a substitute, he had become doubly addicted.[33]

Donald discussed the problem with James C. 'Jimmy' Elder, the Young Marshal's Scottish financial adviser. Elder's father had been director of construction on the Peking–Mukden Railway and had known Chang since they were children. However, their combined efforts to coax Chang into a healthy regime of diet and exercise in the hope of beating his addiction ended in demoralising failure. Donald described Chang as 'a young man of no ambition whatever, rather resentful of the fact that he had responsibilities and that troublesome people should expect him to bestir himself in matters concerning China as a whole'.

Chang Hsueh-liang had been reluctant to join Chiang Kai-shek's Nationalist war effort but on 29 December, shortly after Donald's arrival, he hoisted the Nationalist flag over Manchuria. The commanders of the Kwantung Army had killed the Old Marshal not only for failing to defeat Chiang but also because they saw his son as a weakling who would be easier to manipulate. They regarded the flag episode as nothing more than an act of bravado. Chang then executed two Japanese collaborators among his commanders and made it plain that he intended to govern his own country without Japanese assistance. The Kwantung commanders took this as a grave insult.[34]

Donald's spirits were revived by the arrival of his Russian friend Irina. The beautiful Russian had gone to the United States with her mother, funding the trip by selling a large family diamond. 'I was homesick for China and wrote to Mr William Henry Donald,' she says. 'He gave me a job as his secretary.'[35]

Back in Shanghai, the New Zealander Rewi Alley had taken a job with the Shanghai Fire Department. His duties included inspecting factories for fire hazards, a task which brought him into close contact with the problems of the Chinese workforce. Alley, a man of average height with short-cropped ginger hair, a prominent nose and an unassuming manner, was born in Canterbury, New Zealand, in 1897. His parents named him after Rewi Te Manipoto, a Maori chieftain of legendary bravery. Living up to his name, Rewi Alley won a medal for gallantry with the New Zealand Expeditionary Force in World War I. After the war, he took a half share in a sheep farm as a soldier-settler but was wiped out during the Depression in what he described as 'six years of loneliness and struggle'. The experience turned him into a committed left-winger.

Fire Officer Alley, smartly dressed in cap, greatcoat and muffler, quickly discovered that life as an inspector presented some unexpected hazards. On one occasion an attractive White Russian woman applied for a licence to open a boarding house. Alley inspected the property and noticed that all the fire exits had been blocked with jerry-built bathrooms. 'They'll have to go,' he told her.

'Wait a minute,' the Russian said. She slipped into her bedroom and emerged stark naked apart from a wrap around her shoulder. 'Come in, darlink,' she cooed. Alley, who wasn't remotely interested in women, made his excuses and left.[36]

During this period he learned Mandarin, made friends in the labour unions and became a secret member of the Chinese Communist Party. On his holidays in 1929 he toured rural China helping with famine relief. He adopted a 14-year-old Chinese orphan whom he named Alan and later another Chinese boy called Mike. He lived with both boys in Shanghai and made sure they received a good education.

Alley was a dedicated Communist prepared to risk everything for the party. He sheltered Communist fighters in his home and once washed the blood off money stolen by Red Army soldiers during raids disguised as anti-Japanese protests.[37]

By now, Chiang Kai-shek had achieved the unification of China, but only on paper. His next objective was to develop a workable centralised government under Nationalist single-party control and at the same time complete the annihilation of the Communists. He ordered the military governors in every province to disband their forces and enrol them in the Nationalist Army under his command.[38]

Feng Yu-hsiang, the Christian General who had been pursuing his own anti-British agenda with the aid of Russian money and weapons, had no intention of turning his People's Army over to Chiang. He found a willing frontman in Wang Ching-wei, who had been paying lip service to his old enemy Chiang and was willing to defect. A number of lesser warlords, sensing that the good times were about to end, also loaned their support.[39]

By May 1929, Chiang's commanders were engaged in battles with various rebellious factions from Wuhan to Shanghai, south to Foochow and north to Peking (which Chiang had renamed Peiping – 'Northern Peace'). Casualties were high on all sides and with the country in the grip of famine, Nationalist supply lines were stretched to breaking point.

Late that month the embalmed remains of Sun Yat-sen were placed in an American-made bronze coffin and brought south along his beloved railway line to Nanking. Then, with great ceremony and in front of hundreds of VIP mourners led by

Madame Sun Yat-sen, the coffin was placed in the rotunda of a mausoleum on the slopes of Purple Mountain overlooking the tombs of the Ming emperors.[40]

The heavy symbolism of the occasion seemed to galvanise Chiang Kai-shek. Over the next 12 months he gained the upper hand on the battlefields, receiving a huge boost in September 1930 when Chang Hsueh-liang recognised the Nationalists as his best chance of retaining his autonomy in Manchuria and publicly swore allegiance to him. Chiang immediately appointed the Young Marshal deputy commander-in-chief of the armed forces and governor of North China.

The sudden presence of thousands of battle-hardened Manchurians quickly persuaded the rebel commanders to negotiate a settlement with Chiang. They accepted him as commander-in-chief, while the turncoat Wang Ching-wei was made president of the Nanking executive cabinet. Altogether, the rebellion had cost the lives of an estimated 300,000 people.

Once an uneasy peace had been restored, Chiang travelled to his wife's house in Shanghai and followed through on a plan to convert to Christianity, describing Jesus as 'the first champion of national revolution'.[41]

Chiang's conversion was unlikely to gain favour with radical elements in the *Kuomintang* who regarded all religion – Confucianism, Buddhism, Islam, Judaism, Christianity – as a tool of imperialism designed to keep the people in servitude.[42]

Stalin, meanwhile, had not given up on China following the expulsion of Borodin and his Red Army comrades. In early 1930 Moscow dispatched one of its most brilliant agents, the handsome half-German, half-Russian Richard Sorge, to Shanghai to gather intelligence and foment a Communist revolution. Posing as a pro-Nazi newspaperman, Sorge infiltrated the German military advisers' group at Chiang's forward intelligence HQ. He seduced the disaffected wife of one of the advisers to steal Nationalist codes used in messages between the general staff and the field units attacking the Red Army. These were then passed on to the Communist leaders, enabling Mao Tse-tung to obtain precise intelligence about the movements of Chiang's forces. On 30 December 1930 he threw 40,000 Communist troops and civilians into an ambush against 9000 Nationalists, most of whom surrendered without a fight.

The Nationalist general was exhibited at a mass rally addressed by Mao. To chants of 'Chop his head off! Eat his flesh!', the general was decapitated. His head was sent down the river attached to a wooden door, with a little white flag and a note saying it was 'a gift' for his superiors.

Patrick Givens's Special Branch suspected Richard Sorge of espionage but his cover as a newspaperman held up to scrutiny. He had established himself as an expert on Chinese agriculture, which gave him freedom to travel around the country making contact with members of the Chinese Communist Party. Secretly, the hard-drinking Casanova met the German Soviet spy Ruth Kuczynski and the left-wing American journalist Agnes Smedley, both of whom became his lovers. Sorge was so successful at recruiting new spies that General MacArthur's intelligence chief Charles Willoughby later referred to Shanghai as 'Stalin's vineyard'.

While Richard Sorge was a highly trained and ideologically committed Comintern agent, Alan Raymond, an Australian who stepped ashore from the steamer *Buffington Court* from Sydney in February 1931, would become a spy for purely mercenary reasons. The chance of adventure in a wide-open city like Shanghai appealed enormously to Raymond, a slim, swarthy Australian of 21, with black hair and a pencil-thin moustache.

Alan Willoughby Raymond was born in Melbourne on 27 February 1909. His mother Irene Johnson was English, although she was born at Tulle, France. She married English architect Alan Raymond after arriving in Australia in 1891. Following Irene's death, Alan Sr married Ellen Spice, who already had two daughters, Jean and Dorothy. Alan Raymond Jr was raised and educated in Sydney. His father was killed in a motor accident when he was a child and he found himself the unwanted stepson in a household of women.

At 16, Alan moved to Melbourne to work for Coles department store. After 18 months, he was transferred back to Sydney when Coles opened a new store there. Fate was against him: like his father, he was involved in a motor accident and was laid up for six months. When he recovered, he turned his hand to journalism and spent the next year scraping together his boat fare to Shanghai.[43]

Raymond had no intention of becoming a spy when he stepped on to The Bund, but he was an opportunist and a gambler who was prepared to take unacceptable risks in order to make money. His first job was selling marble for the British firm of Harvie Cooke & Company, even though he had no experience in the marble industry. When he was dismissed from that post, he transferred to one of Harvie Cooke's rivals, the Shanghai Marble Company, for which he travelled around China and Japan.

Shanghai operated on the chit system under which Europeans could get credit in stores and restaurants, provided they settled up on the first of each month. Raymond lost his job again and ran up debts which he was unable to repay. In an effort to get square, he visited the city's pony-racing tracks and the Canidrome greyhound track in Frenchtown. One of the city's biggest gamblers was fellow Australian Dr Bill O'Hara, but whereas O'Hara was a frequent winner, Raymond invariably lost. As his financial problems increased, he wrote a number of dishonoured cheques to business associates and his name was 'posted' at the Shanghai Race Club for unpaid debts.

Shunned by Europeans for his dishonesty – and possibly because of his 'Eurasian' appearance – Raymond socialised with the less-principled members of Shanghai's racing fraternity. 'His association with low Chinese women, Japs and Germans made him an object of loathing among reputable Britishers in Shanghai,' the Sydney branch of the Australian Security Service reported in 1943. Raymond thought this attitude applied to Australians in general. 'During the years I spent in the East,' he wrote in a postwar statement, 'I became conscious that the general attitude on the part of the Britishers here towards Australians was one of superiority and condescension.'

> I also observed that we had little direct communication with China and other countries here and even had to negotiate drafts on Australian banks through London. I came to the conclusion that direct contact was urgently needed if we were to derive the greatest benefit from our geographical location near the Orient.[44]

Meanwhile, Eleanor Hinder had taken over from Lily Haas as the YWCA's industrial secretary. During this period, she and Viola Smith fell in love. They moved into a flat at 8 Young Allen Court and took their holidays together in Australia and the United States. In 1928, they were separated when Eleanor spent several months in Honolulu organising the first Pan-Pacific Women's Conference and then returned to Australia to give a series of lectures on China.

In 1931 she was invited back to Shanghai to advise the Employers Federation on how its members could apply the Nationalist Government's new Factory Act, the first step towards abolishing abuses. 'A Labour Department has been set up and its existence induces the hope that something may ultimately be achieved for the benefit of women and children,' she told an audience of Australian women in Perth. 'It is, of course, impossible to predict whether the Nanking regime will be lasting.'[45]

Eleanor and Viola Smith knew it was essential to persuade the municipal councillors to enforce the new Chinese labour laws. And that meant challenging their all-male preserve. Council membership had gradually changed over the years: there were now 14 councillors of whom five were British, five Chinese, two American and two Japanese. The Shanghai foreign women's clubs made political history when they nominated Viola as the first female candidate to take part in a council election. 'Although Shanghai women have previously considered representation on the council, Miss Smith's nomination constitutes the first attempt to invade the municipal domain,' *The West Australian* reported.[46]

Among Viola's staunchest supporters was Dr Frank Rawlinson's Moral Welfare Society whose avowed aim was to remove the 'iniquitous blemishes on the life of Shanghai'. Sterling Fessenden had resigned as head of the council in 1929 and the new chairman, Hong Kong-born businessman Harry Arnhold, was known to have 'reformist tendencies'. But the ratepayers of the International Settlement weren't quite ready for sexual equality. Viola was defeated in the election – and Arnhold lost his chairmanship.

CHAPTER 17

Japan Strikes

In the summer of 1931 Hallett Abend of the *New York Times* sailed from Shanghai to Dairen after receiving a tip-off from a Japanese contact that Japan was about to solve 'the Manchurian question'. He was astonished to see freight trains loaded with Japanese artillery, ammunition and supplies, plus fodder for the cavalry's horses, trundling along the South Manchurian Railway. The Kwantung Army, whose job was to protect the railway zone, had dispersed perhaps 40,000 troops from Dairen as far north as Harbin and east to the Korean border in contravention of Japan's treaties with China.

At Mukden, there was no sign of the Young Marshal. Anticipating trouble, he had moved the bulk of his 250,000 troops into Jehol, leaving only small garrisons in most towns. He had then travelled to Peking with his entourage, including his two wives, Bill Donald, Irina and Jimmy Elder, and checked himself into the Rockefeller Hospital, where he had rented an entire wing to undergo treatment for his drug addiction.

The local administrators left behind at his Mukden headquarters had no power to deal with Japanese grievances.

Complaints about Chinese treaty breaches were referred to Nanking, which shuffled them back to Mukden without taking any action. The Japanese took this buck-passing as an insult and complained even more vociferously. Their main complaint was that Chinese engineers were building railway lines parallel to the South Manchurian Railway, thus competing for business. All of these wrongs, however, were simply pretexts to support Japan's central claim that China was not really a nation at all and that her proper place in the world was as a Japanese vassal.

At harvest time, as fields of golden Manchurian wheat awaited the threshers, it was clear Japan was preparing to take military action. Hallett Abend travelled to Peking, where he discussed his findings with Bill Donald and asked if he could interview the Young Marshal. Chang Hsueh-liang was still undergoing treatment in a well-guarded wing of the hospital and Donald was reluctant to let the reporter see him. Considering the gravity of the situation, however, he finally relented: perhaps Abend's eyewitness testimony of Japan's intentions in his homeland might strengthen Chang's will to recover.

'I was shocked to see the sickly, emaciated, drug-blurred individual that Marshal Chang had become,' Abend wrote in his memoir. 'When I had first known him, in the autumn of 1926, he had been a husky, red-cheeked young military commander. In 1931, he was obviously a physical and mental wreck.'[1]

On 18 September 1931 a Japanese officer of the Kwantung Army set off a small explosive charge beside the South Manchurian Railway line north of Mukden. The blast occurred shortly before 10.30 pm but damage was so slight that the southbound train from Changchun arrived in Mukden on time.

The 'Mukden Incident' was blamed on Chinese saboteurs. Displaying two damaged railway sleepers, half a dozen fish-plates, one rifle and two Chinese soldiers' caps as evidence, the Kwantung general staff set plans in motion to occupy the three rich Manchurian provinces. The following day Japanese planes from Korea bombed Mukden and Changchun and Japanese troops took control of the Young Marshal's capital.

That evening a shaky Chang Hsueh-liang dined at the British Legation with Bill Donald and then visited the theatre. Despite a lengthy stay in hospital, he was still addicted to opium, morphine and heroin – his 'cure' at the hands of the best physicians Western medicine could provide had failed dismally.

While the Young Marshal stayed in Peking, Bill Donald flew to Nanking in his Ford tri-motor aircraft to discuss the crisis with Chiang Kai-shek.[2] The pragmatic Generalissimo, who had returned to Nanking on 20 September, weighed up his options. As the Chinese armed forces were too weak to defeat Japan in Manchuria, he would leave it up to the peacekeepers of the League of Nations to take action. Meanwhile, the Young Marshal's troops would be used to attack Mao Tse-tung's People's Liberation Army in North China.[3]

None of the Kwantung Army's actions in Manchuria had been authorised by the Imperial Diet or the Japanese Government but they were wildly popular with the masses and received the blessing of Emperor Hirohito and his militarist cabinet. China's protestations to the league and the outrage of the great parliaments of the world were met with Japanese insolence. 'What do those talkative gentlemen know about conditions here?' one Japanese general sneered. 'We are establishing peace and order in Manchuria. Their activities are very tiresome.'

The Japanese had hoped that a quick victory with limited objectives would win Western approval but stubborn resistance from small pockets of the Young Marshal's rearguard forced them to bring in large numbers of reinforcements. The undeclared war rapidly spread to China proper, particularly Shanghai where the Chinese boycotted Japanese goods and formed anti-Japanese societies.[4]

Shelves were stripped of Japanese commodities and burned in the street; 50,000 demonstrators demanded the death penalty for anybody trading with the enemy. Chinese magistrates refused to convict Chinese agitators accused of stealing Japanese goods on the grounds that they were activated by 'patriotic motives'.[5]

In a matter of weeks the godowns on the Whangpoo were bursting with unsold products, slashing Japanese imports by 40 per cent in the last four months of 1931 and by more than 90 per cent in February 1932. Chinese banks in Shanghai refused to do business with Japanese companies, while Japanese spinning mills fell idle. The financial situation became so critical for Japanese manufacturers that in December the Shanghai Japanese Industrialists Association applied to Tokyo for loans to avoid its members going bankrupt.[6]

There was a surprising amount of sympathy for Japan in Europe, especially from her former military ally Britain. 'Technically,' The Times argued, 'there could be no doubt that Japan had put herself in the wrong. But fundamentally it was generally felt that Japan had by no means a bad case.' Even the Foreign Office, believing a Japanese promise that her troops would be withdrawn into the South Manchurian Railway zone once peace and order had been restored, felt that Japan was best suited to end the 'brigandage' that threatened Manchuria's prosperity.[7]

Appeasement was the shameful hallmark of the 1930s, with the Foreign Secretary Neville Chamberlain, The Times editor Geoffrey Dawson and Nancy Astor's 'Cliveden Set' the main offenders. The Chinese boycott in Shanghai had challenged Japan to defend her interests in East Asia and appeasement merely opened the way for her next aggressive move.

At the corner of The Bund and Nanking Road was the Cathay Hotel, built by the businessman–playboy Sir Victor Sassoon in the art deco style and capped by a tower that rivalled Venice's campanile. The Cathay opened to great fanfare as the most luxurious hotel in Asia in 1928. The following year Noel Coward penned one of his most famous plays, Private Lives, in one of its suites while recuperating from a bout of flu. When he recovered, he visited the Shanghai Club and endeared himself to members by placing his cheek on 'the longest bar in the world' and announcing he could see the curvature of the earth's surface.

New Year's Eve 1931 was celebrated in typically extravagant style in the Cathay's ballroom. Sassoon – heir to his family's fortune and a cousin of the World War I poet Siegfried Sassoon – and the Jardine Matheson *taipan* John Keswick, his face covered by a 'grotesquely funny' mask, led 400 guests in bacchanalian revelry. As the Westminster chimes of the Custom House clock rang out midnight, a large turkey was wheeled into the room. Revellers whooped and cheered as an exotic dancer dressed as a little chick jumped from the turkey's breast and shimmied to the rhythms of the dance band.

But the chimes of 'Big Ching', as the Chinese called the clock, heralded a period of doubt and insecurity which not even vintage champagne could obliterate. The Japanese minister in Peking, M. Shigemitsu, added to the gloom in an ominous New Year message in which he declared that 1932 presented Japan and China with 'ponderous problems awaiting adjustment'. Nor could the British consul, Sir John Brenan, offer much hope. 'The best I can suggest for 1932,' he said, 'is that it should help forward all efforts toward international understanding and discourage pessimism.'[8]

The spirit of the times was perhaps symbolised in the actions of a Chinese merchant named Lee Chou, who was jailed for two months on New Year's Eve for selling 69 bottles of counterfeit Hennessy cognac. Lee mixed pure alcohol with brown sugar in the hope that revellers wouldn't notice the difference.[9]

On New Year's Day the Young Marshal's remaining forces in Manchuria began to withdraw south of the Great Wall and west into Jehol. Resistance had been sporadic; some commanders had fought valiantly but others, lacking any assistance from Nanking, had done secret deals with the Japanese. Two days later the last vestiges of Chinese authority evaporated in

Manchuria, leaving Japan in almost total control of its railways, minerals, ports and primary industry.[10]

Japanese jingoists then set about fomenting trouble in Shanghai to distract attention from their war-mongering in Manchuria and to end the crippling anti-Japanese boycott. The task of creating a *casus belli* was given to the military attaché at the Japanese Consulate, an unsavoury character named Major Ryukichi Tanaka.

His first move was to hire a group of Chinese thugs from the San Yu towel factory in Hongkew on 18 January to beat up five Japanese monks and novices belonging to the militant pan-Asian Buddhist Nichiren sect, one of whom later died of his injuries. Other hirelings stoned children on their way to the Japanese Primary School in the International Settlement.[11]

Two days later Tanaka incited 40 members of a *seinedan*, or young men's association, to destroy the San Yu towel factory in a pre-dawn raid. In pouring rain, the Japanese set fire to storage rooms and attacked a nearby police post, stabbing two Chinese constables to death. The culprits were rounded up but under the extrality waiver were released without charge. These crimes were the first committed by Japanese civilian ruffians who would become known in Shanghai as *ronin*, a reference to the lordless *samurai* from the time of the shoguns who operated outside the law.[12]

On the afternoon of the 20th Tanaka organised a protest rally of some 1000 Japanese residents at the Japanese Club in Boone Road. 'Fiery and excited speeches were made, expressing indignation over attacks on the Japanese priests and the insult to the Emperor,' the *North-China Herald* reported. The meeting called on Tokyo to send military units to Shanghai to protect Japanese citizens and suppress anti-Japanese movements. The mob then rampaged through the streets, attacking Chinese citizens and destroying Chinese shops, with the intention of provoking a backlash.[13]

The Japanese consul, Kuramatsu Murai, demanded an apology from the Mayor of Greater Shanghai, General Wu Teh-Chen, for the attacks on the monks, plus compensation and the immediate disbandment of all anti-Japanese organisations, especially the militant National Salvation Association.[14]

On the weekend of 23–24 January 1932 a Japanese cruiser, an aircraft carrier and four destroyers joined the existing force of three cruisers and three destroyers on the river downstream from Shanghai. Mayor Wu hoped to stall the Japanese until he had consulted the Nationalist Government at Nanking but instead was given an ultimatum expiring at 6 pm on the 28th. He immediately took the overnight train to Nanking.

Chiang Kai-shek had reached a deal with Wang Ching-wei under which Wang became prime minister and Chiang took charge of military operations against the Communists. Mayor Wu was informed that Chiang had no intention of fighting the Japanese and thus provoking a full-scale war. The city's defences were to be left to the 19th Route Army, a revolutionary Cantonese force quartered in Chapei. Its young commander, General Tsai Ting-kai, was anti-Japanese and relished the possibility of getting to grips with the enemy.

Bill Donald was in Nanking for a meeting of the Chinese Indemnity Committee. At 11 o'clock on Sunday night, he was asleep in his hotel when Mayor Wu woke him and urged him to come back to Shanghai to help him deal with the Japanese. Donald had intended flying to Peking the following day to rejoin the Young Marshal but 45 minutes later was on a train bound for Shanghai.

'The mayor is a very old friend of mine so I was able to speak frankly to him,' Donald wrote to Herbie Elliston. 'By the time we reached Shanghai, I got him to agree to the acceptance of all the demands without condition, if the residing consuls and municipal authorities were convinced that the Japanese would employ force.'[15]

Early on the morning of Monday, 25 January, Donald ascertained that the general feeling was that the Japanese would use any pretext to send in their armed forces. The Japanese Consulate heard of Donald's intervention and issued a press release that 'Captain Donald, Chang's former adviser' had urged acceptance of the Japanese terms. While Donald was amused at his military title, he realised from the tone of the press release that acceptance was the last thing the Japanese wanted.

During the 26th and 27th of January Mayor Wu persuaded Chinese associations and guilds to call off the boycott. His acceptance of all terms was handed to the Japanese consul Murai around two o'clock on the afternoon of the 28th, four hours before the ultimatum expired. Wu promised that the anti-Japanese boycott would be ended, the assailants of the Japanese holy men punished and anti-Japanese societies disbanded. He had also ordered the suppression of an anti-Japanese newspaper, which had crowed over a recent assassination attempt on Hirohito in a story headlined 'UNFORTUNATELY BULLET MISSED: ASSASSIN ESCAPED'.

The new chairman of the Municipal Council, Brigadier-General E. B. Macnaghten of the British-American Tobacco Company, then gave the Japanese the perfect opportunity to mobilise their forces. Without informing the Chinese, he declared a state of emergency in the International Settlement from 4 pm on Thursday the 28th. The Volunteer Corps immediately deployed along the boundary with Chapei overlooking North Station, where General Tsai's main defences were located; the British Army took up positions along a line extending into open country; and the American Marines were posted on the boundary between the settlement and the country.

The north-eastern sector where Little Tokyo abutted Chapei was the responsibility of the Japanese. That afternoon, the Japanese Naval Landing Force, accompanied by dozens of armed *ronin*, advanced down North Szechuen Road to occupy a salient protruding into the Chinese district.

Meanwhile, the consular body held a meeting at which Murai stated that the mayor had accepted the Japanese demands and that his assurances were considered 'highly satisfactory'. As the British consul, Sir John Brenan, was leaving the meeting, he said to Murai, 'At least we can be sure that there will be no trouble tonight?' The Japanese consul replied in the affirmative.[16]

Japan's military commanders, however, were determined to inflict a humiliating defeat on the Chinese. That evening, Admiral Kiochi Shiozawa told Hallett Abend over drinks in his flagship, the cruiser *Idzumo*, that the mayor's acceptance of Japanese terms was 'beside the point'; he still intended to occupy Chapei to demonstrate Japan's military supremacy over the Chinese.

The Japanese had a garrison of 2000 Imperial Marines at Hongkew and 1200 reinforcements were available in the Japanese warships. As a sign of intent, thousands of Japanese civilians, mostly women, children and the elderly, had been evacuated from Hongkew over the past few days and returned to Japan.

By 8.30 that evening the naval units in Little Tokyo were posing with their war equipment for Japanese news photographers. Then just after 11 pm a detachment of 400 bluejackets stormed into Chapei, with hand-held flares and the searchlights of armoured cars illuminating the darkened and deserted streets. 'I was at the mayor's house in Avenue Haig until 10.30 that night,' Donald relates. 'I got to the Astor House Hotel where I was staying at about 11 o'clock. As I reached Soochow Creek, I could hear rifle and machine-gun firing the other side of North Szechuen Road.'

Admiral Shiozawa was not expecting any organised resistance, but Chinese snipers from the 19th Route Army, reinforced by members of Tu's Green Gang, had taken up positions on top of walls and in the upstairs rooms of buildings. As Japanese patrols approached North Station in the heart of Chapei, they opened fire with rifles and machine-guns at the well-illuminated

Japanese force. Large numbers of bluejackets were caught in the crossfire and mown down.

Misty rain had fallen earlier in the evening but the skies were clear when groups of Westerners in evening dress, hearing gunfire over the sound of the dance bands, poured out of fashionable hotels and restaurants and took taxis to the frontline in North Szechuen Road. As bullets ricocheted off the sides of buildings, they stood around smoking and drinking and eating sandwiches from local cafes.

Hallett Abend lived at Broadway Mansions in Hongkew and had only a short distance to walk. As he joined the spectators, he heard one European man say to another, 'Hope the Japs will teach the cocky Chinese a good lesson.' His companion replied, 'Yeah, Japan is saving the white man the job of bringing the Chinese to reason.'[17]

Japanese reinforcements were cheered as they roared down side streets on motorbikes, with machine-gunners in their sidecars blazing indiscriminately into the dark. The Japanese commanders had expected the Chinese defenders to break and run when confronted by fast-moving mobile units. Instead, their troops soon found it impossible to advance any further against heavy fire from the front, while snipers harassed them from the rear.

The Japanese suffered further casualties when the 19th Route Army opened fire from an armoured train in the sidings at North Station. Forced on the defensive, they erected barbed-wire barricades and posted sentries at intervals of 20 or 30 metres to secure the area.

At a quarter to midnight Mayor Wu rang Donald and said he had received a proclamation from the Japanese admiral, stating that his marines had been sniped at while they were taking up their positions 'to protect the International Settlement'. Donald held the receiver of his telephone out of his bedroom window to confirm that the Japanese were indeed in action in Chapei.

One of the officers at the Chinese Maritime Customs Service was Thomas Macauley, a red-headed Ulsterman and former member of the Royal Army Medical Corps who lived with his Cantonese wife, Ling-ying Lee, his mother-in-law and four young children on the third floor of the Ramus apartment building in Hongkew. 'We were on the crossroads opposite Japanese naval headquarters,' his son Bill Macauley says, 'and we could see the Japanese firing field guns down the road into Chapei.'[18]

Gordon Bowden took his six-year-old son Ivor to the top of the *North-China Daily News* building on The Bund. 'We looked down and could see the fighting in Chapei,' Ivor relates. 'It was night-time and the muzzle flashes of the guns pierced the darkness. My father was taking the family on his leave to England and in the morning our Blue Funnel ship sailed past Chapei and we saw the damage.'[19]

Bill Macauley's family woke up to find their apartment block 'surrounded by Japanese marines with their long bayonets'. During the night, Chinese snipers had fired down on the Japanese from the roof and they had been ordered to search the five-storey building. 'My maternal grandmother was holding on to me because I was scared stiff,' Macauley says.

> The Japanese went rampaging through our flat looking for the snipers but all they found were empty cartridges on the roof. That was my first experience of Japanese anger and I was absolutely petrified. My father organised a convoy and the whole family was evacuated to the Custom House on The Bund. We stayed there until the trouble was over.[20]

That morning Admiral Shiozawa had sent in bombers from his aircraft carriers to bomb Chapei. The main target was the armoured train and the station's modern concrete building, but many bombs were also dropped on residential areas, killing hundreds of Chinese civilians and starting numerous fires.

Eleanor Hinder and Viola Smith witnessed the first night of hostilities from the balcony of their sixth-floor flat in Young Allen Court. In the morning, a young Chinese friend and her child arrived from North Szechuen Road seeking shelter. They invited her to stay but later that day a bomb demolished the house opposite their block. They quickly loaded a few possessions into Viola's Buick coupé and drove to the home of friends in Avenue Haig, Frenchtown. In the words of *The Times* correspondent, the bombing 'created the impression that a policy of frightfulness had been adopted in order to induce the evacuation of the Chinese troops'.[21]

The Japanese sent scores of *ronin* – many of them shopkeepers, bank clerks and factory employees armed with pistols, rifles, swords and baseball bats – into the International Settlement during Saturday 30 January. American Marines detained 14 such gangsters who had infiltrated the American sector with the intention of stirring up trouble and there were dozens in other parts of the city.[22]

As darkness enclosed the war zone, Japanese naval sharpshooters moved up and down the streets of Hongkew, shooting out overhead electric lights. At 8.15 the US Marines in Haiphong Road encountered two groups of armed Japanese who fired over the head of a Marine sentry into a Chinese district. The sentry detained nine of the men.[23]

At 8.25 pm two Chinese were shot and killed by Japanese *ronin* in front of the Japanese marine barracks at 102 Gordon Road inside the American area. Twenty minutes later four more plain-clothed Japanese were detained in the same district, while others were found to have taken charge of a police substation at the corner of Robison and Penang roads. They were evicted by British troops after a fierce struggle.

The *ronin* extended their control from Haining Road up to Soochow Creek. When the Municipal Police withdrew its patrols to avoid clashes, the Japanese were virtually in control of the whole of Hongkew. They assumed police powers and stopped traffic and searched cars and civilians; Chinese citizens came in for rough treatment and a number were bayoneted to death.

'The careless employment of a number of Japanese bad characters as reservists, whose conduct was inexcusable, led to much cruelty and injustice against harmless non-combatants,' *The Times* correspondent commented.[24] The main effect of all this 'frightfulness' was that half a million Chinese in Chapei and Hongkew deserted their homes and sought refuge in the International Settlement, many losing all their possessions in the process. 'From a military point of view,' *The Times* noted, 'the frightfulness had no result.'

For the next 30 days the 19th Route Army battled the Japanese in Chapei. General Tsai's troops outnumbered the Japanese marines ten to one and were winning a decisive victory until the Japanese Army, much to the embarrassment of the Imperial Navy, diverted 20,000 regular troops from Manchuria to save the bluejackets from extinction.

Chiang Kai-shek ordered his two crack National Guard divisions to join the 19th Route Army but placed them under General Tsai's command so they could be passed off as Cantonese units to avoid giving Japan an excuse to extend the conflict.[25] Wang Ching-wei came up with a suitably face-saving slogan: 'Resisting while negotiating'. Chiang's order to General Tsai left little doubt about his intentions: 'The 19th Route Army should take advantage of its victorious position in the last dozen days, avoid decisive fighting with Japan and end the war now.'[26]

Meanwhile, Manchuria's 30 million people living in an area one-third the size of Western Australia were absorbed into the Japanese Empire as members of a puppet state named Manchukuo (Manchu Land) and on 9 March the last Manchu emperor, Pu Yi, was sworn in as president (and a couple of years later elevated to emperor).

Henry Woodhead, editor of the *Peking and Tientsin Times*, had invited Pu Yi to join his bridge club, the illustriously named Tripehounds, after he had given General Feng's guards the slip in Peking and made his way to Tientsin. When Woodhead went to Manchuria in September 1932 to see what conditions were like under Japanese rule, he met Pu Yi in his palace at Chang-chun. Asked whether it was true he had been kidnapped by the Japanese and taken to Port Arthur in a Japanese destroyer, Pu Yi threw back his head and roared with laughter. 'Kidnapped!' he said. 'Kidnapped! No! No!' Manchuria was his ancestral home, he said, and he was a willing collaborator because General Feng had kicked him out of the Forbidden City and confiscated his property, and then the *Kuomintang* had cancelled his pension and treated him with 'studied insolence'.[27]

What infuriated Tokyo most was the refusal of the United States to recognise their new state. The Stimson Doctrine, named after President Herbert Hoover's Secretary of State Henry L. Stimson, declared that the United States would not recognise any territorial arrangements imposed on China by force of arms. Despite that assertion, the United States turned down a Moscow proposal that the USSR, the United States and China form a common anti-Japanese front.[28]

The British, however, rushed the 2nd Battalion of the Argyll and Sutherland Highlanders and No. 1 Mountain Battery up from Hong Kong in HMS *Berwick* to form a full brigade of 3500 troops with the 1st Battalion of the Lincolnshire Regiment, the 1st Battalion of the Wiltshire Regiment and the 2nd Battalion of the Royal Scots Fusiliers.

Sir Howard Kelly, commander-in-chief of the Royal Navy's China Station, was in the Dutch East Indies when the fighting broke out. He returned to Shanghai at full speed in his flagship HMS *Kent* and entered into negotiations with his Japanese naval counterparts. 'One of the popular night amusements,' he noted, 'was to go to the top of the tower of the Cathay Hotel to watch the war in which one was practically taking part.'[29]

Kelly succeeded in arranging a ceasefire between the two sides on 3 March after a new thrust higher up the Yangtze estuary enabled the Japanese to turn the Chinese flank. Having saved face, the Japanese were willing to find a way out of the imbroglio. Sir Miles Lampson, who had been on six months' leave in Britain, had missed most of the war. Over the next two months, the ambassador was able to broker the ceasefire into a formal agreement under which a demilitarised zone was set up around the city.[30]

The Manchurian question reached the League of Nations in Geneva, which sent a commission headed by the Earl of Lytton, former acting viceroy of India and hence an expert on the rights of subject peoples, to Manchuria to investigate China's claim of Japanese aggression. The five-man Lytton Commission spent six weeks in Manchuria in the spring of 1932 on a fact-finding mission after meeting with government leaders in China and Japan. It was hoped the Lytton Report would defuse the growing hostilities between Japan and China and thus maintain peace and stability in East Asia.

Wellington Koo was attached to the commission as assessor and Bill Donald went along as his adviser. He took Irina with him on the six-week assignment. 'I was with the League commission in Manchuria recently and during that time others did a bit of worrying because there was an idea about that the Japanese would try to assassinate some of us,' Donald wrote to his sister Florence Orr in Sydney.

> We had a hectic time of it, being shadowed by detectives and harassed by police. Any Chinese who came near me was arrested. One fellow merely asked if I stayed in the Yamato Hotel at Mukden and for his pains was arrested and held by the Japanese incommunicado for 6 weeks – until the Commission left Manchuria.

'Mr Donald has an exceptional knowledge of the Manchurian situation,' the *Sydney Morning Herald* reported, 'and was therefore of great assistance not only to Dr Koo, but also to the commission.'[31] However, he could do nothing to solve the problems that bedevilled the league in its peacekeeping efforts. General Frank McCoy, the American representative on the commission, told Joseph Grew, the United States ambassador to Japan, that the commissioners were unanimous in finding that Japan's actions in Manchuria were based on two false premises: the argument of self-defence and the argument of self-determination. 'Neither argument is considered sound,' Grew reported to his Secretary of State, Henry Stimson. 'The Commissioners have proved to their satisfaction that the blowing up of the railway and every subsequent incident in Manchuria since 18 September 1931 were carefully planned and carried out by the Japanese themselves.'[32]

Donald flew between Peking and Shanghai six times in three weeks to liaise between the Young Marshal and Nationalist commanders. 'Once I crashed in a storm at Newchwang in a small two-seater,' he wrote to his sister. 'We ended up on our nose with a broken wing, propeller and undercarriage – but that was all the damage. I am organically sound and surviving all the trials and tribulations which beset this country and all who are in it. The redeeming feature about the tribulations is that we have no monotony here: There is always excitement. Wars do not worry us. We are used to them.'

When the Lytton Report was published on 2 October 1932, the commissioners had dodged the main question: the cause of the Mukden Incident. It simply restated the Japanese claim that the Chinese had been responsible, without adjudicating on whether that were true or false. Although there was no doubt as to Japan's guilt among the five commissioners, General Henri Claudel, the French representative, insisted Japan should not be portrayed as the aggressor. As an Asian coloniser herself, France was anxious to avoid angering the Japanese; she was also concerned lest her conquest of Cochin China (Vietnam) attract unfavourable comparison with Manchuria.

Despite the objections of Japan's chief delegate in Geneva, Yosuke Matsuoka, the report was placed before the assembly for its consideration on 24 February 1933. The Chinese delegate, Dr Yen, accepted it, while Matsuoka rejected it on principle. With Siam (soon to become Thailand) abstaining and Japan's negative vote disregarded because she was a party to the dispute, the report was unanimously adopted. Clenching an unlit cigar between his teeth, Matsuoka gathered up his papers and led the Japanese delegation in a dramatic walkout from the assembly's chamber. Japan gave formal notice of its withdrawal from the League of Nations on 27 March 1933.

Meanwhile, Chapei and the other devastated districts of Shanghai were being rebuilt. On 3 January 1933 Eleanor Hinder was appointed chief of Shanghai Municipality's new industrial division responsible for applying the new Factory Act relating to child labour and the employment of women. She approached her task with characteristic vigour. As she feared, diehard conservatives on the Municipal Council refused to pass the necessary bylaws enabling her to enforce the Nationalists' legislation.

The immensity of her task was not lost on the British scholar and aesthete Harold Acton who described the Shanghai of 1932 as 'the most cruel and merciless of cities' in which 'the Japanese textile mills ground the bodies and souls of the girls who toiled in them. Having been bought by contractors and sold to factories, these girls were practically slaves.'[33]

Acton noted that Japan used Hongkew as a base from which to 'spread her tentacles over Shanghai'. He was astonished that few foreign businessmen – 'Old China Hands pickled in alcohol who prided themselves on never mixing with the "natives"' – were perturbed about this. 'Those who had lived here free of taxes, amassing comfortable fortunes, had little to say in favour of the Chinese,' he wrote in his memoir. 'The tone of conversation in the Shanghai Club with its longest bar in the world was intensely anti-Chinese, and when I ventured to protest I was told I wasn't qualified to have an opinion.'[34]

Despite the limitations on her powers, Eleanor Hinder launched a propaganda campaign on health and safety issues, and created the nucleus of a strong factory inspectorate. She was fortunate in the council's choice of Fire Officer Rewi Alley as chief factory inspector. Eleanor and the secret Communist hired Bruno Hader, an Austrian engineer, to examine machinery in textile mills and suggest safety measures, and Chris Bojesen, a Danish electrician, to check electrical circuits. Other inspectors taught Chinese workers how to operate industrial boiler systems.[35]

Rewi Alley described Eleanor as 'an extremely efficient woman who had vision, ability and gave good leadership'. Together, they laid the foundations for safer, cleaner factories. 'We did have some success with things as they were,' he said, 'though only to a limited extent.' One improvement was to persuade silk manufacturers to install central boiling systems in the filatures to eliminate the need for individual boilers that filled each room with steam.

Eleanor admitted many of the problems were insurmountable. Even if she were given powers to enforce reasonable standards, she wrote, many of the factories had no space in which to install machine guards or the money to improve sanitation. Was it right to close down such premises knowing the workforce would face starvation? 'Saving lives by closing dangerous trades means destroying a source of meagre livelihood,' she wrote. It was a bitter decision to have to make and one that caused her immense grief.

CHAPTER 18

Kidnap Crisis

At the beginning of 1933 the Japanese claimed to have found two Chinese bombs at one of their posts at Shanhaiguan, the border crossing point in North China. At the same time, Tokyo announced that Jehol, the rich province north of Peking, was part of Manchukuo. The provincial governor, General Tang Yu-lin, pretended to be in league with the Japanese, while conspiring with the Young Marshal to attack the Japanese with his 140,000-strong army.

As the Kwantung Army advanced into Jehol on 23 February, Chang Hsueh-liang and Bill Donald drove through a blizzard from Peking to the capital of Chengtu to see the situation for themselves. The only troops they could find were guarding General Tang's drug-making factory in the grounds of his palace. Rather than fight the Japanese, Tang's main force had fled north with him to safer parts of his mountainous fiefdom.[1]

By 4 March, the Japanese conquest of Jehol was complete and it was painfully clear the Young Marshal had lost control of the military situation in North China. It was also clear his drug addiction would soon kill him – he could go nowhere without a couple of flunkeys carrying a briefcase containing syringes and other drug paraphernalia.

Four days later Chiang Kai-shek relieved him of his command. 'We came into China proper to effect unification, but the result is that we are now homeless,' the Young Marshal told his troops. 'Although our sacrifice is great, it is worthwhile. After my departure, you must obey Generalissimo Chiang's orders and support the government unanimously. You must be aware of the fact that in permitting me to resign the Generalissimo wishes me well.'[2]

Chang Hsueh-liang's dismissal provided Donald with a golden opportunity. Overriding all objections, he admitted him to a German hospital in Shanghai under the care of Dr Harry W. Miller Jr to undergo treatment for his drug addiction. Miller was a Seventh Day Adventist who had studied medicine at the American Medical Missionary College at Battle Creek, Michigan. He had come to China shortly after the Boxer Uprising. Dressed in Chinese robes and wearing a pigtail, he travelled widely in remote areas of the Celestial Kingdom. He learned a great deal about the effects of opium and over the years had developed a radical treatment for addiction.[3]

Miller put Chang and his two wives, who were also addicted, to sleep for three days with anaesthetics and injected their arms with fluid drawn from blisters induced on their stomachs to cleanse their blood. Miller was delighted when Chang woke up and ordered his execution by firing squad. 'That means we're making progress,' he chuckled.[4] The treatment was successful and Chang and his wives walked out of the hospital drug-free. Chang was then 32; he would live to be 100.

Once he had built up his strength through exercise and a healthy diet, Chang set sail for Europe in April 1933 with Bill Donald, his Scots friend Jimmy Elder, one of his wives and two secretaries – Edith Zhao (his lover and future wife) and Irina, plus a number of nurses and servants. Irina recalled many years later that her role on this trip was to act as secretary to Chang's wife, although it is quite likely that it was Donald who wanted her there, not least because of her linguistic skills.

In May the party arrived in Rome. Chang was introduced to Benito Mussolini and formed a strong impression of Italy's 'national revival' under the blustering Fascist dictator. He gained a similar impression during a tour of Adolf Hitler's Nazi Germany. The best England could offer was the former prime minister Ramsay MacDonald, a discredited figure who compared unfavourably in Chang's eyes with the strutting European demagogues.

Chang rented a house in Brighton, played golf and hosted parties. While he was a social success, people who drank his champagne sniggered behind his back that he was 'the drug addict who lost Manchuria'. In London he took a suite at the Dorchester and met up with T. V. Soong when he arrived on 5 June for a conference on China's economy. Compared with Chang, the thick-set, bespectacled Soong was highly regarded. *The Times* welcomed him as 'a visitor of exceptional distinction' and added, 'Since he took his degree in economics at Harvard University in 1917 Mr Soong has had a remarkable career, as a banker and business manager, as a politician and diplomatist, and for the last five years as the defender of the Chinese Treasury against revolutionary extravagances and militarist depredations.'[5]

If Chang was expecting some of T. V.'s stardust to rub off on him, he was disappointed. Donald later accused Soong of attempting 'to keep the Young Marshal in the background in order that his popularity might not detract from Mr Soong's prominence'.[6] Unfortunately for the Young Marshal, his popularity depended largely on his free-spending habits whereas Soong was seen as the financial wunderkind who had balanced China's budget without recourse to yet another foreign loan. Yet it was Soong who fell from grace soon after his return to Shanghai at the end of August and the Young Marshal who would make a dramatic comeback in China's affairs.

His revival began when he received a cable from his headquarters in Shanghai: 'REVOLT HAS BROKEN OUT IN FUKIEN STOP THERE

IS MOVEMENT UNDER WAY TO GET US TO JOIN FACTIONS AGAINST CHIANG KAI-SHEK STOP COME BACK AT ONCE.' Chang's natural inclination was to pack his bags and take the first ship back to Shanghai. Donald, however, persuaded him to remain in Europe while he went ahead and assessed the seriousness of the situation.

When he reached Shanghai in December 1933, he discovered that the Nationalist government was in disarray. T. V. Soong had resigned as finance minister in protest against Chiang Kai-shek's decision to spend a huge proportion of China's revenue on his anti-Communist campaign. His resignation triggered a long-brewing revolt in which Eugene Chen backed General Tsai Ting-kai, commander of the 19th Route Army, in setting up an anti-Chiang regime in Fukien.

In a hastily compiled manifesto, the so-called 'People's Revolutionary Government of China' belittled T. V. Soong's efforts to sort out China's financial problems and accused Chiang Kai-shek of cowardice over his reluctance to jeopardise his personal military power in the struggle for national independence. Furthermore, it alleged he was committed to supporting Japan's expansionist policy in China.[7]

Donald decided that it would not only be safe for the Young Marshal to return to China but highly desirable. There was a real chance here of mending his relationship with the Generalissimo and at the same time repairing the damage to his reputation. Donald met Chang's ship at Manila and escorted him to Shanghai with a bodyguard of 200 Manchurian warriors to ward off assassination attempts.

Shortly after his return Donald had lunch with W. Langhorne Bond, operations manager of the China National Aviation Corporation (CNAC), and Mayling Chiang. 'What does the Young Marshal want?' Mayling asked. 'Madame,' Donald replied quietly, 'as strange as it may seem to you, the Young Marshal only wants to serve China in the best way he can.'[8]

Mayling reported this conversation to her husband and a reconciliatory meeting between the two commanders was arranged at a resort on the West Lake at Hangchow. Things got off to a shaky start when Chang Hsueh-liang launched into a personal attack on the Generalissimo, telling him how impressed he had been with Hitler and Mussolini as national leaders, and adding, 'Europe doesn't think much of you or China.'

As Chiang sat stony-faced and silent, Donald took over. With Mayling interpreting, he lectured the Generalissimo on the shortcomings of his leadership. 'You are ignorant because no one dares to correct you,' he said. 'Goddamn it, sir, you've all become insufferably stupid!' The country was riddled with graft and corruption, he continued, while millions of ordinary Chinese people died of flood and famine. 'Above all, where is the decency and nobility for the common man?' he demanded. 'China should be ashamed . . . There is the obesity of wealth on the one hand – the hog wallow of poverty on the other. The rickshaw man and the wharf coolie are worse off than the horse and camel in many another lands.'[9]

Mayling was delighted with Donald's outburst. 'You were wonderful,' she told him later. 'Why don't you work for us? We need a brain like yours.' Donald the male chauvinist was unmoved. 'I don't work for women,' he said. 'Why should I try to advise one of heaven's whimsies? They can't take it.' If that were true, Mayling retorted, she wouldn't have dared to translate everything he had said to Chiang. The Young Marshal nodded. 'She even put in our Goddamns,' he said.[10]

Chiang restored the Young Marshal to his former post as second-in-command of the *Kuomintang* forces and appointed him head of 'bandit suppression' – a euphemism for Communist eradication – in the provinces of Honan, Hupeh and Anhwei.

As Chiang had hoped, the Nationalists' crackdown had had a devastating effect on Mao Tse-tung and his followers. Driven out of Kiangsi and Fukien, they headed west on the famous 9000-kilometre Long March that would take them to a new base at Yenan in the remote north-western province of Shensi. For the next 12 months, Chiang's air force bombed and strafed the marchers, while crops and villages in their path were destroyed in an attempt to starve them into submission. Of the original Communist force of 80,000 men and 2000 women, just 5000 survivors made it to Yenan.[11]

Donald spent the first six months of 1934 in the city formerly known as 'Red Hankow'. He had learned a tremendous amount about China's shortcomings during his eight years at the Bureau of Economic Information. In fact, he joked that he intended to write two books, *The Comic History of the Economic Development of China* and *The Comic History of the Political Development of China*, both liberally sprinkled with his tragi-comic observations of the Chinese character.

Chang Hsueh-liang set up a new body, the Central China Economic Investigation Bureau (director: W. H. Donald), with the objective of boosting trade in the interior and developing the country's natural resources. Donald's first action was to urge H. H. Kung, who had replaced T. V. Soong as minister of finance, to increase the size of the customs police force to crack down on the smuggled goods that were finding their way from Manchuria to all parts of China under Japanese protection. The situation was farcical: Japanese products were openly on sale in China at prices lower than the Chinese duty that should have been collected on them. Smugglers swaggered around with pistols in their belts while the Japanese Government demanded that Chinese customs officers at frontier posts on the smugglers' routes should be unarmed to avoid clashes with Japanese soldiers.[12]

Donald informed Chiang Kai-shek, through Mayling, that China's energies should be devoted to manufacturing every item that Japan exported to her. 'Surely China has brains enough for that; has the competent labour; has the energy,' he wrote. 'Of course she has, but she also has the officials who care not one iota for the country or its well-being; who regard it as a bonanza for their exploitation; who bleed it white.'

If China were to take her rightful place among nations, he told Chiang, rotten officialdom would have to be eliminated. 'I am sure that you can help remove it,' he said.

But you will have to be ruthless, and hard, and uncompromising. A big stick can cure a lot of ills in China. The Chinese people are oppressed beyond belief. They are waiting for someone to give just a lead in saving them. Can't you find a big stick lying about somewhere and use it without scruple?[13]

Next, Donald demanded action to stamp out the opium menace. He pointed out to Mayling that the statue of Dr Sun Yat-sen in Hankow overlooked the city's biggest opium shop. In the shop's window was a sign: 'CHEAP SALE OF OPIUM – THOSE WHO MAKE EXTRA LARGE PURCHASES WILL BE GIVEN FREE TICKETS IN THE NATIONAL GOVERNMENT LOTTERY.'

Within 12 hours of hearing this, the Generalissimo issued the first in a series of anti-opium edicts ordering the closure of all opium-smoking shops and the decapitation of anyone dealing in narcotics. The new laws had little effect. Donald saw a postal van loading opium in parcel-post packages in the centre of Hankow. The next day, the *Hankow Herald* published an unsigned article in which he noted: 'Yesterday, I expected to see on the Bund the decapitated heads of a number of persons, including the British commissioner of customs and the French chief of the post office. But there were no heads there at all.'

Within a few months, however, no fewer than 114 Chinese had been brought to the execution block in the Shanghai area for dealing in narcotics.

As with the opium problem, Bill Donald was uncompromising in his attitude towards corrupt officials. 'Make graft, corruption, squeeze, or whatever one might call it, a capital offence,' he told Chiang Kai-shek, 'and shoot a lot of people and soon there would be a change. But start high up and not among the unhappy low-salaried unfortunates.'[14]

Chiang's answer to China's social problems was to launch the 'New Life Movement', based on the four Confucian principles of *Li* (propriety), *Yi* (right conduct), *Lian* (honesty) and *Qi* (integrity and honour). The idea was to build up public morale through Sun Yat-sen's Third Principle of the People – with 'livelihood' substituted for 'socialism'. Goals included courtesy to neighbours, following government rules, keeping streets clean and conserving energy. Chiang urged the Chinese to accept the Confucian and Methodist notion of self-cultivation and correct living. His Blue Shirts, the Chinese equivalent of European fascists, roamed the Chinese districts of Shanghai inflicting harsh penalties on recidivists.

Smoking and drinking were strictly forbidden. Mayling, a heavy smoker, could only light up in private, while Chinese diners hid alcohol in teapots and drank it from teacups.

By now, the Young Marshal, Chang Hsueh-liang, had moved his headquarters to Sian, the provincial capital in southern Shensi, and Bill Donald was working for Chiang Kai-shek on a full-time basis. He warned 'the Gissimo', as he called him, that while the New Life principles were important, it was more important for him to resist Japanese aggression; otherwise, he would lose the support of many of the remaining warlords and the population at large. As usual, he talked to Chiang through Mayling, whom he had known since she was a child. She called him 'Don' or 'Gran' – short for Grandpa; he called her 'the Missimo'.[15]

Donald refused to accept the title 'adviser', describing his mission as 'the development by China of her natural resources. The politics do not interest me at all except where they frustrate progress.'[16] Over the years, he would acquire many nicknames: 'China's No. 1 White Boy' (from Herbie Elliston's revealing portrait in the *Saturday Evening Post*), 'China's publicity-shy Richelieu' (Ilona Ralf Sues in her memoir *Shark's Fins and Millet*) and 'Warwick II' after Warwick the Kingmaker in Tudor England (American journalist Emily Hahn in her memoir *China to Me*), to name but three.

After February 1935 he had to make do without Irina. His Russian secretary had fallen in love with Englishman Joe Cassel and left China to get married. Her husband took her prospecting for gold in New Guinea and they later went farming in the Congo. As Mrs Irene Cassel, she made an interesting observation about her boss in a letter to Professor Lewis in 1969. 'Donald was a man of historic proportions,' she wrote. 'Lots of things did not happen in China because of him and quite a few did happen because of him.'[17]

At Nanking in early November 1935, Wang Ching-wei had just posed for a press photograph with other leading *Kuomintangists* when a gunman posing as a news agency reporter stepped forward and shot him in the left lung, left cheek and left arm. Wang survived but the would-be assassin, Sun Fengmin, died overnight in police custody after apparently claiming that he had acted alone, although Chiang Kai-shek was probably responsible.

Mao's Communist forces and their camp followers were isolated in northern Shensi, but Chiang was determined to pursue his punitive campaign against them. He ordered Chang Hsueh-liang to finish them off. At the beginning of 1936, however, there were reports that Chang's troops were fraternising with the enemy, even supplying them with military materiel from the Sian arsenal. Indeed, Chang had met Mao's chief lieutenant, Chou En-lai, in a Catholic church and after talking all night agreed in principle on the formation of a united Communist–Nationalist front to drive the Japanese from his Manchurian homeland. 'It wasn't that I was sympathetic with them,' he later explained. 'But they were Chinese, so why fight each other?'[18]

Meanwhile, Alan Raymond seemed to attract trouble. He worked for the commodity brokers Payne & Co but was sacked.

He collected money owed to the Sydney firm, Messrs Young & Co, but somehow failed to pass it on to its rightful owner. He engaged in real estate and advertising until 1936 when he established his own marble works and set himself up as one of the city's traders.[19]

His activities caught the attention of the Municipal Police who opened a file on him. A report in this file described Raymond as 'a capable businessman but has always suffered from lack of capital to finance his ventures. This failing is partly due to his spendthrift nature and his fondness for luxuries, insofar as whenever he brought off a good business deal he would squander the money on gambling and pleasure seeking. In this respect, there have been occasions when his clients' money became indistinguishable from his own.'[20]

In 1936 Raymond travelled to Japan to purchase a quantity of marble for the Cosmopolitan Trust of Shanghai. Owing to the explosive political situation between China and Japan, he was told to hold up the final act of purchase and await further instructions. When he ran out of money, he contacted Cosmopolitan's head office in Shanghai and asked them to send him some. 'They failed to do so and virtually abandoned me there,' he wrote in his postwar statement. 'Although in debt to my hotel I received very kind treatment which added to other pleasant experiences gave me a very favourable impression of the Japanese people. I was there almost three months before I was enabled to return to Shanghai.'[21]

The Japanese secret police had thousands of spies, many of whom were hotel clerks, doormen or bartenders who observed Western visitors and filed lengthy reports on their behaviour, attitudes and movements. The authorities were on the lookout not only for enemy agents but also anyone who might be regarded as a potential Japanese spy.

Broke, embittered and anti-British, Alan Raymond fell into the latter category. That he was hired as a paid employee of the Japanese naval intelligence department in Shanghai is beyond question and the three months he was adrift in Japan would have been the perfect time for his recruitment.[22] By the time he got back to Shanghai, China was facing a unique, self-made crisis – one that Bill Donald had no means of preventing but which he was expected to solve virtually single-handed.

On 7 December 1936 Chiang Kai-shek arrived at Sian to launch what he called 'the last five minutes' of his extermination campaign against the severely weakened Reds. The Young Marshal informed him that he was no longer prepared to fight them and pressed for a political settlement between the warring parties. Chiang remained intransigent. If the Manchurians would not fight the Communists, he said, they would be withdrawn to Fukien in disgrace. There was a violent argument and Chiang retired with his staff officers and bodyguard to a pavilion at a hot springs resort outside Sian.

That night Chang discussed the situation with General Yang Hu-cheng, the radical governor of Shensi who was disinclined to fight the Red Army. The two men decided that Chiang must be forced to listen to the case for forming a united front between the Nationalists and the Communists, or, as the Young Marshal's headquarters later put it, 'detained in order to stimulate his awakening to certain national and international problems'. A 25-year-old colonel named Sun Mingjui was ordered to take a raiding party to Chiang's quarters and arrest him.[23]

At dawn on 12 December Chiang heard shooting outside his pavilion. Leaving his dentures on a bedside table, he fled over a wall in his nightshirt, injuring his back in the attempt. He was found shivering and in great pain inside a cave on a nearby hillside. His feet were bleeding and he was exhausted, so Colonel Sun carried him down the slope on his back. At General Yang's headquarters the Generalissimo refused to recognise his captors, telling them to obey his orders or shoot him.[24]

Later that morning Bill Donald was at the Park Hotel in Shanghai when he received an urgent call from H. H. Kung to attend a meeting at his house. When he arrived, he found Mayling and T. V. Soong were also there. Kung explained he had received a call from Chiang's headquarters saying there had been an attack on the Generalissimo's quarters near Sian, his bodyguards had been murdered and he and ten members of his party had been kidnapped.

At Nanking, the government and the Nationalist high command were in turmoil. Some who were less interested in rescuing Chiang than inciting the Young Marshal to murder him wanted to bomb Sian. Others advocated sending in loyal troops garrisoned at Tungkwan, the narrow pass along the Yellow River connecting Honan with Shensi. With the blessing of H. H. Kung, Bill Donald set off from Shanghai on a rescue mission of his own making in the belief that the Young Marshal would at least speak to him on the basis of their long friendship.

Using one of Chiang's aircraft as a taxi, his first stop was Loyang, headquarters of government troops in Honan. There, he conferred with the Nationalist commander and cabled the Young Marshal that he was on his way. Meanwhile, Chou En-lai arrived in Sian from Yenan in another of the Young Marshal's planes to confirm the point that the Communists were indeed willing to join a united front. He found young militants in General Yang's army calling for Chiang's blood over the Communist massacres. They were insisting on giving him a 'popular trial' for his life at an enormous mass meeting.[25] However much he hated Chiang Kai-shek, Chou knew he was the only military leader in the country capable of leading a united front. He argued strongly that his life be spared.

When Donald arrived in Sian the following day, he was escorted to Chang Hsueh-liang's headquarters. There, he handed Chang a section of Chiang Kai-shek's diary, which showed the Generalissimo was more anti-Japanese than supposed.

As outlined in the diary, his plan was to defeat the Communists and then drive the Japanese out of China.

Donald found Chiang lying in bed with a blanket pulled over his head. It was bitterly cold and the room was unheated. He was also in great pain from his wrenched back. 'At 5 pm Donald came to see me,' Chiang wrote in his account of the kidnap. 'I was very much moved by his loyal friendship, especially as he is a foreigner (an Australian) and yet is willing to come so far on such a dangerous mission.'[26]

Donald gave Chiang a letter from Mayling pleading with him to open negotiations with his captors. He then accompanied Chiang to the Young Marshal's house, which had central heating and better security.[27] Meanwhile, the rebels announced the death of one of their captives, Shao Yuan-chung, chief of the government's publicity council, who had been wounded in the attack.

The following day Donald returned to Loyang and then made his way back to Nanking, finally arriving in a taxi after planes were grounded by bad weather. He reported to the cabinet that the Young Marshal realised he 'had a bear by the tail' and that Chiang had no intention of negotiating with him or anyone else. The cabinet decided Donald should return to Sian with Mayling, who might be able to break the deadlock. T. V. Soong, who was authorised to reach a financial settlement with the rebels, would accompany them. Mayling packed a pistol and a spare set of her husband's false teeth. Aware of the torture that the Nationalists had inflicted on female Communists (including Mao Tse-tung's wife), she handed the pistol to Donald and said, 'Please shoot me if any soldiers touch me.'[28]

Chiang had specifically ordered Donald not to bring Mayling with him and was shocked to see her in this dangerous place. Mayling, however, had known the Young Marshal since her days on the Shanghai party circuit and was determined to talk him into freeing her husband. Donald and Chou En-lai had already laid the foundations for a face-saving deal and Chiang finally agreed to speak to his captors, if only to lecture them on the seriousness of their crimes.

On Christmas Day he was released on condition that he suspend the civil war and form a united front against the Japanese as part of a four-point agreement. First, the Communists agreed to discontinue distributing propaganda or forming cells outside their own area; second, they agreed to accept orders from Chiang Kai-shek as head of the armed forces of China; third, Nanking agreed to supply the Communists with a large sum in silver dollars from its revenues every month; finally, Chiang agreed to send the Communist forces monthly supplies of rifles, ammunition and food.[29]

Donald walked out of the compound with the dishevelled and exhausted Generalissimo on his arm. Chiang later claimed that he had given no undertakings to the Communists and in the coming months there were breaches of the truce on both sides.

Instead of joining Chou En-lai and Mao Tse-tung at Yenan, Chang Hsueh-liang insisted on flying back to Nanking with the Generalissimo to face the music.

'I am naturally rustic, surly and unpolished,' the Young Marshal said in a confessional letter to Chiang Kai-shek, which was released to the press to save Chiang's face.

> Because of this I have committed this impudent and criminal act. Now I have penitently followed you to Nanking in order to await a punishment befitting the crime. I shall accept even death if beneficial to my country. Do not let sentiment or friendship deter you from dealing with me as I deserve.[30]

Chang Hsueh-liang was less deferential at his court-martial. At one point he rose to his feet and denounced the court as a bunch of 'crooks and hypocrites'. On hearing this, Mayling burst out, 'How does the young fool expect us to help him if he won't keep his mouth shut?' Indeed, the court sentenced Chang to death but instead of signing the death warrant Chiang commuted the sentence to indefinite detention, initially in a house near Chiang's own home village south of Shanghai. Incredibly, the Young Marshal was kept under house arrest for the next 55 years in various parts of mainland China and later on Taiwan.[31] His followers in Sian rose up in arms against Chiang but the rebellion was crushed and they were driven north, where they joined the Red Army.

The kidnapping – and Donald's role in ending it – made headlines around the world. Just three days after Chiang's release, *Time* magazine published an intimate profile of him in which the hand of one of his former friends, possibly Rodney Gilbert who was working in New York as an editorial writer on the *Herald Tribune*, could be detected. 'Many years ago the health of his wife made it best for her to return to Australia,' the unsigned article said, 'and in China her increasingly polished rough-diamond husband, as the years rolled on, perhaps killed more ladies (in the complimentary, Edwardian sense of "lady-killing") than any other man in China's swift, hard, cheap, international Shanghai–Peking set.'[32]

The writer claimed that on one occasion Donald was invited to a party in Peking to meet a vivacious blonde who had a letter of introduction from a United States publisher. 'I'm afraid I must decline,' he said. 'That kind scratches and bites.'

In Chiang Kai-shek's account – in which Donald almost certainly had a hand – the Generalissimo wrote, 'People have supposed Donald to be an engaged adviser of the government. The fact is that he is a private friend and a frequent guest at my house. I might also add that, although drawn into my circle, he has sternly refused any honours or the name of an adviser.' Six months later Donald, described in *The Times* as 'an unofficial adviser to General Chiang Kai-shek', accepted the award of the Order of the Brilliant Jade with Blue Cravate.[33]

In a letter to his sister Florence Orr in Sydney, Donald ruminated on his life in China. 'Somehow, without any effort,

I have managed to hold the confidences of all political factions in China,' he wrote.

> Lots of people who know China ask me how, seeing that I never learned to speak the language, and all I can tell them is that I have none of the European superiority complex, treat confidences as confidences, play the game and keep smiling. I must have the intuitive understanding of the Chinese character. I tell them exactly what I think of them when they are wrong, which is much of the time, and never humbug them. That is all, except that I can never be bought by them, and this they respect.[34]

The indispensible Donald apart, Chiang Kai-shek employed a large number of foreign advisers to train his armed forces. The Chinese Army's senior adviser was General Alexander von Falkenhausen, a World War I veteran and virulent anti-Nazi, while the tall, blond Aryan archetype Captain Walther Stennes, one-time commander of Hitler's Brownshirts, was charged with moulding Chiang's 3000-strong bodyguard into an elite force similar to the Prussian Guards.[35] Falkenhausen tapped Donald on the chest with his swagger stick. 'My friend,' he said, 'if Japan attacks she will be defeated.'[36]

Chiang took the extraordinary step of putting Mayling in charge of the Chinese Air Force, with the title of secretary-general of the Chinese Aeronautical Affairs Commission. Her senior adviser was Wing Commander Garnet Malley, an outstanding Australian World War I fighter pilot who had been awarded the Military Cross and Air Force Cross for bravery. Born at Mosman on 2 November 1893, Malley had moved to China with his wife Phyllis in 1931 as air adviser to the Nationalist Government and, since 1936, to Chiang Kai-shek personally. His rank was an honorary one, bestowed by the RAAF at the request of the British Foreign Office after Sir Hughe Knatch-bull-Hugessen, who had replaced Sir Miles Lampson as British ambassador the previous year, insisted that he should be of equal rank to an Italian general on the Aeronautical Commission.[37]

China's small air force was built around instructors and aircraft drawn from half a dozen Western nations of which the most prominent was Fascist Italy, conqueror of little Ethiopia. On a visit to Rome in 1934 H. H. Kung had agreed a deal with Mussolini under which Fiat fighters and Savoia-Marchetti bombers would be assembled at Nanchang. The planes were obsolete by the time they rolled off the production line: the fighters turned out to be firetraps in aerial combat while the ancient bombers could only be used as transports.[38]

The Fascist fraud was just one of Malley's difficulties in modernising the Chinese Air Force. His main problem was corruption in the purchase of new planes and aviation equipment involving Kung's wife Ayling Soong, a Chinese general and an American agent named A. L. Patterson. According to the memorandum of a 1937 conversation between the American ambassador, Nelson T. Johnson, and a member of his staff, 'Wing Commander Garnet Malley was satisfied that Patterson had doubled, and in some cases trebled, the price of American aircraft sold to the Chinese Government over the list prices in the United States.

> This was done to provide a larger 'squeeze' to Chinese officials handling the orders. Patterson had even gone so far as to have special catalogues printed in China showing the adjusted prices and purporting to be the American catalogues. Malley said that Madame Chiang had asked him to suggest means of stopping the 'squeeze'.

In one instance Patterson 'had sold to the Aviation Commission one hundred if not two hundred radio sets; not only was the price four times the right price, but the sets themselves were quite unsuitable for use on Chinese military planes, since it was impossible to alter wavelength.'

According to this memo:

General Tzau had been mentioned for some time as the agent of Mrs H. H. Kung in collecting 'squeeze' on the purchase of airplanes. I inquired how it was that Mrs Chiang Kai-shek, Mrs Kung's sister, could take any action which would, if carried to its conclusion, expose Mrs Kung's alleged part in these transactions. [Malley] said that Mrs Chiang Kai-shek had given orders to sift the matter to the bottom and that the bribery in connection with air plane purchases had been the subject of a struggle between the two sisters for some time.[39]

Purchases made for the Chinese Air Force allegedly passed through an entity called the Central Trust, an arm of Dr Kung's Ministry of Finance. The trust was controlled by Ayling Soong and it refused to give orders to any manufacturer not represented by Patterson.[40] The result of all these machinations was that by the summer of 1937 China had 150 competent army pilots, 200 of poor ability and just 91 frontline military aircraft, mostly American fighters, for an outlay of millions of dollars.

Meanwhile, Eleanor Hinder pursued her long-term aim of liberating the slave girls of China. Under the *mui tsai* contract labour system, poor country girls were purchased by members of the Green Gang and brought to Shanghai in batches of 30 or more. The prettiest were sent to work in Chinese-run brothels; the rest ended up as indentured labour in the factories.

After carefully studying a memorandum on the *mui tsai* system from Sir George Maxwell to the League of Nations in 1935, the Municipal Council appointed Eleanor 'protector of the *mui tsai*'.[41] She was careful in addressing the problem to note that a *mui tsai* could only be described as a slave for the period of her life in which she lived as a domestic servant with a family. When she reached puberty, she might be married or taken as a concubine and therefore become part of another family. If she were unlucky, she would be sold again as a prostitute.[42]

It was also important to acknowledge that not all *mui tsai* were mistreated – indeed, some were well cared for and became adopted daughters of the families for which they worked. In her writings on the subject, Eleanor used the term 'slavery' only in the League of Nations context that the *mui tsai* system contained 'elements suggestive of slavery'.[43] She declined to report to the Committee of Experts on Slavery in China but developed a broad study on the role of the authorities 'in the protection of the *mui tsai* and other groups of young persons transferred into the control of others not near relations and exploited by them'.

Eleanor argued it made no sense to liberate slave girls unless the crippling problems of homelessness, kidnapping and the exploitation of child labour in Chinese cities were also solved. It was a valid and humane point; the important thing was that a start had been made in tackling the iniquitous system.

In June 1937 William Arthur Farmer, a young West Australian journalist known as 'Buzz', stepped ashore from the *Ginsu Maru*, a Japanese ship which had brought him from Perth for a holiday in Shanghai. Feeling destiny tugging at his sleeve, he decided to try his luck in Shanghai and took a job as a reporter on the *North-China Daily News*.

Farmer was from Perth where he had attended Basil Riley's *alma mater*, Perth High School (later Hale). He played hockey for the Guildford Club and was the darling of the gossip columnists. 'The entire social whirl of Perth,' 'Jennifer' gushed in the *Western Mail*, 'will be inordinately pleased to hear that Buzz Farmer, so immaculately himself, has at last got rid of that automotive eyesore of his and bought a real car!'[44]

Destiny was indeed at his sleeve. At 10 o'clock on the evening of 7 July 1937 Japanese officers claimed their troops were fired on by Chinese soldiers at the Black Moat Bridge, otherwise known as Marco Polo Bridge after the Venetian explorer who thought it one of the most beautiful in the world. The bridge was near the village of Lukouchiao (Luqouqiao), 32 kilometres west of Peking where a brigade of Japanese troops were garrisoned under the terms of the Boxer Protocol.[45]

At midnight the Japanese commander reported the shooting to the mayor of Peking, General Ching Teh-chun, and requested permission to search nearby Wanping for a missing Japanese soldier who was presumed to have been taken prisoner. As Wanping was an important railway junction on the main line to Hankow, Ching refused the request. To defuse a potentially explosive situation, however, he offered to send a joint commission into Wanping to make inquiries.

This appeared to be agreeable to the Japanese but while arrangements were being made eight truckloads of steel-helmeted Japanese troops tried to force their way into the fortified town. Serious fighting broke out and both sides rushed a battalion of reinforcements to the battlefield. At the same time, the missing man returned to his unit – embarrassingly, he had been enjoying himself at a local brothel.[46]

As Japan was preoccupied with the threat to her northern flank from Russia, it is doubtful she planned to start a full-scale war in North China. The Chinese, however, were unable to decipher Japanese intentions. Determined to resist any further aggression in North China, Chiang Kai-shek ordered four Nationalist divisions into the area.

In Peking the Chinese declared martial law and closed the city gates. In response, Japanese guards inside the city barricaded the Legation Quarter and set up machine-gun posts. Within a week, large numbers of Japanese troops had forced their way into Peking and fighting spread through the streets of the Tartar City.[47]

The Japanese public responded to these events with a show of patriotic fervour. Tokyo newspapers demanded a showdown to eliminate anti-Japanese propaganda in North China and the Japanese War Minister General Sugiyama declared that China 'must be chastised for her insincerity'.[48]

Harold Timperley, the *Guardian*'s Australian correspondent, was staying at the Metropolitan Hotel in Nanking. On 15 July he wrote to Sir Hughe Knatchbull-Hugessen, seeking to enlist his support in a peacekeeping initiative. 'The Chinese do not want to fight if they can possibly avoid it,' he said.

> First, the Central Government has not yet recovered fully from the shock administered by the Sian affair last December; secondly, unification of the provinces under Nanking's rule is still incomplete, though well on the way; thirdly, the Central Government is busily engaged upon a large program of reconstruction which must perforce be interrupted and perhaps abandoned if war comes.[49]

Timperley urged Britain and the United States to intervene between the two belligerents 'before the Japanese preparations are too far advanced for reconsideration to be made possible'. At present, it was still possible to pretend that the issue in North China was merely a local one 'but the longer things are allowed to drift along the more difficult it will be to keep things on that basis'.

By early August, Timperley's hopes had been dashed. All Japanese nationals had been evacuated from Hankow, Nanking and other points in the Yangtze Valley and South China, while Japanese bombers attacked Hangchow, Nanchang, Nanking, Soochow, Chinkiang, and the Shanghai–Nanking Railway. In between air raids, Timperley married Elizabeth Chambers, a young American from Des Moines who was working in Nanking. 'Our married life this far,' he wrote, 'has been punctuated by Japanese bombs.'[50]

Chiang Kai-shek was ridiculed for his 'wait and see' policy and there were calls for his resignation. The Generalissimo announced in an interview, 'I declare again that China does not seek war, but we will accept war if it is forced on us. We have reached the limit of our endurance.'

The situation at Shanghai rapidly deteriorated. On the evening of 9 August two members of the Japanese Naval Landing Party were shot dead when they attempted to enter the Chinese airfield at Hungjao on the outskirts of Shanghai; a Chinese sentry was also killed in the shooting. The Japanese consul, Okamoto, said the incident was of a 'grave nature' and had been reported to Tokyo for appropriate action. Japanese naval authorities at Shanghai announced they would be 'compelled to adopt defence measures'. For the cost of just two lives, a situation had been created which would justify extending the war from North China to Shanghai. Thousands of Chinese in Hongkew and Chapei joined the columns of evacuees pouring into the International Settlement and the French Concession from country districts north of Shanghai.[51]

In desperation the mayor of the Chinese Municipality, O. K. Yui, appealed to the United States and Britain to prevent Japan using Little Tokyo as a base of military operations against China and thereby putting the entire city at risk. When Britain asked Japan to exclude Shanghai from the war zone, her commanders replied this was asking the impossible.

Hand-to-hand fighting broke out in Hongkew when Chinese troops attacked Japanese soldiers landing from warships. British police and American Marines were driven back across Garden Bridge and Hongkew became a no-go area for Westerners. At night, Buzz Farmer could hear Japanese tanks revving up in the back streets. The third Sino-Japanese War was on and the Japanese expected a quick victory. Instead, they would achieve something that had eluded politicians for the past 25 years: the unification of the Chinese people.

CHAPTER 19

Bloody Saturday

On 11 August 1937 the Japanese Third Fleet steamed up the Whangpoo and the cruiser *Idzumo*, Shanghai's talisman of doom, tied up at Garden Point adjacent to the Japanese, British, American and Russian consulates in the heart of the International Settlement. There were now 27 warships anchored off The Bund and several thousand Japanese reinforcements were located on troopships downstream at Woosung. Japanese marines and *ronin* began roughing up Chinese citizens in Hongkew and Chapei.[1]

Gordon Bowden saw the cruiser – flagship of Vice Admiral Kiyoshi Hasegawa, Japanese commander-in-chief – as he drove along The Bund from his home in Frenchtown. Bowden had been Australia's trade commissioner since 1935, the first to be appointed since the departure of the ill-fated Edward Little 11 years earlier. During his long association with Japan, he had learned a great deal about the Japanese and their ambitions to establish their country as the dominant power in East Asia, with Emperor Hirohito as supreme ruler.

Bowden alighted at no. 19, the vast, fortress-like, baroque

building of the Hong Kong & Shanghai Bank, and hurried past the two bronze lions, Stephen and Stitt, at the bank's marbled entrance. Stephen was a ferocious beast, Stitt more affable – characteristics, it is said, of two of the bank's former managers after whom they were named. Bowden would normally rub one of the lions' paws in the Chinese manner for good *joss* but today he had no time for such rituals.[2]

He walked briskly to the trade commission's office on an upper floor of the bank. There, he discussed the mounting crisis with his two aides, Norman Wootton and Arthur Nutt. Bowden's son Ivor was at school in England but his wife and two daughters were in Shanghai and the other men also had families there.

On the morning of Thursday, 12 August, the American journalist Emily Hahn packed an evening dress in a hatbox, put her pet duckling Sweetie Pie into a basket and headed for Nanking. She anticipated spending a couple of nights dining and dancing with one of her beaux, a British naval officer whose first love was navigation.[3]

At North Station the administration building had been rebuilt into ten storeys of white ferro-concrete following the battle against the Dogmeat General a decade earlier. Troop trains were arriving every few minutes packed to the roof with Chinese soldiers from Nanking. Nevertheless, Emily boarded the 8 am express for the five-hour trip up the Yangtze Valley. One of her travelling companions was an Englishman who informed her he was taking some fresh lobster to the British Embassy 'because they're running short of such things'. It was going to be a jolly English weekend.

The train was an hour and a half late leaving Shanghai, a bad omen, according to the Englishman. 'That,' she wrote, 'was the very last train to get through, but we had no way of knowing. Nobody said not to go.' With Japanese bombers prowling up and down the railway corridor and many trains involved in troop movements, progress was painfully slow. She wondered vaguely why so many soldiers were heading for Shanghai when the war was in North China.

The 320-kilometre journey to Nanking took 16 hours and it was after midnight before she arrived in the Nationalist capital and checked into her hotel. There was a sign on the wall which was far from reassuring: 'Visitors are warned that air raids are expected at any time; please keep lights off and shutters closed.'

Back in Shanghai, Inspector Roy Fernandez ventured over Soochow Creek to rescue his wife's father Robert Morgan and his second wife who lived in Kiang Wan, north of Hongkew. They were too scared to move through the Japanese lines, so Roy spent the night with them and in the morning packed them and their pet bulldog Britannia into his car and drove them back to the International Settlement.[4]

In Nanking, Emily Hahn's boyfriend informed her that the railway line had been cut at Soochow, the airport had been bombed and the Nationalists had mined the river below Chinkiang to prevent Japanese gunboats from attacking Nanking. She realised if she didn't return to Shanghai immediately she could be cut off, perhaps for weeks. All through Friday the 13th she tried to find a train heading south but without luck until she heard a whisper that one would be going as far as Soochow in the morning.

That night Bill Donald was at a council-of-war meeting with Chiang Kai-shek and his commanders inside the Nanking Military Academy. A message was handed to the Generalissimo. He passed it to Mayling. 'They're shelling the Shanghai Civic Centre,' she cried. 'They're killing our people.'

'What will you do now?' asked Claire Chennault, a leather-faced veteran of the United States Army Air Force who had been hired to train Chinese pilots. She brushed away her tears and declared, 'We will fight.'

As soon as the war started in North China, the Italian mission had disappeared back to Italy, leaving the combat field open to Chennault. He ordered the Chinese Air Force's Curtiss

Hawk dive-bombers to attack the Japanese cruisers, while its
Northrop light bombers blasted Japanese naval headquarters
aboard the heavy cruiser *Idzumo*.[5]

On Saturday morning a typhoon roared in from the East
China Sea, subjecting Shanghai to 100-kilometre-an-hour
winds and providing, according to *The Times* correspondent, 'blessed relief in the present midsummer heat'. Down on
Nanking Road, beggars and refugees camping out in the street
were scattered about like chaff.[6]

At four o'clock a squadron of ten Chinese aircraft from
Hungjao airfield on the outskirts of the city crossed Frenchtown
and flew north on a course that would take them over the 27
warships, many of them Japanese but also British and American,
on the Whangpoo. Japanese anti-aircraft gunners greeted the
planes with a tremendous bombardment that pockmarked the
air with black puffs of smoke and kept the Chinese pilots at high
altitude. Low-lying cloud cover also caused poor visibility above
the city skyline, making it difficult for them to see their targets.

In the confusion two pilots tried to sink HMS *Cumberland*
and another attacked USS *Augusta* off Woosung, both without
success. 'Neither warship fired, as it was believed that in the
stormy weather the Chinese mistook both ships for Japanese,'
The Times reported.[7]

A few minutes later a Japanese fighter attacked one of the
American-made Northrop bombers carrying two bombs. The
badly wounded Chinese pilot turned towards his airfield but the
Japanese plane was catching him, so he released his bombload
and instantly gained height. He intended the bombs to land on
the open spaces of the racecourse; instead, observers watching
from The Bund saw them disappear at the point where Tibet
Road crossed Avenue Edward VII. 'There followed immediately
a huge belch of red flame and a tremendous explosion,' *The
Times* man reported.

Emily Hahn was now on a Shanghai-bound train that was
taking a roundabout route to avoid the fighting. 'All afternoon

we went slowly through flat, rich country, stopping every few yards,' she wrote. 'Towards evening, a Japanese plane came along directly over us, but that day the Japanese were not bombing trains – not yet.'[8]

Five thousand refugees had assembled at the Great World amusement centre in Avenue Edward VII at the junction with Tibet and Yunnan roads to receive free rice. The traffic lights in the centre of the intersection had just turned red when the crusading American Frank Rawlinson drove up Yunnan Road with his wife and daughter in his small car. He stopped the car at the lights and, hearing planes overhead, opened his door and stepped out on to the road to investigate. Just as his feet touched the ground, he uttered a cry, threw up his arms and fell down.[9]

His wife Florence Lang Rawlinson dragged his body back into the car and drove off towards the hospital unaware that he had been shot through the heart by a machine-gun bullet. The car had just turned the corner into Tibet Road when the crowded plaza exploded behind them.

Tragically, both bombs had fallen 300 metres short of the racecourse and landed on refugees, pedestrians and assorted vehicles. Dozens of cars were peppered with shrapnel and their occupants incinerated by exploding petrol tanks, while hundreds of pedestrians were knocked down like skittles for a block in every direction. The worst carnage was among the refugees in front of the Great World, so often the scene of Chinese festivities. Mangled bodies with most of their clothing burned away littered the pavement in smouldering heaps.[10]

Dr Rawlinson's friends Viola Smith and Eleanor Hinder had driven from their flat in Bubbling Well Road to visit the cable office at the Cathay Hotel. They found Nanking Road blocked and had to turn around. As they drove down Hankow Road to Tibet Road, frightened people fleeing from the first blast climbed over the hood of their car. It was impossible with the crush of bodies to turn left, so Viola swung right. Just as she did so, the second bomb, which must have had a delayed fuse, exploded at the intersection. They missed the blast by three blocks.[11]

John Powell was standing on the roof of the American Club, opposite the vast Municipal Administration building in Foochow Road, watching the dogfights between Chinese and Japanese planes when the bombs struck the plaza. 'The explosion shook the entire city,' he said. 'I hurried to the scene, and for the first time in my extensive coverage of battles, I actually saw human blood running in the gutters.'[12] The two bombs killed 450 people and wounded 850.

Buzz Farmer had scrambled on to the roof of the *Daily News* building on The Bund. The hands of the nearby Cathay Hotel clock now showed 4.20. He had a good view of the thousands of homeless refugees milling around the intersection of The Bund and Nanking Road, with the *Idzumo* clearly visible at its moorings near Garden Bridge.[13]

Suddenly, he saw several Chinese chasing a Japanese student wearing a baseball cap. They knocked him down with half a brick and proceeded to beat him to death. Farmer watched appalled. Then the sound of more aircraft engines approaching from the south dragged his eyes away from the scene to the river.[14]

Within a few minutes of the first bombing five Chinese bombers came droning down the Whangpoo between The Bund and Pootung towards the *Idzumo*. Every Japanese ship on the river threw up an ear-splitting barrage of anti-aircraft fire. The bomber crews had been trained to drop their bombs at a fixed air speed from a height of 620 metres. According to Claire Chennault, bad weather forced the pilots to attack at a lower altitude, which put the planes into a shallow dive that increased their air speed. Tragically, the pilots neglected to adjust their bomb sights for the new conditions.

Five bombs were dropped. All missed their target and two plunged towards the Palace and Cathay hotels. 'I watched both bombs skim 50 feet overhead,' Farmer said. 'One disappeared into Nanking Road. Then the roof of the Palace Hotel erupted.'

Farmer was showered with debris. He ran downstairs. On the corner of The Bund and Nanking Road, a decapitated Sikh policeman lay with his arms outstretched as though resisting the traffic. People were burning to death in blazing motor vehicles.[15]

The blue clothing of hundreds of coolies turned red with blood. Refugees lay in grotesque heaps in doorways. 'The sticky-sweet stench of blood hung in my nostrils until I could taste it,' Farmer said. The young West Australian walked up the left-hand side of Nanking Road counting the dead. Across the tramline sprawled the body of a tall European man, his white flannel suit unmarked, so neatly had his head been separated from his torso. The body count had reached 200 when the Australian heard his name. 'Come and have a drink, Farmer,' shouted his news editor Percy Finch, 'before they mistake you for a corpse.'

Late that night Emily Hahn made it home to discover that more than 1200 Chinese and 26 foreigners had been killed in Shanghai's 'Bloody Saturday', including an Australian-born American barmaid known to Shanghai drinkers simply as 'Dodo Dynamite'. She was one of several people killed in the entrance of the Palace Hotel.[16]

Probably the most remarkable escape of all was that of 28-year-old Australian nurse Elsie Farrell. Miss Farrell had just left the Palace Hotel through that same entrance and was about to take a lift in a rickshaw to her home in Frenchtown when Montagu Smith, the British manager of ICI, offered her a lift in his car. As they drove along Tibet Road, the car was suddenly engulfed in 'a dark grey haze'.[17]

'The next thing I knew,' Miss Farrell says, 'I was scrambling over a pile of bodies. I could not see because of blood pouring down my face. I put up my hand to feel my eyes. When I found they were there, I felt so happy I couldn't think of the poor wretches over whom I was stumbling. All I had in mind was to get away.'

She was taken to the French Hospital where it was discovered she had a piece of shrapnel embedded in her head. As the hospital was packed with wounded and there would be a long delay before she could be treated, she took a rickshaw to the Country Hospital in Great Western Road where she worked.

Gordon Bowden visited her there in his capacity as an officer of the Australia and New Zealand Society and found her 'comfortable and cheerful'.[18] Montagu Smith had lost an eye and one of his arms but survived.

'Nobody deplores more than we the terribly tragic accidental bombing by two damaged Northrop planes,' Mayling Chiang said in a statement from Nanking.

> It is officially confirmed that both pilots were wounded and that [anti-aircraft shots] damaged the bomb racks, which caused the bombs to break loose. Both wounded pilots are in Shanghai hospitals. It is incredible that the belief exists in some places that China deliberately bombed the International Settlement. What for?[19]

On 17 August the first contingent of 800 British women and children was evacuated from Shanghai. 'The ship taking us to Hong Kong dropped anchor at the mouth of the Yangtze River out of sight of the combatants and we were rushed down the river in a British destroyer,' Stephanie Sherwood, Roy Fernandez's daughter, says. 'It was quite frightening to hear the shelling over the ship. Everyone knew that we could be hit at any time.'[20]

American civilians were also ordered to evacuate. Carl Crow, who had retired from newspapers to launch a successful advertising agency, was evacuated to Manila with his wife Helen in the Dollar Line steamship SS *President Hoover*. After 36 years' hard work in China, he left with just one suitcase and his new camel-hair overcoat. 'Leaving the servants was the most difficult problem we had to face,' he wrote, 'for, in Chinese style, we had been adopted by them and were members of their family.'[21]

The evacuees included a group of American tourists, one of whose members had been killed in the Palace Hotel, many nightclub entertainers – tap dancers, crooners and minstrels, and two Filipino orchestras – and 'a surprisingly large number of American prostitutes'.[22]

Alan Raymond also chose this moment to quit the city. He would later claim the war had destroyed his marble business but it seems likely that pressure from his creditors played a hand in his departure. Raymond moved to Hong Kong and got a job on one of the local newspapers as a journalist. He also became a jockey and trainer, but his racing career ended abruptly when he was expelled from the Hong Kong Jockey Club over 'an incident connected with the running of a pony at the Macao Races'.[23]

Hallett Abend was in North China and missed Bloody Saturday. When he returned to Shanghai on 18 August, he found himself cut off from his flat and the *New York Times* office, both of which were on the sixteenth floor of Broadway Mansions in Hongkew. He and his assistant Anthony Billingham, a 35-year-old former US Marine, moved into a hotel near The Bund.

Late on the morning of 23 August the two Americans went shopping for new clothes and other essential items in Nanking Road. Abend was parked outside the Wing On department store while Billingham bought the last item on their list, a pair of binoculars in order to watch the fighting close-up. Big Bertie, the clock at the Shanghai Race Club building 50 metres away, had just struck one when he noticed Chinese pedestrians gazing skywards at the silvery shape of an aircraft. Moments later, a bomb exploded in Nanking Road. It blew in the side of the Sincere department store and sent thousands of metal fragments crashing through the windows of the Wing On.[24]

Abend stepped over the bodies of the dead and dying and entered the department store to look for Billingham. The electrical circuits had fused and in the semi-darkness the orderly department store had been turned into a charnel house of human limbs and headless bodies. 'Chinese shop girls lay on one side of the wrecked silk counters and customers were piled on the other,' Buzz Farmer later wrote. 'Toys from a burst window covered one big heap of mangled people.'[25]

Billingham had been seriously injured and was bleeding profusely. Abend found him but then lost him in the crush.

Dr Bill O'Hara, the Gallipoli veteran, was in his surgery on the fifth floor of the China United Building, three blocks from the blast. He dashed to the scene with his medical bag and treated some of the injured and then drove in his car to the Country Hospital to offer his assistance to the overstretched medical staff. The bomb had killed 612 people and wounded 482. While he was there, Hallett Abend arrived looking for Billingham. He found him being unloaded from an ambulance. O'Hara checked Billingham's injuries and operated immediately. It was after 4 pm when he emerged from the theatre. Abend was still waiting for news of his assistant's condition. 'You look pretty badly shaken up,' the Australian said. 'You need a double jolt of brandy and so do I.'

They drove to the British Country Club in Bubbling Well Road. When Abend stepped out of the car, O'Hara asked, 'Why are you limping?' Abend was so shell-shocked he was unaware he had a large piece of glass imbedded in his right foot and a shrapnel wound at the back of his neck.[26]

Three days later Sir Hughe Knatchbull-Hugessen was badly wounded on the Nanking–Shanghai road when a Japanese fighter pilot machine-gunned his Armstrong-Siddeley sedan, despite the large Union Jack marking on its roof. Tokyo blamed 'outrageous Chinese soldiery' for the attack and denied any Japanese aircraft were anywhere near the scene.

Minutes later, on the same road, the open-top tourer carrying Madame Chiang Kai-shek and Bill Donald from their Nanking base on a morale-boosting mission to the besieged city crashed into a bomb crater. Madame Chiang was thrown over the

Australian's head and knocked unconscious. As she lay on the road, Donald recited a couplet over her prone figure:

> *She flies through the air with the greatest of ease*
> *This daring young woman who fights Japanese.*[27]

Mayling had broken a rib in the accident. 'It hurts to breathe,' she gasped. 'Then don't breathe,' Donald growled (but said to himself, 'She's broken a rib'). Mayling carried on bravely with her visit to wounded Chinese soldiers in Shanghai hospitals and returned to Nanking in the morning. 'Why were you so cruel out at the wreck?' she asked Donald. The Australian smiled. 'Because,' he said, 'once you let a woman lie down and think she's hurt, she never gets up.'[28]

Every day the Japanese increased the pressure on Chiang Kai-shek's battered legions. Japanese shells from Chapei screamed over the foreign concessions on a five-kilometre arc to explode in Nantao where 20,000 Chinese troops were holding out. Japanese destroyers moved up and down the Whangpoo like mobile artillery batteries, indiscriminately pounding civilian and military targets in the Chinese districts.[29]

Donald claimed the Japanese had made a serious blunder in believing that the Chinese Government would follow precedent and seek peace on any terms in the face of Japan's mechanised units and terror bombing. 'The situation is that because China refused to comply, the Japanese have suffered grave loss of prestige,' he wrote from Nanking in his old newspaper, *The Argus.*[30]

In Chapei, a so-called 'Doomed Battalion' of 500 Chinese troops held the Continental Bank godown on the north bank of Soochow Creek, sheltering behind sacks of rice as the building was torn to shreds by Japanese machine-gunners. One night a brave girl guide swam the creek to present the troops with a Nationalist flag, which flew defiantly from the top of the building.[31]

Eleanor Hinder had taken on the additional task of supplying rice to destitute Chinese families. She kept in touch with Florence Rawlinson, who had returned to the United States following her husband's death. 'What a terrible tragic month it has been,' she wrote on 14 September.

> Yesterday the Chinese made a strategic retreat to their first line of defence taking themselves out of the area within sound and range of the navy's guns . . . They are of course still in Pootung and so we are not finished with the naval bombardment. Nor the air raids, nor the dropping of shells in the foreign areas.
>
> I am still at work trying to rescue food stocks and get them into circulation. We are alright for the present and the coastal ships have now opened up a trade and are bringing in some cargoes. The Council has imported rice – 7000 tons which it is holding as a reserve.
>
> My own work [as industrial secretary] will open up again very slowly. I have computed that 70% of the small-scale industry and 60% of the large-scale industry were in the Northern and Eastern districts, and these for the moment are all out of commission. What will be found to be intact when it is possible to return to these areas no one can tell. Even in the areas not occupied only about one-fourth of the workers in the cotton mills and less in the case of small industries are back at work. It will be many a long day before Shanghai recovers.[32]

Chapei blazed again. 'Hundreds of thousands of Chinese homes, shops and small factories were destroyed in that fearful holocaust,' Buzz Farmer wrote. 'It illuminated the roof of our world, as though the dome of hell had been lifted for a night.'

The arsonists were Chinese soldiers who had begun to implement a scorched earth policy on Chiang's orders to deny these properties to the Japanese.[33]

After a siege lasting four days, the survivors of the 'Doomed Battalion' made a fighting retreat over the Tibet Road Bridge to the International Settlement. The 377 men, women and children included seven smartly uniformed girls, who carried the battalion's standard, and a boy of 14 who had a wooden sword in one hand and a grenade in the other.

Three Welsh Fusiliers remained in the blockhouse beside the bridge under heavy fire all night to disarm the Chinese fighters and give first aid to the wounded. They reported that the Chinese rifles were still hot when they were handed over.[34]

Buzz Farmer watched the survivors march off to an internment camp. 'They looked as though a high wind would blow them away,' he wrote. 'A few carried oiled-paper umbrellas. One actually carried a canary in a cage. Many walked hand in hand. It seemed preposterous that these thin, tattered boys had held up the conquest of Chapei for four days.'[35]

Apart from the streets of the foreign concessions, the only safe place for refugees was the 'Jacquinot Zone', a patch of ground between Frenchtown and Nantao, which the Japanese and Chinese armies promised to respect. It was named in honour of Father Jacquinot de Besange, a one-armed Jesuit priest who worked tirelessly to feed and clothe thousands of Chinese families who packed into the safety zone's makeshift shelters.[36]

Harold Timperley was instrumental in setting up the safety zone and organised medical aid for hundreds of apprentices who worked without pay in Shanghai's sweatshops, some of whom had been locked in by factory owners to prevent them running away. He urged Westerners to help refugees who were sleeping in alleyways of the settlement 'with only a thin ragged cotton blanket as protection'.[37]

Timperley watched boy scouts and rickshaw pullers carry the wounded to hospital where the volunteer nursing staff included taxi dancers. 'A large section of the population has been thrown out of employment,' he wrote in the *Guardian*, 'many farmers have been prevented from planting or harvesting their crops, thousands of businessmen have been ruined, officials, teachers and the like have suddenly been deprived of their livelihood.'[38]

Les Lawrance, the former Queensland speedway star, spent three weeks besieged in the telephone exchange while it was peppered with bullets by both sides. Bill O'Hara was made homeless when the Japanese destroyed his lovely house 'for military reasons'. The very heart was being ripped out of Old Shanghai, leaving the foreign concessions as small, over-crowded oases in the middle of a vast wilderness.[39]

When the fighting started, Rewi Alley had been in London on long leave. He returned to find his house in Hongkew had been looted. His two adopted sons, Alan and Mike, now teenagers, informed him they wanted to join the Red Army to fight the Japanese. The youths had been in Nanking Road on Bloody Saturday and Alan was slightly wounded by flying shrapnel. Alley gave them permission to make the long, dangerous journey to Yenan like thousands of other volunteers to join Mao Tse-tung's forces 'for that was what I would have done'.[40]

From the rooftops of the International Settlement, Alley and his American friend Edgar Snow, who was covering the Battle of Shanghai for the London *Daily Herald*, watched the Japanese Army dismantling and burning the factories, mills and work-shops of Pootung. He estimated that 600,000 displaced Chinese workers were dying in the city's freezing streets at the rate of 10,000 a month. The price of a dance ticket and drinks at one of the big hotels, he noted sourly, could have saved the lives of a dozen men.[41]

By November, the Japanese had broken out of Shanghai into open country and were advancing rapidly up the Yangtze Valley to converge on Nanking.[42] At 44, Claire Chennault had never flown a combat mission himself (an omission he was about to rectify) but he was a master tactician. Promoted to colonel by Mayling Soong, the Texan taught Chinese fighter pilots how to intercept unescorted Japanese bombers. They were so successful in shooting them down that the Japanese abandoned unescorted daylight bombing. The Chinese then shot down night bombers as well – seven out of 13 in one night – but the Japanese were fast learners. By September, they were escorting their bombers with strong fighter groups, which inflicted heavy losses on the Chinese.

Bill Donald watched the dogfights from his house in parkland east of the city. He churned out a constant stream of news stories about the Battle for Nanking on his Hermes Baby typewriter or dictated letters to a Chinese stenographer. His letters carried the letterhead 'HEADQUARTERS OF THE GENERALISSIMO' and sometimes ran to 20 or 30 pages. His stories were cabled to many newspapers, including *The Argus* and the *Sydney Morning Herald*.

'Eighteen Japanese bombers and pursuit planes arrived among the clouds over Nanking at 11 o'clock this evening,' he wrote to both papers in late September.

> With glasses, I counted them streaming in pairs, the steady droning of their engines suddenly punctuated by anti-aircraft detonations. While the American Ambassador and his staff fled, the British and French have refused to budge. The British Embassy staff took refuge in separate dugouts in order to avoid the possibility of one bomb killing them all. The dugout of Mr R. G. Howe, the British *chargé d'affaires*, was named 'Journey's End'.[43]

Back in Shanghai at 11 am on 3 December, the Japanese exercised their right as a partner in the city's municipal government to stage a victory march through the International Settlement. Starting at Jessfield Park on the western outskirts, 3000 troops in well-worn field kit marched three abreast down Avenue

Edward VII between the settlement and the French Concession, up Tibet Road and into Nanking Road.[44]

'Dozens of *ronin* and Japanese civilians invaded the settlement from Hongkew,' Buzz Farmer wrote. 'They were madly
excited. They carried little paper flags. They pushed to the fore-
front through throngs of sullen, silent Chinese.'[45]

Outside the Sun Sun department store a Chinese man
threw a grenade which slightly wounded two Japanese soldiers,
one Japanese civilian and a British police officer. The officer
actually pushed a Japanese spectator away and stood between
him and the bomb, thus protecting him from flying fragments. The Japanese column immediately halted and the troops
deployed in case of further trouble. A Chinese policeman shot
the grenade-thrower dead and the column then moved along
The Bund and crossed Garden Bridge into Hongkew.

However, a group of Japanese soldiers who had stayed behind
threw a barbed-wire barricade across Nanking Road at the Sun
Sun store and subjected Chinese pedestrians to brutal interrogation. They withdrew at 9 pm after a conference between the
Municipal Police Commissioner Frederick W. Gerrard and a
representative of Lieutenant-General Iwane Matsui, commander-
in-chief of Japanese forces in the Central China Area.

The West Australian friends Colin McDonald of *The Times*
and Harold Timperley of the *Guardian* travelled up the Yangtze
to report on the battle. As the Chinese Army withdrew towards
the Nationalist capital, they again applied Chiang Kai-shek's
rigorous scorched earth policy to whole towns and villages.
Foreign military observers in Nanking were amazed by the
extent of the Chinese destruction, most of which served no
military purpose except to force the Japanese invaders to sleep
in tents instead of buildings.

The fighting now constituted a direct threat to British interests north of the Yangtze Valley. Britain was a signatory to the
Nine-Power Treaty that guaranteed China's sovereignty but
the British foreign secretary, Sir John Simon, refused to take

any action to stop the Japanese advance. Neville Chamberlain, now prime minister, told his cabinet he 'could not imagine anything more suicidal than to pick a quarrel with Japan at the present moment when the European situation had become so serious'.[46]

The West continued to sell weapons to both sides in the undeclared war. American and Australian scrap iron used in the production of weapons-grade steel flowed into Japanese foundries. Robert Menzies, Australia's attorney-general and deputy leader of the United Australia Party, was branded 'Pig Iron Bob' by Australian unionists for breaking a strike of workers opposed to the export trade with Japan.

'The Chinese are grateful to the Australian wharf labourers who refused to load pig-iron at Port Kembla,' Bill Donald wrote to a friend. 'Their gratitude goes, too, to all those in America and Great Britain who boycott Japanese products and protest against Japanese inhumanities.'

At dawn on 7 December Chiang Kai-chek, Mayling Chiang and Bill Donald flew from Nanking to Hankow, the new capital, in Chiang's fast American-made Beechcraft plane. Before he left the doomed city, Donald handed the keys of his European sports car to his friend George Fitch, an American missionary who was staying behind as director of the Safety Zone, an area which the Japanese had agreed through their embassy in Peking to leave untouched.

Since arriving in Nanking on 8 November James McHugh, now a captain and assistant naval attaché at the American Embassy, had visited Donald every day at his residence to keep abreast of developments for his intelligence reports to the US ambassador, Nelson T. Johnson. 'I have been regaled ever since my arrival in Nanking with stories of how the American aviation salesmen swindled China and brought about the collapse of the Chinese Air Force at the beginning of the present war,' he wrote to Johnson.

W. D. Pawley [president and sole shareholder of the Inter-continent Aircraft Corporation of Miami, Florida] came in for the lion's share of the blame because he had done the most business. Donald, in relating some of the details, once remarked that when he and Madame Chiang had taken over administration of the air force and had begun to trace some of the deals and the 'squeeze' which had been paid to various members of the Aviation Commission, they found that the trail led to the doors of the Central Trust, special purchasing division of the Ministry of Finance; that at this point Madame had gone to the Generalissimo and asked if he wanted the investigation to continue; and that he had emphatically approved that it should. When I inquired why they did not take action against those people who received the 'squeeze', I was told that everyone in the air force was guilty and that they needed their services to fight the war.[47]

Thanks to Donald, McHugh was able to spend time with Mayling, describing himself in one intelligence report as 'the only foreigner not in the employ of the Government with this entrée'. She offered him a lift to Hankow in her big American Buick, which was transporting members of the Moral Endeavour Association who handled many of her personal affairs.[48]

'If the Japanese continue their present rate of advance they will soon be at the gates of Nanking,' Colin McDonald wrote in a dispatch to The Times on the day the Nationalist government abandoned the city.[49] While Timperley remained in Nanking, McDonald boarded the United States gunboat Panay to accompany diplomats and civilians who were being evacuated upstream. These included George Atcheson Jr, second secretary in charge of the United States Embassy at Nanking, and A. L. Patterson, the dodgy aviation middleman.

McDonald, a shy, retiring man, was born at Cottesloe in 1899 to John and Florence McDonald. His father and L. R. Menzies had discovered the Menzies goldfields north of Kalgoorlie in 1894. At 12, Colin was sent to Daniel Stewart's College, Edinburgh, and began reporting for *The Scotsman* while still a pupil there.[50]

At 17, he returned to Perth and worked as a court reporter on *The West Australian*. In 1920, he moved to the *China Mail* in Hong Kong and then the *South China Morning Post*. He moved to Peking in 1931 and worked as a freelance reporter for *The Times* and other clients for six years before being appointed *Times* staff correspondent, the first since David Fraser. He travelled to London in 1937 to marry his Perth sweetheart Phyllis Margaret Allum, daughter of the superintendent of the Perth Mint, then returned to Peking with his bride after visiting relatives in Australia.

At 11 am on Sunday 12 December, McDonald was on board the *Panay* when she dropped anchor on a broad stretch of the Yangtze 45 kilometres above Nanking. On the way upriver she had been constantly shelled from the shore but was so far undamaged. As she was flying the Stars and Stripes and had two newly painted American flags on her top deck, nobody paid much attention when several aircraft appeared high overhead an hour and a half later. The weather was clear and sunny and the planes were identified as Japanese. 'The first bomb, dropped at 1.38 pm, struck the main gun on the forward deck, snapped the mast in half, wrecked the bridge, and put the wireless out of action in the middle of a message,' McDonald later wrote. 'The force of the explosion broke the captain's leg and blackened his face with powder.'[51]

McDonald was typing a dispatch in a makeshift pressroom, which had been set up in the sick bay. He dashed on deck and saw a red roundel like a large blood spot on the wings of the attacking planes as they launched 'a deliberate and systematic attempt to destroy the gunboat and all on board'.

The *Panay*'s machine-gunners fought back. 'I had a vivid picture of American sailors, stripped to the waist, grimly firing on the oncoming aeroplanes,' McDonald wrote. 'The chief boatswain's mate, who was bathing when the bombing began, was out on deck naked directing the fire and afterwards manning the gun himself.'

Eric Mayell of British Movietone News filmed the attacks in which three American sailors were killed and 50 wounded. The gunboat was holed in several places and was settling on the riverbed by the starboard bow when the order to abandon ship was given at five past two. The 54 survivors packed into lifeboats and landed on a mudflat on the riverbank. Through the reeds, they watched the Japanese planes return to bomb two Standard Oil barges on the river. One of the survivors was an American diplomat. He recalled Colin McDonald as 'a slight, gentle, thinnish fellow with spectacles' who went without food and sleep, was one of the last to leave the ship and who offered to lie on a wounded man ashore to protect him from machine-gun bullets. McDonald also used his knowledge of Chinese to obtain help from local villagers. The survivors were finally rescued by the British gunboat HMS *Ladybird* and the *Panay's* sister ship USS *Oahu* on 15 December and taken to Nanking and thence to Shanghai.

The Japanese Government regretted the '*Panay* incident', offered its apologies, promised to punish the transgressors and paid an indemnity. President Franklin D. Roosevelt had no intention of going to war with Japan and saw to it that the faces of Japanese pilots, clearly visible in newsreel footage, were excised before transmission in the United States, rather than contradict the Japanese version that the pilots had been too far away to recognise the American flags.

McDonald later testified to the United States naval committee that he thought the attack was a deliberate act of aggression designed to test the extent of American support for China. He was one of the few non-American, non-military recipients of America's highest award for bravery, the United States Congressional Medal of Honor.

In the meantime, Nanking had fallen to the Japanese on 13 December. Harold Timperley had begged Britain to protest, hoping that a strong line would deter the Japanese from its usual practice of slaughtering Chinese males of military age. But most British diplomats in Nanking had gone on summer holiday despite the growing crisis and Timperley accused the staff of 'criminal negligence'.[52]

Timperley, McDonald and Tillman Durdin of the *New York Times* alerted the world to the Rape of Nanking in which up to 300,000 Chinese men, women and children were butchered. Timperley's main sources were Percy Fitch, John Rabe and Miner Searle Bates, all members of the International Committee. This small group of foreigners witnessed many of the atrocities, including the rape and murder of Chinese women of all ages.

'On Tuesday [14 December] the Japanese began a systematic searching out of anyone even remotely connected with the Chinese Army,' Colin McDonald wrote in *The Times*.

> They took suspects from the refugee camps and trapped many soldiers wandering in the streets. Soldiers who would willingly have surrendered were shot down as an example. No mercy was shown. The hope of the populace gave place to fear and a reign of terror.[53]

Shops were looted. Nurses at the American University Hospital were robbed. Young men were assembled in groups for execution. Babies were thrown in the air and impaled on bayonets. The streets were littered with bodies, including those of harmless old men. The atrocities were at their height when McDonald passed through the city the following day. They would go on for six weeks and include thousands of rapes and murders, leading to theories that the Japanese high command intended to terrorise the Chinese into submission.

'Unfortunately,' *The Times* lamented, 'the Japanese Government has virtually no control over the fighting services, and the fighting services in their turn are powerless – and often reluctant – to control the ebullience of junior officers. Add to this a low standard of education among the officers; a fanatical patriotism fired by the intoxication of conquest; and the effects of propaganda directed against this country and (to a less extent) against the white races in general. It will readily be grasped how precarious is the self-control of a military machine thus composed and directed.'[54]

As well as wholesale rape and murder, the Japanese Army had also gone into business in opposition to the Green Gang. On the outskirts of Shanghai, Japanese officers were receiving $500 per day from each of 300 gambling houses, which also sold opium and were connected to brothels. 'The whole Japanese Army is incurably honeycombed with criminal tendencies,' Bill Donald wrote angrily to his friend Kenneth Cantlie in England. 'Officers and men are money-minded like the pirates of old, and no method of accumulating wealth is too mean or too despicable.'[55]

By the end of 1937, the Chinese Air Force had virtually been destroyed. Garnet Malley and Claire Chennault put together an International Air Corps consisting of 86 European pilots, including two Australians and one New Zealander. Many of the mercenaries flew twin-engined Glenn Martin bombers under the command of American veteran Colonel Vincent Schmidt. The men were paid US$500 a month plus bonuses and operated effectively until the Glenn Martins were caught on the ground during a Japanese air raid and most of them were destroyed.

One of the Australians, John Whitehead of Sydney, was shot down when his bomber ran into a flight of Japanese fighters south-east of Hankow. His rear gunner was shot through the head and the plane riddled with bullets. Whitehead bailed out and was shot through the spine as he parachuted down.

'They would have made me look like a sieve if I hadn't gone limp and pretended to be dead,' he said. Mayling Soong visited him in hospital and arranged for him to be flown to Hong Kong for specialist treatment.[56]

Just after Christmas, Shanghai Municipal Police handed a Chinese patriot who hurled a grenade into a boat full of Japanese troops on Soochow Creek over to the Japanese military authorities. The prisoner admitted he belonged to the 'Dare or Die' corps of Chinese soldiers pledged to terrorise Japanese forces in Shanghai. His fate can only be imagined.

PART IV (1938–1949)

Chains

'Donald is a red-faced, serious man, with an Australian accent and a large, sensible nose – a pleasant surprise; for most of our informants had led us to expect an oily, iron-grey, evangelical figure, with a highly developed manner.'

CHRISTOPHER ISHERWOOD ON MEETING W. H. DONALD
IN CHINA, 1938

CHAPTER 20

Celestial Twilight

By the New Year, Shanghai had reached the tipping point. Although members of the Shanghai Club and the Cercle Sportif Francais (to give the French Club its proper title) would take some time to realise it, the glory days under the colonial powers had passed forever. Gypsy violinists still played at Joe Farran's, the White Russian taxi dancers at Del Monte still charged 20 cents a dance, Americans still drank their sodas at the Chocolate Shop in Nanking Road and Sid's Syncopators still tootled at the tea dance in the ballroom of the Cathay Hotel; but the old magic had evaporated in the sulphurous air.

John Keswick, younger brother of the Jardines *taipan* Tony Keswick, acknowledged that times were changing. He served in the Shanghai Volunteers and raised money for refugee relief, 'but otherwise we worked in our offices, played tennis and polo, and danced and dined at night, an exciting, rather unreal life'.[1]

The Japanese moved quickly and skilfully to consolidate their victory. Apart from isolated pockets of resistance, they now controlled the Chinese Municipality of Greater Shanghai. Chapei, Nantao, Yangtzepoo and Pootung, which had all suffered huge damage, would later be included in a collaborationist regime under Wang Ching-wei. Much of Hongkew had virtually been wiped off the map. Over the next three years, 18,000 German Jews and 4000 Polish Jews were allowed to settle in 'Little Tokyo' as part of a Japanese program of urban regeneration. The sight of Hitler's allies helping stateless Jewish refugees to find a new home added a surreal dimension to the Shanghai panorama.[2]

Despite protests from the British Foreign Office and the newly knighted inspector-general, Sir Frederick Maze, all customs revenues held in the Hong Kong & Shanghai Bank were transferred to the Yokohama Specie Bank.[3] The Japanese Consulate also insisted that the number of Japanese in the Municipal Police Force be increased, that Japanese applicants be given senior administrative posts in the council; and that the overall number of Japanese in council employment be enlarged.[4]

Each of these measures was designed to increase Japan's stranglehold on the British sector of the divided International Settlement. At crossing points, Japanese sentries were given free rein to humiliate Westerners. Face-slapping became a hazard for Chinese and Europeans alike. Emily Hahn reported the case of an Englishwoman who crossed Garden Bridge on what was, according to new, unannounced Japanese rules, the wrong side.

'The sentry shook her arm, hustled her across to her proper place, and slapped her face,' she wrote in the New Yorker. 'She reported it to the British Consulate. They made representations. Next day she prudently went down to another bridge to do her crossing and all unwittingly walked through a gap reserved, for no particular reason, for rickshaw coolies. She was again slapped, and again she reported the incident to the British Consulate. They made representations . . .'[5]

Alfred Turner had joined the Municipal Police in 1937 as a 21-year-old probationary sergeant. At 3 pm on 6 January 1938 he complained to a Japanese constable about the rough handling of some Chinese hawkers who wished to pass into the British sector at the Brenan Road crossing. The Japanese constable punched Turner on the nose and shouted, 'It's none of your damned business!' Several Japanese soldiers then dashed across the boundary line and dragged Sergeant Turner into occupied territory, threw him to the ground and beat him.[6]

When Inspector Frederick West was informed that the Japanese were holding one of his men, he drove to the crossing and ordered his release. Instead, West was also grabbed and savagely beaten. The two British policemen were freed only when a senior Japanese police officer arrived at the scene and restored order. Once again the British consul Herbert Phillips made representations . . .[7]

Harold Timperley and Colin McDonald returned to Shanghai where Timperley wrote a new account of the Nanking atrocities and filed it to the *Guardian* at one of the settlement's three cable offices at 8 pm on Thursday 16 January. The Japanese had installed censors in each office to suppress critical news dispatches and at 10.45 the following morning he learned his story had been stopped and that his presence was requested at Japanese military headquarters.

The Japanese, however, sent a copy of Timperley's cable to the Japanese Foreign Office in Tokyo, which radioed a truncated form of the message in the Japanese diplomatic code to their foreign embassies. This was intercepted by an American listening station and sent to Washington for deciphering. The telegram read:

Since return [to] Shanghai [a] few days ago I investigated reported atrocities committed by Japanese Army in Nanking and elsewhere. Verbal accounts [of] reliable eye-witnesses and letters from individuals whose credibility [is] beyond question afford convincing proof [that] Japanese Army behaved and [is] continuing [to] behave in [a] fashion reminiscent [of] Attila [and] his Huns. Not less than three hundred thousand Chinese civilians slaughtered, many cases [in] cold blood.[8] Robbery, rape, including children [of] tender years, an insensate brutality towards civilians continues [to] be reported from areas where actual hostilities ceased weeks ago. Deep shame which better type [of] Japanese civilian here feel – reprehensible conduct [of] Japanese troops elsewhere heightened by series [of] local incidents where Japanese soldiers run amock [in] Shanghai itself. Today North China Daily News reports [a] particularly revolting case where [a] drunken Japanese soldier, unable [to] obtain women and drink he demanded, shot [and] killed three Chinese women over sixty and wounded several other harmless civilians.[9]

The Americans kept Timperley's message secret – disclosure would have revealed that the United States had broken the Japanese diplomatic code. Timperley protested to the British consul Herbert Phillips about the attempt to muzzle him. He refused to report to Japanese military headquarters and filed two further stories on Nanking, which were also suppressed. Phillips made representations . . .

Then in April Timperley left Shanghai for London to publish a book entitled *What War Means: The Japanese Terror in China*, containing graphic testimony on the Rape of Nanking. The book had been written, he explained in the preface, because of the suppression of his *Guardian* stories 'by the censors installed by the Japanese authorities in the foreign cable offices at Shanghai'. Japanese claims that the reports were 'grossly exaggerated' had spurred him to find documentary proof to confirm his information. He had had 'no difficulty in discovering a wealth of corroborative evidence from unimpeachable sources'.

He also smuggled a cine-film out of China showing scenes of Nanking before, during and after the Japanese occupation and including the first filmed shots of the Japanese atrocities to reach the West.

Upriver in Hankow, the American attaché Jimmy McHugh resumed his daily conversations with Bill Donald in Donald's large, ramshackle flat on The Bund. Donald was now 63 and his nerves were as frayed as anyone's over the Japanese bombing and the constant military setbacks. As a release from the ever-present tension, he talked to McHugh about the past.

'It slowly dawned upon me that he expected me to accept as master to pupil, without argument or question, his version of events in China,' McHugh noted in an intelligence report dated 20 January 1938.

> In fact he irritably rebuked me on more than one occasion when I attempted to cross-question him or suggest that any conditions other than those which he was describing might exist. I therefore gradually assumed the role of meek listener.[10]

One of Donald's main concerns was a Soong family feud which had simmered in the background ever since H. H. Kung had replaced his brother-in-law T. V. Soong at the Ministry of Finance four years earlier. T. V. was currently governor of the Bank of China in Hong Kong but Ayling and Mayling wanted to find a solution which would enable him to rejoin the government without bringing the whole edifice crashing down.

Mayling was the channel for several offers from the Generalissimo to T. V., who not only rejected them but made his loathing of Chiang and Kung abundantly clear. Pleading ill-health and the need for a rest, Mayling flew to Hong Kong on 11 January to try to break the deadlock. As usual, Donald was at her side but she had taken a fancy to Jimmy McHugh and invited him to accompany them. 'She is undoubtedly a woman of outstanding ability and personality,' McHugh wrote to his ambassador.

> She radiates it, in fact, and hardly ever fails to captivate those who meet her. She is thoroughly feminine and makes full use

of those attributes. She impresses one as being more Western than Chinese in her mental processes. She speaks English perfectly in a pleasing, well-modulated tone of voice which never fails to attract attention. She always presents an attractive, well-groomed appearance and, although by no means a beautiful woman, her eyes have a lustrous, appealing quality which at once command attention and leave the impression of having been in the presence of a lovely creature. I believe she married her husband purely for position and that she has been a deciding factor in his subsequent rise.[11]

The family feud erupted almost as soon as Mayling's plane touched down in Hong Kong. Ayling, Chingling, T. V. and another brother T. L. Soong were all there, as well as one of Ayling's sons, David Kung, who was driving around in a Cadillac. Mayling, Ayling and T. L. all supported Chiang Kai-shek and were therefore working towards a rapprochement, whereas Chingling's devotion to the Communist cause made her anti-Chiang and therefore a natural ally of T. V.

Donald's position was difficult: he was aware of the allegations against the Kung faction regarding 'squeeze' from American aviation salesmen but his loyalty to Mayling put him firmly in that camp, despite what Jimmy McHugh described as his 'frantic but rather futile efforts' to stamp out corruption. Furthermore, he had once jokingly suggested to T. V. that the young man should make himself dictator of China and had been appalled when he later raised the subject with him in all seriousness. Since then, Donald had 'lost no opportunity to stress both to Madame Chiang and the Generalissimo that Soong was ambitious, unscrupulous, selfish and domineering'.[12]

McHugh found himself the 'unwitting confident [sic] of parties on both sides'. Two days after he arrived, T. V. Soong told him that Dr Kung was trying to have him dismissed as head of the Bank of China. He had turned down other government posts, he said, because he did not want to become 'tainted' by working with him. Chiang had written him a very bitter letter for declining to rejoin his government and Soong's attitude towards him remained one of contempt, bitterness and aloofness. Soong also denounced the 'venality' of the Ministry of Finance. 'They are spending the reserves which I built up, without any regard for the future,' he said. 'All they think of is lining their own pockets and after that they don't care.'

'The present dissension is an advanced stage of a struggle for the control of China which has existed for several years between Mr Soong and Generalissimo Chiang Kai-shek,' McHugh wrote in his report of the conversation.

> The question of the moment concerns the terms under which Mr Soong might agree to make peace with his family and accept a post in the Government thereby assuring a united front for continued resistance to Japan. The alternative thrown at him by his family is the cancellation of his last remaining governmental connection – his post as head of the Bank of China.[13]

McHugh then approached Cyril Rogers of the Bank of England who had come to China in 1935 with Sir Frederick Leith-Ross, the British Government's chief economic adviser, to initiate banking and currency reforms. Over dinner, Rogers described Ayling Soong as a 'modern Borgia'. He warned there would be serious repercussions on the stability of China's finances and credit status abroad if T. V. Soong were dismissed. Moreover, Rogers would sever his connections with the Nationalists and return to London, thereby withdrawing Britain's direct financial support to China.

'I have reason to believe,' McHugh wrote, 'that the state of China's credit abroad has been seriously misrepresented to Chiang Kai-shek by Dr Kung in connection with the latter's recent elevation to the post of President of the Executive Yuan [effectively making him premier of China].' There was deep unrest over the conduct of the war and great dissatisfaction over Chiang's failure to sweep away a large group of corrupt politicians and militarists and replace them with more reputable figures.

Shortly after McHugh's meeting with Rogers, Donald exploded angrily when an article appeared in the Hong Kong press announcing Mayling's presence in the colony. 'She apparently arrived on Tuesday by air with General Chiang's Australian adviser, Mr W. H. Donald, and other officials,' *The Times* correspondent reported from the colony. 'Additional interest is lent to her visit by the presence of several other notables, including her brothers, Mr T. V. Soong and Mr T. L. Soong; her sisters, Mme H. H. Kung and Mme Sun Yat-sen. Rumours that Mme Chiang is here for important conferences are denied in trustworthy quarters.'[14]

Donald blamed Jimmy McHugh's meddling in the Soong family's affairs for the leak, a charge the American hotly denied. However, he was getting too much sensational inside information about the workings of the Nationalist government to drop his central role in the drama, even at the risk of offending Donald. On the afternoon of the 18th, he saw T. V. Soong again. 'Their whole organisation is rotten and about to fall apart,' Soong confided. 'The time will come, and very soon, when they will have to come to me on bended knee and ask me to save them.'

McHugh suggested that Chiang Kai-shek had become a symbol of Chinese resistance to the Japanese. 'That is just the impression which Donald works to create,' Soong replied. 'Actually, [Chiang] is a second-rate militarist and possesses a medieval mind. China can never make real progress while he is in control.'

Regarding corruption, McHugh added in his report that Donald had complained to him many times that he and Mayling had pressed Chiang to shoot corrupt members of his government but he refused to do so. T. V. Soong also claimed that Dr Kung was 'a mere figurehead and puppet in the hands of his wife and the Generalissimo'. Having been one of the wealthiest men in China before joining the government, Kung had been the target for an added measure of criticism over Ayling's activities and his own ministry. He was, admittedly, a sick man, suffering from heart trouble.

Nothing was resolved at any of the meetings and Mayling, Donald and McHugh flew back to Hankow on 19 February. Mayling complained bitterly that people believed the reason China was losing the war was because it had a 'petticoat government'. Even the fact that the railways were congested was blamed on the inefficiency of her Aviation Commission.

On Donald's advice, Mayling resigned as chief of the Chinese Air Force, citing the injuries she had suffered in the car accident on the road from Shanghai to Nanking in August the previous year. Nothing must be allowed to diminish her aura in the eyes of the world. 'Donald often claims that his sense of humour is the only thing that has permitted him to survive all of these years in China and until recent months I know him to have been a remarkably cheery person,' McHugh noted. 'Of late, he has exhibited increasing signs of irritability and short temper. He possesses a blind faith in Madam Chiang Kai-shek. He has put up with the conditions in the belief that he can get Madam Chiang away from the influence of her family and set her up as the saviour of China.'

In late February the new British ambassador to China, Australian-born Archibald Clark Kerr, arrived in Hong Kong on his way to Shanghai. He intended spending several days there meeting diplomats and Chinese dignitaries. Soon after his arrival, however, he received a telegram from Bob Howe, the British *chargé d'affaires* who had been holding the fort since the attack on Sir Hughe Knatchbull-Hugessen. He informed Clark Kerr that the Japanese had displayed 'aggressive, intolerant disregard of the ordinary rules of international intercourse' towards the

British community in Shanghai. Morale had hit rock bottom and a firm hand was needed to rescue British prestige.[15] Clark Kerr cancelled his plans and hastened to Shanghai.

To make matters more difficult, Anthony Eden had resigned as foreign secretary on 20 February over the manner in which Prime Minister Neville Chamberlain's Government was appeasing Germany, Italy and Japan. His replacement was the lanky giant Lord Halifax, one of the arch appeasers who was liable to bend even further in the face of the Japanese typhoon.

The British Embassy was now located on the top floor of the Jardine Matheson building on The Bund, directly across the river from Pootung. Sir Archibald and Lady Clark Kerr moved into a well-appointed villa called 'Number One House' in Frenchtown, adjacent to the smoking ruins of Nantao.

Archie Clark Kerr was a robust, barrel-chested man, with extensive experience in the diplomatic gladiatorial ring. He had been born at his grandparents' house, 'Clovelly', at Watsons Bay, Sydney, on 17 March 1882 and christened Archibald John Kerr Clark. He added a final 'Kerr' to his name to make it appear he had been born at the Kerr family's Scottish seat. Indeed, he was so keen to appear Scottish that on joining the Foreign Service in 1906 he omitted any mention of his Australian origins in his entry in *Who's Who*.[16]

Lady Kerr, known as Tita, was the former Maria Theresa Diaz Salas, the beautiful blonde daughter of a Chilean millionaire. The couple had met in March 1929 while Clark Kerr was based in Santiago and had been married one month later when he was 47 and she just 18. Their marriage had survived the rigours of their previous posting – Iraq – but it would not survive China.

Around this time, a small dinner party was held at the home of John Alexander, a young secretary at the British Embassy, which would have a profound effect on Clark Kerr's term of office and on China's war effort. The guests were Emily Hahn, Ed Snow and his wife Helen Foster Snow, a.k.a. Nym Wales.

According to Emily Hahn's version, Alexander asked Ed Snow what he thought about the English co-operative movement. Snow had just written his classic work *Red Star over China* on the Chinese Communist Party after travelling to Yenan with the help of Rewi Alley to interview Mao Tse-tung and Chou En-lai. He confessed he knew nothing about co-operatives, so Alexander explained the concept to him.

Coincidentally, Rewi Alley had been thinking for some time about how his practical experience as a factory inspector might be used to advantage in the resistance movement. 'Now look here, Rewi,' Nym Wales told him a day or so after Alexander's dinner party, 'what China wants today is industry everywhere. Drop this job of making Shanghai a better place for the Japanese and get out and do something.'[17]

Alley wrote down his ideas for creating a chain of industrial co-operatives stretching thousands of kilometres inland and giving workers a stake in each enterprise. He gave the document to John Powell of the *China Weekly Review* to print as a pamphlet.

Meanwhile, the English novelist Christopher Isherwood arrived in China with his chum, the poet W. H. Auden, to write a travel book entitled *Journey to a War*. They spoke no Chinese, had little knowledge of Chinese affairs and described themselves as 'not real journalists but mere trippers'. Nevertheless, Isherwood would write a darkly humorous account of his observations and Auden would pen 27 insightful poems.[18]

On 9 March they called on Bill Donald in his flat on the Hankow Bund. Donald had a cold and was treating himself with a variety of medicinal remedies. Isherwood noted, 'Donald is a red-faced, serious man, with an Australian accent and a large, sensible nose – a pleasant surprise; for most of our informants had led us to expect an oily, iron-grey, evangelical figure, with a highly developed manner.'[19]

A few days later Donald wrapped himself in a voluminous fur coat with an astrakhan collar and took the visitors to meet

Mayling Soong Chiang at Wuchang, the all-Chinese city on the south bank of the Yangtze where the Generalissimo's standard flew in bold defiance of the Japanese and their Chinese collaborators. Isherwood noted that she was 'vivacious rather than pretty and possessed an almost terrifying charm and poise'. He was impressed with the fact that she sometimes signed death warrants in her own hand, but he was even more taken with her perfume, which he described as 'the most delicious either of us has ever smelt'.[20]

Unknown to Donald, the knives were out for him in Hong Kong. In April, Jimmy McHugh flew back to the colony to see the banker Cyril Rogers again. At this meeting Rogers revealed he had sent a memorandum to the Bank of England in which he described Donald as a megalomaniac and accused him of wrongly taking credit for the success of the Leith–Ross mission to put China's finances on a more stable footing. Rogers added he had also got in touch with Clark Kerr soon after his arrival 'to debunk Donald and make sure that the new ambassador did not fall under his influence'. Donald would have been outraged to hear of Rogers's perfidy but despite his apparent friendship with McHugh, the American told him nothing on his return to Hankow on 22 April.[21]

Back in Shanghai, the Committee for the Promotion of Industrial Co-operatives held its first meeting. As an emblem, Alley had a workshop in Shantung Road stamp out some enamel badges with the words '*Gung Ho*', translated as 'work together', on them. The committee liked the sound of Gung Ho and adopted it as the name of the co-operative movement.

John Alexander gave a copy of Rewi Alley's pamphlet to Archie Clark Kerr and arranged a meeting with Ed Snow and Nym Wales. Snow pitched the Gung Ho idea to him and suggested Rewi Alley as the leader of the movement. Clark Kerr saw the scheme as a basic form of socialism and thus a possible antidote to the more extreme menace of Communism. He was due to see Chiang Kai-shek at Hankow in June and on 27 May invited Snow and Alley to the embassy to answer questions about Gung Ho prior to that meeting.

Although Clark Kerr could rightly describe himself as liberal and anti-Fascist, he knew the Chinese were bound to see him as an imperialist like his predecessors. At Ed Snow's suggestion, he saw Chingling Soong in Hong Kong on his way to Hankow and outlined the Gung Ho scheme to her. She gave it her blessing.

At Hankow, Clark Kerr invited the Snows' friend and kindred spirit Agnes Smedley to dinner. Agnes was raising funds to provide medical supplies for the 8th Route Army, the Communist element in the Nationalist forces which had caught the public imagination with their daring resistance to the Japanese in Shansi province. Clark Kerr wanted to hear all about this and later made several contributions to Agnes's medical fund, as well as providing her with such personal essentials as a Christmas pudding and a bottle of Scotch.

Agnes turned up at the dinner in a borrowed dress, expecting to meet 'some devil of a British imperialist' but was pleasantly surprised. 'He didn't much resemble a devil, but he certainly had the charm of one,' she wrote in her memoir. 'He was a lean, brown, Scotchman with a keen, tough mind and a scintillating sense of humour.' She wondered whether he was really the militant democrat he appeared to be or merely a clever diplomat.[22]

Over dinner Clark Kerr raised the question of Rewi Alley's plan for industrial co-operatives. When one of the other guests, a diplomat, replied that Alley seemed 'something of an illusionist chasing a will-o'-the-wisp', he replied that might not be a bad thing. At the end of the evening, Agnes concluded Clark Kerr was 'a good Scotchman fallen among diplomats'.

Shortly afterwards the ambassador laid the Gung Ho plan in front of Chiang Kai-shek, Mayling and, despite Cyril Rogers's warning, Bill Donald. He admitted that while the plan was a form of socialism, he believed it would prevent the spread of Communism rather than assist it. And he pledged British financial aid to get Gung Ho off the ground. Chiang accepted the offer and, on his return to Shanghai, Clark Kerr persuaded the Municipal Council to release Rewi Alley from the factory inspectorate to take up his new duties.

H. H. Kung, however, was violently opposed to the scheme, which he believed would place power in the hands of ordinary Chinese who were more likely to support the Communists than the Nationalists. He called a meeting of conservative Chinese industrialists in Hankow with the intention of sabotaging it. Donald heard about the meeting and tipped off Mayling, who stormed into the room. 'You have spoiled every project that I tried to carry out,' she shouted at Kung, 'but you will not spoil this one.'[23]

Then she swept out into the hot afternoon, with Dr Kung in a blue silk dressing gown waddling along after her trying to say something. The following morning Rewi Alley was given the green light to make Gung Ho a reality. Soon, the forges and factories of every town in the Yangtze Delta not under Japanese control were being dismantled and carried or shipped west to Szechuen.[24]

On 25 May the two trippers Christopher Isherwood and Wystan Auden reached Shanghai. As their car crossed Soochow Creek, they saw the stark contrast between the cratered and barren moonscape of Hongkew on one side and the jostling crowds in neat, well-swept streets on the other. They had been invited to stay with Sir Archibald and Lady Clark Kerr at 'Number One House' in Frenchtown and were relieved to see police guards on the front gate and smiling Chinese servants waiting to greet them.

Isherwood, who had chronicled the cosmopolitan lowlife of the Weimar Republic in Goodbye to Berlin, a.k.a. Cabaret, was impressed with Shanghai's 'Sin City' reputation. 'The tired or lustful business man will find here everything to gratify his desires,' he wrote.

> If you want girls or boys, you can have them, at all prices, in the bath-houses and the brothels. If you want opium you can smoke it in the best company, served on a tray, like afternoon tea. Good wine is difficult in this climate, but there is whisky and gin to float a fleet of battleships.[25]

Archie Clark Kerr threw a garden party at the ambassadorial residence at which the guests included several hissing Japanese generals, as well as Chinese dignitaries and foreign diplomats. Scottish pipers played on the lawn and Chinese waiters dressed in lemon silk dispensed cocktails; the clink of ice cubes provided a neat counterpoint to the rattle of machine-guns next door in Nantao, where Chinese guerrillas were holding out.

Isherwood noted that the Japanese never ceased trying to find collaborators to prop up their puppet government. 'Blackmail and bribes coerce or tempt a few prominent Chinese to negotiate with the enemy,' he wrote, 'but would-be traitors seldom live long enough to be of much use to their new masters . . .'[26]

Despite the self-deprecating description of themselves as 'mere trippers', Isherwood's words and Auden's poems provide a riveting portrait of the dying world of Shanghai. 'In this city, the gulf between society's two halves is too grossly wide for any bridge,' Isherwood wrote. 'There can be no compromise here. And we ourselves, though we wear out our shoes walking the slums, though we take notes, though we are genuinely shocked and indignant, belong, inescapably, to the other world. We return, always, to Number One House for lunch.'

The foreigners' world was one of garden parties, nightclubs, hot baths and cocktails, a fool's paradise in which one European businessman could write to the *North-China Daily News* that Chinese refugees should be turned out of the settlement because they smelled, while another seriously suggested that the Japanese should be asked to drive Chinese farmers from a plot of land enclosing a grave-mound which spoiled the appearance of his garden.[27]

Before departing Shanghai, Isherwood and Auden visited the Shanghai Club, where the longest bar in the world 'proved to be far shorter than we had expected'. It was left to the Australian author Frank Clune, who followed in their footsteps a few weeks later, to disprove the myth entirely. He measured the bar at 35 paces and declared, 'The Australia Hotel bar in Sydney is half as long again but nobody skites about it.'[28]

Meanwhile, Buzz Farmer booked his ticket to return to Australia and resigned from the *North-China Daily News*. 'The war had rolled northward,' he explained. 'There seemed no point in remaining in the Far East.' On the eve of his departure a Nationalist official offered him the chance to become involved in the Chinese war effort with Hollington Tong's Ministry of Information. Farmer told the official he knew nothing about propaganda; he replied that didn't matter. Farmer accepted the well-paid job of editor in the ministry's international department and reached Hankow via Hong Kong.

Chiang Kai-shek had kept the Foreign Ministry, the Ministry of Information and his military headquarters in the Wuhan triangle but moved his government beyond the Three Gorges to Chungking, a city atop the precipitous cliffs of the Yangtze in Szechuen. After being driven out of Shanghai, Chiang's strategy had been to 'trade space for time' in Central China in order to protect his forces from total destruction at the hands of the Japanese. His enemies, however, accused him of selling out the country to Japan little by little to amass arms to fight Mao's Communists.

Indeed, Nationalist forces were still attacking the Communists in Shensi but it was also true that the grim realities of war had dictated a new course. Hitler had recalled his German advisers to the Fatherland and although they had trained a force of some 80,000 troops, it was nowhere near big enough to tackle the Japanese Army.

Also, China now had just a few squadrons of serviceable aircraft and many of her best pilots were dead or badly wounded. Garnet Malley's optimistic reports to his friend Air Marshal Richard 'Dick' Williams, head of the RAAF, on China's Air Force managed to convey completely the wrong impression about the true state of affairs. 'I might add that the [Chinese] Air Force is a Service to be reckoned with these days,' he wrote in May 1938.

> It has developed enormously and the Japanese have by no means wiped it out the many times they would have the world believe. As a matter of fact, they had a very bitter lesson right over our heads last week, when they lost over 30 machines in one of the most spectacular battles I have ever seen. There were over 130 machines involved, and I quite felt I was back again in 1918, but as a spectator this time![29]

In another letter to Dick Williams, Malley recalled a tour of inspection he had made of China's airfields some time earlier, 'landing on aerodromes that were all polished up for inspection, being met by provincial dignitaries and lavishly entertained . . .'

> When landing on most large Airports, it was most impressive seeing hundreds of Officers and personnel lined up in parade formation, and smartly turned out in white. Bands were playing, and then one was whisked away by motor-car to some sumptious [sic] banquet.[30]

At the time he was writing, China's planes were being shot out of the sky and dozens of Chinese civilians were being killed in air raids. Chiang appealed for international help and

Russia – the only responder – sent four fighter and two bomber squadrons, complete with pilots, ground crews and supplies. The Kremlin figured that while the Japanese were fighting the Chinese they would be too tied up to attack the Soviet Union across the Manchurian border with Siberia.

The Japanese had battered their way to within 100 kilometres of Hankow and Chiang Kai-shek was anxious that the Russian pilots should stop them. 'At present, the Japanese are exerting every piece of military and naval strength that they possess to take Hankow,' Donald wrote to Kenneth Cantlie on 2 July 1938. 'When they do get here, it will be an empty shell, while the Chinese will have started for fresh fields and pastures new . . .'

At 5 am on 7 July – the first anniversary of the start of the 'China Incident' on the Marco Polo Bridge – Chinese freedom fighters threw 18 bombs at targets in the International Settlement and shot dead two Japanese millworkers in the street. British troops, Shanghai Volunteers and American Marines swooped on Chinese premises and arrested more than 1000 Chinese, two of whom were found with bombs. The Chinese otherwise observed the anniversary by a three-minute silence.[31]

Buzz Farmer met Donald for the first time that month when Donald, 'big as a buccaneer', strode into the Ministry of Information office in the former Japanese Club. 'What the hell, Holly?' he addressed Hollington Tong. 'If the Ruskies start hammering the Japs, your fat generals along the Yangtze will just lie back, open their tunics, fan their fat bellies and let the Russians do all the fighting. Better beat them yourselves, without the Russians.'

The young Australian fell under the Donald spell. He got the first-ever interview with the mysterious W. H. Donald who described his childhood in Australia and told how he came to Hong Kong. 'I could smell the place 40 miles away: it was terrible, but I liked it!' he said. 'Ashore, everyone was in duck suits and topees. My heavy blue suit and bowler hat started a procession. I don't believe I even noticed the crowd of grinning Chinese. China gripped me that day and has never let go. I thrill every time I see a junk.'[32]

The Russian pilots were short and squat and seemed surly to other Europeans. They lived in quarters near the airfield and shared their mess with their Russian ground crews. 'They had the necessary patience to understand the Chinese and struck up instant friendship with the Chinese fliers and mechanics,' Buzz Farmer wrote. 'It was said of the Russian airmen that they would be speaking Chinese within a month and living with a Chinese girl within five weeks.'[33]

Stalin was keen to give as many Soviet pilots as possible combat experience, so the tour of duty was just four months. But despite their undoubted bravery there was little the Russians could do to halt the Japanese advance. The supporters of Wang Ching-wei bided their time, 'banqueting and whoring', in the words of Agnes Smedley, until they could form a puppet government for the enemy.

'Their sons and daughters dance in the night clubs, neither knowing nor caring about the fate of their country,' she wrote in the *Guardian*. 'Outside, on the streets streams of refugees pour through the city, while the roads from the north, east and south are endless lines of wounded soldiers . . .'[34]

In August Donald was stricken with fever while on a trip to Yunnan and was flown to hospital in French Indochina for treatment. Jimmy McHugh informed Washington he was certain Donald had come to realise that reports of Dr Kung's ineptitude in managing China's finances were in fact true. 'His present trip to Yunnan, while genuinely necessary for purposes of health, embodies the two-fold object of getting away from the Kung regime for a time if possible,' he wrote. 'Opposed to this is his loyalty to Madame Chiang which I believe in the end will dominate and force him to return.'

Donald was incapacitated for almost three months but on 22 October returned to Hankow from Hanoi. 'Japanese pursuit planes were apparently waiting for me at sunset at Hankow, but I landed up-river,' he wrote to Kenneth Cantlie. 'I arrived next morning at Hankow on top of a bombing raid.'[35]

The war news was grim. The Japanese had made a surprise landing at Bias Bay, only 56 kilometres north-east of Hong Kong, and marched to the outskirts of Canton.[36] Fearing a repeat of the Rape of Nanking, many Cantonese fled up the Pearl River in sampans or took to the hills; the remainder abandoned the city within hours of the Japanese occupation. The Japanese then edged their way down the Chinese coast and sealed off Hong Kong. Chiang Kai-shek warned Archie Clark Kerr that he was witnessing the 'life and death turning-point in British Far Eastern policy'.[37]

Donald's illness had added to a growing sense of disillusionment. He could see the republicans' democratic achievements being swept away on the in-rushing Japanese tide. Moreover, he was powerless to curb the corruption that was bleeding China white. His bad temper and irritability were aggravated by the relentless flow of bad news. 'The strategic policy for the first phase of the war was to hold positions as long as possible, and then withdraw to new lines,' he wrote in one newspaper article at this time.

> This policy ended after the withdrawal from Hankow and the capitulation of Canton. The first phase lasted from the outbreak of the war in July 1937 to the end of October 1938. The second phase is now developing. The strategy now being followed is that of nationwide mobile fronts, with intensification of guerrilla warfare and reinforcement of Chinese military and political strength behind the Japanese lines. Henceforth there is to be more intensive training of the fighting forces before they go into action.[38]

Shortly afterwards he saw an ambulance bought by American funds pull up outside a Hankow bank in which one of the senior Nationalist officials had a big stake. He stood in the crowd, watching, as armed guards loaded the official's fortune into the back of the ambulance. That afternoon, the president of an American university rang him to complain about the blatant profiteering of Dr Kung and members of the Soong family, adding, 'Lord, haven't they any sense of decency?'[39]

Donald knew he would get nowhere with Chiang, so he raised the matter with Mayling, citing the wife of an official who was not named but who was clearly her sister Ayling. Mayling turned on him angrily. 'You may criticise the government or anything in China,' she said, 'but there are some persons even you cannot criticise.' Donald had always prodded, cajoled and goaded Mayling into action. With a heavy heart, he realised his days in China were drawing to an end.

On the night of 24 October Donald left Hankow with Chiang Kai-shek and Mayling just hours ahead of the advanced Japanese units. They spent six weeks visiting Nationalist positions along the Yangtze, passing through many undefended towns and villages that had been bombed for no reason other than the Japanese being intent on bringing the Chinese to their knees through a reign of aerial terror. 'The Chinese people, however, are blessed with a patience and a philosophy that enable them to face colossal calamity,' Donald wrote.

> They are used to natural catastrophes which wipe out great sections of the population in one fell swoop. They have been used to civil wars for the past 20 years which have burned them out of house and home, so they understand that life is full of bitterness and sudden death. They have never before experienced the death that rains upon them from the heavens and blows them to fragments.[40]

As the Japanese marched further into the interior, they demanded that the Chinese provide 'comfort women' for their men. The authorities at Wenshui, 80 kilometres south-west of Taiyuan, Shensi, received such an order. 'The brothels on Ho Chia Hsiang have only four prostitutes, minus those with disease,' Donald wrote. 'This number is far from sufficient. Instructions have therefore been issued by the Imperial Army requiring the number to be increased within three days. It has been decided that a certain number should be selected from among the women in the city, while each village must contribute one girl for prostitution.'

Hankow fell while the Chiangs were travelling. They reached Chungking in early December. Buzz Farmer and the Ministry of Information were there, along with a large number of foreign correspondents and members of the diplomatic corps. Most of the Russian squadrons transferred to the north-west to protect supplies reaching Chungking on the overland route from Russia.

But the new capital proved too small for Chiang and the disloyal Wang Ching-wei. On the second anniversary of the Sian Incident, Wang flew to Kunming and, making his way south to Hanoi, issued a public plea for China to start peace talks with Japan. The Japanese installed him at Nanking as the head of a puppet government to aid 'China's rebirth and mutual co-operation among Japan, Manchukuo and China'.

On Christmas Eve news came in that the Japanese had bought another 150,000 tons of American scrap iron, a Christmas present that would be delivered to the Chinese in the form of shrapnel. Sure enough, more than 200 people were killed in air raids on Chungking on Sunday, 15 January 1939.

'Many of the victims were literally blown to pieces, the debris of the houses being splashed with blood and the gory fragments of what, a few moments before, were live people,' Donald wrote. 'The shocking thing about it is that the material from which these bombs are made mostly comes from the Democratic countries whose people are sympathetic with the Chinese.'

Donald had planned to leave China in 1935. A boat-building friend, Edward Cock, chief engineer of the Hong Kong

& Whampoa Dock Company, had built a yacht to his speci-
fications. He named it *Mei Hwa*. 'Unhappily, I got tied up with
the Generalissimo and Madame Chiang and the boat is still
sitting on the water in Hong Kong,' he reminisced.

> Unusual in a yacht, I built in a large writing desk and I
> imagined I would get anchored in some congenial place, pound
> away at the typewriter until I got tired of it, then I would sail
> to some other locality and stay there as long as I liked it.
> However Madame Chiang proved to be such an earnest worker
> that I decided to stand by and see if we could not really do
> something with this country.

Donald was no quitter but he was fast reaching the conclusion
that his mission to make Mayling the saviour of China was no
longer viable. It was time to go sailing.

CHAPTER 21

Goodbye Chungking

Thirty-six years after he had set foot in Hong Kong, Bill Donald made his first attempt in the summer of 1939 to break free of the emotional bonds that tied him to China. He flew from Chungking to Hong Kong. His plan was to load his yacht *Mei Hwa* on to a New Zealand-bound freighter and go sailing in the South Pacific.

As soon as Jimmy McHugh heard about Donald's departure, he wrote to Mayling offering his services. On 16 June 1939 she replied in a letter from the Headquarters of the Generalissimo, Chungking. 'Two days ago I received a wire from Mr Donald saying he was sailing for Surabaya [in the Dutch East Indies] and will, upon his arrival there, determine where he will go later. It seems that the boat for New Zealand on which he was expecting to sail had only one empty berth in a three-berth cabin, and as he felt that he could not bear to have anyone cooped up with him he decided not to take passage.'[1]

But Donald did not sail to Surabaya; the timing didn't seem right or perhaps he felt he was running away. Much to

McHugh's chagrin, he returned to Chungking and resumed his old duties.

On the evening of Sunday 3 September Neville Chamberlain's grim words announcing the outbreak of World War II were relayed to China over the BBC. In Australia, Bob Menzies – who had survived the 'pig-iron' crisis to become prime minister following the death of Joe Lyons – committed his country to war against Germany without the formality of a parliamentary vote.

By then, Chungking, which had endured Japanese bombing for more than a year, had established itself in the eyes of the world as the bastion of resistance against Japanese aggression, even if foreign diplomats fated to serve there were warned they 'had best do it under a mosquito net' to avoid catching malaria from the prevalent anopheles mosquito.[2] After one air raid, Buzz Farmer encountered Bill Donald walking through the rubble. 'I'll be damned if the Japs have left a chemist shop standing in this city,' he said. He had been attacked by hordes of mosquitoes and was looking for something to put on the bites.[3]

After a year in Chungking, Farmer was given leave. He made a roundabout journey through the beautiful lakeside city of Kunming to Hanoi and then took one boat to Hong Kong and another to Shanghai. He wanted to see his former colleagues on the *North-China Daily News* and perhaps enjoy the kudos of having been in Chungking. On a visit to the newspaper office, he found that many of his friends had left and there was a chronic shortage of staff. Charlie Tombs, the little Australian news editor, prevailed on him to help out for a few weeks.

Back on the news beat, Farmer discovered that Shanghai had become the scene of a vicious turf war. The *Kempeitai* (the Japanese Gestapo) and their collaborators controlled the densely populated Chinese districts and existed in an uneasy alliance with the *gendarmes* in Frenchtown. In the International Settlement, the Japanese continued to jostle for power in the Municipal Police Force, while gangs of *ronin* roamed the streets beating people up. Crime was out of control. 'Assassins, kidnappers, plug-uglies and extortionists held Shanghai in a terrible grip,' Buzz Farmer wrote. 'Shanghai's underworld, heavily armed and fiercely audacious, had declared war on the Settlement.'[4]

Bank raids and payroll heists were commonplace. One evening Farmer and Charlie Tombs attended a birthday party for a retired American army captain who ran a servicemen's club opposite the China Press building. Four hours later at Ciro's, Victor Sassoon's nightclub on Bubbling Well Road, a police inspector told them the American had been killed while trying to prevent the escape of an armed gang who had raided the China Press office.

The gangsters fled to 'the Badlands', an area in once-salubrious western Shanghai where power rested in the hands of the Kempeitai and their puppet allies. Night after night, Farmer watched Wang Ching-wei's dinner-jacketed lieutenants share 'the gaming tables, the bars, the opium rooms and the gaudy prostitutes with the rank-and-file of Japan's hireling Chinese'.

The Nationalists hit back through Chiang Kai-shek's Blue Shirts and the Green Gang, many of whose members were strongly anti-Japanese. 'General' Dai Li, Chiang's secret service chief, co-ordinated resistance through the Juntong, an organisation so secret that it appeared on no official Nationalist list. Dai was a dark-haired, white-faced man with a mouthful of gold teeth. He described himself as Chiang's 'claws and teeth' and had the privilege of being the only man allowed to enter the Generalissimo's bedroom armed at any time of day or night.[5]

General Milton Miles of the United States Navy supplied Dai's men with training and equipment for use against the Japanese. On first meeting Dai, he thought him 'a pansy' but soon changed his view: 'he might have been a skunk and all those things – an assassin, a poisoner, a saboteur of the first water but I found out he was a great man [and] I liked him.'[6]

supine = failure to act from cowardice

He also found out that Dai was using American resources to fight Chiang's domestic enemies rather than tackle the Japanese Army. Dai split his operations into two 'special operations units' to assassinate prominent members of the Japanese community and Japanese collaborators. One squad, led by a former bomb-thrower, targeted pro-Japanese bank officials, newspaper publishers and judges.[7] Whenever one of the assassins was arrested in the foreign concessions, he was handed over to Wang Ching-wei's police and taken to their headquarters at 76 Jessfield Road in the centre of the Badlands. There, interrogation methods were so harsh that Juntong and other Nationalist agents broke within a few days. When the torturers had finished their grisly work, the prisoners were taken into a courtyard and shot.[8]

Few Westerners suffered more than Jean Armstrong, the Sydney journalist who had helped set up the Australian stall at the Shanghai fair with Rose Venn Brown back in Edward Little's time as trade commissioner. Jean was now 47 and edited the *Catholic Review* from an apartment at 25 Rue du Consulate, Frenchtown. Given no protection by the supine French police, she was harassed by *ronin* over her Christian beliefs. When she refused to be intimidated, the Japanese ruffians beat her up, permanently injuring her hands.[9]

By 1940, the Year of the Dragon, China had been divided into three countries with ever-changing borders: Japan controlled much of the coastline and the north-east; Chiang Kai-shek's Nationalists held the south-western inland and Mao Tse-tung's Communists the remote north-west around Yenan.

In January Chiang Kai-shek asked Donald to fly to Rangoon to meet the left-wing British politician Sir Stafford Cripps and escort him up the railway line to Lashio and then over the Burma Road to Kunming in south-western China. Cripps was making an unofficial tour of India, China and Russia in the belief that these countries held the key to the future. Although he had no official status, Donald advised Chiang to meet him.

Donald flew to Kunming and was about to descend the Burma Road when Chiang received reports that Japanese agents were plotting to assassinate him en route. Forewarned, Donald waited for Cripps at Kunming and then flew back to Chungking with him in the middle of January.

Meanwhile, Harold Timperley was in the United States on a secret mission for Chiang Kai-shek after visiting Chungking and joining Hollington Tong's Ministry of Information. In the autumn of 1939 he travelled to Paris and London to interest the French and British governments in negotiating treaties with China under which Chinese troops would be provided for the defence of Hong Kong and French Indochina. It was a bold move. In Paris, Timperley put the idea to the minister of colonies and it was favourably received, although he was told a final decision would depend very much on the attitude of the British Government.

In London Timperley ran into a brick wall. Since the outbreak of hostilities in Europe, Westminster was committed to a Far Eastern policy that involved the least risk of upsetting the Japanese, and the idea of allowing Chinese troops to join the Hong Kong garrison was considered wildly provocative. Bob Howe, now chief of the far eastern division of the Foreign Office, suggested that Timperley visit Washington and dispel the notion that, thanks to appeasement, the British were pro-Japanese and might 'sell China down the river'.

At the State Department on 2 April 1940 Timperley met one of Howe's counterparts, George Atcheson Jr, whom he had known in Nanking and who had escaped from that city in the ill-fated *Panay*. 'Mr Timperley said that Mr Howe had told him that the British Government had given continuous emphatic assurances to the Chinese Government that the British had no idea of that kind and that any rumours or reports to the contrary were entirely without foundation,' Atcheson wrote in a memorandum of conversation to his superiors. 'The

British Government was, of course, adopting a conciliatory attitude toward Japan because of the exigencies of the situation in Europe.'

During the meeting it dawned on Atcheson that the personable Australian with brushed-back greying hair and an engaging smile hadn't crossed the Atlantic simply to pass on this fairly anodyne message but, when pressed, Timperley 'did not seem disposed to furnish information as to the particular matters which had brought him to Washington'.[10] As we shall see, Timperley's visit was a precursor to a much bolder venture that would completely change China's fortunes in the undeclared war with Japan.

Back at the Headquarters of the Generalissimo, Bill Donald lost no opportunity to inject his anti-Nazi views into the speeches he wrote for Chiang Kai-shek. According to Donald's biographer, Chiang sent one speech back with a curt note: 'I'm not at war with Germany.' Donald even more curtly replied, 'I am.'

It was the perfect exit line. The Chinese Government had failed to adopt an uncompromising anti-Axis policy, he told his friend Harold Hochschild, and he no longer wanted to continue as adviser to Chiang Kai-shek.[11] The date was May 1940. He was now ready to make the break. He said a brief goodbye to Mayling and flew to Hong Kong where the *Mei Hwa* was loaded on to the deck of a southbound freighter. He was not alone. His travelling companion was 18-year-old Ansie Lee, daughter of a Hong Kong merchant who was an old friend of his. She would be his secretary on a voyage to the South Seas while he bashed out his memoirs on his Hermes Baby typewriter.

Back in Chungking, Claire Chennault was in the process of forming his famous 200-strong American Volunteer Group, known as the Flying Tigers after the tiger-shark snouts painted on the noses of their aircraft. He was furious over the manner of Donald's departure. 'It was a tragedy for all China in 1940 when

Donald's attempt to rout reactionaries from their high places in the *Kuomintang* government failed, and he was banished from the place behind the Generalissimo's chair,' he wrote in his memoir, *Way of the Fighter*.

placated
— appeased
or
bribe.

> Donald readily grasped the decisive significance of airpower in modern warfare. He became one of my strongest supporters, because he felt the urgent need to build a strong Chinese Air Force while there was still time. It was Donald who introduced me to the inner circles of the Chinese Government where the intricate wheels within wheels revolved. It was Donald who, through ready access to the Generalissimo, carried my problems directly to the supreme authority. *unable to be appeased*

Chennault saw Donald as an implacable foe of Chinese kick-backs and inefficiency. He had been defeated, he thought, because reforming the Chiang regime was like wrestling a sponge-rubber statue that yielded easily but resumed its original shape as soon as pressure relaxed.[12] Whether Donald was 'banished' from Chungking or left of his own accord remains debatable: it was probably a bit of both. Chiang Kai-shek must have grown tired of his endless lectures on corruption. Indeed, Archie Clark Kerr, who spent a lot of time with Chiang on his frequent visits to Chungking, described his fellow Australian as 'a garrulous old man'.

Jimmy McHugh was also critical of Donald, even though he owed his intimate contact with the Nationalist leaders almost entirely to his goodwill. 'Don was a newspaperman through and through,' he wrote, 'but he was also a fierce protagonist of China and almost a fanatic about China's potential and future. He was always giving Chinese advice about what they should be doing for their country. He was blunt to the point of being rude at times.'

But Donald was a far more complex character than that. During his visit to Chungking in March 1939, Harold Timperley had discussed the Donald enigma with McHugh. According to McHugh's record of that conversation:

> Timp characterised Don as (1) a genuine and loyal supporter of China, (2) a loyal and most potent supporter of British interests and (3) as the victim of a very human desire for power. Under the latter he confirmed [Cyril] Rogers' characterisation of Don as a megalomaniac – dogmatic and self-centred, jealous of his position and power and unwilling to share it with others. His sincerity of purpose, unselfishness, self-sacrifice, honesty and integrity, however, remained unquestioned.[13]

Indeed, Timperley received a letter from Donald on 14 July 1937 which backed up his 'very human desire for power'. After complaining about various difficulties he was having with Chiang Kai-shek's regime, Donald added, 'but the lack of foresight, and so on, is what has always confronted me all my life with these people and still does. That is why I just took hold of the Revolution (1911) and ran things myself at that time.'[14]

In July 1940 the Japanese prime minister, Prince Konoye, demanded that Britain withdraw her garrison from Shanghai and shut down the Burma Road to prevent America's Lend-Lease supplies reaching China. Faced with the prospect of a Nazi invasion across the Channel following the collapse of France, Churchill agreed to the troop withdrawal and to a three-month closure of the Burma Road during the wet season. His agreement to Japanese demands earned him Chiang Kai-shek's undying enmity.

Alan Raymond chose this inauspicious moment to return to Shanghai. He stepped ashore on The Bund on 3 July from the SS *Husimi Maru*. It was a time of grave uncertainty in China and few Western civilians were actually heading *towards* the fighting. But like the ship itself – which was once the steamer *Hobart* – Raymond had pinned his colours to the Japanese mast. He had run away from Australia to avoid the possibility of military service and having to fight in a war that was, in his opinion, of Britain's making.

After 18 months in Hong Kong, Raymond had arrived back in Melbourne on 11 December 1939. Based on his experiences in China and Japan, he applied to become Australian trade commissioner in East Asia, the post currently held by Gordon Bowden in Shanghai. 'I called on the Minister of Commerce and Mr Murphy the permanent Secretary of the Department to whom I submitted a report on various matters concerning the East,' he wrote in his postwar statement. 'I sought an appointment which would give me scope to use my experience in the Orient in the service of my country.'

While waiting for the department to make up its mind, Raymond moved to Sydney and rented a flat in Darlinghurst Road, Potts Point. He went surfing, courted a girl called Mavis (who married someone else and moved to Brisbane) and 'made arrangements' to go into a stockbroker's office. This prompted a letter to Frank Cade, a respected journalist on the Melbourne *Sun News-Pictorial* whom he had known in Hong Kong and whose name he had given as a reference. On 4 January 1940 he wrote to Cade, 'I have included your honourable name so if one Ralph W. King should inquire of me kindly use the full power of your journalistic talents in a description of my unique and unrivalled abilities and reputation in Hong Kong (the better side of course).'

After a long wait, he received a letter of rejection from the department. In retaliation, he wrote a stinging article in *The Bulletin* on 22 May 1940 in which he attacked Australia's trade representation in China and urged recognition of the fact that Japan had been 'completely successful' in her war against China, and that Chiang Kai-shek had no chance of regaining lost territory in northern China and the Yangtze basin.

Gordon Bowden pulled no punches in the letter he wrote to the Department of Commerce. 'Raymond is a man of no standing whatever in the business community of Shanghai and on the moral and personal side he does not bear a good name,' he said. He added that while it was perhaps a natural democratic tendency to accept men at face value, 'in the case of Raymond it is a form of misrepresentation that might enable him to make arrangements with business houses or others in Australia which, in evidence of his past career, would be more likely to bring theirs or Australia's name into discredit rather than achieve any good for them'.

But despite his record in Shanghai, Raymond was back to stay. It was evident he welcomed the Japanese presence and saw Shanghai as a place of opportunity. He later claimed in his postwar statement that he had been greatly disturbed by Australia's involvement in the European war, 'which I regarded as unwarranted and as a selfish action on the part of Britain'. He continued, 'I did not wish to participate in such a war and decided to return to the Orient where I could live a quiet detached life. I remained strongly of the opinion that either our government acted precipitatedly [sic], unwisely or that we had been forced into the war in consequence of our national status in relation to Britain.'[15]

Bill Donald's South Seas idyll began, ironically, in the calm waters of Tulagi in the Solomon Islands, soon to be the scene of horrendous fighting between the Japanese and United States Marines. From there, he headed for New Zealand via the New Hebrides (now Vanuatu). In Auckland it was clear his heart was still in Chungking. 'I am not going back to Australia,' he said. 'I left there 38 years ago and have never been back. With Australia's politics as they are, I shall not go there.' He criticised the Australian and New Zealand governments for trading with Japan and sending her materials that could be used against China. 'If it had not been for the stand which China has made,' he added, 'Japan by now would have carried out her preparations of southward expansion. The Chinese feel very bitterly about the attitude of the democracies.'[16]

On 27 August 1940 a 28-year-old Australian *femme fatale* named Wynette Cecilia McDonald arrived in Shanghai in the Dutch steamer *Tjibadak*. She was travelling with a Swedish seaman-turned-Melbourne hairdresser named Henry Olof Lindquist. McDonald was the daughter of Ewan Cameron McDonald, a Melbourne botanist, and his wife Winifred Grace née Le Blanc. Known as Wyn, she was a willowy, dark-eyed beauty with a number of broken relationships behind her, including marriage to a man named Porter who had divorced her.

Lindquist, her current lover, had sold his hairdressing salon in Swanston Street, Melbourne, 'because Australians suspect everybody who has any trace of a foreign accent and that there was a public movement to intern all foreigners'. The couple had travelled to northern Queensland and Western Australia hoping to make a fortune from minerals. They had no luck and had taken a ship from Darwin to Java with the intention of prospecting for gold. When that scheme failed and their funds ran out, they headed for Shanghai to find work.[17]

'McDonald went to the secretary of the Municipal Council to look for employment,' Gordon Bowden wrote in a report to Colonel H. E. Jones of the Australian Security Service in Canberra on 27 December 1940, 'and he referred her to me as president of the Australian and New Zealand Society of Shanghai.' Bowden also met 39-year-old Lindquist whom he regarded as 'a derelict', although he thought McDonald 'not without intelligence and a good deal of spirit'.[18]

He gave her a number of addresses where she could apply for work but she returned to his office a few days later saying she and Lindquist 'had been staying at a boarding house called Chelsea House and that they were to be put on the street that afternoon, minus their baggage, as they were unable to pay their bill'.

Bowden, on behalf of the society, paid the bill of $108.87 and gave McDonald $20 spending money. He also found her accommodation at the YWCA International Hostel in Great Western Road, where the society guaranteed her board and lodging for one month at a cost of $116. Shortly afterwards, he learned McDonald had been given a job as a teacher by Mrs Ruby Taylor, the Australian proprietor of the Peter Pan School for infants. The job paid only $185 per month but Bowden noted that 'she seemed by then to have begun to receive money from Australia and even to have bought clothes'.[19]

Like Alan Raymond, Wynette McDonald was violently anti-British. Bowden learned from the hostel manageress that she 'expressed very strong views about the war and seemed very bitter against England'. He also learned that 'she was twice reported to the British Intelligence Officer here for having spread reports regarding the alleged ill-treatment of interned Germans in the Netherlands East Indies'.

Furthermore, it was noted that she preferred the company of German and Japanese residents. To the Japanese, she was openly critical of the White Australia policy. She told Bowden on her second visit to his office that 'a senior Japanese officer in the Shanghai Municipal Police had been very kind in helping her'.

Bowden decided to write to Colonel Jones after he learned from Ruby Taylor on 21 December 1940 that she had caught McDonald trying her hand at spying. 'After she had been with me for about three months,' Mrs Taylor related in a statement,

> she stayed away from the school at the weekend. I had to take her class over and on looking through her desk found some documents which appeared to be in code. I contacted an official of the British Consulate and showed him these documents which he later told me contained a copy of the secret code used by the Royal Navy in Hong Kong.

As well as the coded message, there was a sheet of paper on which McDonald had been trying to decipher it. Bowden discussed the case with a British naval officer who deduced that Lindquist probably stole the message from the wireless operator of a Moller Line ship on which he had found work. 'This suggests a deliberate – even if clumsy – attempt at spying,' Bowden wrote, 'and lends colour to doubts that I have felt about them ever since I first heard their story.'[20]

Meanwhile, T. V. Soong had finally accepted a role in Chiang's government. As a follow-up to Harold Timperley's American visit, he was sent to Washington as his brother-in-law's special envoy to negotiate a huge loan to finance China's continuing resistance against Japan. In exchange for funds, T. V. explained to President Roosevelt and the Secretary of the Treasury, Henry Morgenthau, at a meeting in the White House, China would keep 1,125,000 Japanese troops tied up in China indefinitely and force the Japanese Fleet to continue its blockade of China's shores.[21]

As the United States armed forces were in the early stages of rearmament, Roosevelt saw the wisdom of T. V.'s proposal. He ordered Jesse H. Jones, the Federal loan administrator, to enter into negotiations with Soong for loans to stabilise China's markets and purchase war materials.[22]

While the talks were in progress that September, the Japanese occupied the northern part of French Indochina to close down the rail link between Haiphong and Kunming along which supplies were ferried into China, bringing matters to a swift resolution in Washington. On 24 September Roosevelt ordered a complete embargo on the sale of all types of iron and steel to Japan and 24 hours later he announced a loan of US$85 million to Chiang Kai-shek through the Export–Import Bank.

On 27 September Japan signed the Tripartite Pact in Berlin under which she recognised the leadership of Hitler and

Mussolini in 'the New Order in Europe', while Germany and Italy supported Japan's dominance in 'Greater East Asia'.

Around this time, Ralph Shaw, an English reporter on the *North-China Daily News*, was walking in the public gardens on The Bund when a rotund figure in flowing saffron robes started haranguing him in heavily accented English. 'I hate the British,' he shouted. 'You, young man, should be ashamed of your race. You will not win the war.'

The stranger then launched into a tirade against the perfidy of the British, their hypocrisy, dishonesty and inferiority to the Germans. 'One day,' he concluded, 'I will walk in the ruins of London. I will see you a conquered race.'[23] Shaw later learned that the man was Trebitsch Lincoln, the fraudster and former arms dealer who ran his own monastery in Shanghai. His anti-British prejudice stemmed not only from his treatment at the hands of British justice but also from the fate of his favourite son Natzl who was hanged for murder. Lincoln had dashed to Britain from China to see the young man before his execution but was not permitted to land. He returned to China a sworn enemy of the British people.[24]

Since the Japanese invasion in 1937 Lincoln had espoused the Japanese cause and when World War II broke out, he volunteered his services as a Nazi propagandist. Lincoln's biographer, Bernard Wasserstein, described him as a 'low-level German agent'. He would soon have a fanatical Australian disciple.

CHAPTER 22

Betraying Australia

Trebitsch Lincoln's anti-British ranting was music to the ears of Wynette McDonald. Now broke and jobless, she started attending his Shanghai monastery looking for a handout. She needed little encouragement to offer her services to the Germans. Either Lincoln or one of his acolytes suggested she see Baron Jesco von Puttkamer, a 38-year-old German aristocrat who ran the German Information Bureau from a penthouse suite at the Park Hotel.

Puttkamer worked closely with the Shanghai branch of the Nazi Party and reported to Goebbels's Propaganda Ministry in Berlin. In a statement after the war, he said that McDonald and Olof Lindquist approached him with an extraordinary proposition: if the Nazis would provide a boat, they would fill it with pro-Nazi propaganda, such as books and leaflets, and sail back to Australia. They would smuggle the material ashore and distribute it to sympathisers in Australian cities. Puttkamer thought the plan 'too fantastic' and politely showed them the door.[1]

The Japanese were more receptive. According to an English-born resident of Shanghai, Georgina Fuller, proprietor of a hostel called the Clarendon Club who got to know McDonald well during the war, 'McDonald and Lindquist handed over to the Japanese the records and photographs of their travels in Northern and North-eastern Australia. These documents, among other details, told of the nature of the bush and the obstacles to be met with.'

Hearing that Gordon Bowden had been making inquiries about her, McDonald sent him a letter threatening libel proceedings against anyone who made derogatory remarks about her. 'These and other incidents in connection with her case,' Bowden concluded, 'led me to feel that she is not quite normal mentally.'

One of the arms dealers selling guns to Wang Ching-wei's gangsters was an Australian, John Joseph Holland. The 35-year-old black sheep of a respectable West Australian family arrived in Shanghai in 1938 and ran up debts he was unable to pay from his earnings as a freelance journalist. At some point he linked up with 'General' One-Arm Sutton, former chief of staff of the Old Marshal in his battles with his rival warlord Wu Pei-fu.[2]

'One-Arm' Sutton – a.k.a. Francis Arthur Sutton, an Old Etonian and former British Army officer – was fond of Australians: he had formed a mixed company of miners consisting of Anzacs and British volunteers at Gallipoli to blow up Turkish positions. He had been awarded the Military Cross for gallantry after losing a hand while throwing enemy grenades back into their trenches.[3]

Sutton had found a willing apprentice in Holland, a dreamer and a schemer whose failed schemes included an attempt to buy a ship, the SS *Karoola*, and take Australians and New Zealanders on Anzac excursions to the Gallipoli battlefield.

Holland was five-feet seven-inches tall, with brown hair and a slight build. He had been born at Kanowna, Western Australia, on 5 July 1907 and educated at Christian Brothers College, New Norcia Catholic College and Perth High School.

He worked as a jackeroo on the Wooleen Station on the Murchison River for three years and then on a stud farm, but after returning to Perth and arguing about money with his father, John Joseph Holland Sr, a respected Perth physician, he stowed away on a ship bound for Sydney.

In 1932 he married Doris Radeski – 'an excellent type of woman', according to a security report – at St Mary's Cathedral. Within a matter of months, he had been convicted of forgery after stealing a cheque for £78 and passing it off at Anthony Horderns department store as his own. He served six months at Emu Plains Prison Farm.[4] On his release, he moved to Brisbane with Doris but in 1937 abandoned her after she objected to him seeing other women.

Holland left Australia with the intention of becoming a war correspondent in Hong Kong. He got no further than Singapore, where he worked in the car trade. Doris joined him there in August 1940 in the hope of saving her marriage but after a few weeks her husband told her 'he had lived too long with Chinese women to be associated with a European female'.[5]

He abandoned his wife once more and moved to Hong Kong where he got a job on the *China Press*, ran up debts including one of $340 to his landlord at Dina House and then, on 10 October 1938, disappeared. 'Hong Kong has seen neither hide nor hair of John Holland since his fly-by-night,' one of his former colleagues wrote to a friend in Melbourne on 18 August 1939. 'Shall I ever forget it? Rumour hath it he deserted at the first port, Haiphong, but there is no confirmation. Rumour also had it that the ever-faithful Margaret [Holland's girlfriend] was, as the Australian papers say, in a certain condition . . .'

Holland surfaced in Shanghai where he met 'One-Arm' Sutton. He came to the attention of the authorities in March 1941 when he attempted to sell seven bombers to the French vice-consul for service in Indochina. The French political police investigated Holland's associates and reported that they included 'a number of well-known swindlers', one of whom had 'special relations' with the Japanese. The French concluded that Holland may well have been acting as an *agent provocateur* in a Japanese attempt to embarrass the French Government had it accepted his offer.[6]

Even for a conman like John Holland, Shanghai was in a different league for crime compared with Hong Kong or Singapore. Kidnapping and murder grew naturally out of the struggle between the Nationalists in Chungking and the collaborators in Shanghai. Chiang Kai-shek maintained banks in the foreign concessions, while Wang Ching-wei's regime issued its own currency through banks in the Chinese districts. The trouble escalated in early 1941, the Year of the Serpent, when Dai Li's Juntong assassination squads launched bomb attacks against Wang's banks and their employees.[7]

Wang's gunmen retaliated. Posing as police officers, they entered the company dormitory of one of the pro-Chiang banks. The gunmen turned on the lights and opened fire into the beds. Five men were killed and six others left wounded among the blood-stained blankets. At 3 am that same night squads of puppet police and Japanese military police raided another pro-Chungking bank compound in the Badlands. They dragged 128 bank employees out of bed, locked them up at 76 Jessfield Road and announced that three hostages would be killed for the death of every collaborationist bank employee.[8]

When Juntong assassins hacked to death a senior accountant of the puppet Central Reserve Bank in the presence of his family, three senior accountants among the hostages were executed. That evening the remaining employees of Nationalist banks fled from their dormitories.[9]

In Chungking, Chiang Kai-shek's strategic problems increased immeasurably when it was announced in Tokyo that Matsuoka, now Japan's foreign minister, had negotiated a non-aggression treaty with Stalin. The five-year Soviet–Japanese Neutrality Pact, signed in Moscow on 13 April 1941, secured

Japan's northern flank and would enable her to remove many divisions from Manchuria to take part in the conquest of China proper.

Meanwhile, Bill Donald and Ansie Lee had reached Tahiti in a sugar boat from Fiji, having sent *Mei Hwa* back to Hong Kong as deck cargo. 'I came here because I fondly thought that this is the farthest spot from China where one might live in peace for a time, but alas and alack!' he wrote to Herbie Elliston from Papeete on 3 June 1941. 'Before I arrived here Madame Chang Kai-shek wrote me a letter asking me to fly back. I wired that I must have from four to six months' notice to catch a steamer.'[10]

Donald then set sail on a month's cruise in a schooner. When he returned to Tahiti, there was a telegram from Mayling urging him to go to a more accessible place or to find his way back to Hong Kong. Donald ignored that cable and several more like it but soon afterwards made an important decision: he would abandon his book because 'I would have to do too much debunking and hurt too many people'.

The decision meant he had nothing to do and he found himself monitoring short-wave radio bulletins for news about the fighting in China and the 'Washington conversations' between Secretary of State Cordell Hull and the Japanese envoys, which were supposed to settle matters between Japan and the United States. When Mayling cabled that she was planning a goodwill tour of America and wanted him on hand as her adviser, the pull was too strong. He cabled back, 'I am returning.'[11]

In Shanghai, Gordon Bowden had been ordered to close down the Australian trade commission. At the same time, he was transferred from the Department of Trade to the Department of Foreign Affairs. The three Bowden children were sent to school in Sydney and Melbourne, and in September Gordon and Dorothy arrived in Singapore where he opened a new office in the Union Building at Collyer Quay, with Norman Wootton as commercial secretary and John Quinn as political secretary.[12]

'As official representative of Australia at Singapore, V. G. Bowden will have high diplomatic status,' *The Argus* reported. 'Australia's trade representation at Shanghai will cease and all the Commonwealth's commercial relations with China will be controlled by Sir Frederic Eggleston, Australian minister for Chungking.'[13]

Indeed, Eggleston, lawyer, politician and head of the Commonwealth Grants Commission, had been knighted and sent to the wartime capital as Australia's first minister to the Chinese Republic. Aged 66, he suffered from arthritis and gout and weighed 200 pounds. His huge bulk had to be carried everywhere in a sedan chair borne by four coolies rather than the usual two. Despite his immobility, he was remarkably successful in the post. At the Australian Legation, he opened a salon to which he invited a wide range of Chinese intellectuals and young scholars. Visiting journalists including Douglas Wilkie of the Melbourne *Herald*, Selwyn 'Dan' Speight of the *Sydney Morning Herald* and Wilfred Burchett of the Sydney *Daily Telegraph* and the London *Daily Express* were offered French wine from the well-stocked ambassadorial cellar while listening to his collection of Beethoven, Bach, Mozart, Chopin and Schubert records.[14]

Burchett made trips to the fronts in Chekiang, Fukien and Kiangsi and reported on the fighting to Eggleston when he returned to Chungking. 'Burchett is a most interesting and enterprising man and deserves a very high reputation as a war correspondent,' the minister wrote in his diary. 'He is always where the firing is.'[15]

Eggleston proved to be a natural diplomat capable of presenting Canberra with a shrewd analysis of the Chungking political scene. 'The China I do see is interesting but not inspiring,' he wrote to his friend Robert Menzies. 'One or two heroic figures like Chiang, a few very fine minds, a lot of intriguing politicians and a mass downtrodden by landlords, moneylenders and profiteers, tolerating with smiling faces and full but undernourished bellies what could not stand for a moment with us.'[16]

Eggleston held weekly meetings with Archie Clark Kerr when he was in Chungking, dined with H. H. Kung and consulted Chou En-lai who ran the Communist office there until he left abruptly for Yenan to present Mao Tse-tung with an ultimatum from Chiang Kai-shek.[17]

Throughout the troubles, Viola Smith and Eleanor Hinder had been actively involved in their duties for the Municipal Council and the American Consulate respectively. Viola, who had been promoted to consul, took a leading role in the evacuation of American civilians from Shanghai. Then in October 1941 she left Shanghai on home leave expecting to be away four months. The separation affected Eleanor deeply. On 9 October she wrote:

> Just 24 hours since the tender pulled out. They have been heavy hours. How devastation can invade and possess one while outwardly one is carrying on. I have a weight on my heart like the Dunkirk days, as if my body cannot contain the pressure that is within it. I was determined that you would leave me calm, that I would not make it harder for you than it was, that I would show no tears. But the effort at control can build up a suffering which is almost unbearable . . . By the time this can reach you, of course, this too will have passed, as other griefs have passed. So you can read it knowing that I will soon be alright.
>
> Goodnight, my ownest one. How silent the house is!
> My love, my dear dear one.
> Your Bug.[18]

Meanwhile, Harold Timperley was on a lecture tour of Australia after spending that summer in Chungking. 'The ruined and blackened areas of Chungking tell their own story today,' he said in an interview with Geoffrey Hutton of *The Argus*.

> In the spring of 1939 I was staying in a small hotel in Chungking. The hotel has gone now. A bank was built on its ruins. That has gone, too, and there is another building there . . . Summer is the bombing season in Chungking – in winter the mountains are covered in cloud and the Japanese do not risk a flight. So each summer the city is painfully destroyed and each winter it is rebuilt.[19]

Later that month Timperley was on his way from Australia to the United States when Bill Donald and Ansie Lee boarded his ship in Auckland. The two Australians were delighted to see one another. The meeting convinced Donald that fate was drawing him back to China. Timperley told him he had been in Canberra for the fall of the Fadden Government and had renewed his acquaintance with the new prime minister, John Curtin, 'who was formerly a journalist colleague of mine in WA'.[20]

Donald and Ansie Lee left the ship at Honolulu and sailed for Hong Kong in the freighter SS *Robert Dollar* which was carrying arms and equipment for the Canadian expeditionary force that had been sent to protect Hong Kong after Britain turned down Chiang Kai-shek's offer of Chinese troops. Before they sailed, Donald wrote to Harold Hochschild, 'The heat of war is steaming up. Whether or not Japan will risk an encounter with America and Britain will be known in a week or so.'

On the night of 7–8 December 1941 the Japanese occupied The Bund – British troops had been evacuated to Hong Kong at Japanese insistence and there was nothing to stop them walking over Garden Bridge and taking possession of the rest of the International Settlement. The lone British gunboat on the Whangpoo, HMS *Peterel*, deprived of most of her guns following Japanese protests, was sunk by Japanese naval gunfire when her captain, Lieutenant-Commander Stephen Polkinghorn, refused to surrender.

Later that same morning the SS *Robert Dollar* was south of Ambon in the Dutch East Indies when the captain told Donald, 'Pearl Harbor has just been bombed. There's war with Japan.' As reports came in of Japanese attacks on Malaya and Hong Kong, the *Robert Dollar* headed for Manila.

Shanghai awoke to the sight of Japanese soldiers setting up barricades and taking control of newspapers and radio stations. The office of the *North-China Daily News* was sealed and the paper shut down. Allied officials were corralled at Cathay Mansions, a British-owned residential hotel across the street from the French Club in Rue Cardinal Mercier.

When the Japanese tried to enter the Custom House, Captain Charles Woodfield of the Shanghai River Police barricaded the heavy bronze doors. Born in South Shields, County Durham, Woodfield had worked his way up in the municipal police from 1907 to 1923 when he transferred to the river police section of the customs service. 'Uncle Bill was the last man in the building – he'd got everyone out in the old tradition of the captain being the last man on the ship,' says his great-niece Elizabeth Fay Woodfield. 'The Japanese broke in and as they were coming up the stairs, he hanged himself.' It was a tragic end for a brave man who had devoted his life to protecting the people of Shanghai.[21]

After months of violent crime, many Europeans found compliance with the occupiers the easier option. The savage efficiency of the Japanese authorities in imposing their will was an important factor in the city's comparative calm. On 9 December Viola Smith wrote to Eleanor Hinder from California:

Buggie, BUGGIE, DARLING!
The zero hour has struck. Flora [Gramber, a mutual friend] and I first heard it from a radio truck in the courtyard of the lovely Mission Inn at Riverside . . . We got only the barest details of attacks on Manila and Honolulu. We stood riveted

in the spot. It seemed incredible that after 21 years of living
on a tinder box in China that I should be in America, standing
alongside Flora, and amidst all that the Mission Inn stands
for. The anguish of the last 48 hours without any news or any
possibility of getting news of you has been terrible . . . My heart
aches for you darling darling mine but I can serve you best by
trying to be reasonable. God keep you safe and grant that this
letter reaches you.[22]

Always your devoted VEE.

Hubert 'Hugh' Collar, chairman of the British Residents' Association, was halfway through lunch in the upstairs dining room
at the Shanghai Club when there were muffled sounds of disturbance from below. 'Ward, the club secretary, entered the dining
room accompanied by a Japanese Naval Officer and two ratings
armed to the teeth,' he wrote. 'Ward called for silence and
announced in a very agitated voice that the Japanese had come
to take over the club, and that the whole premises must be
completely vacated in 20 minutes.' Several resident members
went up to their room to pack, while the remainder continued
their meal, 'and apart from a certain heightening in the level
of conversation no one would have realised that the members
were about to be submitted to the indignity of being turned out
neck and crop from these sacrosanct premises'.[23]

The vast administrative building where Eleanor Hinder
worked on the corner of Kiangsi and Foochow roads was
occupied by Japanese personnel and guards were placed at the
entrance. Along with all Australian, New Zealand, British,
American, Belgian and Dutch citizens, she lined up on a wet,
cold December morning to register with the *Kempeitai* at their
new headquarters in nearby Hamilton House. The queue
extended around the block and many people had to return
several times before they could get in.

'The Japanese appeared to enjoy our discomfort and took
motion pictures of us waiting in line,' Arch Carey of the Asiatic

Petroleum Company wrote. 'Most people turned their backs on the photographers [and] we all kept up a cheerful front.'[24] Allied nationals were also required to bow and raise their hats whenever they passed one of the Japanese flags that had suddenly appeared over the entrances of many of the city's most prominent buildings. Most solved that problem by leaving their hats at home and going bareheaded, despite the icy winds whistling down from Manchuria.

Inspector Roy Fernandez had sent his wife Sybil and children Roy Jr and Stephanie to Australia via Hong Kong in the Butterfield & Swire steamer SS *Anhui* on 6 December. As soon as war was declared, the captain was ordered to head for the nearest port, which happened to be Manila. 'Manila didn't really want us,' his daughter Stephanie says. 'We were left out in the bay being bombed. The Red Cross took us in and we were sent from place to place.' When the Japanese took over Manila, Sybil and her two children were interned in a camp at Sulphur Springs in the hills outside the capital.[25]

Meanwhile, Colin McDonald had been steadfastly reporting the war for *The Times*. He was in Hong Kong when it surrendered to the Japanese on Christmas Day 1941 and ran the Japanese blockade to cable his dispatch to his newspaper. He filed 500-word reports every day not knowing whether they would reach their destination owing to frequent disruption of the telegraphic service.[26]

Bill Donald and Ansie Lee reached Manila just as General Douglas MacArthur declared it an open city and withdrew his troops to the Bataan Peninsula to make a last desperate stand. In a press interview, Donald revealed that Britain had secretly turned down Chiang's offer to protect Hong Kong with 200,000 Chinese troops. The British declined the offer, he said, because they feared acceptance would offend Japan.[27]

George Morrison's eldest son, Ian, was working for Rob Scott at the Ministry of Information in Singapore. He and his Czech-born wife Maria were asleep in their flat when the city was bombed for the first time. He dashed on to the balcony and saw searchlights probing the skies and heard the drone of Japanese bombers and the sound of explosions from the docks and the city centre.

Gordon Bowden joined the Far East War Council as Australia's representative under the chairmanship of Churchill's emissary Duff Cooper. At the first meeting, Sir Robert Brooke-Popham, Commander-in-Chief Far East, and the Governor of Singapore, Sir Shenton Thomas, made it plain they had no intention of taking orders from Cooper. Bowden's cables warned Canberra of the looming disaster, but as the Japanese advanced down the Malay Peninsula, there was nothing he could do to prevent the council from lapsing into impotence. Cooper proved incapable of overcoming the opposition and fled back to England at the earliest opportunity.

Ian Morrison escaped in one of the last freighters to leave Singapore and made his way to Melbourne where he wrote a scathing account of Britain's greatest military catastrophe in a book entitled *Malayan Postscript*. Gordon Bowden, Norman Wootton and John Quinn, however, were told to hold on in Singapore until the very last minute. 'The department ordered my father, Wootton and Quinn to stay,' Ivor Bowden says. 'It was a question of face and they also wanted the latest reports. But my father cabled my mother that he would have sent Wootton and Quinn away and stayed himself but they refused to leave without him.'[28]

Gordon Bowden's final cable said, 'Our work completed. We will telegraph from another place at present unknown.' The message was transmitted on a small handset located at the point where the cable entered the water. In the early hours of 15 February, Bowden and his two colleagues left Singapore in the motor launch *Mary Rose*, which ran into the Japanese Navy at the entrance to Banka Strait. The men were taken to Muntok Harbour, where Bowden was involved in an altercation with a Japanese guard. He was led outside and half an hour later two shots were heard. Gordon Bowden had been forced to dig his own grave and was then executed.

'It could well have been my father's knowledge of Japanese that cost him his life,' Ivor Bowden says. 'One of the soldiers tried to remove his gold watch and he remonstrated with him. He had also been told to state that he was a member of the diplomatic corps and that he had immunity. He probably demanded to speak to the soldier's commanding officer and that was the last thing the soldier wanted. He would have thought my father was going to complain about the watch, so he killed him.'[29]

To celebrate the fall of Singapore, Wynette McDonald drove along The Bund in an open-top car with a Japanese naval officer in a Japanese victory parade, an act that brought universal condemnation from the city's Anglo-Australian community. Then on the evening of 7 March she joined Alan Raymond and the former Australian arms dealer John Holland at a 'Break Away from Britain' meeting in Room 106 of the Palace Hotel.[30]

At midnight on 11 March, Radio Berlin reported that an 'Australian Independence Movement' had been founded in Shanghai under the leadership of Alan Raymond. Raymond was quoted as saying that Australia should demand complete independence from Britain 'in so far as she is able to determine her own destiny at the conclusion of the present conflict'. He would appeal to his fellow countrymen in radio broadcasts because 'it looks as though Japan will win the war or force a peace on Australia'.

At the second meeting of the Independent Australia League Raymond told his followers (and Lieutenant Kazumaro Ueno, a member of the Japanese Army's intelligence section who turned up to check the progress of the embryonic organisation), 'Since the Japanese government has intimated its desire to save Australia from the horrors of war, the Commonwealth should negotiate for an honourable peace.' The *Shanghai Times* reported under the headline 'Australians urged to end pointless war' that 'the gathering has grown to twice the number of

Australians who attended the first meeting'. Since there were eight Australians among the 11 people at the first meeting, this meant an increase to perhaps 16, although that figure was never substantiated. One of them was Jacqueline Valerie Everett, 'a pleasant and capable personality' who was described as the league's social secretary. Indeed, it transpired that most of the members were more interested in social activities than getting involved in politics.[31]

Lieutenant Ueno suggested that the renegade Australians be given a three-hour daily program on Station XMHA entitled 'Australia Calling' and consisting of items urging Australians to withdraw from the war. 'Should this program fail,' he declared, 'it is the intention of the Japanese authorities to contact all Australians in occupied areas and give them a chance to go with the Japanese to Australia and there run the administration.'[32]

Prior to the Japanese takeover, Station XMHA at 445 Racecourse Road had a proud record of resistance. Its star broadcaster was 40-year-old Carroll Alcott, a beefy American who broadcast three times a day on Asian matters. It was said Tokyo lost face every time he opened his mouth. Using a transmitter based in a room at the Astor House Hotel, the Japanese jammed his broadcasts, so Alcott opened his show by singing 'Jell-O, Jell-O, Jell-O', the name of a popular brand of jelly.

When the Japanese denied they were jamming him, he announced the room number of their operations. When they threatened his life, he bought a bullet-proof vest. After they tried to drag him out of a rickshaw, he drove to work in a Packard with bullet-proof glass and a couple of Russian bodyguards. He finally left Shanghai when the United States Marines were recalled to the Philippines prior to Pearl Harbor, donning a Marine uniform and marching out with them.[33]

The Japanese brought a man named Peterson from Hong Kong to organise 'Australia Calling'. According to Georgina Fuller in her postwar interview, Peterson had stolen the identity papers of an Australian seaman and his true identity was unknown. Soon afterwards, Wynette McDonald started calling herself 'Mrs Peterson'.

Understandably, the collaborators used pseudonyms, with the exception of Alan Raymond who made no attempt to hide his identity: after a lifetime of rejection and failure, people were listening to his views for the first time and he was enjoying the notoriety. John Holland, who started broadcasting from the German station XGRS in the Kaiser Wilhelm School on Great Western Road on 13 February, sometimes called himself 'David Lester'. According to an anonymous informant in Holland's file in the Australian National Archives, 'He took over the Walla Walla* broadcast news from "Pat Kelly" (Frankie Johnston, Shanghai-born Irishman, Free State passport) when that worthy disgraced himself by a shady deal on classical records.' For that misdemeanour, Johnston had served 14 days in the Bridge House, a former apartment block in North Szechuen Road in Hongkew, which the *Kempeitai* had turned into Shanghai's chamber of horrors.

Holland said in a postwar statement, 'I was asked to read a commentary written especially for the Australian audience urging Australians to refrain from any further participation in the Pacific War.' The Germans were impressed with his delivery and diction and quickly increased his pay and gave him more responsibility.

As 'Australia Calling' took to the air to the imitation call of a kookaburra, 78,000 American and Filipino troops were being driven at bayonet point into captivity on the notorious Bataan Death March. Raymond made no mention of that in any of his broadcasts, or of the *sook ching* massacres of thousands of Chinese men and boys following the fall of Singapore, or of the Parit Sulong atrocity in Malaya in which 133 Allied prisoners, including many Australians, were machine-gunned, bayoneted, drenched with petrol and set alight.

---

*   Named after a small town in southern New South Wales

Australian listening posts monitored Raymond's broadcasts and the director-general of security labelled him the 'Australian Lord Haw-Haw' after the Nazi propagandist on German radio.[34] Raymond's readiness to join the Japanese war effort and the ease with which he slotted into its propaganda machine suggest he was already a Japanese agent when he returned to Shanghai in August 1940.

Meanwhile, Wynette McDonald worked as assistant to Berthel Alexander MacKenzie, who made anti-British broadcasts to Australia under the pseudonym 'Roy Stewart'. He read letters from Shanghai residents to friends and relatives in Australia and warned of the dire consequences of resisting the Japanese. Some of Shanghai's 200 Australian residents allowed their names to be used simply as a means of letting their families know they were alive but most recognised it as a propaganda trick and refused to take part.

The Japanese magazine *Freedom* of 10 June 1942 reported that 'Roy Stuart [sic]', who was connected with the 'Break away from Britain League', was an Australian 'whose voice was well known over the Australian Radio 3AW'. The magazine added that the aim of the league and its leader Alan Raymond was to see 'an Australia free from British influence and living at peace in co-operation with Japan's projected East Asia Co-prosperity Sphere'.

Berthel MacKenzie claimed to have been born in Melbourne and to have attended Scotch College and the University of Melbourne but H. S. Austin, an Australian security officer who had worked with the Shanghai police, described him as 'a renegade Britisher, a Scotsman who obtained his discharge from a Scottish regiment while stationed in Shanghai'. He also noted that MacKenzie was 'opposed to Imperialism and bore a bitter hatred for the Royal Family'.[35]

In April the Japanese rewarded Wynette McDonald's treachery with her own radio slot, 'Woman's Hour', on XMHA over the long-wave transmitter. According to A. V. Cattel, the station's chief engineer, her contribution 'consisted mainly of persuading local women of the advantages to everyone of being under Japanese control'.[36]

Expatriate women in Shanghai, such as Georgina Fuller, thought that although the program was meant to be serious, it was regarded as a joke and they tuned in for a laugh. Some of McDonald's claims, however, were highly defamatory. In one broadcast, she described John Curtin as 'an evil and corrupting influence' and accused him of poisoning the former prime minister Joe Lyons who had died of natural causes in February 1939.[37] According to Georgina Fuller, 'a close relationship sprang up between McDonald and Suyana, Chief of Police in Shanghai, and Hayashi, who subsequently became camp commandant of the internment area'.

In the Philippines, Donald and Ansie Lee were interned with 400 other anti-Axis foreigners in the camp at Sulphur Springs. Several internees recognised Donald and greeted him as a celebrity but he asked them to keep his identity a secret and they agreed. The commandant, a decent old German named Dahlan who had fought against the British in World War I, registered him as 'William Donald of Edinburgh', rather than 'W. H. Donald of Chungking'. He also stored Donald's papers and diaries in a locked shed and looked after them until the end of the war.

One of those who kept the secret was 13-year-old Roy Fernandez Jr. 'There were no Japanese guards at Sulphur Springs, so we had a grown-up and a boy on the gate to see who was coming into the camp,' he said. 'I was there one day with Mr Donald. He was a nice person with short-cropped hair and a pleasant manner. He saw I was reading a book on India and asked me about it. We were quite close for the next six weeks and he gave me some guidance on what sort of books to read. Then we were sent to Santo Tomas.'

Donald was in a group of internees who were moved to the huge internment camp at Santo Tomas University in Manila. There, things became more difficult – it was always possible he would bump into a Japanese officer who had served in the China theatre and who knew him by sight.

The prospect of becoming *gauleiter* of the Australian media following a Japanese victory over Australia appealed enormously to Alan Raymond. He followed up his broadcasts with a vitriolic article entitled 'Australians play with fire' in the 'Double Seventh Anniversary' issue of the *Shanghai Evening Post* commemorating 'the very unhappy day [7 July 1937] on which that sad series of events began which is called the China Incident'. The cover of the edition showed a chilling, four-colour drawing of a fully armed Japanese soldier standing on a map of Asia with the words 'Guardian of East Asia's Co-prosperity Sphere'.

'The bogey of the Japanese was a thing which the British continually waved ominously before our eyes,' Raymond wrote with unconscious humour. 'We were constantly told that if the British did not protect us, the Japanese would get us.' Describing Australia as a 'British lacky [sic]', he urged Australians to forge an independent path – as members of Japan's Co-prosperity Sphere.[38]

Raymond kept up his anti-British barrage in a series of columns called 'An Aussie's Point of View' in the Japanese-controlled *Shanghai Times*. But Japan's hour had already passed. The shattering defeat of the Imperial Fleet in the Battle of Midway in June 1942 had destroyed any chance she might have had of making the Co-prosperity Sphere a permanent fixture in Asian life.

CHAPTER 23

Behind Barbed Wire

Ever since 8 December 1941 the *Kempeitai* had been picking up certain British and American nationals and taking them to their interrogation centre at Bridge House. They included Bill Gande, a wine importer, Eddy Elias, a stockbroker, A. H. Gordon, a photographer, and other seemingly ordinary people who were accused of 'espionage designed to undermine the Japanese Empire'.

'Victims were taken from all walks of life, without rhyme or reason,' Hugh Collar wrote. 'When they eventually came out, they were changed and badly shaken men. None of them talked and with cause.'[1]

Each man, however, had been reported at some point in the past as being a member of a security organisation, or for being 'anti-Japanese' and marked down for interrogation. The most prominent American among this group was John B. Powell, whose anti-Japanese views were well known through his writings in *China Monthly Review*.

On 20 December half a dozen members of the *Kempeitai* raided his room at the Metropole Hotel on Foochow Road and seized papers and letters. He was driven to Bridge House and, after being stripped of his possessions, taken downstairs to the building's former retail section, which had been converted into 15 prison cells of varying size.[2]

Powell was thrown into cell no. 5, a filthy room crowded with European and Asian prisoners. For the next 68 days, he was interrogated in an attempt to link him with American and British intelligence services. When this failed, he was accused of having 'dangerous thoughts' and of being 'disrespectful to the Emperor'. Finally, he was transferred to Kiangwan prison to be court-martialled on a trumped-up charge of espionage. The penalty would be death, although it was doubtful he would live long enough to be executed: by then, he had lost half his body weight through starvation.

Despite the fact that there was a price of 100,000 pesos (£15,000) on Bill Donald's head, he found himself among a group of people at Santo Tomas who would rather die than betray him. One of them was Carl Mydans, a photographer for *Life* magazine, whom he had first met in Chungking. Mydans had been caught in Manila with his wife Shelley. He had what he described as 'furtive talks' with Donald until September 1942 when he and his wife were shipped off to Shanghai on the first step of a prisoner exchange program.

Donald also met Jack Percival of the *Sydney Morning Herald* who was interned with his wife Joyce and baby son Jack Jr. 'Years ago he worked for my father on the *Bathurst Advocate*,' Percival recalled, 'and he teased me about wheeling me around Machattie Park in a pram.'[3]

All of Santo Tomas's 3500 internees faced the same problem: a chronic shortage of food. 'For many months the internment camps were deprived of all our staple foods and we got nothing but rice and corn and now and again a little green stuff,' Donald wrote in a letter to his daughter Muriel after the war. 'In a land where the coconut grows more prolifically than anywhere else on earth we could not get coconuts. Nor sugar. Nor any other fruit. We were slowly being starved and many people died of malnutrition.'[4]

Donald lost 25 kilograms in weight 'but was not as badly off as many'. Although there were rigid rules against trading with the enemy, the time came when Japanese soldiers roamed through Santo Tomas offering food in exchange for watches, diamonds and jewellery. '"Watchee, watchee," they cried out – or "ling, ling", or "diament",' Donald wrote. 'For a $750 diamond, the Jap traders gave 2 or 3 kilos of sugar; 1 or 2 kilos of rice and some ears of corn – total value before the war of about one peso.'

In common with many of the internees, Donald built a shanty out of bits of wood and branches in the university grounds and kept out of sight of the Japanese guards as much as possible. He became a favourite with the camp's children, telling, in the words of one mother, 'wonderful fairy stories of "Winkie Doodle" – interspersed with bits of his own true life story in China'.[5]

After seven months in captivity Sybil Fernandez and her two children were sent back to Shanghai from Manila in the hold of a cargo ship with a number of other families whose menfolk were in the Shanghai Municipal Police Force. Roy Fernandez heard a ship was due in from the Philippines and went to the dockside. 'He was very surprised to see us,' Stephanie Fernandez says. 'He thought we'd gone to Australia.'[6] Roy moved his family into a house in the police compound in Bubbling Well Road. The Japanese were gradually taking over the running of Shanghai – in the first eight months 80 senior British police officers had been replaced with their own people. Until that process was complete, Roy would continue to work at the Central Police Station in Foochow Road with a Japanese 'shadow' who would take his job when he was interned.[7]

The Japanese also occupied the ranking posts in the council secretariat, the health department and the industrial and social division, although Eleanor Hinder says that division went on under her direction for the first eight months. She also managed to have a book entitled *Life and Labour in Shanghai* printed in a Japanese-run print works after first removing any mention of foreign countries.[8] 'Many enterprises have closed down and more than 80 foreign plants are operating under the supervision of Japanese authorities,' she wrote in a letter on 10 July 1942. 'We struggled to get satisfactory pay-off allowances for the workers dismissed and to get some travel facilities for those desiring to return to the country. Finally we got half fares third class on the trains.'

Her own salary was drastically reduced and she was forced to move out of the big flat she shared with Viola into one room. She kept a bolthole at the home of friends in Frenchtown simply to get away from the misery of downtown Shanghai. 'It is so difficult to get about at night that one cannot get the escape of visiting friends and getting home again,' she wrote. 'It is a question of staying out once one goes out. There is no disguising the anguish of heart that one experiences even though one is living in comparatively good circumstances.'

The Japanese had seized all ten Allied banks and frozen the funds of Allied nationals. By queuing outside one of the banks in the freezing cold – waiting was not permitted inside the doors – those who had personal accounts were allowed to draw $2000 a month (US$50) in weekly instalments of $500.

Arch Carey, who lived with his father in Rue Ratard in Frenchtown, found it almost impossible to make ends meet. 'By pooling their resources, four people could live together sparingly on eight thousand Chinese dollars per month,' he wrote. 'But it was impossible for one person or even two persons to exist on this small amount, especially those who had to pay rent. The object was to bring our standard of living down to the same level as that of the lower-class Chinese and thus make us "lose face" in the eyes of the native population.'[9] For a time, fresh food and vegetables were readily available but a thriving

black market soon put most of these out of reach. By the end
of the war, prices in Shanghai had risen to 4000 times their
prewar level.

In August 1942 Eleanor Hinder received a telegram from
Viola Smith through the International Red Cross: 'ILO [INTER-
NATIONAL LABOUR ORGANISATION] OFFERS YOU POST EARLIEST
OPPORTUNITY STOP URGE YOU ACCEPT.' Behind the scenes, the
British Residents Association had placed Eleanor's name on a
list of people to be exchanged for Japanese nationals, while the
American Department of Labour co-operated with the Inter-
national Labour Organisation, formerly an agency of the League
of Nations, to offer her the ILO post.

On 14 August 1942 she sailed in the *Kamakura Maru* to
Lourenco Marques in Portuguese East Africa (now Mozam-
bique) to be swapped for a Japanese pearl fisherman who was
being held in Australia. 'My own Darling Darling,' she wrote
to Viola from Lourenco Marques on 9 September. 'For the
first time in these many months I can write to you without the
thought that other people would see what I have written! How
long these months have been! How I have missed you, longed
for you, yearned for you!' From Africa, Eleanor made her way
to London and then, despite the U-boat danger, crossed the
Atlantic to Canada, where she was reunited with Viola Smith
and took up her post with the ILO.

She had escaped just in time. On 21 September Japanese
military headquarters announced that enemy nationals
in Shanghai over the age of 13 must wear red armbands
whenever they left home. The armbands had 'B' for British
(which included Australians such as the Fernandez family),
'A' for Americans, 'N' for the Dutch and 'X' for others, such as
South Americans. 'I was only 11 at the time and I was jealous
of my brother because he had an armband and I did not,'
Stephanie Fernandez says. 'Far from shaming people they had

the opposite effect; they became a badge of honour.'[10] They were also an easy way of identifying people for internment.

That evening Carl and Shelley Mydans arrived in Shanghai in the Japanese transport *Maya Maru* with a group of American internees from Santo Tomas who were due to be exchanged for Japanese nationals in the United States. There was no blackout and Mydans was amazed to see European men dressed in immaculate white jackets and shorts standing under the bright street lights on The Bund watching the gathering on the dockside. After rollcall, a Japanese guard told the internees, 'You may go.'

It took a few moments for the message to sink in that after eight months' captivity in Manila they were free to move around as they pleased. Someone shouted, 'The Palace Hotel!' and they all bolted down The Bund clutching their little bundles of clothing. In the lobby Mydans found Chinese and European civilians mixing with Japanese officers. 'The strange war world of Shanghai fell into perspective,' he wrote, 'and by the time our Chinese room boys came for our bags and we followed them across the busy lobby to the elevator we were already ourselves becoming part of it.'[11]

Within a week of Mydans's arrival, however, squads of troops began rounding up Allied nationals and putting them in concentration camps, euphemistically known as 'civil assembly centres'. Like many others involved in essential services, Henry F. Pringle, the 40-year-old bespectacled head of the Shanghai Telephone Company, had remained free until now. His luck changed on 6 October – 'one of those beautiful Shanghai autumn days' – when he was arrested by the *Kempeitai* and taken to Bridge House.

Harry Pringle had been born in China of British parents and spoke fluent Chinese. He was thrown into a lice-infested cell with 20 other European prisoners, some of them barely recognisable as human beings. The Japanese accused him of being 'second in command' of a Chinese cell which passed information gleaned by tapping Japanese telephones to the Soviet authorities. When Pringle refused to confess, he was tortured.

'One of them clapped a towel over my eyes while another sprayed water over my body,' he says. 'The next thing a searing shock passed through my body as they applied an electrode to my navel and then passed another electrode over my breast, lips, throat, eyes and ears. The agony was terrible and I shrieked with pain.'

The torture went on for days. It included waterboarding in which he was tied down and a wet towel placed across his mouth and water poured over it until he believed he was drowning. When Pringle still refused to confess, the Japanese lost interest in him and moved on to more likely prospects. He was sent to the all-male Haiphong Road camp, which was reserved for Chinese speakers and those likely to be involved in subversion.

On 10 October – China's National Day commemorating the Double Tenth Revolution in 1911 – the governments of Great Britain and the United States quietly informed the Nationalists in Chungking that they were relinquishing their extraterritorial rights. The unequal treaties that had caused the Chinese such grief expired with barely a whimper after exactly one hundred years.

The next month Brigadier George Walker, the Australian-born officer in charge of the Salvation Army in Shanghai, was separated from his wife Jesse and dragged off to Haiphong Road. The Japanese wanted Walker to broadcast messages to Allied nationals, urging them to reconsider their position on the war. A highly principled man with a strong Christian faith, he refused to co-operate with his captors. Even torture over a long period at Bridge House failed to break his spirit.

Unlike George Walker, John Holland was only too willing to collaborate with the enemy. On 25 July 1942, he wrote to his father in Perth from his home at 47 Rue de Roi Albert:

I have not the space to go into great detail as to why or wherefore, but I belong to an Australian Political Party here which is interested in endeavouring to promote a separate peace with Japan. I broadcast over XGRS, which is a German station, every evening, so if this gets through the Australian Censor you may listen in. Naturally this is a serious statement for me to make, but I am prepared to stand by the results of it, as we people in the Far East have better conception of what the score is than you folks at home. Results of the war to date should bear this out. I am able to hear the ABC Station in Melbourne quite frequently so am well aware of what is going on in Australia. I do hope you will not condemn me until we get the chance to explain things more clearly to each other, after all we are entitled to our own politics.

After broadcasting for the Germans for some months in Shanghai, Holland offered his services to the Japanese, who flew him to Tokyo and put him up in a hotel.[12] On 6 December, he gave a talk on Tokyo radio on the eve of the first anniversary of the Japanese attack on Pearl Harbor. 'Roosevelt believed that Japan was exhausted through four years of war in China,' he said.

He thus believed he could adopt a bullying attitude towards the Japanese envoys. It is obvious the USA did not want peace with Japan. While Japan was trying to avert war, the USA was preparing for it. The USA, through Roosevelt, precipitated a crisis which burst on December 8. America thus provoked a war which it has been unable to prosecute.

In the New Year, Roy Fernandez and his family were ordered to report to the 'civil assembly centre' at the Public School in Yu Yuen Road to be interned. They arrived at the gates with a Chinese wheelbarrow full of tinned food that Roy had carefully accumulated over the previous months. The internees included almost the entire hierarchy of the Shanghai Municipal Police, Fire Brigade and Municipal Council. The camp representative was Kenneth Bourne, the police commissioner.

Freda Howkins had been working as a secretary at the British Embassy in the Jardine Matheson Building on The Bund. On the day war broke out, she was visiting Hong Kong with an embassy official. Along with thousands of Allied foreigners, she was interned at Stanley Camp but was then shipped back to Shanghai where she was reunited with her parents. As her father worked for the power company, the family remained free until 1943. 'As I'd already been interned in Hong Kong, I knew what to do,' Freda says.

> I said to mother, 'We must take in a side of bacon.' She looked at me with horror. I had managed to buy a bicycle and cycled to the market and came back with a side of bacon. It worked – it lasted quite a while. We filled a big trunk full of tinned food and a silver wedding cake for my parents because their anniversary was coming up in two months' time.[13]

Just as Bill Donald was starting to believe he might survive in Santo Tomas, his old enemy T. V. Soong almost put a noose around his neck. Having been appointed China's foreign minister, Soong was on a visit to London in August 1943 when he announced to the press that 'the Australian W. H. Donald, a former personal adviser to General Chiang Kai-shek, is a prisoner of the Japanese in Manila'. The story was published around the world that Donald had been trapped on the Philippines en route to China when the Japanese attacked and was now their prisoner.[14]

The *Kempeitai* heard the story and sent a detachment to Santo Tomas to find him. Donald was repairing books in the library with Ansie Lee and was unaware of the danger as the commandant thumbed through the camp register. When he reached Donald's entry, he shook his head. 'No, there is no

W. H. Donald of China here,' he said. 'We only have William Donald of Scotland and he's 68 years of age.' The *Kempeitai* had been led to believe that 'Donald of China' was a much younger man and left without asking to see him. Donald's luck had held but soon afterwards he volunteered to transfer to a new internment camp being set up in an agricultural college at Los Banos on the southern tip of the Philippines' largest lake, Laguna de Bay. It would be safer there and there might be more to eat . . .

Back in Shanghai, the Australian Independence Party collapsed after half a dozen meetings. Nevertheless, Alan Raymond and his cronies were allowed to stay in comfort at the Astor House Hotel and Broadway Mansions. Raymond said in his postwar statement, 'Personally I was able to engage in tea trading and as a broker on the Chinese stock exchange owing to my fluent knowledge of Chinese and my many Chinese connections, and so support myself and my Mother whom I had been able to rescue from an internment camp in Hong Kong.'

Such privileges were unheard of among expatriates during the Japanese occupation. While Raymond claimed after the war that he had never been in Japanese pay, he was not interned and his own statement makes clear that he benefitted financially from his collaboration.

As it became known that Japan was losing the war, there were visible signs of stress among the Sons of Nippon. They began squabbling among themselves in front of the internees whose meagre rations were cut even further in an attempt to kill off as many witnesses to their vile regime as possible. For thousands of prisoners, it was now a daily battle for survival against hunger and disease. There were also signs of friction in the collaborators' camp. Wynette McDonald physically attacked Alan Raymond after a furious argument. As a result, she was dismissed from the radio station and in April 1943 found herself interned at Lunghwa camp, which had just opened outside Shanghai.

Lunghwa was a township in itself, with large barrack rooms, a school, hospital, churches, clubs and even beautiful gardens. It was home to some 2000 internees, including *Empire of the Sun* author J. G. Ballard and his parents. 'The majority worked hard with little food, doing menial and dirty jobs throughout the boiling hot summers and bitter cold wet winters,' says one of the camp's former internees, Irene Kilpatrick. 'There were grumblers, but the British always grumble; it is their safety valve and keeps people calm.'[15]

The camp commandant was McDonald's friend Tomohiko Hayashi. According to Ruby Taylor, her former employer at the Peter Pan School who was also an inmate, she became a constant visitor to the quarters of Japanese officers. McDonald, however, claimed after the war that she was anxious to escape and on New Year's night 1944 dyed her skin with iodine and walnut oil to appear Chinese and slipped past the guards in the company of two young Chinese men. She said she was recaptured and placed in solitary confinement. Other internees, however, claimed her 'escape' was a ruse organised by Hayashi and that she lived out the war in a furnished apartment where she entertained her Japanese friends and lovers.[16]

McDonald's entry in the camp's nominal roll – published in Greg Leck's voluminous record of internment, *Captives of Empire* – contains the note 'failed escape' after her name and adds that she was transferred to Ward Road Jail in December 1943, an entry that could easily have been manufactured by Hayashi or one of her other Japanese friends among the guards.[17]

Meanwhile, John Powell had developed a form of gangrene in his feet due to starvation and neglect. Despite many attempts by the Swiss consul to locate him, the Japanese denied all knowledge of his whereabouts and then forced him to sign a statement saying he was 'all right and satisfied with his treatment'. By the time he was given medical aid, it was too late. He was taken to hospital where both feet were amputated.

The Japanese dropped the trumped-up charges against him and he was repatriated to the United States.

Carl and Shelley Mydans were also repatriated. In September 1943, they sailed in the *Teia Maru* to the neutral port of Goa in Portuguese India, where they were transferred to the Swedish American liner *Gripsholm* for the trip to New York. Carl went back to work as a war photographer for *Life* in the Battle for Europe and after VE day moved to the Pacific theatre.[18]

In Tokyo, the West Australian collaborator John Holland had fallen out with his Japanese masters. He had been writing a daily commentary on the Pacific War for a program called 'Asia's Views on the News'. When he was asked to do more work, he demanded higher pay. The Japanese turned him down. When he threatened to walk out, he was told he would be unable to earn a living if he did so. Regardless of the consequences, Holland quit his job and on 24 April 1943 he was arrested.[19]

Holland was secretly tried on charges of 'attempting to disturb the morale of the Japanese people and disturbing the public peace and safety'. He spent 30 months behind bars during which he lost six stone in weight and developed beri beri through malnutrition. He was forced to sit cross-legged on the floor for 14 hours a day winding pieces of string into balls. When he grew tired, the guards threw water over him. He was made to stand for hours on end and at other times beaten unconscious.[20] He had learned the hard way that Japanese militarists were hard taskmasters and even more ruthless enemies.

At dusk on 3 February 1945 Carl Mydans was with Company B of the United States 44th Tank Battalion when it liberated Santo Tomas camp after a firefight with Japanese guards. 'Carl Mydans walked in the big door of the Main Building in his fatigues with his camera over his shoulder,' one of the internees,

Catherine 'Kay' Cotterman, recalls. 'Betty Wellburn, who had been a good friend of his, called out, "My God, it's Carl Mydans!" Everybody just cheered. When I saw Carl Mydans there, I knew it was all over.'[21]

Then at dawn on 23 February the liberating forces moved in on Los Banos camp when two columns of phosphorus smoke rose near the camp to guide American paratroopers to their drop zone. Shortly afterwards, two more columns of smoke rose from the beach of Laguna de Bay as markers for 59 Amtracs (amphibious tractors) that would carry the internees to safety. At the same time, other troops linked up with Filipino guerrillas and started killing Japanese sentries.

The Japanese commandant and most of his officers and men were doing their daily exercises when they were attacked from all sides. As they scrambled for their weapons, paratroopers hit the jump area and Amtracs thundered into camp from the lake. 'I was sitting on the roadside waiting for rollcall when I saw the planes tip out the paratroopers,' Donald recalled. 'Then guerrillas began shooting and in no time the Japs were dead. We were loaded on to "alligators" which rode us to the lake and took us to the other side. We left all we had in the camp and it was burning before we got out.'

Jack Percival, who had been released from Santo Tomas earlier that month and was working as a war correspondent for the *Sydney Morning Herald*, greeted Donald as he crossed Laguna de Bay in one of the Amtracs. He was shocked to see that Donald was now 'a walking skeleton', the result of malnutrition and lack of medical care for a chronic lung condition. 'The first question he asked,' Percival recalled, 'was, "Where's Madame Chiang?" I told him she was in New York.' The internees were taken to Bilibid Prison in Manila for medical treatment and to start the process of building up their strength.

Donald was furious to discover that in mid-February an Associated Press reporter in Manila had filed a story that he had been released from one of Manila's prison camps. 'I escaped by good fortune and by virtue of the stupidity of the Japanese,' he wrote to Muriel.

> But at no time was the risk raised until American troops dropped on Los Banos camp from parachutes and rescued us. That was on February 23, though newspapermen had reported that I had escaped from Santo Tomas camp. The war correspondent who first reported this said that he was putting up a smoke screen. But had the Japanese seen this notice in the newspapers (especially *Time*) they had plenty of time to pick me up and dispose of me.[22]

Through sheer stamina and luck Donald had outlived the Empire of the Sun. He was also mightily relieved to discover that Ansie Lee had survived 37 months' detention in Santo Tomas. She had fallen in love with another internee, Henry 'Hank' Sperry, an American banker, and was engaged to be married.

But it was in many ways a pyrrhic victory. Donald's own life was in ruins. He had lost all his possessions and his health was broken. 'This war has now relieved me of everything that I possessed,' he said. 'I ought to get to China to try to rescue something.'

There was no chance of that, so Donald left Manila in the Holland America Line's SS *Noordam* bound for San Francisco where he was reunited with his daughter, Muriel, who was living in California. His estranged wife, Mary, had worked as a nurse but had fallen ill and Muriel supported her on her wages as a newscaster on a TV and radio station. Donald had no wish to see his wife. 'Your mother seems to think I have a lot of wealth,' he told Muriel. 'I came out of the camp without anything, either clothes or coin, and unless the house stands in Peking I have lost everything in China.'

He stayed with his friend H. Scott Martin at 2907 College Avenue, Berkeley, the university suburb across San Francisco Bay. He told reporters that Stalin would declare war on Japan as soon as he had 'tied up the knots in Europe'. He had no plans 'except to go to New York and visit Madame Chiang'.[23] Mayling had been in the United States so long there was talk of a rift between her and the Generalissimo. 'There is much speculation as to whether Donald will be able to reconcile the Chiangs,' Creighton Burns wrote in *The Argus*.[24]

By coincidence, the largest gathering of foreign ministers in history was meeting in San Francisco to draft the World Organisation Charter of the United Nations. Publicly, Australia's representatives, Foreign Minister Dr Bert Evatt and Deputy Prime Minister Frank Forde, were in accord that the new body should concentrate on economic and social issues rather than global peacekeeping. Privately, Evatt and Forde were at daggers drawn over who was in charge of the delegation. Someone spread the story that Forde had rung room service at his hotel and said, 'This is the Honourable Francis Michael Forde speaking, Deputy Prime Minister of the Australian Government and Leader of the Australian Delegation to the Conference of the United Nations. Send me up a hamburger.'[25]

'I have seen the Australian delegates, and they want me to go back to Australia,' Donald wrote to Muriel. '"Come and be the Far Eastern Adviser" to the Government, they say. And I say, "What do I know of the Far East that you people do not know, since you turned down all my advice prior to the war?" They retort, "That was another government." It was.'[26]

Donald was more concerned about having his teeth fixed before he set off across country on 20 June in the 'City of California' express for New York via Chicago. 'I am still unable to chew and am in pain and uncomfortable,' he told Muriel.

On the 19th he wrote to Muriel again. 'I have said goodbye to most of the conference people whom I know and today called and said hail and farewell to the Premier of New Zealand, Mr Peter Fraser. Everyone seemed glad to see me alive and well and one lady presented me with a typewriter. She had heard my Baby Hermes had been burned in camp and insisted on giving me another one.'

Just before the train left on 20 June a dentist filed down Donald's upstanding molars 'without mercy', and he was able to chew food properly for the first time in years.

Donald reached New York in early July. In a prophetic interview with David McNicoll of *The Argus*, he said the Japanese people would continue fighting as long as their emperor told them they were invincible. 'The Japanese have thrown off the veil of civilisation and have returned to the Samurai era,' he said. 'We must kill them off to beat them. They will not surrender.' He said he doubted that bombing would bring them to their knees, adding, 'The final battles against the Japanese will be fought in Manchuria.'[27]

Donald was reunited with Mayling at her Manhattan hotel. They hadn't seen each other for five years and it was an emotional moment. Mayling's standing in the world had risen to great heights with the help of Henry Luce, publisher of *Time* and *Life* magazines, but had then fallen dramatically after she made a number of political gaffes. No one knows for sure what transpired between them, although Donald later indicated she wished him to resume his former role at her side. 'Madame Chiang expects me to return to China, so does her brother T. V.,' he wrote to Lieutenant Bob Tierney of the United States Army who had escorted him across the Pacific. 'I may or may not go there. Though I am now recovering my strength I still feel against returning and have a lurking wish to go back to New Zealand.'[28]

As well as spending a couple of weeks in New York, Donald stayed with Harold Hochschild at his country home, 'Eagle Nest', at Blue Water Lake in the Adirondacks, and with a Chinese friend, K. C. Li, on Long Island. To his regret, he never found time to see Radio City Music Hall, the great entertainment palace in the Rockefeller Center.

All this time, the United States armed forces were making their way closer to the sacred Home Islands of Japan. The names of Saipan, Iwo Jima and Okinawa were written into the annals of war in the blood and sacrifice of thousands of

young men. Alan Raymond greeted the Allied advance with a
sneer. In his broadcast on 11 April 1945, he said, 'The American
policy to send over greater numbers [of planes] against Japan
gives a welcome increase of the targets for the Japanese special
attack units.'[29] And on 20 July he assured listeners, 'Despite the
approaching battle, Shanghai continues as normal. In point of
gaiety and excitement, there is no other community anywhere
in the world like this.'[30]

CHAPTER 24

Return to Shanghai

At 08.15 on the morning of 6 August 1945 bombardier Major Thomas Ferebee released a four-tonne uranium device named Little Boy from an American B-29 aircraft over the south island of Japan. Forty-three seconds later the first atomic bomb exploded at a height of 305 metres above the courtyard of the Shima Hospital in the heart of Hiroshima with the force of 12,500 tonnes of TNT. Around 70,000 people were vaporised in the first nuclear attack on a civilian population.

As Bill Donald had predicted, the Red Army then attacked Japanese forces in Manchuria. On 8 August Stalin's legions fell upon the dispirited defenders with 70 divisions in a four-pronged offensive. The Japanese had anticipated this moment for eight years and when it came their 40 divisions were completely overwhelmed.

At 11.02 the following morning, 9 August, Fat Man, a plutonium bomb bigger than Little Boy, was dropped on the civilian port of Nagasaki, killing 50,000 people and injuring many thousands more. Ironically, it was the threat of a Russian invasion of the sacred homeland rather than the effects of two atom bombs that most terrified the Japanese hierarchy.

At midday on 15 August a Japanese radio announcer asked all listeners to stand 'respectfully' in front of their radio sets. The familiar strains of the Japanese anthem were played and then in a high-pitched, tremulous voice Hirohito announced Japan's unconditional surrender.

The Pacific War – and more importantly to Donald and 400 million Chinese, the Sino-Japanese War – was over. While 200,000 Japanese prisoners of war were transported to Siberia, the American Air Force flew thousands of Nationalist troops to Shanghai, Nanking and Peking to take the surrender of the local garrisons and beat the Communists to vast dumps of Japanese arms.

Wilfred Burchett, the Australian war correspondent, arrived in Japan with General Douglas MacArthur's occupation forces. At great personal risk, he joined a queue at Tokyo central station and took a train to Hiroshima. 'I was the first non-Japanese person into Hiroshima,' he said. He was also the first reporter to write about the 'atomic plague' that would kill thousands of Japanese from leukaemia and other forms of cancer.

Like many Old China Hands, Bill Donald was unforgiving. 'I hope MacArthur has the determination to strip those little people of everything they possess that might help them to recover,' he wrote to Bob Tierney. 'I do not like the way in which they are hoping to retain their military machine. I want to see them be made to pay for their atrocities towards Americans, Filipinos, Spaniards, British and Chinese.'[1]

Roy Fernandez and his family had been moved to another camp in the Sacred Heart Chinese Hospital downriver at Yangtzepoo. 'Our commandant got up and told us the Japanese would fight to the last man,' Stephanie Fernandez says. 'We woke up one morning to find they had disappeared and we were free.'[2] Then a van with the Australian flag tied to both sides came trundling into the camp – the Australian Red Cross had got through the lines to deliver food. They also gave every woman in the camp a box containing soap, shampoo, talcum powder, lipstick, face powder, underwear, a nightdress and sanitary towels. 'Someone in Australia had been really thoughtful,' Stephanie says, 'and I was a very proud young Australian.'[3]

While thousands of ecstatic Chinese citizens swarmed through the streets of the International Settlement, Lieutenant-General Chen Shu-sun of the Third Chungking Army took the Japanese surrender from the deputy chief of the Japanese 13th Army, Lieutenant-General Toji Minfu, at the Cathay Hotel.

Reviewing the status of Shanghai following the end of the loathsome extraterritorial privileges for foreigners, the War Minister General Ho Ying-shin announced, 'Shanghai is now completely under Chinese sovereignty and no one, regardless of nationality, is to observe any law other than that of this country. No one is to have any privilege whatsoever.'[4]

The Nationalists restored the Shanghai Power Company to its American owners and the waterworks to the British, but the American-owned Shanghai Telephone Company was the subject of negotiations.

'Although 8500 Allied internees in Shanghai have been freed, including Australians, the majority of them have no money and are homeless,' Herbert Mishael reported in the *Sydney Morning Herald*. 'They are compelled to stay in the internment camps until they can be reached by friends.'[5] Keith Officer, the Australian *chargé d'affaires*, flew down from Chungking and set up a residential centre in a building in downtown Shanghai as a temporary home for 70 Australians. A large Australian flag was draped over the entrance of the 'Southern Cross Club' and Fred Drakeford, brother of the Australian Minister for Air Arthur Drakeford, was appointed manager.[6]

Major H. W. Jackson, who arrived in Shanghai with the 3rd Prisoner of War contact and inquiry unit, compiled nominal rolls of 240 Australian internees in the Shanghai area and interviewed many of them about their experiences. One of the saddest cases was Jean Armstrong, the journalist who had been beaten by *ronin* prior to internment. Now 53, Jean suffered badly from arthritis, anxiety and loss of memory. She described herself as a 'woman who has gone through Hell'. 'Can't gather thoughts accurately but think I went into camp around 15 April 1942,' she later wrote. 'Doctors tried to keep me out of camp, said I was not fit to go in.' Jean was initially interned at Lunghwa but was then admitted to the invalids' camp at Columbia Country Club before being sent to Yangtzepoo. After being liberated, she was taken to an American hospital ship, then to the British Hospital in Shanghai, where she was interviewed by the investigating committee and signed a statement. 'Formerly I was a worldly Australian citizen,' she wrote to Henry Stokes, a member of the Australian Legation at Chungking who visited her at Yangtzepoo, 'now I come to you "beaten & broke".'

Internees were informed they would be sent by ship as soon as possible to Manila, where an Australian reception centre had been established. Fred Drakeford, however, flew out in a Catalina flying boat, courtesy of his ministerial brother. The plane also took Douglas Murdoch, a cousin of Sir Keith Murdoch, and his wife Joyce back to Australia.[7]

Murdoch, an engineer with Cable & Wireless in Hong Kong, was suspected of collaboration after accepting a Japanese offer to transfer from Stanley camp in Hong Kong to Shanghai where he and his wife were given an apartment at the Cathay Hotel. After the war, Murdoch claimed he had been 'interrogated' for six months because the Japanese believed he had diplomatic connections. Australian investigators concluded that he had flirted with the idea of collaboration but had changed his mind and was then interned at Yangchow internment camp.[8]

The former telephone supremo Harry Pringle had the satisfaction of seeing his torturers sentenced to long terms of imprisonment. In November 1945, he was reunited with his wife Isabella and two daughters Elizabeth and Eileen in Australia. For many years, he worked at Nicholson's Music Store in George

Street, Sydney, and retired to Canberra. He died in 1987 at the age of 84.

Peace negotiations between Chiang Kai-shek and Mao Tse-tung opened in Chungking on 28 August but had little effect in stopping clashes between the Communists and Chiang's commanders. 'If the Communists are ready to give up their arms, then we may hope for peace in China,' Bill Donald said in an interview. 'However, I can't believe that they are ready; they will never be satisfied until they dominate China completely.'

On his way back to California, Donald developed feelings of impending doom. 'When I came out of the camp, I had nothing and I thought I was lucky,' he wrote to Muriel from Chicago. 'Now I have accumulated two suitcases, one duffel bag and they are too much and I feel unlucky.'

On 25 October 1945 Donald sailed for New Zealand with the intention of stopping in Tahiti for a while and then travelling from New Zealand to Australia to see his family before finally heading north to China. 'Be of good cheer,' he counselled Muriel, 'and don't throw dirty water away till you can get clean. With warmest regards and affectionate wishes. As ever, with love, Dad.'[9] Donald never saw his daughter again.

With the defeat of Japan, Chiang Kai-shek, pale-faced and almost bald, claimed in an interview in October 1945 to have all but united China with the exception of the Communists and, according to Herbert Mishael, 'he has gone a long way towards achieving that in spite of almost insurmountable difficulties and differences'.[10]

In late December, General George C. Marshall, America's brilliant wartime chief of staff, arrived in Shanghai as President Harry S. Truman's special representative, 'a midwife to deliver the peace child to China'.[11] His mission was to arrange a truce between Communist and Nationalist forces and establish a coalition government with the objective of resisting Stalin's attempts to take over Manchuria. Truman had little regard for Chiang Kai-shek or the Nationalist Government. He had met Mayling once and, according to Vice President Wallace, 'did not like her'.

Mayling had returned to China from her extended stay in the United States in September. Eleanor Roosevelt issued this stinging verdict on her former guest: 'She can talk beautifully about democracy, but she does not know how to live democracy.'[12]

Mayling threw herself into the negotiations between Marshall and her husband, interpreting at their meetings but also attempting to take control of the talks. On 10 January 1946 Marshall succeeded in negotiating a ceasefire which began to take effect three days later. By the 25th, there was no fighting in China for the first time in 18 years.

Meanwhile, Bill Donald had been taken ill in Tahiti and admitted to the French Hospital. A doctor told him one of his lungs had collapsed and his other lung was full of fluid. Donald cabled Mayling asking for help and a request for assistance was sent from the Headquarters of the Generalissimo to the United States naval base at Pearl Harbor. The Navy dispatched a flying boat to Tahiti which took Donald to Honolulu. He was admitted to the Aiea Naval Hospital where tests showed he was suffering from terminal lung cancer.

When he was allowed visitors, the first people through the door were reporters anxious for his views on the new drama unfolding in China. Donald was as outspoken as ever: America, he said, was playing into the hands of the Chinese Communists by making aid to China contingent on certain political and economic changes. 'The Reds live from the land and since they have never been recipients of aid from anyone, including the Russians, their position is not affected,' he said. 'Since they have no intention of laying down their arms their strength may grow purely because the areas under *Kuomintang* will weaken.'[13]

To Muriel, he wrote on 22 February 1946, 'I am still here, looking forward to going back to Shanghai to see how things are there. To tell you the truth I feel nothing. I never did feel anything in the way of sensation and I feel no more or less today.'

One of the reporters who interviewed him was Earl Albert Selle of the *Honolulu Advertiser*. Selle had worked in Shanghai in the 1930s and talked to Donald about old times and the characters they had known. Knowing he was dying of lung cancer, Donald decided to collaborate with Selle on his life story and paid him US$5000, which he could ill afford, to take over the work immediately.

Selle had had a mixed career in journalism, ranging from police reporter on the *Seattle Star* to news reporter on the *Shanghai Evening Post* under the editorship of Carl Crow, as well as working for brave John Powell on the *China Weekly Review*. He had also lectured in journalism at the University of Shanghai, worked as publicity director for the Democratic Party in Washington State and written movie scripts for RKO Pictures in Hollywood.

One of the difficulties the authors had to overcome was that Selle had gone blind during the war. He recorded interviews with Donald on a dictaphone and corresponded with some of Donald's friends and family through his wife, then set about dictating the book, *Donald of China*, to a secretary.[14] After four weeks of interviews, Bill Donald called a halt; he was too sick to continue. He cabled the Chiangs that he wanted to die in China, so in March they sent his old friend Hollington Tong to Hawaii to take him back to Shanghai in a Nationalist aircraft.

'In Shanghai, we are going to grieve a lot before we are through the jungle,' he wrote to Muriel. 'But we shall get through some way or other.' When his plane took off on the evening of 15 March, he was wearing a lei of Hawaiian flowers around his neck, a panama hat on his head and a broad smile on his face. Donald of China was going home.

It came as no surprise that Shanghai had changed. In this new postwar world, the warships of the United States Seventh Fleet rode at anchor on the Whangpoo. On The Bund, a wooden building bearing the sign 'US Navy Hamburger Stand' sat opposite the regal Hong Kong & Shanghai Bank, now restored to its rightful owners. The moneychangers in Szechuen Road no longer based their rates on the pound sterling but on the American dollar. And at the Canidrome, previously the scene of greyhound races, spectators now queued up to watch American football games.[15]

Millions of Chinese had turned out to welcome Chiang Kai-shek when he returned to Shanghai from Chungking in early 1946. But his minions unleashed such a ruthless takeover of so-called 'enemy property' – much of which had been seized from its Chinese owners in the first place – that public opinion quickly turned against him. The Nationalists were dubbed 'Chungking Man' and, it was said, they were interested only in the 'five *zi*' – *tiaozi* (gold bars), *fangzi* (houses), *nuzi* (girls) *chezi* (cars) and *guanzi* (restaurants).[16]

Donald was admitted to the Country Hospital in Great Western Road. On 5 August 1946 he received a cable informing him that his house in Peking, although dilapidated, was still intact. He sent orders back for the house to be sold. His visitors included George Morrison's middle son Alastair Morrison, now a captain in the British Army, and Harold Timperley, who was back in Shanghai working for the United Nations Relief and Rehabilitation Administration (UNRRA). Alastair recalled, 'He was a frail and gentle man who could joke about the solemn way a group of doctors told him he had terminal lung cancer.'[17]

Reporters still consulted him. 'If China has the wisdom of the Serpent – and I believe she has – she will become the leading industrial power in Asia in the next ten years,' he told one.

Harold Timperley's colleague at UNRRA, Ida du Mars, had known Donald since 1923. She took him for walks in the garden, to the movies, to H. H. Kung's mansion for dinner and for drives in Chiang Kai-shek's car.[18] 'They are very kind to me,' Donald wrote to Harold Hochschild. 'They allow me to buy nothing and anticipate all of my wants, even to the point of embarrassment.'[19] Mayling visited him several times, once with George Marshall's wife Katherine.

Donald made frantic efforts to put his affairs in order. He wrote to Muriel on 12 October 1946:

> On October 9th there was sent to you from the sale of my Peking house the sum of US$16,000. As it is now very difficult in China to arrange for gold dollar exchange, I have had the entire amount sent directly to you in one lump sum. It is my wish that you accept US$10,000 of this amount for yourself and deposit the balance of the amount, ie US$6000, in my account with the National City Bank of New York, 22 William Street, New York City. I am still in hospital and now that the hot summer weather is past, I am very hopeful that I will regain some of the strength I lost during the terrifically hot weather. I spend most of my time either in bed or sitting in my armchair on the verandah. I have had several operations since I last wrote to you and on the whole everything is going as well as can be expected.
>
> With love to you and hoping that you are well.
> As ever, Dad (W. H. Donald)

As the Shanghai nights drew in, the man known to the Japanese as 'the evil spirit of China' approached what he called 'the bourne where none return'. He cried out for Mayling who set off for Shanghai from Nanking but her plane was delayed and it seemed she might not arrive in time. Ida du Mars was at his side as he listened anxiously for the sound of her footsteps in the hall. She entered the room with the words, 'Gran, here's your boss.' She sat beside his bed, picked up the Bible and read the 23rd Psalm. His last words to her were, 'We'll meet again in the next world.'[20]

Donald's last wish was to see Dean A. C. S. Trivett of the Holy Trinity Cathedral, who hurried to the hospital and offered prayers for his salvation. Dr James T. Cheng said Donald lost consciousness late that night, his breathing became laboured and 'in about five minutes it was all over'.[21]

W. H. Donald died at 1.15 am on 9 November 1946 at the age of 71. The following day he lay in state in a coffin draped in the Chinese flag, with a cross of yellow and white chrysanthemums and a ribbon inscribed 'In memory of an Old and Valued Friend – Generalissimo and Madame Chiang'.[22]

The mourners at his funeral included Mayling Soong Chiang, H. H. Kung, T. V. Soong, Lieutenant-General Claire Chennault and Harold Timperley. They heard Tao-fan Chang, chairman of the Central Cultural Movement, deliver the eulogy. 'It has pleased the Almighty to give you eternal peace and rest in Paradise,' he said. 'We, your admiring Chinese friends, find some consolation in this thought. Nevertheless, we feel utterly desolate because our country has lost in you such a dear friend.'

Later that day Donald was buried at the International Cemetery. 'I spent nearly seven months with him, visiting him twice daily and latterly I slept at the hospital,' Ida du Mars wrote to Muriel. 'Except for a special nurse I was alone with him when he passed away.'

'Hank' Sperry, now married to Ansie Lee, was one of Donald's last visitors. After discussing his book project with Mayling during one of her visits, Donald had decided – for the second time – that his life story should remain unwritten to avoid embarrassing the Chiangs and hurting other people. He tried to cancel his agreement with Earl Selle and wrote to friends and members of his family withdrawing permission for them to speak to the writer. He also retrieved as many of his personal papers as he could locate. 'On his deathbed in Shanghai,' Sperry later said, 'he asked me to burn those he still had and I did so.' Thus the life of 'Donald of China' went up in smoke in a Shanghai fireplace.

Less than ten years later Mayling Soong Chiang was asked about Donald at a private dinner party at Chiang Kai-shek's home in Taiwan. It was the spring of March 1955 and her guests were Denis Warner and his wife Peggy and Sir Wilfred and Lady Kent Hughes. Donald? Oh yes, Mayling said, he was 'a funny little man'.

Denis Warner was a respected foreign correspondent for the Melbourne *Herald* Group. Well aware of Donald's Olympian reputation among his peers, he pressed Mayling for an explanation. She scoffed at the suggestion that Donald had been her husband's adviser and said he had worked in Chungking in some minor capacity. He was, she said, 'someone of absolutely no consequence'.

The reason for Mayling's attitude towards her long-time adviser and the man she called 'Gran' wasn't hard to divine. Her popularity on the world stage, especially in the United States, had plummeted after Donald withdrew his careful guiding hand and left Chungking. Then in 1948, just as the Chiang regime was collapsing, Earl Selle's book *Donald of China* appeared with its unquestioning hero-worship of Donald. As Donald had feared, the book presented the Chiangs as bit players in a great drama in which W. H. Donald was producer, director and star performer.

Mayling would have read the book, plus the numerous obituaries in which Donald was hailed as a hugely significant figure in the history of the Chinese Republic, a man who exercised enormous influence on Chiang Kai-shek and herself. The easiest way to kill questions about his role was to dismiss him as 'a man of no consequence'.

It was also partly true. The tragedy of W. H. Donald was that he had played no part in the events culminating in Japan's defeat. With his plain-talking, down-to-earth approach and vast experience of Chinese affairs, he would have been the perfect man to intercede in the highly personal clashes between Chiang Kai-shek and his irascible American chief of staff, General Joseph 'Vinegar Joe' Stilwell, that had crippled much of China's war effort.

Typical of Stilwell's venom was his description of Chiang as 'a grasping, bigoted, ungrateful little rattlesnake'. Donald might have agreed with these sentiments but, realising the importance of the Sino-American pact, would have hammered out a working relationship between them. As things were, James McHugh sided with the Chiangs and put the knife into Stilwell in letters to Washington. On Chiang's insistence, Vinegar Joe was recalled to the United States.

Languishing in a Japanese internment camp during those tumultuous years, Bill Donald was indeed 'a man of no consequence' to Chiang Kai-shek and his wife. His terminal illness then cruelly robbed him of a second chance to get back into the game for the final showdown between Chiang and Mao Tse-tung.

Donald's rightful place is beside George Morrison as the two most influential Australians in modern Chinese history. Like Morrison, his record wasn't perfect but he set a standard for honesty and decency that was hard to beat. 'Australia can be proud of Donald who served as a better Ambassador of Goodwill than could have any career diplomat,' the *China Press* wrote in an editorial. 'For in his every word, in his every deed, Donald showed the marks of the tradition of democracy which has made Australia what she is today. Yet Donald was more than an Australian, more than a man of "European" background. He was something far greater, far finer – a citizen of the world.'

There seemed to be no justice. On 24 October 1945 the Australian Crown Solicitor, H. F. E. 'Fred' Whitlam, father of the future prime minister Gough Whitlam, decided there was insufficient evidence to charge Alan Raymond or Wynette McDonald with treason. Captain Wilfred Blacket, a Sydney barrister serving with the Australian Security Service, was ordered to interview all three collaborators to extract more information.

On 10 November 1945 Blacket flew out of Sydney and six days later stepped off a plane in Tokyo. On the orders of Brigadier-General Elliott R. Thorpe, chief of counter-intelligence at MacArthur's headquarters, John Holland had been arrested at gunpoint by three of Thorpe's officers at Sapporo on the north island of Japan. The Americans found him sitting in a barber's chair at the Grand Hotel while one girl shaved him and another manicured his nails. They believed his plan was to escape to Manchuria.[23]

Holland was flown to the war criminal stockade at Yokohama and then confined in Sugamo Prison where many Japanese war criminals were under lock and key. After interviewing him and reading Thorpe's dossier – which included a signed statement from Holland admitting he had worked for the Japanese – Blacket concluded there was a prima facie case of treason against him.

Meanwhile, Wynette McDonald turned up at the Australian Legation in Shanghai demanding financial assistance. The legation occupied two large rooms in the consulate-general's office in Avenue Joffre. There was a queue of people waiting in the drab corridor to be seen but McDonald and two of her lovers pushed passed them into the office of Henry Stokes. 'I put the lovers out of court,' Stokes related, 'and was very blackbrowed with the wide and innocent eyed Miss McDonald.' McDonald brassily told him she had had 100 lovers 'but says that No 67, the Japanese guard when she was in the jug, was the only one she really loved'.

After she had left, Stokes 'applied to have the harlot incarcerated immediately' so that Blacket would arrive 'to find the gentry all detained for questioning, including Raymond and McDonald'. But as Britain and the United States had given up their extraterritorial rights, the Chinese authorities refused to co-operate with Stokes and the pair were still free when Blacket flew into Shanghai.

When Blacket tracked them down, they admitted having been members of the Independent Australia League and making radio broadcasts for the Japanese. Raymond was unrepentant. He said that at no time was he under any form of compulsion and nor had he been paid for his services: he had worked for the Japanese because he believed Australia should be free of its imperial bonds. He expressed a desire to return to Australia but was most anxious that nothing should interfere with a psychology course he was taking at St John's University.[24]

At his home in Frenchtown on 5 December, he handed Blacket a signed statement in which he claimed he had 'made the decision to sacrifice myself if necessary' for the benefit of Australia.

> After the fall of Singapore the outlook for Australia was indeed black [he wrote]. I did not broadcast until after that time. Myself and a group of friends decided that if we could get Australia to declare independence she could not only take care of her own dire situation in a more realistic manner, but could also prepare for a better future. Accordingly we formed the Independent Australia League . . . I admit that I have worked constantly to lessen the effects of the war on Australia [and] I have always prayed that the Allies would win the war and that Australia would be safe.

At 9.45 am the following day Captain Blacket interviewed Wynette McDonald at 585 Yu Yuen Road, where she was living with her current lover, 24-year-old Carlos Henrique de Rosa Ozorio, a British subject of Portuguese extraction who had also been interned at Longhwa camp.

By the most twisted of logic, McDonald told Blacket that her broadcasts were actually an attempt to assist the Allied war effort. 'I at no period had intended to co-operate with them,' she said, 'but had walked in fear of the Bridge House.' She had found a Japanese travel book, which contained information that might be of use to the Nationalist regime in Chungking. She asked for permission to broadcast a program called 'Japan and the Japanese' in order to disseminate this information, but was 'caught out' when the Japanese told her she would have to make a political broadcast as well. She agreed to do so, and her lover Olof Lindquist wrote a political commentary for her – presumably the one about John Curtin and Joe Lyons.

McDonald admitted she had broadcast material that was abusive to the Allies and of assistance to Japan, but insisted her intention all along was to help Australia. 'I am of the opinion,' Blacket concluded, 'that there is not sufficient evidence obtainable to warrant the laying of a charge of treason against McDonald.'

McDonald also told Blacket that Alan Raymond was 'on a good thing with the Japs – they set him up in a tea business'. She added she was prepared to give evidence against him. His stepmother was contacted and also agreed to testify against him in exchange for a berth in a repatriation ship back to Australia. Blacket asked the Chinese authorities to arrest Raymond and McDonald but once again they refused to take orders from a foreign officer.[25]

Back in Canberra, lawyers studied the statements made by Raymond and McDonald and concluded there was little chance of getting a conviction on a charge of treason. In Raymond's case, there was 'little doubt he was guilty of treason but there was not sufficient evidence to support an indictment'.

Meanwhile, Wynette McDonald returned to Australia in the SS *Bonaventure* and moved in with her sister in Melbourne. From Chungking on 13 April 1946, the new Australian minister to China, Sir Douglas Copland, cabled Canberra demanding to know why 'this notorious collaborationist' had not been taken into custody on arrival in Australia, thus increasing 'criticism in Shanghai that we are not planning to take action against such persons'.

In fact, there was evidence aplenty against Alan Raymond back at Sugamo Prison where, on 20 March 1946, Japanese spy chief Ikushima Kichizo revealed under interrogation that the Australian had served as a paid employee of Japanese naval intelligence in Shanghai.[26] The Australian Legation in Washington followed this up in a message to the Department of External Affairs on 19 April 1946 which actually named Raymond as a Japanese agent:

> The Military Intelligence Service of the [United States] War Department have asked us to transmit to you for information and appropriate action the following extract from a report forwarded from JICA [the Joint Intelligence Collecting Agency], Shanghai:

> Report no. R-5005-CH-45: The following list of foreign agents of the Japanese, formerly active in Shanghai, has been submitted to General Dai Li [head of Chiang Kai-shek's secret service][27] as of primary importance:

> Pat Kelly, alias Frankie Johnston, British;
> Alan Raymond, Australian.

On 20 May 1946 Fred Whitlam wrote to the Department of External Affairs that 'it seems to me that the best course to adopt would be to give all possible assistance to the Chinese to have Raymond arrested and tried under Chinese law'. But the Nationalist regime took no action against him. Raymond's identification as 'an agent of primary importance' was of little concern to Dai Li, who was involved in a life-and-death struggle with Communist infiltrators. He did nothing.

One resident was so infuriated about Raymond he consulted British Intelligence at the British Consulate. 'Although they have a complete dossier on his record during the war, they are powerless to bring him to book without the co-operation of the Chinese,' he said in a statement to the Australian Security Service. 'Any unilateral act on the part of the British in this matter would be regarded by the Chinese as an infringement of their sovereignty, a point upon which they are absurdly touchy at the present time.'

As Raymond had wished, he was permitted to continue his studies in psychology at St John's University. He also got married, a fact that emerged when he applied for Australian passports for himself and his Chinese wife. His application was turned down. Wynette McDonald was permitted to leave Australia and astonishingly took a job with the United States Army. John Holland was brought back to Australia where he was freed without charge.

To former internees who had listened to the collaborators' broadcasts and then endured abuse and incarceration at the hands of the Japanese, it seemed monstrously unfair. One resident who saw Raymond lunching at the Palace Hotel with Chinese friends said, 'It is galling to think that this man, who did so much to assist the enemy, should still be enjoying a full measure of freedom.'

CHAPTER 25

Mao's Triumph

Chinese Red Army units rampaged over Manchuria, besieging the Nationalist forces in Mukden, Changchun and Chinchow. Fearing the emergence of a strong Communist China under Mao Tse-tung on Russia's eastern borders, Stalin had sent military supplies to Chiang Kai-shek throughout the war. But in the summer of 1946, he suddenly dumped the untrustworthy Chiang and handed the Communists 1226 field guns, 369 tanks, 300,000 rifles, 4836 machine-guns and 2300 vehicles, all of which had been seized from the Japanese.[1]

As the military pendulum swung heavily in Mao's favour, James McHugh also changed tack. 'The more I hear and see of this situation out here, the more I am inclined to think that we should pull out completely and let this civil war take place,' he wrote in a letter to his wife. 'It would unseat Chiang and T. V. and all of the other crooked politicians, all of whom are growing rich now on all that we have given China.'[2]

The Australian minister, Sir Douglas Copland, concurred. He informed Canberra that the Nationalists were 'inefficient, corrupt and intractable, and seemed destined to lose China to the Communists'.[3] Although Chiang had an advantage in numbers and weapons, the peasants believed it was the Communists who had actively resisted the Japanese. It was the peasants who would decide the outcome of the civil war and they overwhelmingly supported Mao Tse-tung.

General Marshall realised that the Communists were not merely 'land reformers', as they presented themselves to foreign diplomats and journalists, but full-blooded Leninists, and that his mission to unite two diametrically opposed forces was doomed to fail. When he was recalled to Washington, the United States ended its efforts at mediation. As Nationalist troops deserted en masse rather than fight the Red Army, Dr John Leighton Stuart, the academic who served as the last American ambassador to Chiang's government in mainland China, could do little except report the collapse of the regime.

In October 1946 Captain Wilfred Blacket returned to Japan to gather further evidence from the Japanese that would enable a charge of treason to be brought against John Holland. But Holland had slipped the net. After visiting his family in Perth, he left Fremantle in the SS *Tai Ping Yang* bound for Norway via the United Kingdom. His Australian passport had expired, so he travelled on a seaman's document of identity.

Through Scotland Yard, the Australian Security Service traced him to an address in England. The question then arose of whether he should be tried in a British court or returned to Australia under the Fugitive Offenders Act. The solicitor-general, Kenneth Bailey, sought the advice of the English director of public prosecutions, Sir Theobald Mathew (who would gain international notoriety in 1960 over his decision to prosecute Penguin books for obscenity after it published *Lady Chatterley's Lover*).

On 7 February 1947 he replied to Bailey that Holland could be charged in Britain under Defence Regulation 2A which dealt with 'renegades who were not thought to be deserving of death, which is the only penalty for treason'. As Holland was a British subject and the offences had been committed in Shanghai and Tokyo, he did not foresee any jurisdictional difficulty and he had been supplied with enough evidence to obtain an arrest warrant.

On 18 February Holland was arrested aboard an oil tanker at Hull. When he appeared at the Old Bailey on 25 March, he pleaded guilty before the Lord Chief Justice, Lord Goddard, to engaging in subversive activities in China and Japan. 'It was vanity which caused you to think that a person like yourself could have some influence on the policy of Australia,' Goddard told him. 'But what you did in lending yourself to the Japanese came back on you like a boomerang and landed you in this torture of hell in Japanese prisons for two and a half years.' Holland was bound over in the sum of £10 to be of good behaviour for the next five years.

At the Old Bailey on 24 March Lord Goddard had sentenced Thomas John Ley, a former minister of justice in New South Wales, to be hanged for arranging the murder of a barman he wrongly suspected of having an affair with his mistress. Describing Goddard's leniency towards John Holland as 'surprising', Theobald Mathew wrote in a letter to Kenneth Bailey, 'Perhaps he felt that having sentenced an Australian ex-Minister of Justice to death on the previous day it was time that the Commonwealth had a break!'*

Bailey replied there was 'a great deal of disappointment' in Australia at Holland's lenient sentence. 'I think most people had a kind of uneasy feeling that perhaps British Courts were not disposed to treat collaboration with the Japanese with the same realism as they had displayed in dealing with the collaborators with the Germans.'

---

* In the event, Ley's death sentence was commuted and he was committed to Broadmoor hospital for the criminally insane where he died in July 1947.

Wynette McDonald surprised everybody by returning from abroad with a new husband, Carlos Ozorio; she was also pregnant. On 22 July 1947 Frederick G. 'Black Jack' Galleghan, former commander of the 2/30th Battalion in the Battle of Malaya and now deputy director of the Commonwealth Investigation Service in Sydney, sent a secret memorandum to Canberra that McDonald had been under surveillance while in Australia in 1946 but 'was permitted to leave Australia and proceed to employment with the United States Army and returned to Australia per the SS *Haleakala* en route to Melbourne on Saturday, 19 July 1947'.

Fellow passengers told an investigator who met the ship in Melbourne that they 'were of the opinion that Ozorio and McDonald were man and wife, and their conduct on the voyage was such as to strengthen this impression'.[4] Carlos Ozorio was born at Swatow, China, on 1 February 1921 and had been one of McDonald's lovers during the war. They were now living at her parents' home in Alma Place, St Kilda, and Carlos was working as a radio technician with the Department of Civil Aviation at Essendon Airport.

'This man avers that he was married to Wynette McDonald on the 3rd or 4th January 1943 at a small Chinese church outside Lung Hua [sic] Internment Camp,' says a secret memorandum dated 23 September 1947 in the Commonwealth Investigations Service files.

> The parties are living together as man and wife, and a child is expected in December. She does not hold a marriage certificate and, as she indicated that they will probably go through a form of marriage here, it might be taken as an indication that there was no consummation [sic]. It can now be stated that Miss McDonald is not engaged in any activity of a subversive nature. She spends most of her time at home and would appear to have adopted the role of housewife.

As the Red Army approached the Yangtze and rice riots broke out among the starving masses in Shanghai, Ian Morrison wrote in November 1948, 'My own prediction is that the Communists are going to get the whole of China – and fairly soon. There is nothing to stop them. The question is not whether they are going to come out on top, but what sort of Communists they are going to be.'[5]

This was the question that exercised the Foreign Office, which feared for the future of British investment in China. The Communists, however, refused to speak to British diplomats or even recognise the existence of the British consul-general in Shanghai. Whitehall called in the British Secret Service and as a result Commander John Proud joined the staff of the British Consulate in early 1949.

John Charles Rookwood Proud had been born in Melbourne on 13 October 1907. He had enlisted in the Royal Australian Navy Volunteer Reserve in August 1939 and had served in Singapore in 1941–42. On his return to Australia he had run Section D, the military propaganda section of the Allied Intelligence Bureau.[6]

His sudden appearance in Shanghai in the once important but now defunct role of 'land consul' mystified the foreign community. Proud was in fact a secret agent who had been trained in London with other agents including the Russian spy Kim Philby. During training exercises on how to lose an enemy tail, both men could be seen dashing up and down escalators in Harrods department store in Knightsbridge.

Proud was described as a dark-haired man with a wry, sardonic sense of humour and a thin figure 'which seemed to slide into a chair rather than sit'. His mission in Shanghai was to recruit spies for the British Secret Service and make contact with the Communists with a view to protecting British investments.[7]

The curious thing about John Proud was that he had been named in an Australian secret intelligence report on 18 October 1948 as 'a suspect member of the Australian Communist Party'.

R. Williams, the deputy director of security, noted that after being demobilised Proud had worked for the Daily Telegraph and had subsequently run the 'Forum of the Air' program on the ABC. 'It is reported that Proud in the course of his duty did not lose an opportunity of placing a Communist Party speaker on this program,' Williams wrote, adding, 'It is thought that some interest should be paid to Proud's activities overseas.' Clearly, he had no idea about Proud's war service in intelligence or his present role in the British Secret Service.[8]

Proud's second wife Roberta was also 'suspected to possess Communist sympathies' after an informant reported a conversation at a Sydney drinks party in February 1948. When Tommy Thompson, advertising manager of Frank Packer's Women's Weekly, commented that one of the guests was a Fascist, Roberta had replied she was 'glad to meet someone after her own heart'. This was taken to the absurd length of meaning that she was a Communist and that 'she was here to contact members of the Party and pass on information'. Such was the anti-Communist paranoia in postwar Australia, mirroring the extremist McCarthyist mindset in the United States.

Australia's representatives in China also faced a daunting task in negotiating with either Nationalist or Communist regimes. The Minister for Immigration Arthur Calwell was quoted in the Shanghai press in March 1949 as saying there would be 'no appeasement, no quota system for the admission of Asiatics' to Australia. 'No matter how violent the criticism, no matter how fierce and unrelenting the attack upon me personally may be,' he said, 'I am determined that the Flag of White Australia will not be lowered.'[9]

In advance of the Battle of Shanghai, the deciding battle in the 'War of Liberation', Mao Tse-tung sent hundreds of fifth columnists south to spread propaganda among the workers. Driven out of Nanking, Chiang Kai-shek arrived in Shanghai and announced,

'We will fight to the end. There will be no surrender.' Graham Jenkins, a handsome, quietly spoken Melbourne reporter who was covering the war for Reuters, escaped on the last plane out of the doomed Nationalist capital before it fell to the Communists. On 24 April 1949 he reported in a Reuters dispatch that Communist forces under General Lin Piao had crossed the Yangtze in several places. The cities of Soochow to the north of Shanghai and Kashing in the south were in Communist hands and the Red Army was heading for Shanghai itself.

This report appeared in the *North-China Daily News* and several other Shanghai newspapers the following morning. The news that the Communists were so close to Shanghai caused panic among Chinese civilians. The streets filled with crowds stockpiling rice, flour and tinned foods for the impending siege. Later that morning, Jenkins and George Vine, the *Daily News*'s British assistant editor who had been on duty the previous night, were arrested by Chiang's secret police and the paper's British owners, the Morriss family, were ordered to suspend publication of the newspaper.[10]

At police headquarters in a derelict building in Avenue Haig, Frenchtown, Colonel Yang demanded to know Jenkins's sources among the Communists. The Australian refused to tell him. 'I can sentence you to death under martial law,' the colonel warned. Jenkins was a confident, strongly built man nicknamed 'Gunboat'; he had no intention of being intimidated. 'You do that,' he replied. 'I will,' the colonel shouted and told Jenkins that he would be shot at dawn.

Colonel Yang's commander was General Mao Sen – known as 'Bloody Mao' – chief of Chiang's Secret Intelligence Corps following the death of Dai Li in a suspicious plane crash in 1946. General Mao had been responsible for scores of disappearances in Shanghai in a campaign to stamp out subversive elements undermining Nationalist morale. Yang harangued Jenkins and Vine for 'rumour-mongering' and then passed the same death sentence on the British journalist.

The newsmen were saved when Clyde Farnsworth, a veteran reporter who had the phone number of police HQ, rang up and inquired after the welfare of his colleagues. Colonel Yang allowed Jenkins to come to the phone to prove he was still alive. 'I am detained over the story,' he said. 'It is very serious. We are being treated all right.' To save face, the two newsmen were interrogated for a further 36 hours and then released, minus a few teeth. To his family's despair, an American news agency had already carried a report that Jenkins had been executed by firing squad.[11]

As a warning to Western newsmen, two Chinese 'rumour-mongers' were executed by Bloody Mao for spreading 'false reports', and a further 60 university students were arrested for possessing banners welcoming the Communists to Shanghai. To avoid further problems with the authorities, Reuters ordered Jenkins back to Hong Kong and then sent him to cover postwar events in Vietnam and Indonesia. He later launched his own newspaper, *The Star*, a daily tabloid in Hong Kong.

Later that day, the Chinese prime minister Ho Ying-chin announced at a meeting of government, military and civil leaders in Shanghai that the Nationalists were determined to make a stand there; he then packed his bags and departed for Canton, while the executive *yuan* announced plans for the removal of government officials to that city.

Chiang Kai-shek flew out of Shanghai for the last time in early May, a broken and embittered man. He said he was 'ashamed to be back in Canton in the present circumstances of retreat and failure. I cannot but admit that I must share a great part of the defeat.'

On the night of 24–25 May thousands of Red Army troops, clad in coarse green uniforms and clutching captured American Tommy guns, slipped silently into the sleeping city. At dawn, they began the peaceful occupation of the French Concession and then, with the guns of the Nationalist rearguard booming from other sectors of the city, systematically took over The

Bund. By 8 am, the fighting was all over on the southern side of Soochow Creek.[12]

Across Garden Bridge in Hongkew, however, the garrison held out in the Post Office, the Embankment Building and Broadway Mansions. Well over one thousand foreigners had been herded on to the third, fourth and fifth floors of Broadway Mansions, with the heavily armed Nationalists on the ground floor. To break the siege, the Communists simply crossed the creek and turned the position, which gave the defenders the alternative of surrendering or fighting to the death, with the ultimate destruction of the buildings and heavy loss of life. They chose to surrender.

The rest of Chiang Kai-shek's forces melted away to Canton, leaving the Communists free to celebrate their victory with a gigantic parade through the streets of Shanghai. With consummate ease, the same crowds that had hailed the Nationalists just a few days earlier waved flags and cheered lustily for the new conquerors. When shipping companies cautiously approached the authorities for permission to bring in their ships, they were told the port was open for business.[13]

Commander John Proud felt 'an enormous sense of relief, maybe we can do something now'. But he knew he must move quickly: the Communists would shortly proclaim themselves rulers of China, so the question of whether Britain and Australia would recognise the new regime or stick with Chiang Kai-shek's discredited government was a matter of extreme urgency.

One of Proud's Chinese agents informed him that Chou En-lai had arrived in Shanghai and introduced the Australian to Norman Watts, an English scholar who once saved Chou's life while fighting with the Communist guerrillas against the Japanese. Watts and Proud agreed that the only way to protect British and Commonwealth interests in China would be immediate diplomatic recognition by those governments. Watts arranged for Proud to meet Chou in an apartment at Cathay Mansions in Frenchtown. Chou let Proud speak and then replied he did not see any reason why Britain and China should not be friendly. 'There will be conditions,' he added, 'and above all it must be on the basis of equality.'

There was no chance of equality and, with the United States in the grip of anti-Communist hysteria, no chance of diplomatic recognition from that quarter either. After the Nationalists abandoned Shanghai, Ambassador Stuart had flown to Washington, where the administration shunted him aside. He died shortly afterwards in obscurity. Members of America's so-called 'Dixie Mission' to Yenan in 1944, who had argued that the Communists were more worthy of US support than Chiang Kai-shek, lost their jobs in the State Department. The Truman administration had washed its hands of 'the China problem'.

On 1 October 1949 Mao Tse-tung, now formally entitled 'Chairman Mao', stood on a platform in Tiananmen Square surrounded by a massive chanting, cheering, fist-clenching crowd and proclaimed the founding of the People's Republic of China, with its capital at Peking, renamed Beijing (Northern Capital). One of the guests of honour was Chingling Soong – Madame Sun Yat-sen – who was met at the station by Mao, Chou En-lai and other dignitaries. 'Today, Sun Yat-sen's efforts at last bore fruit,' she said.

The new regime announced that it intended to establish diplomatic relations with friendly nations. The following day the Soviet Union became the first country to recognise the new republic. Keith Officer, who had replaced Frederic Eggleston as Australian minister, was living in Shanghai. Fully expecting Australia to follow suit shortly, he packed his bags and prepared to move to Peking. But from the United States, Britain and Australia, there was only moody silence.

On 10 December Chiang Kai-shek retreated to Formosa, taking with him the vast treasure trove of Chinese art that had been stored in caves around Chungking for safekeeping during the Sino-Japanese War. Local legend had it that the island had been created by a fire-breathing dragon but Chiang's own fire was almost extinguished – he presided over a population of just two million Nationalist refugees and 11 million Formosans.

President Truman announced in the New Year that the United States 'would not provide military aid or advice to Chinese Forces on Formosa'. But although Truman was fed up with Chiang, the United States bluntly refused to recognise the new Communist government as the legitimate ruler of China and blocked her membership of the United Nations. The Australian cabinet under Labor prime minister Ben Chifley hesitated despite the advice of its professional advisers that early recognition was highly desirable. Then Chifley's self-important Foreign Minister Bert Evatt sided with Dean Acheson, the hawkish American secretary of state, who demanded that Mao demonstrate that his regime actually controlled the country, that it was capable of carrying out its international obligations and that it was supported by the free will of the majority of the people. The result was stalemate.[14]

Any chance of friendly relations between China and the Allies evaporated over the issue of Korea. At 4 am on Sunday, 25 June 1950 the North Korean People's Army – the *In Min Gun* – stormed across the 38th Parallel, the demarcation line between the Communist North ruled by Stalin's tyrannical protégé Kim Il Sung and the capitalist South controlled by the corrupt and brutal Syngman Rhee. The following year Australia joined the United Nations forces expelling the *In Min Gun* from South Korea. Chou En-lai, now Chinese premier, warned the United States that 'an American intrusion into North Korea will encounter Chinese resistance'. General MacArthur, the American commander, paid no heed to the warning and sent American and Australian troops over the border. As Allied forces approached the Yalu River on the Manchurian frontier, Mao Tse-tung unleashed a massive 'human wave' counter-attack against them.

By then, Wynette McDonald and Carlos Ozorio had moved to Rabaul in Papua New Guinea with their two children. Ozorio was employed as a radio technician with the Commonwealth Department of Civil Aviation. The 'notorious collaborationist' had got away with it.

Life, however, wasn't so simple for many of the Australians who had seen the war at close quarters. Colin McDonald's career as a war correspondent had come to an end in late 1942 when he was taken chronically ill with dengue fever, tonsillitis and eyestrain. He resigned from *The Times* and sailed to England but returned to Perth in 1948, where he worked for the ABC and *The West Australian* until his retirement. He died in 1983.[15]

His life-long friend Harold Timperley worked for the United Nations and its specialised agencies for seven years after cutting his ties with Chiang's Ministry of Information. On resigning from UNESCO in 1950 he went to Indonesia as a technical expert attached to the Indonesian Foreign Office where his main task was training young Indonesians for diplomatic service. He returned to England after contracting a tropical illness and was working as secretary and treasurer for the War on Want campaign when he was admitted to hospital in Sussex. He died there on 26 November 1954.[16]

And what of the other irrepressible West Australian, William Arthur 'Buzz' Farmer? Having escaped from China in late 1939, he made his way to London where he covered the war in Europe, including the Normandy landings on D Day, for the Melbourne *Herald*. Under the name 'Rhodes Farmer', he published *Shanghai Harvest*, his graphic account of the Sino-Japanese War, to wide acclaim in 1945. He chose the name 'Rhodes' because his father, who had taken part in the 1895 Jameson Raid on Johannesburg, was an admirer of Cecil Rhodes, the prime mover behind the insurrection. When he returned to Australia at the end of the war, Buzz Farmer went to live on Rottnest Island, travelling to the mainland or making overseas trips in the winter. At the age of 75, he died in Perth on 12 October 1979.

Ian Morrison had led a charmed life covering the Pacific War for *The Times* – he was slightly wounded in the Battle of Buna in New Guinea in 1942, fractured his vertebrae in a plane crash in December 1943 and was later shot in the thumb, while a second bullet grazed his thigh. 'He was in danger most of the time,' *The Times* official historian wrote. 'He reported from near the firing lines; he shared the soldier's life in the jungles; he was wounded more than once and was ill at times. His dispatches always brought clarity and colour out of the confusion of war.'[17]

During a spell in Hong Kong, Ian fell in love with Rosalie Chow, a beautiful Eurasian doctor who had written an important war book, *Destination Chungking*, under the pen-name Han Suyin. Rosalie had previously been trapped in a violent marriage to one of Chiang Kai-shek's officers, during which she had been beaten and abused. Her husband had been killed in the Chinese civil war.

At 37, Ian Morrison was one of the first war correspondents into Korea to cover the fighting, eager to be there and to get to the heart of the story without fear or favour. On 12 August 1950 he and the British military historian Christopher Buckley were being driven by an Indian Army officer towards a destroyed North Korean tank when their jeep struck a landmine, killing all three instantly. At his funeral, an American guard of honour fired a salute and the Last Post sounded as fellow war correspondents bore his coffin to the graveside at a little mission cemetery at Taegu.

In his last dispatch, published in *The Times* on the day he was killed, he warned that early American military successes should not be overrated but rather be seen in relation to 'the whole weakness of the allied position in Korea'. He was proved right – the war dragged on until a ceasefire was finally agreed in 1953.

Writing as Han Suyin, Rosalie chronicled their love affair in her most famous novel, *A Many-Splendored Thing*.[18] Ian's character was called Mark Elliott and when Hollywood turned the book into the Oscar-winning film *Love Is a Many-Splendored*

Thing, he was transformed into an American, played by William Holden. As Ian was still married to Maria at the time of his death, he would have appreciated that.

'He was a cultivated and gentle man and no swashbuckler,' his brother Alastair Morrison says, 'but he had an insatiable curiosity about events in Asia.'[19]

EPILOGUE

Better City, Better Life

Britain finally recognised Mao's People's Republic as the legitimate government of China on 6 January 1950 but for the next 17 years abstained from votes that would permit its membership of the United Nations. Australia, whose ANZUS Alliance with America had become the cornerstone of her defence policy, was even more recalcitrant. It was not until 1972 that the newly elected Labor Prime Minister, Gough Whitlam, gave formal recognition and celebrated the event with a personal visit to Beijing.

Televised coverage of the visit reached the home of a 15-year-old schoolboy in the small Queensland town of Nambour and inspired the young Kevin Rudd to learn Mandarin and join the diplomatic service. Thirty-five years later Rudd himself would become Australia's twenty-sixth prime minister and the only Western leader able to converse fluently with his Chinese counterparts in their own language.

Australia then played a key role in replacing the Eurocentric G8 with the G20 – including both China and Australia – to monitor and direct the global economy. China replaced Japan as Australia's biggest trading partner. Australia's mineral exports to China created boom conditions for the foreseeable future; its biggest company, BHP Billiton, donated the gold, silver and bronze medals at the 2008 Beijing Olympics. And a total of 8,182,259 people visited the striking Australian pavilion at the Shanghai World Expo 2010. A relationship that began badly in the riotous days of the gold rush in the mid-19th century has been utterly transformed. China has become Australia's third biggest source of immigrants after Britain and New Zealand.

Kevin Rudd's domestic political expertise did not match his international diplomacy and he was replaced three years later by his deputy, Julia Gillard, though he retained the important Foreign Affairs portfolio. He is well placed. The inherent Occidental suspicion of Oriental motives – inflamed by the Communist takeover and fanned by conservative propaganda during the Vietnam War – still smoulders beneath the surface. American concerns over the woken giant, its growing strength and ambition – combined with the repressive nature of the Beijing government – still act as a brake on a broadly based and open-hearted relationship.

However, the international pace of change is itself increasing exponentially and as information technology batters down the walls of censorship and secrecy, new generations are bringing global perspectives to bear. Shanghai itself is the perfect exemplar of this new paradigm. Visitors travel from the international airport to the city on the Maglev train, flying above the rail on a cushion of pure energy at 480 kilometres an hour, faster than anywhere else in the world. Some 25 per cent of the world's building cranes are transforming the city into a futuristic behemoth.

The chunky, colonial skyline of The Bund preserves a memory of the city's old-world charm and in the opalescent morning light elderly Chinese couples dance in dignified measure to the steps of yesteryear. At night, ghostly multitudes pass along the waterfront and from the terrace of M on The

Bund we suddenly hear again the crackle of machine-gun fire and the sound of screaming, only to realise they are firecrackers and squeals of delight from a brightly coloured riverboat gliding downstream to the Yangtze. Shanghai has lived down its frenetic, disreputable, violent past and now strives to live up to its Expo theme: 'Better City, Better Life'.

Men and women of many nations have found a place in the city's story. Most were bit players, anonymous extras in a pageant of millions. Some were touched by greatness and only now can their contribution be revealed and measured. Among them are the five Australians, George Ernest Morrison, William Henry Donald, Eleanor Mary Hinder, Harold John Timperley and Colin Malcolm McDonald. They devoted themselves to China, yet remain little known there and less again in their native land.

But history has a way of separating the dross from the hidden gems. Perhaps their time has come.

And no one would deserve recognition more than Tse Tsan Tai, a.k.a. James See of Sydney and Grafton. Thomas Reid, former editor of the *China Mail*, wrote to him in 1912 after the revolution had become a reality, 'You have the great satisfaction of knowing that you assisted in placing 400 million of your fellow men on the road to a better and more humane life and in initiating a movement that will go down in history as one of the most momentous in the records of the world.'

APPENDIX 1

Dramatis Personae

Abend, Hallett: *New York Times* correspondent in Shanghai from 1928 to 1941. He used W. H. Donald as a go-between with the Young Marshal, Chang Hsueh-liang, and Chiang Kai-shek.

Alley, Rewi: New Zealander who worked with Eleanor Hinder's factory inspectorate and founder of the Gung Ho industrial co-operative scheme.

Anderson, Dame Adelaide: Melbourne-born member of the Shanghai Labour Commission, who tackled the problem of child labour in Shanghai sweatshops.

Anderson, Roy Scott: China-born American who worked with W. H. Donald on the Double Tenth Revolution and later shared a compound with him in Peking.

Armstrong, Jean: Sydney journalist targeted by the Japanese for her Christian beliefs and whose health was ruined by incarceration during World War II.

Auden, W. H. and Christopher Isherwood: Celebrated British writers who travelled to Shanghai in 1938 in search of a war and wrote a darkly humorous book about their experiences. They met W. H. Donald in Hankow who introduced them to Mayling Soong Chiang.

Bennett, James Gordon: Proprietor of the *New York Daily Herald* who hired W. H. Donald as South China Correspondent in 1905 and agreed to him moving to Shanghai in 1911.

Blacket, Captain Wilfred: Member of the Australian Security Service who travelled to Shanghai and Tokyo in an attempt to bring three Australian collaborators to justice.

Borodin, Michael (real name: Mikhail Markovich Gruzenberg): Americanised Russian adviser to Sun Yat-sen who organised the *Kuomintang* along Soviet lines. Expelled from China in 1927, he died in a Siberian labour camp after falling foul of Stalin.

Bowden, V. G. 'Gordon': World War I hero, novelist and businessman who became Australia's trade commissioner to Shanghai in 1935. Bowden moved into the International Settlement with his wife **Dorothy** and three young children, **Ivor**, **June** and **Doreen**. The young Australian diplomats **Arthur Nutt** and **Norman Wootton** worked at his side advancing Australia's political and commercial interests. Wootton was with him when he was murdered by a Japanese soldier in February 1942. After three and a half years in a POW camp on Sumatra, Wootton returned to Shanghai as commercial counsellor. He never recovered from his wartime experiences and later committed suicide.

Chang Hsueh-liang (Zhang Xueliang, the Young Marshal): Manchurian warlord and opium addict who employed W. H. Donald as adviser and who kidnapped Chiang Kai-shek in 1936 but released him after Donald's intervention. Although under house arrest for many years, he eventually settled in Hawaii and lived to be 100.

Chang Jen-chun: Viceroy of Canton and Nanking who befriended W. H. Donald after he door-stepped his Cantonese *yamen* on an overnight trip from Hong Kong.

Chang Tso-lin (Zhang Zoulin, the Old Marshal): Chang Hsueh-liang's father who captured Peking and was then assassinated by the Japanese for losing it to Chiang Kai-shek.

Chennault, Claire Lee: Head of the Flying Tigers, a group of

American airmen who volunteered to fight the Japanese in China. He was a great supporter of W. H. Donald.

Chiang Kai-shek, Generalissimo (Jiang Jieshi): Nationalist leader who purged the Communists in Shanghai in 1927 and won a power battle with **Wang Ching-wei (Wang Jingwei)** for control of the *Kuomintang*. During the Sino-Japanese War, he was suspected of conserving his military strength to fight the Communists. In the end, he lost China to **Mao Tse-tung (Mao Zedong)**.

Chou En-lai (Zhou Enlai): Mao Tse-tung's chief lieutenant who attempted to set up a Shanghai commune in 1927 and narrowly escaped assassination during Chiang's anti-Communist purge. Rose to become prime minister and foreign minister of the People's Republic of China.

Clark Kerr, Sir Archibald: Australian-born British ambassador to China who supported Rewi Alley's Gung Ho industrial co-operative scheme to save China's secondary industry from the Japanese.

Clune, Frank: Australian author who travelled widely in China – and who exposed the Shanghai Club's claim to have the longest bar in the world.

Copland, Sir Douglas: Australia's Minister to China in 1946 who complained about the non-prosecution of Australian collaborators and who warned that Chiang Kai-shek would lose his battle with the Communists.

Deng Xiaoping: Veteran of the Long March, he survived Mao's Cultural Revolution to lead China into an age of 'socialism with Chinese characteristics'.

Donald, William Henry: Lithgow-born journalist and friend of **George Ernest Morrison** who wrote **Sun Yat-sen**'s manifesto after the Chinese Revolution of 1911 in which he played an important role. He was a complex man with a secret lust for power and was close to the centre of Chinese politics until 1940. His wife Mary left him in 1919 and he never forgave her. He was interned in the Philippines but survived the war only to die of lung cancer in Shanghai in November 1946.

Eggleston, Sir Frederic: Australia's first Minister to China in 1941 was based at Chungking and was noted for the stimulating conversation at his salon and the clarity of his reports to Canberra. Denounced the embryonic pan-Asian movement as a threat to colonial supremacy.

Farmer, William Arthur 'Buzz': Australian reporter who arrived in Shanghai for a holiday in 1937 and was pressed into service as a war correspondent. He later joined Chiang Kai-shek's Nationalists and worked with Donald in Hankow and Chungking. Wrote a first-class war book, *Shanghai Harvest*, under the name **Rhodes Farmer**.

Feng Yu-hsiang (Feng Yuxiang, a.k.a. the Christian General): Famous for baptising his troops with a garden hose, his men were responsible for the murder of Australian reporter **Basil Riley**.

Fernandez, Roy: Australian orphan who became inspector of the Shanghai Municipal Police and was interned in Shanghai in 1943.

Fernandez, Roy Jr: Australian diplomat who was raised in Shanghai and was interned in the Philippines with W. H. Donald and then in Shanghai with his father.

Galen, General (Vasily Konstantinovich Blucher): Soviet general who played a major role in Chiang's early victories was expelled from China in 1927 and executed on Stalin's orders.

Gilbert, Rodney: American journalist who started a freelance agency with W. H. Donald in Peking and later wrote *What's Wrong with China*.

Hinder, Eleanor Mary: Australian-born feminist who waged war on child labour and the *mui tsai* slave system as industrial secretary of the Shanghai Municipal Council. Stranded in Shanghai in 1941, she was repatriated to Canada the following year.

James, John Stanley (a.k.a. Julian Thomas, The Vagabond): Journalist who wrote brilliant colour articles about Shanghai for the Melbourne *Argus* in 1881 which formed the basis of his excellent book *Occident and Orient*.

Jenkins, Graham: Reuters correspondent who was sentenced to death by Chiang Kai-shek's secret police for revealing that the Red Army had crossed the Yangtze and was heading for Shanghai.

Kung, H. H.: Chinese banker who married Ayling Soong, eldest of the three Soong sisters, and became China's minister of finance. Suspected of corruption.

Lawrance, Les: Queensland speedway star who returned to Shanghai after a professional visit to work as head of the transport section of the Shanghai Telephone System, a position that put him in the frontline in the 1937 Battle of Shanghai.

Li Hung-chang (Li Hongzhang): China's most prominent statesman for 25 years, an extraordinary feat of survival in the treacherous Manchu Court. He died of natural causes shortly after signing the Boxer Protocol in 1901.

Li Yuan-hung: Chinese general who became military governor of Hunah during the Double Tenth Revolution, then vice president under Yuan Shi-kai and ultimately president of the Chinese Republic.

McDonald, Colin Malcolm: Australian reporter who followed in the footsteps of G. E. Morrison as Peking correspondent of *The Times*. He was on board the USS *Panay* when it was sunk by Japanese planes.

McHugh, James M.: Naval attaché at the American Embassy, Nanking, and officer in charge of Far Eastern intelligence, he befriended Donald and used him to get close to the Chiangs.

Mao Tse-tung (Mao Zedong): Founding member of the Chinese Communist Party who saw clearly that the battle for China would be decided by its peasantry. Escaped to Yenan with the Long March in 1934 and led the fight against the Nationalists and the Japanese throughout the Sino-Japanese War. Triumphed over Chiang Kai-shek in the Chinese civil war and announced the founding of the People's Republic of China on 1 October 1949.

Marshall, General George M.: United States chief of staff during World War II who came to China in 1945 to arrange a ceasefire between Chiang Kai-shek and Mao Tse-tung.

Morrison, George Ernest 'Chinese': Geelong-born physician who became famous as *The Times* correspondent in Peking during the fall of the Manchu Dynasty and later joined President Yuan Shi-kai as political adviser only to die of pancreatic cancer in England in 1920.

Morrison, Ian: Peking-born son of 'Chinese' Morrison, who was a correspondent for *The Times* in World War II and who warned the West that Chiang Kai-shek would lose to the Communists. Killed in the Korean War in August 1950.

O'Hara, Dr William 'Bill': Captain-surgeon with the 7th Light Horse at Gallipoli, he built a successful medical practice in Shanghai and developed a reputation as one of the city's biggest gamblers.

Proud, John: Former Royal Australian Navy officer who came to Shanghai as a secret agent to open talks with Chou En-lai aimed at preserving Britain and Australia's interests following the Communist takeover. According to recently declassified files in the National Archives of Australia, Proud and his wife **Roberta** were wrongly suspected of being Communists.

Raymond, Alan Willoughby, Wynette Cecilia McDonald and John Joseph Holland: The treacherous trio who founded the Independent Australia League in Shanghai and who made anti-Allied broadcasts for the Japanese during the Pacific War. Raymond and McDonald went even further: Raymond spied for Japanese naval intelligence and McDonald concocted a plot to smuggle pro-Nazi propaganda material into Australia.

Rasmussen, Dr Otto Durham: Australian-born eye doctor who treated Chinese patients, including child factory workers, for trachoma and other ophthalmic diseases for 30 years and who became one of China's most outspoken defenders with his book *What's Right with China*.

Riley, (Frank) Basil: Rhodes Scholar and son of the Archbishop of Perth, who was murdered by Chinese soldiers in 1927 while reporting the civil war between the Nationalists and the Communists for *The Times*.

Smedley, Agnes (a.k.a. Marie Rogers, Agnes Brundin, Alice Bird, Alice Reed and Mrs Chattopadhyaya): Left-wing American journalist who was born in poverty on a tenant farm in Missouri and raised in mining camps in Colorado. Suspected of being a Comintern agent, she refused to join the American, Indian or German Communist parties and was denied entry into the Chinese Communist Party. She wrote on China for *The Guardian* and other newspapers, and her memoir *Battle Hymn of China* concerned her experiences with the Red Army.

Smith, (Addie) Viola: American diplomat and lover of Eleanor Hinder who was responsible for helping many Americans evacuate Shanghai at the outbreak of the 1937 war.

Snow, Edgar 'Ed': American author of *Red Star over China*, the first book about the Chinese Communists which he wrote after interviewing Mao Tse-tung and Chou En-lai in Yenan.

Snow, Helen Foster (a.k.a. Myn Wales, also known as Peg): Left-wing American writer and wife of Edgar Snow.

Soong, Ayling (Song Ayling): Eldest of the three Soong sisters and wife of H. H. Kung. She was noted for her corrupt financial dealings.

Soong, Charles Jones: Methodist preacher, businessman and father of the six Soong children (three girls and three boys). He was one of Sun Yat-sen's main supporters until Sun married his middle daughter Chingling.

Soong, Mayling (Song Mayling): Youngest of the Soong sisters who entered into an arranged marriage with Chiang Kai-shek. With W. H. Donald's help, she became an international symbol of China's resistance to the Japanese.

Soong, Chingling (Song Qingling): Middle Soong daughter who married Sun Yat-sen and supported the Communists against Chiang Kai-shek.

Soong Tzu-wen (T. V. – Song Ziwen): Eldest of the three Soong sons, he was an ambitious financier and banker who rose to become China's foreign minister and negotiate huge loans with the United States.

Sorge, Richard: Handsome Comintern agent sent to Shanghai in early 1930 to gather intelligence and foment revolution. He was later Stalin's most successful spy in Japan although Stalin refused to believe his reports that Hitler was about to invade the Soviet Union. Captured by the Japanese and hanged.

Stilwell, General Joseph: American supremo in the China, Burma, India (CBI) theatre in World War II who clashed repeatedly with Chiang Kai-shek and was finally sacked by **President Franklin D. Roosevelt**.

Stokes, Henry: Australian *chargé d'affaires* in postwar Shanghai who tried unsuccessfully to have the Australian collaborators arrested.

Sun Yat-sen (Sun Zhongshan): The 'Father of the Chinese Republic' who asked W. H. Donald to write his manifesto for the *Kuomintang* and who later formulated the Three Principles of Democracy. Became the first president of China in 1912 but was forced to hand over to the warlord **Yuan Shi-kai**, heralding the start of the Warlord Era. Died in 1925 without ever realising his dream of a united China.

Taylor, Ruby: Proprietress of the Peter Pan School in Shanghai who hired Wynette McDonald and caught her spying.

Timperley, Harold John: Australian correspondent of *The Guardian* in China who reported on the Rape of Nanking and worked hard to alleviate the hardship of Chinese refugees.

Tong, Dr Hollington: Graduate of Columbia University who became China's minister in the United States at 27 and later head of the Ministry of Information during the Sino-Japanese War.

Tu Yeuh-sheng (Du Yeusheng, a.k.a. Big-Eared Du): Boss of the Shanghai Green Gang (Qingbang), who helped Chiang Kai-shek wipe out trade unionists and left-wing agitators in the anti-Communist purge of 1927.

Tzu Hsi (Cixi): The Dowager Empress who became the de facto ruler of China under two emperors, one of whom she probably poisoned.

Venn Brown, Rose: Australian businesswoman and Red Cross worker who witnessed much of the fighting during the Chinese Civil War in the 1920s.

von Puttkamer, Baron Jesco: Head of German propaganda in Shanghai who turned down an offer from Wynette McDonald to smuggle German propaganda material into Australia.

Walker, Brigadier George: Salvation Army officer who was arrested and tortured by the Japanese for refusing to make pro-Japanese broadcasts on Shanghai radio.

Wang Ching-wei (Wang Jingwei): Chiang Kai-shek's rival for control of the *Kuomintang* and puppet ruler of China under the Japanese. Suffering from diabetes, he died in Japan of natural causes on 10 November 1944.

Yuan Shi-kai: Chinese general who became president of the Chinese Republic in 1912 and who then attempted to restore the monarchy with himself as emperor.

APPENDIX 2

Chinese place names then and now

Provinces:

Anhwei – Anhui

Chekiang – Zhejiang

Fengtiang – Lioaning

Formosa – Taiwan

Fukien – Fujian

Honan – Henan

Hopeh – Hebei

Hupeh – Hubei

Kansu – Gansu

Kiangsi – Jiangxi

Kiangsu – Jiangsu

Kirin – Jilin

Kwangsi – Guangxi

Kwangtung – Guangdong

Shansi – Shanxi

Shantung – Shandong

Shansi – Shaanxi

Shensi – Shaanxi

Sinkiang – Xinjiang

Szechuen – Sichuan

Cities and towns:

Amoy – Xiamen

Anking – Hefei

Canton – Guangzhou

Chapei – Zhabei

Chefoo – Yantai

Chengchow – Zhengzhou

Chengtu – Chengdu

Chihli – Zhili

Chinkiang – Zhenjiang

Chungking – Chungqing

Dairen – Manchuli

Foochow – Fuzhou

Hangchow – Hangzhou
Hankow – Hankou
Huashan – Hwasang
Kalgan – Zhangjiakou
Kiukiang – Jiujiang
Kuling – Guling
Mukden – Shenyang
Nanking – Nanjing
Newchwang – Yingkou
Ningpo – Ningbo
Pakhoi – Beihai
Peitaiho – Beidaihe
Peking (Peiping) – Beijing
Port Arthur – Lushan

Saianfu – Xiangyang
Shasi – Jinsha
Sian – Xian
Soochow – Suzhou
Swatow – Shantou
Tientsin – Tianjin
Tsinan – Jinan
Tsingtao – Qingdao
Wenchow – Wenzhou
Whangpoo River – Huangpu River
Wusih – Wuxi
Yangtze River – Yanzi
Yunnan – Kunming

The 'Big Four' department stores
Sincere – Xianshi
Wing On – Yong'an
Sun Sun – Xinxin
Sun Company – Daxin

APPENDIX 3

Currency and measures

Dollar values in Imperial China were quoted as 'dollars mex' after the Mexican silver dollar. The Chinese yuan was introduced in 1889 at par with the Mexican peso. In 1914, the Silver Dollar was established as the currency of the Republic of China. To make matters more complicated, the *tael*, equivalent to one ounce of silver, was the currency for banking and wholesale transactions for rentals and taxation (and indemnities) prior to 1935.

In November 1935 the *fapi* was introduced as a national currency and the circulation of Silver Dollar coins was prohibited to prevent the drain of silver from China. Most prices after that date were expressed in *fapi* or Chinese dollars. The present currency of the People's Republic of China is the Renminbi (RMB), with the units Yuan and Jiao (1 Yuan = 10 Jiao).

The currency denoted by the $ sign in this work is the Chinese currency at the time. American dollars are represented as US$. No differentiation is made between pounds sterling and Australian pounds.

Distances and altitudes in the narrative have been expressed, where practicable, in (rounded) metric units; but in quotations from other works, the original units have been retained.

The displacements of ships – expressed in tons – are not converted because of the difficulty of knowing whether long (UK) or short (US) tons are referred to. A similar difficulty applies in the difference between British and international knots in referring to a vessel's speed.

Metric equivalents:
1 inch = 25 millimetres
1 foot = 30 centimetres
1 yard = 0.914 metre
1 mile = 1.6 kilometres
1 pound = 0.45 kilograms
1 long (UK) ton = 1.016 tonnes
1 short (US) ton = 0.907 tonne
1 acre = 0.4 hectare
1 knot (distance in sea miles travelled in one hour)
    = approximately 1.85 kilometres per hour

BIBLIOGRAPHY

Abend, Hallett, *Japan Unmasked*, Bodley Head, New York, 1941

—— *My Years in China 1926–1941*, Bodley Head, New York, 1944

—— with Anthony J. Billingham, *Can China Survive?*, Ives Washburn, New York, 1937

Acton, Harold, *Memoirs of an Aesthete*, Methuen, London, 1948

Albinski, Henry S., *Australian Politics and Attitudes to China*, Princeton University Press, Princeton, 1965

Allman, Norwood, *Shanghai Lawyer*, Whittlesey House, New York, 1943

Andrews, E. M., *Australia and China: The ambiguous relationship*, Melbourne University Press, 1985

Auden, W. H. and Christopher Isherwood, *Journey to a War*, Faber & Faber, London, 1939

Ballard, J. G., *Miracles of Life*, Harper Perennial, London, 2008

Barber, Noel, *The Fall of Shanghai: The Communist Takeover in 1949*, Macmillan, London, 1979

Barrett, David D., *Dixie Mission: The United States Army Observer Group in Yenan, 1944*, University of California, Berkeley, 1970

Basil, George C., *Test Tubes and Dragon Scales*, John C. Winston, Chicago, 1940

Baumler, Alan, *The Chinese and Opium under the Republic*, State University of New York, 2007

Belden, Jack, *China Shakes the World*, Harper, New York, 1949

Bennett, Milly, *On Her Own: Journalistic adventures from San Francisco to the Chinese Revolution 1917–1927*, Foreign Languages Press, Beijing, 2003

Bickers, Robert, *Britain in China: Community, culture and colonialism 1900–1949*, Manchester University Press, Manchester, 1999

—— *Empire Made Me: An Englishman Adrift in Shanghai*, Allen Lane, London, 2003

—— *The Scramble for China: Foreign Devils in the Qing Empire, 1832–1914*, Allen Lane, London, 2011

Bland, J. O. P., *Houseboat Days in China*, Earnshaw Books, Hong Kong, 2008

Bloodworth, Dennis, *An Eye for the Dragon: South-east Asia Observed 1954–1970*, Secker & Warburg, London, 1970

Bonavia, David, *The Chinese*, Lippincott & Crowell, New York, 1980

—— *China's Warlords*, Oxford University Press, Oxford, 1995

Bonavia, Judy and Richard Hayman, *Yangzi: The Yangtze River and the Three Gorges*, Odyssey, Hong Kong, 1999

Booker, Edna Lee, *News Is My Job: A correspondent in war-torn China*, Macmillan, New York, 1940

Brunero, Donna, *Britain's Imperial Cornerstone: The Chinese Maritime Customs Service*, Routledge, London, 2006.

Burchett, George and Nick Shimmin (editors), *Memoirs of a Rebel Journalist: The autobiography of Wilfred Burchett*, University of New South Wales Press, Sydney, 2006

Cameron, Nigel, *Barbarians and Mandarins: Thirteen Centuries of Western Travellers in China*, Walker/Weatherhill, New York, 1970

Carey, Arch, *The War Years at Shanghai*, Vantage Press, New York, 1961

Chambers, Roland, *The Last Englishman: The double life of Arthur Ransome*, Faber, London, 2009

Chennault, Major-General Claire Lee, *Way of a Fighter*, Putnam, New York, 1949

Clifford, Nicholas R., *Spoilt Children of Empire*, Middlebury College Press, Hanover, 1991

Clune, Frank, *Sky High to Shanghai*, Angus & Robertson, Sydney, 1939

Coble, Parks M., *Facing Japan: Chinese politics and Japanese Imperialism 1931–1937*, Harvard University, Cambridge, Massachusetts, 1919

Collar, Hugh, *Captive in Shanghai*, Oxford University Press, Oxford, 1990

Collis, Maurice, *Foreign Mud: being an account of the opium imbroglio at Canton in the 1830s and the Anglo-Chinese war that followed*, Faber, London, 1946

Conn, Peter, *Pearl S. Buck: A cultural biography*, Cambridge University Press, Cambridge, 1996

Cradock, Percy, *Experiences of China*, John Murray, London, 1994

Crossley, Pamela Kyle, *The Manchus*, Blackwell Publishing, Oxford, 1997

Crow, Carl, *Foreign Devils in the Flowery Kingdom*, Earnshaw Press, Hong Kong, 2007

—— *400 Million Customers*, Earnshaw Books, Hong Kong, 2008

Day, David, *Reluctant Nation: Australia and the allied defeat of Japan 1942–5*, Oxford University Press, Oxford, 1992

Deacon, Richard, *The Japanese Secret Service*, Frederick Muller, London, 1982

Deane, Hugh, *Good Deeds and Gunboats: Two centuries of American-Chinese encounters*, Foreign Languages Press, Beijing, 2003

Denison, Edward, and Guang Yu Ren, *Building Shanghai: The Story of China's Gateway*, Wiley-Academy, Chichester, 2006

Dong, Stella, *Shanghai: Gateway to the Celestial Empire 1860–1949*, FormAsia, Hong Kong, 2005

Duus, Peter, Ramon H. Myers and Mark R. Peattie (editors), *The Japanese Wartime Empire 1931–1945*, Princeton University Press, 1996

Earnshaw, Graham, *Tales of Old Shanghai*, Earnshaw Press, Hong Kong, 2008

Eber, Irene (editor), *Voices from Shanghai: Jewish Exiles in Wartime China*, University of Chicago Press, 2008

Elphick, Peter, *Far Eastern File: The Intelligence War in the Far East 1930–1945*, Hodder & Stoughton, London, 1997

Eldridge, Fred, *Wrath in Burma: The uncensored story of General Stilwell*, Doubleday, New York, 1946

Fairbank, John King, *The Great Chinese Revolution 1800-1985*, Harper & Row, New York, 1986

—— (editor) with Katherine Frost Bruner and Elizabeth MacLeod Matheson, *The I.G. in Peking: Letters of Robert Hart, Chinese Maritime Customs, 1868–1907*, Belknap Press of Harvard University Press, New York, 2 volumes, 1976

Farmer, Rhodes, *Shanghai Harvest: A diary of three years in the China War*, Museum Press, London, 1945

Farndale, Nigel, *Last Action Hero of the British Empire: Cdr John Kerans 1915–1985*, Short Books, London, 2001

Farnsworth, Robert M., *From Vagabond to Journalist: Edgar Snow in Asia 1928–1941*, Foreign Languages Press, Beijing, 1996

Fearn, Anne Walter, *My Days of Strength: An American Woman Doctor's Forty Years in China*, Harper, New York, 1939

Fenby, Jonathan, *Generalissimo Chiang Kai-shek and the China he Lost*, The Free Press, London, 2003

—— *China: The Fall and Rise of a Great Power 1850–2009*, Penguin, London, 2008

Figes, Orlando, *A People's Tragedy: The Russian Revolution 1891–1924*, Jonathan Cape, London, 1996

Fitch, George A., *My Eighty Years in China*, Self-published, 1974

Fitzgerald, John, *Big White Lie: Chinese Australians in White Australia*, University of New South Wales Press, Sydney, 2007

Fleming, Peter, *One's Company: A Journey to China*, Jonathan Cape, London, 1934

—— *The Siege at Peking*, Rupert Hart-Davis, London, 1960

French, Paul, *Carl Crow – a Tough Old China Hand: The life, times and adventures of an American in Shanghai*, Hong Kong University Press, Hong Kong, 2006

—— *Through the Looking Glass: China's Foreign Correspondents from Opium Wars to Mao*, Hong Kong University Press, Hong Kong, 2009

Friedman, Irving S., *British Relations with China: 1931–1939*, Institute of Pacific Relations, New York, 1940

Gage, Berkeley, *It's Been a Marvellous Party*, Self-published, 1969

Gelber, Harry G., *The Dragon and the Foreign Devils*, Bloomsbury, London, 2007

Gilbert, Rodney, *What's Wrong with China*, Murray, London, 1925

Gillies, Donald, *Radical Diplomat: The life of Archibald Clark Kerr, Lord Inverchapel, 1882–1951*, I. B. Tauris, London, 1999

Hahn, Emily, *The Soong Sisters*, Cedric Chivers, Bath, 1942

—— *China to Me*, Doubleday, New York, 1944

Han Suyin, *Birdless Summer*, Jonathan Cape, London, 1968

Henriot, Christian, *Prostitution and Sexuality in Shanghai: A social history 1849–1949*, Cambridge University Press, Cambridge, 2000

Hershatter, Gail, *Dangerous Pleasures: Prostitution and Modernity in Twentieth-Century Shanghai*, University of California Press, Berkeley, 1997

Hinder, Eleanor M., *Life and Labor in Shanghai: A decade of labour and social administration in the International Settlement*, Institute of Pacific Relations, New York, 1944

History of The Times: *The Tradition Established 1841–1884*, The Office of The Times, Printing House Square, 1939

—— *The Twentieth Century Test 1884–1912*, Macmillan, New York, 1947

—— *The 150th Anniversary and Beyond 1912–1948*, The Office of The Times, Printing House Square, 1952

—— *Struggles in War and Peace 1939–1966*, Times Books, London, 1984

Hotz, Robert (editor), *Way of a Fighter: The Memoirs of Claire Lee Chennault*, G. P. Putnam, New York, 1949

Hughes, Richard, *Foreign Devil: Thirty years of reporting from the Far East*, Century, London, 1972

Isaacs, Harold R., *The Tragedy of the Chinese Revolution*, Stanford University Press, Stanford, 1951

Jordan, Donald A., *China's Trial by Fire: The Shanghai War of 1932*, University of Michigan Press, Ann Arbor, 2001

Jukes, Geoffrey, *The Russo-Japanese War 1904–1905*, Osprey, London, 2002

Maggie Keswick (editor), *The Thistle and the Jade: 175 years of Jardine Matheson*, Francis Lincoln, Hong Kong, 1982

Knightley, Phillip, *Australia: A Biography of a Nation*, Vintage, London, 2001

Kuhn, Irene, *Assigned to Adventure*, Harrap, London, 1938

Lamont-Brown, Raymond, *Kempeitai: Japanese Dreaded Military Police*, Sutton, England, 1998

Lary, Diana, *The Chinese People at War: Human Suffering and Social Transformation, 1937–1945*, Cambridge University Press, New York, 2010

Lattimore, Owen, *China Memoirs: Chiang Kai-shek and the war against Japan*, University of Tokyo Press, 1990

Leck, Greg, *Captives of Empire: The Japanese Internment of Allied Civilians in China 1941–1945*, Shandy Press, 2006

Lethbridge, H. J., *All About Shanghai: A standard guidebook*, Oxford University Press, Oxford, 1983

Leo Ou-fan Yeh, *Shanghai Modern: The flowering of a new urban culture in China 1930–1945*, Harvard University Press, Cambridge, Massachusetts, 1999

Lo Hui-Min (editor), *The Correspondence of G. E. Morrison, 1895–1912*, Cambridge University Press, Cambridge, Massachusetts, 1976

Long, Gavin, *The Six Years War*, Australian War Memorial, Canberra, 1973

Lynch, Michael, *The Chinese Civil War 1945–49*, Osprey, London, 2008

Li, Laura Tyson, *Madame Chiang Kai-shek: China's eternal First Lady*, Atlantic Monthly Press, New York, 2006

McDonald, Lachie, *Bylines: Memoirs of a war correspondent*, Kangaroo Press, 1998

Macmanus, James, *Ocean Devil: The Life and Legend of George Hogg*, Harper Perennial, London, 2008

Marder, Arthur L., *Old Friends, New Enemies: The Royal Navy and the Imperial Japanese Navy – Strategic illusions 1936–1941*, Clarendon Press, Oxford, 1981

Meo, L. D., *Japan's Radio War on Australia 1941–1945*, Melbourne University Press, Melbourne, 1968.

Morrison, Alastair, *The Road to Peking*, Self-published, Canberra, 1993

Morrison, G. E., *An Australian in China*, Oxford University Press, Hong Kong, 1985

Murphey, Rhoads, *Shanghai: Key to modern China*, Harvard University Press, Cambridge, 1953

Mydans, Carl, *More than Meets the Eye*, Hutchinson, London, 1961

Osmond, Warren G., *Frederic Eggleston: An intellectual in Australian politics*, Allen & Unwin, Sydney, 1985

Pakula, Hannah, *The Last Empress: Madame Chiang Kai-shek and the birth of modern China*, Weidenfeld & Nicholson, London, 2010

Pal, John, *Shanghai Saga*, Jarrolds, London, 1963

Pott, F. L. Hawks, *A Short History of Shanghai*, Kelly & Walsh, Shanghai, 1928

Pottinger, George, *Sir Henry Pottinger, First Governor of Hong Kong*, Sutton Publishing, England, 1997

Powell, John B., *My Twenty-Five Years in China*, Macmillan, New York, 1945

Preston, Diana, *The Boxer Rebellion: China's War on Foreigners 1900*, Constable & Robinson, London, 1999

Pringle, Henry F., *The Experiences of a Civilian Prisoner-of-War in Shanghai and Beijing, China, 1942–1945*, Privately published, Canberra, 2005

Ransome, Arthur, *The Chinese Puzzle*, Allen & Unwin, London, 1927

Rasmussen, O. D., *What's Right with China: An answer to foreign criticisms*, Commercial Press, Shanghai, 1927

—— *The Reconquest of Asia*, Hamish Hamilton, London, 1934

Rea, Kenneth W. and John C. Brewer, *The Forgotten Ambassador: The Reports of John Leighton Stuart, 1946–1949*, Westview Press, Boulder, 1981

Roberts, Andrew, *Salisbury, Victorian Titan*, Weidenfeld & Nicolson, London, 1999

Sayer, Geoffrey Robley, *Hong Kong, 1862–1919: Years of discretion*, Hong Kong University Press, Hong Kong, 1975

Seagrave, Sterling, *The Soong Dynasty*, Harper & Row, New York, 1985

—— *Dragon Lady: The Life and Legend of the Last Empress of China*, Macmillan, London, 1992

Sergeant, Harriet, *Shanghai*, John Murray, London, 1991

Service, John S., *The Amerasia Papers: Some problems in the history of US-China relations*, University of California, Berkeley, 1971

Shaw, Ralph, *Sin City*, Everest Books, London, 1973

Sheean, Vincent, *Between the Thunder and the Sun*, Macmillan, London, 1943

Sherwood, Stephanie, *Shanghai Recollections*, Mini-Publishing, Sydney, 2004

Smedley, Agnes, *China Correspondent*, Pandora Press, London, 1984

—— *China Fights Back*, Left Book Club, London, 1938

Spence, Jonathan, *To Change China: Western advisers in China 1620–1960*, Little, Brown, 1969

—— *The Gate of Heavenly Peace: The Chinese and their Revolution 1895–1980*, Penguin, London, 1982

—— *The Search for Modern China*, W. W. Norton, New York, 1999

Schedvin, Boris, *Emissaries of Trade: A History of the Australian Trade Commissioner Service*, Department of Foreign Affairs and Trade, Canberra, 2008

Springfield, Maurice, *Hunting Opium and Other Scents*, Norfolk and Suffolk Publicity, Halesworth, Suffolk, 1966

Stead Sisters, The, *Stone-Paper-Scissors: Shanghai 1921–1945*, Oxon Publishing, 1991

Spurling, Hilary, *Burying the Bones: Pearl Buck in China*, Profile Books, London, 2010

Sternberg, Josef von, *Fun in a Chinese Laundry*, Mercury House, New York, 1988

Stilwell, Joseph W., *The Stilwell Papers* (arranged and edited by Theodore H. White), Macdonald, London, 1949

Sues, Ilona Ralf, *Shark's Fins and Millet*, Little, Brown, Boston, 1944

Sun, Youli, *China and the Origins of the Pacific War 1931–1941*, St Martin's Press, New York, 1993

Tennant, Kylie, *Evatt: Politics and Justice*, Angus & Robertson, Sydney, 1970

Timperley, H. J., *What War Means: The Japanese terror in China*, Victor Gollancz, London, 1938

Thorne, Christopher, *The Limits of Foreign Policy: The West, the League and the Far Eastern Crisis of 1931–1933*, Hamish Hamilton, London

—— *The Far Eastern War: States and societies 1941–45*, Counterpoint, London, 1980

—— *Allies of a Kind: The United States, Britain and the War against Japan 1941–1945*, Hamish Hamilton, London, 1978

Trevor-Roper, Hugh, *Hermit of Peking: The hidden life of Sir Edmund Backhouse*, Penguin, England, 1979

Tse Tsan Tai, *The Chinese Republic: Secret History of the Revolution*, South China Morning Post, Hong Kong, 1924

Tuchman, Barbara W., *Stilwell and the Experience in China 1911–45*, Macmillan, New York, 1970

Twomey, Christina, *Australia's Forgotten Prisoners: Civilians interned by the Japanese in World War Two*, Cambridge University Press, Melbourne, 2007

Vagabond, The (John Stanley James), *Occident and Orient: Sketches on both sides of the Pacific*, George Robertson, Melbourne, 1882

Wakeman Jr, Frederic, *Policing Shanghai 1927–1937*, University of California Press, Berkeley, 1995

—— *The Shanghai Badlands: Wartime terrorism and urban crime 1937–1941*, Cambridge University Press, Cambridge, 1996

—— *Spymaster: Dai Li and the Chinese Secret Service*, University of California, Berkeley, 2003

Warner, Marina, *The Dragon Empress: The Life and Times of Tzu Hsi 1835–1908*, Vintage, London, 1972

Wasserstein, Bernard, *Secret War in Shanghai: Treachery, Subversion and Collaboration in the Second World War*, Profile Books, London, 1998

Wasserstrom, Jeffrey N., *Global Shanghai 1850–2010*, Routledge, London, 2009

Wickert, Erwin (editor), *The Good German of Nanking: The Diaries of John Rabe*, Little, Brown, London, 1999

Willoughby, Major-General Charles A., *Sorge: Soviet Master Spy*, William Kimber, London, 1952

Wood, Frances, *No Dogs and Not Many Chinese: Treaty Port Life in China 1843–1943*, John Murray, 1998

Woodhead, H. G. W., *A Journalist in China*, Hurst & Blackett, London, 1934

Wright, Arnold (senior editor), *Twentieth Century Impressions of Hong Kong, Shanghai and Other Treaty Ports of China*, Lloyds, London, 1908

Wright, Mary Clabaugh, *China in Revolution: The First Phase 1900–1913*, Yale University Press, New Haven, 1968

Lectures

George Ernest Morrison Lectures 1932–1941, *East Asian History*, Number 34, December 2007, Institute of Advanced Studies, Australian National University, Canberra

Magazines and newspapers

Harper's Magazine
Life Magazine
The New Yorker
The New York Review of Books
Time Magazine
United China Magazine

The Advertiser, Adelaide
The Age, Melbourne
The Argus, Melbourne
The Brisbane Courier
The Canberra Times
The Courier-Mail, Brisbane
The Daily Telegraph, Sydney
The Manchester Guardian (later *The Guardian*, London)
The Herald, Melbourne
The Mercury, Hobart
The New York Times
Sydney Morning Herald

The Times, London
The West Australian, Perth
The Western Mail, Perth

ENDNOTES

Chapter 1: Barbarians

1 Bonavia and Hayman, p. 37
2 The Third Principle is often given as 'people's livelihood' rather than the more pejorative 'socialism'
3 Lindsay, H. H. and Karl Gutzlaff, 'Report of Proceedings on a Voyage to the Northern Ports of China', House of Commons, London, 1834
4 Hugh White, 'Power Shift: Australia's future between Washington and Beijing', *Quarterly Essay*, Issue 39, 2010
5 'Davidson, Walter Stevenson (1785–1869)', *Australian Dictionary of Biography*, Volume 1, Melbourne University Press, 1966
6 'Union Insurance Society of Canton: 100 years of continuous progress', *The Times*, 11 July 1935
7 Blake, p. 18
8 *Asiatic Journal*, December 1839. Walter Davidson left China in 1822 to invest his ill-gotten gains in Australia and Britain. He increased his land holdings in the Australian colonies and became a large investor in and director of the Australian Agricultural Company. He also imported Saxon merino sheep for his properties, notably the 5000-acre (2024 ha) property 'Collaroi', on the River Krui near Cassilis in NSW. His connections with Australia continued until his death in 1869. 'Davidson, Walter Stevenson (1785–1869)', *Australian Dictionary of Biography*, Volume 1, Melbourne University Press, 1966
9 Deane, p. 47
10 British opium was grown in India, American opium in Turkey
11 Craddock, p. 6
12 Professor Griffith Taylor, 'Shanghai and its environs', *Sydney Morning Herald*, 5 March 1927
13 *The Courier*, Hobart, 25 November 1842
14 Crossley, *The Wobbling Pivot*, p. 80

15 Blake, p. 104

16 Murphey, p. 15

17 Douglas M. Peers, 'Balfour, Sir George (1809–1894)', *Oxford Dictionary of National Biography*, Oxford University Press, 2004

18 George Lanning, *A History of Shanghai*, 1923, p. 134

19 Blake, p. 125; Hibbard, p. 289. The Ewo Building is now no. 27, The Bund

20 J. H. Haan, 'Origin and development of the political system in the Shanghai International Settlement', University of Amsterdam, undated

21 Wright, Arnold (senior editor), in *Twentieth Century Impressions of Hong Kong, Shanghai etc*, p. 62

22 Keswick, p. 21. Jardines inherited 'Ewo' from one of its Cantonese compradors, the old *hong* of Howqua. Ewo also served as its China brand for beer and other products.

23 Crossley, *The Wobbling Pivot*, p. 82

24 Hibbard, p. 289

25 Foldout illustration of The Bund in 1849 in *The Model Settlement* (*Shanghai Mercury* editors, Shanghai, 1893)

26 Andrews, p. 4; Bickers, *The Scramble for China*, pp. 160–1

27 Deane, p. 55

28 Fenby, *China*, p. 19

29 Spence, *God's Chinese Son*, p. 325

30 Hsu, p. 245

31 Ibid, p. 236

32 Henriot, p. 207

33 Crossley, *The Wobbling Pivot*, p. 102

34 Begley, p. 30

35 'A morning stroll through Shanghai', *Sydney Morning Herald*, 3 March 1858 (reprinted from *The Times* of 15 December 1857)

36 Ibid

37 Rasmussen, *The Reconquest of Asia*, p. 319

38 *The History of The Times, Volume 2: The Tradition Established*, The Times, 1939, p. 292

39 'The statement of Mr Parkes', *The Times*, 29 December 1860

40 Bonavia, p. 84.

41 'The War in China', *The Times*, 15 December 1860, quoting the *Overland China Mail* of 29 October 1860

42 'China: The peace of Peking', *The Times*, 28 December 1860

43 Warner, p. 61

44 Spence, *China Helpers*, p. 74

45 Victor Hugo letter to Captain Butler, 25 November 1861 ('The Sack of the Summer Palace', *UNESCO Courier*, November 1985)

46 'Visit of the rebel forces to Shanghai', *New York Times*, 17 November 1860

47 'Visit of the rebel forces to Shanghai', *New York Times*, 4 September 1860

48 'Visit of the rebel forces to Shanghai', *New York Times*, 17 November 1860; Crossley, *The Wobbling Pivot*, pp. 112–3

49 'Progress of the Taiping Rebellion towards Shanghai', *The Argus*, 27 December 1861

50 Hibbard, p. 217

51 Spence, *God's Chinese Son*, p. 300

52 Mrs Archibald Little, *Li Hung-chang*, p. 17

53 'Visit of the rebel forces to Shanghai', *New York Times*, 17 November 1860

54 Sir Halliday Macartney was related to Lord Macartney, the first British envoy to China in 1793 whose mission ended in humiliation and failure.

55 Mrs Archibald Little, *Li Hung-chang*, p. 24

56 Spence, *God's Chinese Son*, p. 305

57 Warner, p. 79

58 'General Gordon obituary', *Sydney Morning Herald*, 12 February 1885

59 Fairbank, *The Great Chinese Revolution*, p. 106; Fenby, *China*, p. 27

60 Spence, *God's Chinese Son*, p. 325

61 'The Ever Victorious Army', *Sydney Morning Herald*, 13 October 1868

62 *All About Shanghai*, p. v

63 'China', *The Times*, 12 September 1864

64 The Vagabond, 'Chinese Sketches', *The Argus*, 17 September 1881

65 Spence, *God's Chinese Son*, p. 311; Carr, p. 97

66 Murphey, p. 11; *Tales of Old Shanghai*, p. 27

67 'China and Japan', Hobart *Mercury*, 29 March 1865

68 Murphey, p. 7

69 The Vagabond, 'Chinese Sketches II', *The Argus*, 8 October 1881

70 John Fitzgerald, *Big White Lie*, p. 87; 'Tomb of Ching rebel found in Hong Kong', *China Daily*, 17 November 2004

71 John Fitzgerald, 'Chinese Masons in Australian history', Trans-National History Symposium, ANU, Canberra, 2004; Rodney Noonan, 'Grafton to Guangzhou: The revolutionary journey of Tse Tsan Tai', *Journal of Intercultural Studies*, Volume 27, Issue 1 & 2, February 2006

72 Crossley, *The Wobbling Pivot*, pp. 116–7

Chapter 2: Distorted Images

1 Andrews, pp. 5–6

2 Ibid, p. 47

3 John Fitzgerald, quoting Taiwanese scholars Liu Daren and Tian Xinyuan, 2004

4 John Daniel Fitzgerald, 'A Celestial Gentleman', in Ethel Turner (editor), *The Australian Soldier's Gift Book*, 1918

5 John Fitzgerald, 'Chinese Masons in Australian history', Trans-National History Symposium, ANU, Canberra, 2004

6 Tse, p. 6

7 Ibid, p. 7. Tse calls this organisation 'the Chinese Independence Party of Australia'.

8 Ibid, p. 6; Pearl, p. 280

9 Tse, p. 7

10　Margaret Tart, *The Life of Quong Tart*, pp. 1–2

11　John Fitzgerald, *Big White Lie*, p. 113; Willard, pp. 26–7

12　E. J. Lea-Scarlett, 'Mei Quong Tart (1850–1903)', *Australian Dictionary of Biography*, Volume 5, Melbourne University Press, 1974, pp. 234–5

13　'Mining News', *Sydney Morning Herald*, 9 July 1872

14　'Sketches of the Braidwood district', *Sydney Morning Herald*, 14 April 1874

15　'Death and burial of a Chinese storekeeper', reprinted from the *Bathurst Times* in the *Maitland Mercury and Hunter River General Advertiser*, 8 August 1874

16　Fenby, *China*, p. 36

17　Mrs Archibald Little, *Li Hung-chang*, p. 5

18　Hibbard, p. 123; Fenby, *China*, p. 34

19　Mrs Archibald Little, *Li Hung-chang*, p. 121

20　Pearl, p. 98

21　Fearn, p. 129

22　Fairbank, *The Great Chinese Revolution*, p. 4

23　Calling himself Julian Thomas, The Vagabond had arrived in Sydney from the United States in 1875 'sick in body and mind and broken in fortune'. He made his mark in journalism with well-written articles on the seamy side of Australian life in *The Argus* and *Sydney Morning Herald* which were collected in *The Vagabond Papers* (1876). It wasn't until 1912 that his true identity was established. His real name was John Stanley James and he had been born on 15 November 1843 in Walsall, Staffordshire. (J. B. Cooper, 'Who was The Vagabond?' *Life* magazine, Melbourne, 1 January 1912; John Barnes, 'James, John Stanley (1843–1896)', *Australian Dictionary of Biography*, Volume 4, Melbourne University Press, 1972, pp. 469–70)

24　The Vagabond, 'Chinese Sketches', *The Argus*, 8 October 1881; *Occident and Orient*, p. 86

25　Pearl, p. 85

26　*Occident and Orient*, p. 83

27　Ibid, p. 84

28　The Vagabond, 'Chinese Sketches', *The Argus*, 10 December 1881

29　Woodhead, p. 24

30　The Vagabond, 'Chinese Sketches', *The Argus*, 10 December 1881; *Occident and Orient*, p. 150

31　Ibid, p. 151

32　'Notes of a voyage from Queensland to China and Japan', *Brisbane Courier*, 28 May 1894

33　Morrison, p. 2

34　'Notes on a voyage from Queensland to China and Japan', *Brisbane Courier*, 24 May 1894

35　Ibid, 26 May 1894

36　Fenby, *China*, p. 48

37　Thompson and Macklin, p. 179

Chapter 3: Mission Massacre

1   Fenby, *China*, p. 49
2   Warner, p. 129
3   Crossley, *The Wobbling Pivot*, p. 95
4   Fenby, *China*, p. 51
5   'Tartar Dynasty Doomed', *New York Times*, 2 December 1894
6   Fenby, *China*, p. 51
7   Crossley, *The Wobbling Pivot*, p. 96; Thompson, *Pacific Fury*, p. 17
8   Sergeant, p. 23
9   Andrews, p. 22
10 'Stewart mentions the Saunders sisters', *The Argus*, Melbourne, 7 August 1895
11 'The Massacre in China: Australian ladies included', *Sydney Morning Herald*, 7 August 1895
12 Quoted in 'Troubles in China: women missionaries to blame through lack of judgment', *New York Times*, 25 June 1892; Andrews, p. 254 n
13 'The Letters of Miss Saunders', *The Argus*, Melbourne, 8 August 1895
14 Williams, p. 428
15 'The Massacre at Kucheng: Statement by the survivors', *The Argus*, Melbourne, 4 September 1895
16 'H. S. Phillips statement', *North China Herald*, 9 August 1895
17 Ibid
18 'The Kucheng Massacre: How the missionaries were butchered', *Brooklyn Eagle*, New York, 8 August 1895
19 'The Massacre of the Missionaries', *The Times*, 6 August 1895
20 'The Massacre in China: Australian ladies included', *Sydney Morning Herald*, 7 August 1895
21 *The Age*, Melbourne, 7 August 1895
22 Schiffrin, *Sun Yat-sen: Reluctant Revolutionary*, p. 23; Deane, p. 54
23 Spence, *The Gate of Heavenly Peace*, p. 44
24 Cantlie, p. 31
25 Hsu, p. 457
26 Hsu'eh, C, 'Sun Yat-sen, Yang Ch'u-yu'n, and the Early Revolutionary Movement in China', *Journal of Asian Studies* 19.3 (1960)
27 Tse, p. 8
28 Ibid
29 Ibid
30 Schiffrin, p. 70; Hsu'eh, C, 'Sun Yat-sen, Yang Ch'u-yu'n, and the Early Revolutionary Movement in China', *Journal of Asian Studies* 19.3 (1960)
31 W. Hutcheon, p. 40
32 Schiffrin, *Sun Yat-sen and the Origins of the Chinese Revolution*, pp. 72–3
33 Ibid
34 'Lord Salisbury and the Chinese Legation', *The Times*, 24 October 1896
35 Schiffrin, *Sun Yat-sen and the Origins of the Chinese Revolution*, p. 60
36 Ibid, p. 82

37 Cantlie, p. 40
38 Kenneth Cantlie letter, *The Times*, 6 June 1975
39 Spence, *The Gate of Heavenly Peace*, p. 44
40 Ibid, p. 88
41 Ibid
42 Cantlie, pp. 42–3
43 Ibid
44 Letter, *The Times*, 26 October 1896

Chapter 4: Silk and Steel

1 Thompson and Macklin, p. 159
2 Thompson, *Pacific Fury*, p. 14
3 Fenby, *China*, p. 63
4 Tse, p. 12
5 Ibid, p. 11
6 Fairbank, *The Great Chinese Revolution*, p. 134
7 Lo, p. 86
8 Hsu, p. 415
9 Spence, *The Gate of Heavenly Peace*, p. 52
10 Hart, p. 1
11 Irish-born John Otway Percy Bland joined the Imperial Customs Service in 1883 and had served as Sir Robert Hart's private secretary for two years. In 1896, he became secretary of the Shanghai Municipal Council. He represented *The Times* in Shanghai from 1897 to 1907. He was later co-author with the forger Sir Edmund Backhouse of two sensational books on China.
12 'The situation in China', *The Times*, 26 September 1898
13 Ibid
14 Fairbank, *The Great Chinese Revolution*, p. 137
15 Ibid
16 Waley, p. 10
17 *The Model Settlement*, p. 5
18 Morrison, p. 4
19 H. H. Lowry, 'The Chinese resentment', *Harper's Magazine*, October 1900
20 Dent & Company had already imploded with bad debts in 1867.
21 Hart, p. 2
22 'The murder of the Rev Sydney Brooks', *The Times*, 16 January 1900
23 Seagrave, p. 300
24 'China', *The Times*, 6 January 1900
25 'The Siege of the Legations', *The Times*, 13 October 1900
26 Seagrove, pp. 202–3
27 'Before the fighting: an Australian's experience', *Brisbane Courier*, 16 July 1900
28 Preston, p. 80
29 *Daily Telegraph*, Sydney, 7 July 1900. French (p. 72) claims Morrison 'was caught napping by the Boxers, as he was out of town on a snipe-hunting expedition'.

He also says (p. 74) Morrison 'had smuggled himself into the British Legation and then been promptly immobilised by a gunshot wound in the thigh'.

30 Cornelia Spencer, p. 49
31 Spurling, p. 35

Chapter 5: China force

1 'The last stand: Europeans shoot their women and children', *Sydney Morning Herald*, 17 July 1900

2 Thompson and Macklin, pp. 237–8

3 'China: The Peking Massacre', *Sydney Morning Herald*, 18 July 1900

4 *Daily Telegraph*, Sydney, 27 July 1900

5 'The Siege of the Peking Legations', *The Times*, 15 October 1900

6 Hart, p. 4. Sir Robert Hart's essays were published in a book, *These from the Land of Sinim* (Chapman & Hall, London, 1901). Hart, who saw himself as a lay missionary preaching the gospel of peace and progress, took his title from the Bible: 'Behold, these shall come from far: and, lo, these from the north and from the west; and these from the land of Sinim.' – Isaiah 49.12

7 Hart, p. 53

8 Ibid, p. 5

9 Ibid, pp. 54–5

10 Thompson and Macklin, pp. 248–9

11 Pearl, p. 127. Arthur Henry Adams, poet, playwright and novelist, was born at Lawrence, New Zealand, on 6 June 1872. On leaving China, he spent three years as a freelance journalist in England, where he published his first novel, *Tussock Land*. In 1906, he joined *The Bulletin* as editor of the 'Red Page'; in 1909 he succeeded Frank Fox as editor of *Lone Hand*, and in 1911 he became editor of the Sydney *Sun*.

12 Andrews, p. 30

13 'Back from China', *Brisbane Courier*, 12 April 1901

14 Ibid

15 Ibid

16 Ibid

17 'Rebel ringleaders beheaded', *The Advertiser*, Adelaide, 22 January 1901

18 Nicholls, p. 91

19 Morrison Papers, Mitchell Library

20 'The Germans in Chi-li', *The Times*, 31 December 1900

21 Pearl, p. 129

22 Waldersee, Count Alfred von, *A Field Marshal's Memoirs*, Hutchinson, London 1924

23 'Loot and indemnity in China', *New York Times*, 26 January 1901

24 'Australians in Peking', *Daily Telegraph*, 10 January 1901. Although Wynne was officially the *Daily Telegraph* representative in China, his dispatches were also published in other newspapers. Sometimes his reports and those of Arthur Adams appeared under the same byline of 'Our Special Correspondent'.

25 Ibid
26 Andrews, p. 35
27 Crossley, *The Wobbling Pivot*, pp. 139–40
28 A. B. 'Banjo' Paterson, 'Dr Morrison: a notable Australian', *Evening News*, Sydney, 21 January 1903; reprinted in Paterson
29 Fairbank (editor), *The I. G. in Peking*, p. 76
30 Kevin Rudd, George Morrison Lecture, Canberra 2010

Chapter 6: Lithgow Express

1   Winston G. Lewis, 'Donald, William Henry (1875–1946)', Australian Dictionary of Biography, Volume 8, pp 317–8.
2   'Macquarie's acting architect', *Sydney Morning Herald*, 27 June 1935
3   '"Chinese" Donald – mystery man', *Sydney Morning Herald*, 4 April 1945
4   'Lithgow', *Maitland Mercury and Hunter River General Advertiser*, 7 May 1881
5   'Chinese doctors', *The Argus*, 22 June 1875
6   'The Medical Society and the Chinese doctor', *The Argus*, 17 June 1875; *Brisbane Courier*, 14 July 1875
7   French (p. 72) claims Morrison 'had canoed across Australia', a physical impossibility.
8   L. Petocz, Lithgow District Historical Society, National Library of Australia; 'George Donald obituary', *Sydney Morning Herald*, 11 July 1930
9   David McNicoll, 'Life in China: Australian's gift', *Sydney Morning Herald*, 13 February 1937; '"Chinese" Donald – mystery man', *Sydney Morning Herald*, 4 April 1945
10 'Personal', *Brisbane Courier*, 21 January 1901
11 C. F. Yong, 'The Chinese Revolution of 1911: Reactions of Chinese in New South Wales and Victoria', *Australian Historical Studies*, 12:46, 1966
12 'The Chinese reform association', *Sydney Morning Herald*, 4 July 1900
13 'Presentation', *Sydney Morning Herald*, 4 May 1901
14 Petrie Watson, *The Future of Japan*, p. xii
15 Ibid, p. vi
16 Selle, p. 5
17 Tse, p. 15
18 Spence, *The Gate of Heavenly Peace*, pp. 60–1; Rodney Noonan, 'Grafton to Guangzhou: The revolutionary journey of Tse Tsan Tai', *Journal of Intercultural Studies*, Volume 27, Issue 1 & 2, February 2006
19 John Fitzgerald, *Big White Lie*, p. 87
20 Tse, p. 21
21 John Fitzgerald, 'Chinese Masons in Australian history', Trans-National History Symposium, ANU, Canberra, 2004
22 Tse, p. 21
23 L. E. Armentrout, 'The Canton Rising of 1902–1903: Reformers, Revolutionaries and the Second Taiping', *Modern Asian Studies* 10.1 (1976)
24 Tse, pp. 22–3

25   L. E. Armentrout, 'The Canton Rising of 1902–1903: Reformers, Revolutionaries and the Second Taiping', *Modern Asian Studies* 10.1 (1976)

26   Tse, p. 22

27   'Arrival of Dr G. E. Morrison', *Sydney Morning Herald*, 23 January 1903

28   L. E. Armentrout, 'The Canton Rising of 1902–1903: Reformers, Revolutionaries and the Second Taiping', *Modern Asian Studies* 10.1 (1976)

29   'The governorship of Queensland', *The Argus*, 9 November 1888. Sir Henry Blake's rejection had more to do with the issue of non-consultation between the Colonial Office and the Queensland Government than with his fitness for office.

30   Margaret Klam, Lithgow District Historical Society, National Library of Australia. Federal Parliament met in the Victorian Parliament House, Spring Street, from 1901 until 1927 when it moved to its new home in Canberra. During those years the Victorian Parliament deliberated in the Royal Exhibition Building.

31   Lo, p. 3; Selle, p. 6; Wright, Arnold (editor), *Twentieth Century Impressions of Hong Kong, Shanghai etc*, p. 349

32   French, p. 94. Many inaccuracies have been written about Donald. Here, French seems to have relied on Ilona Ralf Sues, who wrote in *Shark's Fin and Millet* (Little, Brown, New York, 1944) that Donald 'was so poor that he could not pay his passage but worked his way across as the cook's helper. He was lucky in Shanghai (*sic*). One of the big dailies was looking for a thing unheard-of in Shanghai – a reporter who neither drank nor smoked.' While there is no doubt that Sues met Donald in China, it is clear he didn't illuminate her on how he got there.

33   Henry James Lethbridge, 'Adventurers in Hong Kong', University of Hong Kong website.

34   Wright, Arnold, *Twentieth Century Impressions of Hong Kong, Shanghai etc*, p. 349

35   H. B. Elliston, 'China's No. 1 White Boy', *Saturday Evening Post*, 19 March 1938

36   W. H. Donald, 'The Press', in *Twentieth Century Impressions of Hong Kong, Shanghai etc* (Arnold Wright, senior editor), p. 347

37   Lo, p. 215

38   Ibid, p. 406

39   Ibid, p. 406; *The Times*, 15 June 1903

40   Robin Hutcheon, p. 1

41   Tse, p. 24

42   Robin Hutcheon, p. 15

43   Lynch, *The Path of Empire*, p. xv

44   Witte, p. 127

45   Ibid; Figes, p. 169

46   David S. Crist, 'Russia's Far Eastern Policy in the Making', *Journal of Modern History*, Volume 14, No. 3 (September, 1942)

47   Morrison to Bland, 19 July 1903, Bland Papers

48   Chirol to Morrison, 25 August 1903, Morrison Papers

49   Witte, p. 126

50 Woodhead, p. 21

51 Neville, p. 161

52 Kagan and Higham (editors), p. 185

53 'War begun: Russian warships torpedoed', *The Times*, 10 February 1904

54 Pearl, p. 146

55 'America and the Far East: Australian war correspondents', Adelaide *Advertiser*, 2 April 1904.

56 Martin Donohoe was born in Galway in 1869 but had been raised in Sydney and was often referred to as Australian.

57 'America and the Far East: Australian war correspondents', Adelaide *Advertiser*, 2 April 1904.

58 Charles Belmont Davis (editor), p. 299

59 Fox, p. 50

60 Charles Belmont Davis (editor), p. 301

61 Sakuye Takahashi, *International Law applied to the Russo-Japanese War*, Stevens, London, 1908, pp. 387–8

62 Morrison to Moberly Bell, 9 June 1904, Morrison Papers

63 Ibid; Sir Claude MacDonald to Morrison, 20 May 1904, Morrison Papers

64 John Fox Jr, p. 182

Chapter 7: War and Marriage

1 Selle, p. 23

2 'Japan in Wartime', Adelaide *Advertiser*, 6 July 1904

3 Selle, p. 23

4 'Japan in Wartime', Adelaide *Advertiser*, 6 July 1904

5 Smiler Hales linked up with George Kingswell, New Zealand-born representative of the *Daily Mail* in China, but they got nowhere near the front. Instead, they crossed the Gobi Desert into Russia and made their way to Moscow. Hales wrote a series of forceful articles, 'The Far East as I saw it', for the *Daily News* in which he predicted that Russia would win the war ('London personal notes', Adelaide *Advertiser*, 10 October 1904).

6 Kagan and Higham (editors), p. 196

7 Fox, p. 177

8 Ibid, p. 183

9 'War correspondents quit', *New York Times*, 3 September 1904

10 'Mikado honors Americans', *New York Times*, 4 July 1907

11 'General Stoessel's last proclamation', *The Times*, 25 January 1905

12 'Port Arthur from Within', *The Times*, 25 January 1905

13 Marder, p. 5

14 'Grave breaches of neutrality', *The Times*, 8 May 1905

15 'The Russian Armada', *Brisbane Courier*, 25 April 1905

16 Donald's report in the *China Mail*, 10 May 1905; Winston G. Lewis, 'The quest for William Henry Donald (1875–1946), that other Australian in China', *Asian Studies Review*, 12:1, 23–29

17 W. H. Donald, 'Battle of Tsushima: How the Russians met their doom', *Brisbane Courier*, 22 June 1905

18 Ibid

19 Ibid

20 Ibid

21 Pearl, p. 150

22 Calvocoressi, Wint and Pritchard, p. 628.

23 'Tsushima and its lessons', *Brisbane Courier*, 1 June 1905

Chapter 8: Mixed Emotions

1 Fearn, p. 135

2 The Chinese Exclusion Act, originally passed in 1882, excluded all Chinese skilled and unskilled labourers and Chinese employed in mining from entering the United States for ten years under penalty of imprisonment and deportation. The 1904 re-enactment enforced the earlier suspensions of Chinese immigration without a time limit.

3 'Chinese boycott is beyond control', *New York Times*, 14 September 1905

4 Ibid

5 Mary Backus Rankin, 'Nationalistic Contestation and Mobilisation Politics: Practice and Rhetoric of Railway Rights Recovery at the end of the Ching', Modern China, Volume 28, no. 3 (July 2002)

6 'Chinese version', *New York Times*, 21 August 1905

7 'Chinese boycott succeeds', *New York Times*, 30 July 1905

8 'Scope of Shanghai boycott', *New York Times*, 15 September 1905

9 Lo, p. 406

10 Hsu, p. 463

11 Spence, *The Gate of Heavenly Peace*, p. 88

12 'Chinese boycott is beyond control', *New York Times*, 14 September 1905

13 Ibid; 'Shanghai boycott over', *New York Times*, 26 September 1905; 'Editorial', *New York Times*, 25 February 1906; Crossley, *The Wobbling Pivot*, p. 149

14 Crossley, *The Wobbling Pivot*, p. 146

15 Woodhead, p. 27

16 'Fracas in a court of justice', *The Times*, 11 December 1905

17 'Chinese girl slavery and the Shanghai Municipality', Letter to *The Times*, 1 November 1906

18 'The Shanghai disturbances', *The Times*, 11 May 1907

19 Entry 12 December 1905, Sir Ernest Satow's Peking Diary 1904–1906

20 Entry 16 December 1905, Ibid

21 'The Shanghai Mixed Court Affair', *The Times*, 14 December 1905; *The Times*, 16 December 1905

22 'Shanghai under arms', *Kalgoorlie Western Argus*, 30 January 1906

23 'Mr E. Lynch', *Sydney Morning Herald*, 28 July 1930

24 Rasmussen, *The Reconquest of Asia*, p. 109

25 'Shanghai under arms', *Kalgoorlie Western Argus*, 30 January 1906

26 Fearn, p. 136

27 'The Shanghai disturbances', *The Times*, 21 December 1905

28 'Disturbances at Shanghai', *The Times*, 19 December 1905. The Japanese consul-general in Shanghai claimed that Bland had mistaken queueless Chinese students in European clothes for Japanese ('The attitude of the Japanese', *The Times*, 24 December 1905).

29 Entry 22 December 1905, Sir Ernest Satow's Diary 1904–1906

30 Fearn, pp. 137–8

31 Woodhead, p. 29

32 Selle, p. 54

33 'Death of Mr James Gordon Bennett', *The Times*, 15 May 1918

34 'The man who made news', *New York Times*, 22 November 1942

35 'Caprice and whims of *Herald*'s late owner', *New York Times*, 19 May 1918

36 Bennett launched the *New York Evening Telegram* and the *Paris Herald* (later the *International Herald Tribune*). He also gave rise to the phrase 'Gordon Bennett!' to express exasperation or disdain.

37 Selle, p. 11

38 Farmer, p. 166

39 Selle, p. 14

40 Farmer, p. 166

41 Selle, pp. 16–17

42 Letter W. H. Donald to Muriel Donald, 15 September 1945, Lewis Papers, Mitchell Library

43 Selle, p. 42

44 Ibid

45 Selle, p. 55

46 'J. K. Ohl, editor, dies of heart disease', *New York Times*, 28 June 1920

47 'Hong Kong University marks its golden jubilee', *The Times*, 20 March 1961; 'Mr W. H. Donald', *The Times*, 11 November 1946

48 'British influence in China: the Hong Kong University', *The Times*, 7 June 1913

49 'Hong Kong University marks its golden jubilee', *The Times*, 20 March 1961

50 Thomas F. Millard, 'Arms from Japan for revolt in China', *New York Times*, 6 May 1908

51 Crossley, *The Wobbling Pivot*, p. 150

52 Ibid

53 'Japan's ultimatum delivered to China', *New York Times*, 8 March 1908

54 'Indignation in Canton', *The Times*, 23 March 1908

55 'China boycotts Japan,' *New York Herald*, 10 April 1908

56 Selle, p. 47; 'China and her foreign relations', *The Times*, 22 September 1908

57 John Garnaut, 'Shopping palaces spread gospel from Down Under', *The Australian*, 6 February 2010

58 John Fitzgerald, *Big White Lie*, p. 191. Anthony Hordern (1819–1876), born in London and raised in Melbourne, opened a drapery on Brickfield Hill, Sydney, with his brother Lebbeus in 1855. Anthony started on his own in the Haymarket

which became the first premises of Anthony Hordern & Sons. In 1879, his sons Anthony and Samuel opened the 'Palace Warehouse' and the 'Palace Emporium' in the Haymarket and according to the *Bulletin* of 22 May 1880 'fairly rule[d] the retail trade of the metropolis and the colony in general'. (Ruth Teale, 'Hordern, Anthony (1842–1886)', *Australian Dictionary of Biography*, Volume 4, Melbourne University Press 1972, pp. 423–4.)

Chapter 9: Battle Stations

1   'The Crisis in China', *The Times*, 19 July 1912
2   'China and her foreign relations', *The Times*, 22 September 1908
3   Selle, p. 47
4   Thompson and Macklin, p. 304
5   'Dismissal of Yaun Shi-kai', *Sydney Morning Herald*, 9 January 1909
6   Fenby, *China*, p. 112; 'Dismissal of Yaun Shi-kai', *Sydney Morning Herald*, 9 January 1909; Selle, p. 52
7   'China and Australia', *Sydney Morning Herald*, 18 March 1909
8   'China's awakening', *Sydney Morning Herald*, 17 March 1909
9   'China and Australia', *Sydney Morning Herald*, 18 March 1909
10 'Unrest in China', *The Mercury*, Hobart, 6 June 1910
11 'Mr Hugh Ward returns', *Sydney Morning Herald*, 4 December 1909
12 Fitch, p. 33; Woodhead, pp. 14, 92. Under the terms of the Anglo-Chinese Opium Agreement of 1907 and 1911, Britain gradually reduced imports of Indian opium until they were completely prohibited from 1 April 1913. The American missionary George Fitch was a member of the official party who burned the remaining stores of opium from the Whangpoo hulks in 1915. The trade continued illegally.
13 Most reference books place the Shanghai Club at no. 2 The Bund. Contemporary reports, however, give its address as no. 3.
14 Scotch and soda
15 Hibbard, p. 93
16 Denby, p. 2
17 Robert A Bickers and Jeffrey N. Wasserstrom, 'Shanghai's "Dogs and Chinese Not Admitted" sign: Legend, history and contemporary symbol', *The China Quarterly*, No 142, June 1995. Various signs were displayed at the gardens over the years, the most offensive of which said, '1. No dogs or bicycles are admitted. 5. No Chinese are admitted except servants in attendance upon foreigners.' This was later changed to, '1. The Gardens are reserved for the foreign community. 4. Dogs and bicycles are not admitted.'
18 Hibbard, p. 212 *passim*
19 On 17 December 1925, Hayley Morriss, 37, and his 20-year-old wife Madeline were found guilty of procuring young girls for immoral purposes at his home at Pinningford Park, Nutley, Sussex. Morris was sentenced to three years' imprisonment and his wife to nine months.
20 Lo, p. 489; 'Mr Montague Bell', *The Times*, 8 November 1949

21 Powell, p. 9
22 Ibid, p. 10
23 'Mr O. M. Green', *The Times*, 5 October 1959
24 Thomas F. Millard, 'China changing and struggling for reform', *New York Times*, 28 June 1908
25 'The rebellion in China', *The Advertiser*, 13 October 1911
26 Laura Tyson Li, pp. 22–3
27 Fenby, *Chiang Kai-shek*, p. 134
28 Powell, p. 30; Hsu, p. 465; 'Revolutionaries in China', *The Times*, 28 August 1911
29 'Revolutionary scare in Canton', *The Times*, 16 August 1911
30 Powell, p. 30; Hsu, p. 465
31 Selle, p. 68
32 Powell, p. 20; Woodhead, p. 39
33 Fitch, p. 34
34 Fearn, p. 130
35 Fairbank, *The Great Chinese Revolution*, p. 137
36 Lo, p. 622
37 Schiffrin, p. 150; Hsu, p. 467; Fenby, *China*, p. 115
38 Hsu, pp. 467–8
39 A tael is a Chinese coin weighing one ounce of silver.
40 'Chinese press subsidies', *The Times*, 3 May 1900
41 'The floods in the Yangtze Valley', *The Times*, 15 August 1911
42 'The floods in the Yangtze Valley', *The Times*, 23 August 1911
43 Ibid
44 'Starts a paper in Shanghai', *New York Times*, 30 August 1911
45 'Plague in Shanghai', *The Times*, 2 September 1911
46 Hsu, p. 468; Mary Backus Rankin, 'Nationalistic Contestation and Mobilisation Politics: Practice and Rhetoric of Railway Rights Recovery at the end of the Ching', Modern China, Volume 28, no. 3 (July 2002)
47 Lo, p. 622

Chapter 10: Revolution

1   Thompson and Macklin, pp. 313–4
2   Fenby, China, p. 119
3   Hsu, pp. 468–9; Thompson and Macklin, p. 314
4   Crossley, *The Manchus*, p. 194
5   G. E. Morrison, 'The rising in China', *The Times*, 13 October 1911
6   Schiffrin, p. 153
7   'Details of the Rising', *The West Australian*, 22 November 1911
8   G. E. Morrison, 'Crisis in China: Manchu Dynasty in danger', *The Times*, 14 October 1911
9   Braham to Morrison, 13 October 1911, Morrison Papers
10 Selle, p. 74
11 Hsu, p. 463

12 Ibid

13 Selle, p. 77; Pearl, p. 236

14 Thompson and Macklin, pp. 314–5

15 Fenby, *China*, p. 121

16 Thompson and Macklin, p. 316

17 'Revolt at Shanghai', *The Times*, 4 November 1911

18 Dong, pp. 87–8

19 'Massacre at Nanking', *The Times*, 11 November 1911

20 'Imperialist excesses at Nanking', *The Times*, 16 November 1911

21 Morrison diary entry, 6 December 1911

22 Morrison to Braham, 29 December 1911

23 'Nanking cut off', *The Times*, 17 November 1911

24 'Imperialist excesses at Nanking', *The Times*, 16 November 1911

25 'The Revolutionary Programme', *The Times*, 17 November 1911

26 Morrison to Braham, 17 November 1911

27 'Roy S. Anderson dies in Peking', *New York Times*, 13 March 1925

28 Selle, p. 82

29 On 4 August 1914, King George V granted Arthur Pope a royal licence to wear the insignia of the fifth class of the Order of the Excellent Crop conferred on him by the President of the Republic of China in recognition of his services to China.

30 'Imperial and foreign intelligence', *The Times*, 2 December 1911

31 'The Fall of Nanking', *The Mercury*, Hobart, 16 January 1912

32 Thompson and Macklin, p. 318

33 Morrison to Braham, 29 December 1911; Crow, *China Takes Her Place*, p. 216

34 Hsu, p. 470; Schiffrin, pp. 156–7

35 Ibid

36 Ibid

37 Morrison to Braham, 8 January 1912

38 Donald to Morrison, 4 July 1912

39 Schiffrin, p. 157

40 Li Yuan-hung speaking in July 1913, quoted in Pearl, p. 264

41 C. F. Yong, 'The Chinese Revolution of 1911: Reactions of Chinese in New South Wales and Victoria', *Australian Historical Studies*, 12:46, 1966

Chapter 11: The Sinking Sun

1 Now Huan-lung Road

2 Pearl, p. 233

3 Thompson and Macklin, p. 329

4 Ibid, p. 321

5 Morrison to Braham, 16 January 1912

6 'Attempt to murder Yuan Shi-kai', *The Times*, 17 January 1912; 'Peking bomb outrage', *The Times*, 19 January 1912

7 Schiffrin, p. 160; Rasmussen, *The Reconquest of Asia*, p. 115

8   Reinsch, p. 49

9   Morrison's diary, 28 February 1912, Morrison Collection

10   Author in conversation with Alastair Morrison, Canberra, 2004

11   *Sydney Morning Herald*, 19 February 1923; Wearne, Albert Ernest MC (Major) 1871–1954, PRO1739, UK National Archives

12   Pearl, p. 253

13   Donald to Morrison, 25 May 1912, Morrison Papers

14   Donald to Morrison, 4 July 1912, Morrison Papers

15   Donald to Robert Tierney, 2 August 1945, Winston G. Lewis Papers

16   James M. Macpherson, 'The canny Scot who advises China's president', *New York Times*, 11 August 1912

17   Donald to Morrison, 4 August 1912, Morrison Papers

18   Donald to Morrison, 11 August 1912, Morrison Papers

19   'Wedding of Dr Morrison', *The Guardian*, 27 August 1912

20   Powell, p. 142

21   'Rodney Gilbert, columnist, dies', *New York Times*, 12 January 1968

22   Selle, p. viii

23   Selle to Mary Donald, 1 September 1949, Winston G. Lewis Collection

24   Selle to Muriel Donald, 8 January 1957, Winston G. Lewis Collection

25   Thompson and Macklin, p. 356

26   Fenby, *China*, p. 131

27   Pearl, p. 283

28   Donald to Jennie Morrison, 1 June 1913, Morrison Papers

29   Pearl, p. 253

30   Ibid, p. 280

31   Ibid, p. 290; Fenby, *China*, p. 134; 'Siege of Nanking', *The Times*, 1 September 1913

32   Fenby, *China*, p. 134

33   A. E. Wearne, 'Dr Morrison, Australian adviser to China', *Sydney Morning Herald*, 14 February 1914

34   Ibid

35   'Dr Morrison on China', *The Times*, 25 June 1914

36   'Dictator of China', *The Times*, 2 July 1914

Chapter 12: Perfidious Albion

1   Donald to Morrison, undated but probably 1915, Morrison Papers

2   Fenby, *China*, p. 141

3   George Bronson Rea, *Japan Times*, 7 October 1928

4   Schiffrin, *Sun Yat-sen: Reluctant Revolutionary*, p. 183

5   Fenby, *Chiang Kai-shek*, p. 37

6   C. F. Yong, 'The Chinese Revolution of 1911: Reactions of Chinese in New South Wales and Victoria', *Australian Historical Studies*, 12:46, 1966

7   Selle, pp. 178–9; 'Obituary: The Strong Man of China', *The Times*, 7 June 1916

8   'Yuan Shi-kai dead', *The Times*, 7 June 1916; Fenby, *China*, p. 138

9   Powell, p. 55
10   Donald to Morrison, 4 February 1917, Morrison Papers
11   Summerskill, Michael, *China on the Western Front*, p. 175
12   Fenby, *China*, p. 140
13   Powell, pp. 55–6
14   Now no. 7 Xiangshan Road, next to the Sun Yat-sen Museum
15   Thompson and Macklin, p. 420
16   Ibid, p. 425
17   L. F. Fitzhardinge, 'William Morris Hughes (Billy)', *Australian Dictionary of Biography*, Volume 9, Melbourne University Press, 1983, pp. 393–400
18   Hsu, pp. 501–2; Fenby, *China*, p. 142
19   Reinsch, p. 361
20   Kuhn, p. 175
21   'Asia divided up, Millard says', *New York Times*, 26 July 1919
22   A. J. Hill, 'Gullett, Sir Henry Somer (1878–1940)', *Australian Dictionary of Biography*, Volume 9, Melbourne University Press, 1983, pp 137–9; 'Unguarded Australia', *Sydney Morning Herald*, 26 July 1919
23   Schedvin, p. 28
24   Fitch, p. 213
25   'Exhibition at Shanghai', *The Argus*, 21 August 1923
26   W. Farmer Whyte, 'Mr E. S. Little's defence', *The Advertiser*, Adelaide, 15 December 1923
27   Fitch, p. 238
28   *North-China Daily News*, 12 January 1924; Fitch, p. 235
29   Hsu, p. 517
30   Spence, *The Search for Modern China*, p. 312
31   Mary Clabaugh Wright (editor), p. 2
32   'China today: Vivid inside picture', *Sydney Morning Herald*, 16 November 1920

Chapter 13: Bitter Endings

1   Various documents, Winston G. Lewis *Papers*
2   Noel Croucher, born in England in 1891, arrived in Hong Kong in 1905 and worked his way up from Post Office clerk to the multi-millionaire founder of the Croucher Foundation for the advancement of medical science in Hong Kong.
3   Mary Donald to Noel Croucher, undated but 1966–67, Winston G. Lewis Papers
4   'Pain in the heart', *Time* magazine, 28 December 1936
5   'Woman gets 73 bank-note shares', *New York Times*, 11 October 1930
6   Donald to Mrs Jennie Morrison, 9–10 October, 26 October, 14 December 1920, Morrison Papers
7   Alastair Morrison, p. 1
8   'George Bronson Rea: Character of and Activities in Far Eastern Affairs', Winston G. Lewis Papers
9   'Mr Rea packs a wallop', *Washington Post*, 28 December 1934
10   'George Sokolsky, columnist, dies', *New York Times*, 14 December 1962

11 Harold K. Hochschild to Winston G. Lewis, Winston G. Lewis Papers

12 Selle, p. 227

13 Pal, pp. 55–6

14 Clifford, p. 10

15 Pal, p. 59

16 Baumler, p. 144

17 Ibid, p. 89

18 Ibid, p. 90; Fenby, *Chiang Kai-shek*, p. 112

19 Robert H. Murray, 'The most hated Americans in China', *Cosmopolitan* magazine, October 1908; Eileen P. Scully, 'Taking the low road to Sino-American relations', *Journal of American History*, Volume 82, No. 1, June 1995

20 Sergeant, p. 116

21 Fearn, p. 264

22 Ibid, p. 143

23 Pal, p. 85

24 Booker, p. 26

25 Ibid, p. 44

26 Ibid, p. 52

27 'Wu Pei-fu', *The Times*, 6 May 1922

28 'Sun Yat-sen: a brilliant failure', *The Times*, 13 March 1925

29 Bennett, p. 297

30 Fairbank, *The Great Chinese Revolution 1800–1985*, p. 211; Fairbank, 'His Man in Canton', *New York Review of Books*, 28 May 1981; Bennett, p. 223

31 Sergeant, p. 69

32 Deng, p. 169

33 Sergeant, p. 69

34 Powell, p. 94

35 Booker, p. 145

36 'Bandits carry off 300 passengers', *The Times*, 7 May 1923; 'Raid on passenger train', *The Times*, 8 May 1923; 'The Shantung outrage', *The Times*, 9 May 1923

37 Powell, p. 108

38 Carl Crow, 'Sharks' fins and ancient eggs', *Harper's Magazine*, September 1937

39 'Roy S. Anderson dies in Peking', *New York Times*, 13 March 1925

40 W. Farmer Whyte, 'China's millions: From Mukden to Peking', *Daily Telegraph*, Sydney, 15 March 1924

41 Harold K. Hochschild to Winston G. Lewis, 13 October 1969, Winston G. Lewis Papers

42 'Fighting in China', *The Argus*, 1 November 1924

43 'Wu Pei-fu: Leading Chinese general', *The Times*, 1 May 1923

44 Donald to Mrs and Mrs N. Peter Rathvon, 1 October 1924, quoted in Selle p. 233

45 Ibid

46 Rasmussen, *The Reconquest of Asia*, p. 115

47 Arthur Huck, 'Mathews, Robert Henry (1877–1970)', *Australian Dictionary of Biography*, Volume 10, Melbourne University Press, 1986, pp. 443–4

48 'Chaotic China', *Sydney Morning Herald*, 13 July 1925
49 'Melbourne Letter', *Western Mail*, Perth, 1 July 1920; 'Soldiers' Friend', *Brisbane Courier*, 18 January 1933
50 Sues, p. 183
51 'The Old Eleventh', *The West Australian*, 17 September 1918
52 'Fighting in China', *The Argus*, 1 November 1924
53 Arthur Huck, 'Mathews, Robert Henry (1877–1970)', *Australian Dictionary of Biography*, Volume 10, Melbourne University Press, 1986, pp. 443–4
54 'Sun Yat-sen dead', *The Times*, 13 March 1925
55 Selle, pp. 236–7

Chapter 14: Shanghai Fury

1 Wakeman, p. 9; Acton, p. 292
2 Leo Ou-fan Lee, p. 8
3 Clifford, pp. 39–41
4 Sternberg, pp. 82–3
5 Author's interview with Ivor Bowden, May 2010
6 Clifford, p. 60
7 Alley, *Rewi Alley: An Autobiography*, pp. 46–7
8 Ibid
9 Meta Zimmeck, 'Anderson, Dame Adelaide Mary (1863–1936)', rev., *Oxford Dictionary of National Biography*, Oxford University Press, 2004
10 Ibid
11 'Dame Adelaide Anderson dead', *The Guardian*, 31 August 1936
12 'Obituary: Dame Adelaide Anderson', *The Times*, 29 August 1936
13 Wheelhouse, p. 9
14 Rigby, p. 17
15 'Dame Adelaide Anderson's experience', *The Guardian*, 6 October 1925
16 Ibid
17 *The Times*, 17 June 1925
18 Rigby, p. 34
19 Ibid, p. 23
20 Rasmussen, *The Reconquest of Asia*, p. 109
21 'At Shanghai', *Sydney Morning Herald*, 27 April 1925
22 Hsu, p. 534
23 Ibid; Rigby, p. 19
24 Bickers, *Empire Made Me*, pp. 163–4
25 'The Shanghai riots: evidence of the police', *The Mercury*, Hobart, 17 October 1925
26 Rigby, p. 34; 'The Shanghai riots: evidence of the police', *The Mercury*, Hobart, 17 October 1925
27 Bickers, *Empire Made Me*, p. 164
28 'The Shanghai riots: evidence of the police', *The Mercury*, Hobart, 17 October 1925

29 Donald to Mr and Mrs N. Peter Rathvon, 7 July 1925, quoted in Selle, p. 240
30 'The Boxer Indemnity', *The Times*, 4 January 1926
31 Dong, pp. 124–5
32 Pal, p. 106
33 Fairbank, *The Great Chinese Revolution*, p. 175
34 Deane, pp. 21–2; Farnsworth, p. 28
35 Dong, pp. 97–8
36 Higham, p. 63 *passim*
37 Ibid, p. 72; Moseley, p. 10 *n*
38 Dong, p. 125. The Municipality of Greater Shanghai, covering an area of 828.8 square kilometres, finally came into being on 14 July 1927.
39 Dong, p. 165
40 Clifford, p. 75
41 Author's interview with Roy Fernandez Jr, May 2010
42 Toomey, p. 142
43 Roy Fernandez, 'Police expert defends the paraffin test', *Sydney Morning Herald*, 1 March 1954
44 Author's interview with Ivor Bowden, May 2010; Ivor Bowden to Winston G. Lewis, 1 July 1969, Winston G. Lewis Papers
45 'Personal', *The Argus*, 3 May 1946
46 Hsu, p. 534; Fairbank, *The Great Chinese Revolution*, p. 212; Bickers, *Empire Made Me*, p. 172
47 'Life in Shanghai', *The Argus*, 22 April 1927
48 Rasmussen, *What's Right with China*, dedication
49 Bernard Wasserstein, 'Trebitsch Lincoln', Oxford Dictionary of Biography, 1989

Chapter 15: Yangtze Thunder

1 Chang and Halliday, p. 43
2 Bennett, p. 239
3 Hsu, p. 527; 'Obituary: Chiang Kai-shek', *The Times*, 7 April 1975; Fairbank, *The Great Chinese Revolution*, p. 215
4 Sergeant, p. 70
5 Jonathan D. Spence, 'Portrait of a Monster', *New York Review of Books*, 3 November 2005; Chang and Halliday, p. 48
6 Fenby, *China*, p. 172
7 'Scenes in China', *Sydney Morning Herald*, 3 February 1927
8 Ibid
9 Fenby, *China*, p. 152, 'Obituary: Wu Pei-fu, soldier and poet', *The Times*, 5 December 1939
10 'Editorial: Hankow and After', *The Times*, 2 December 1926
11 'Chang Tso-lin's warning to Bolshevists', *The Times*, 25 September 1925
12 Clifford, p. 177
13 Ibid, p. 178
14 'The Hankow Riots', *The Times*, 2 February 1927

15 'British prestige in China', *Brisbane Courier*, 1 February 1927

16 'Scenes in China', *Sydney Morning Herald*, 3 February 1927; Rigby, p. viii

17 'The Hankow Riots', *The Times*, 2 February 1927

18 'Hankow: British Concession invaded', *The Times*, 5 January 1927

19 'The Hankow Riots', *The Times*, 2 February 1927

20 'The Lesson of Hankow', *The Times*, 8 January 1927

21 Ibid

22 Clifford, p. 181

23 Bennett, p. 327

24 Sergeant, p. 74

25 Woodhead, p. 160

26 Clifford, p. 178

27 'Editorial: Hankow and After', *The Times*, 2 December 1926

28 Robert Bickers, 'Changing Shanghai's "Mind": Publicity, reform and the British in Shanghai 1928-1931', lecture, China Society, 1991

29 Arthur Ransome, *The Chinese Puzzle* (London, 1927), pp. 28–32

30 Rasmussen, *The Reconquest of Asia*, p. 76

31 Ibid

32 Powell, pp. 145–6

33 Clifford, p. 200

34 Isaacs, p. 134

35 Ibid, pp. 135–6

36 Clifford, p. 217

37 Dong, p. 180; Clifford, p. 218

38 'Lord Gort's narrow escape', *The Times*, 23 March 1927

39 Dong, p. 180

40 'Parliament', *The Times*, 29 March 1927

41 'The Nanking Outrages: Refugees' sworn statements', *The Times*, 31 March 1927

42 'British victim at Nanking', *The Times*, 25 March 1927; 'The Nanking Settlement', *The Times*, 11 August 1928; 'Looting of Nanking', *The Times*, 28 March 1927

43 Fenby, *Chiang Kai-shek*, p. 143; Spurling, p. 176

44 'The Nanking Outrages', *The Times*, 26 March 1927

45 Bennett, p. 240

46 Dong, p. 181

47 Sergeant, p. 70

48 Fenby, *Chiang Kai-shek*, p. 153

49 Sergeant, p. 75

50 Jonathan D. Spence, 'The Underground War for Shanghai', *New York Review of Books*, 20 April 1995

51 Isaacs, pp. 142–3

52 Fenby, *China*, pp. 177–8

53 'Raid on Shanghai Reds', *The Times*, 13 April 1927

54 Dong, p. 184

55 Alley, p. 44

56 Sergeant, pp. 222–3; *The Australian*, 29 December 1987

57 Author's interview with Freda Ingham née Howkins

58 Bennett, p. 240

59 Spence, *The Search for Modern China*, p. 342

Chapter 16: Donald's Dilemma

1   James M. McHugh ms, Box 3, James M. McHugh Papers, courtesy of the Division
    of Rare and Manuscript Collections, Cornell University Library

2   'Russian refugee works in war-wracked China', *Sydney Morning Herald*, 22 October
    1936; 'Life of adventure in New Guinea', *Sydney Morning Herald*, 11 August 1938

3   Selle, p. 225

4   'Wu Pei-fu: Leading Chinese general', *The Times*, 1 May 1923

5   Jo Gullett to Winston G. Lewis, 18 April 1969, Winston G. Lewis Papers

6   'Kermit Roosevelt back with a panda', *New York Times*, 13 June 1929

7   Harold K. Hochschild to Winston G. Lewis, 18 August 1969, Winston G. Lewis
    Papers

8   Wheelhouse, p. 20

9   Professor Taylor Griffith, 'China: Is she awakening?', *Sydney Morning Herald*,
    1 February 1927

10 Ibid

11 'Obituary: Mr Basil Riley', *The Times*, 11 November 1927

12 'A young man in China: Mr F. B. Riley's letters', *The Times*, 12 November 1927

13 'Mr Riley's disappearance', *The West Australian*, 28 July 1927

14 Bennett, Introduction, p. xv (A. Tom Grunfeld editor)

15 'Reds bribe to Feng', *The Times*, 14 June 1927

16 Bennett, p. 348

17 Fenby, *Chiang Kai-shek*, p. 154

18 Bennett, pp. 361–2; Hsu, p. 529

19 'The Hankow Regime: Leaders fear of Chiang', *The Times* 13 July 1927. This
    story was datelined: 'Hankow, July 9 (delayed)', so it is impossible to ascertain
    exactly when it was filed.

20 'China for the Chinese', *The Times*, 4 July 1927

21 'Murdered by soldiers', *The West Australian*, 12 November 1927

22 'The fate of Mr Riley', *The Times*, 11 November 1929

23 *United China Magazine*, July 1932

24 'The Murder of Mr Riley', *The Times*, 11 November 1927. It is odd that another
    source (the Scoop database which lists profiles of thousands of journalists) says of
    Riley: 'Appointed special correspondent for *The Times* in China, 1927 and was
    tortured and murdered by the troops of General Feng Yu-hsiang, his death being
    reported to the British Consul by a German woman doctor, Carla Schreyer.' On
    11 October 1927, four weeks before *The Times* released its report, the *Northern
    Territory Times* published this report from London: 'The little hope which still
    lingered that F. Basil Riley, son of the Archbishop of Perth, WA, might still be
    alive, is now dispelled by the German woman who reported that Riley had been

murdered by Chinese troops. She supplied full details of the crime to Sir Sidney Barton, the British Consul-General [in Shanghai].' If so, Barton and *The Times* suppressed them.

25 'A young man in China: Mr F. B. Riley's letters', *The Times*, 12 November 1927

26 W. H. Donald to his sister, Mrs Florence Orr, 7 July 1932, Winston G. Lewis Papers

27 Woodhead, p. 159

28 Fenby, *Chiang Kai-shek*, p. 160

29 Dong, p. 190

30 'China: Tribute to an Australian', *Sydney Morning Herald*, 19 May 1931

31 Winston G. Lewis, 'The Quest for William Henry Donald (1875-1946) that other Australian in China', *Asian Studies Review*, 12: 1

32 Hallett Abend, 'Manchurian ruler broken by intrigue: Turned to opium smoking', *New York Times*, 22 October 1928

33 Selle, pp. 255–6

34 Abend, *My Years in China*, p. 150

35 'Russian refugee works in war-wracked China', *Sydney Morning Herald*, 22 October 1936

36 'Gung Ho – Rewi Alley of China', documentary, 1980, NZ On Screen

37 'Writer Rewi Alley dies aged 80', *The Guardian*, 28 December 1987

38 Jonathan Spence, 'Before the East was Red', *New York Times*, 29 February 2004

39 Crossley, *The Wobbling Pivot*, pp. 185–6

40 'China honours the national hero', *The Observer*, 2 June 1929

41 Farmer, p. 115

42 James M. Yard, 'Christianity in the Chinese laboratory', *Journal of Religion*, volume 8, number 4, October 1928

43 Alan Willoughby Raymond, Item 63, Security Service, 2 February 1943, A6126XMO, National Archives of Australia

44 Alan Willoughby Raymond, statement to Captain Wilfred Blacket, Shanghai, 5 December 1946, A4144/1, 244/1946, National Archives of Australia

45 'Back from China', *The West Australian*, 2 March 1929

46 'First woman candidate', *The West Australian*, 24 February 1930

Chapter 17: Japan Strikes

1 Abend, *My Years in China*, p. 151

2 Ibid, p. 167

3 Youli Sun, p. 21

4 Thorne, *Limits of Foreign Policy*, p. 205

5 'The Shanghai Fighting', *The Times*, 7 March 1932

6 Fenby, *China*, pp. 234–5

7 'Editorial: Manchuria and the League', *The Times*, 11 December 1931

8 'Welcoming the New Year', *North-China Daily News*, 1 January 1932

9 *North-China Daily News*, 31 December 1931

10 Hallett Abend, 'Japanese threat to Pieping', *New York Times*, 3 January 1932

11 Thorne, *Limits of Foreign Policy*, p. 206; Wakeman, p. 187

12 Jordan, p. 12

13 *North-China Herald*, 26 January 1932

14 Abend, *My Years in China*, p. 175

15 H. B. Elliston, 'China's No. 1 White Boy', *Saturday Evening Post*, 19 March 1938

16 'The Shanghai Fighting', *The Times*, 7 March 1932

17 Abend, *My Years in China*, p. 190

18 Author's interview with William Macauley

19 Author's interview with Ivor Bowden

20 Author's interview with William Macauley

21 'The Shanghai Fighting', *The Times*, 7 March 1932

22 Wakeman, pp. 191–2

23 C. S. Hirsch, 'How Japanese took Chapei', *North-China Daily News*, 31 January 1932

24 'The Shanghai Fighting', *The Times*, 7 March 1932

25 Jordan, p. x

26 Youli Sun, p. 27

27 Woodhead, pp. 207–8

28 Jordan, p. x

29 Thorne, *Limits of Foreign Policy*, p. 209

30 Paul G. Halpern, 'Kelly, Sir (William Archibald) Howard (1873–1952)', *Oxford Dictionary of National Biography*, Oxford University Press, 2008

31 'League commission in Manchuria', *Sydney Morning Herald*, 11 August 1932

32 Memo from Joseph Grew, United States Ambassador to Japan, to Secretary of State, Henry L. Stimson, Washington, 16 July 1932

33 Acton, pp. 287, 291

34 Ibid, p. 291

35 Alley, pp. 46–7

Chapter 18: Kidnap Crisis

1   Fenby, *Chiang Kai-shek*, p. 220

2   Selle, p. 281

3   Ian Stewart, 'The China Doctor still practising', *New York Times*, 12 August 1973

4   Fenby, *Chiang Kai-shek*, p. 222; Selle, p. 283

5   'Mr T. V. Soong', *The Times*, 5 June 1933

6   'Present Political Situation in China', 20 January, 1938, MLSMSS 7594/3/10, James M. McHugh Papers, courtesy of the Division of Rare and Manuscript Collections, Cornell University Library

7   'The Fukien Coup', *The Times*, 24 November 1933

8   W. L. Bond to Professor Lewis, 3 September 1969, Winston G. Lewis Papers

9   Selle, pp. 289–90

10 Ibid

11 Abend, *My Years in China*, p. 195

12 'Pain in the heart', *Time* magazine, 28 December 1936

13 Donald to Madame Chiang Kai-shek, 24 February 1934, quoted in Selle, pp. 292–3

14 Donald to Madame Chiang Kai-shek, 13 April 1934, quoted in Selle, p. 295
15 Farmer, p. 109
16 Donald to James M. McHugh, 11 July 1935, James M. McHugh Papers, courtesy of the Division of Rare and Manuscript Collections, Cornell University Library
17 Irene M. Cassel to Winston G. Lewis, 14 August 1969
18 Fenby, *China*, p. 270
19 Alan Willoughby Raymond, V. G. Bowden report, A6126/XMO, National Archives of Australia
20 Shanghai Municipal Police report 15 July 1940, quoted in Wasserstein, p. 178
21 Alan Willoughby Raymond, statement to Captain Wilfred Blacket, Shanghai, 5 December 1946, A4144/1, 244/1946, National Archives of Australia
22 Wasserstein, p. 179
23 Powell, p. 270
24 Fenby, *Chiang Kai-shek*, p. 2
25 Snow, p. 389
26 'Chiang fought captors by spiritual strength', *New York Times*, 22 April 1937
27 Barratt, p. 18
28 Powell, p. 275
29 Selle, pp. 328–9; Abend, *My Years in China*, p. 231
30 'General Chang's letter', *The Times*, 28 December 1936
31 After his release, Chang Hsueh-liang moved to Honolulu, where he died in October 2001 at the age of 100
32 'Pain in the heart', *Time* magazine, 28 December 1936
33 'In brief', *The Times*, 7 July 1937
34 'Life in China: Australian's gift', *Sydney Morning Herald*, 15 February 1937
35 Li, pp. 132–3
36 Fenby, *Chiang Kai-shek*, p. 286
37 C. D. Coulthard-Clark, 'Malley, Garnet Francis (1892–1961), *Australian Dictionary of Biography*', Volume 15, Melbourne University Press, 2000
38 Gillison, p. 149; Chennault, p. 38
39 Nelson T. Johnson Papers, Library of Congress, quoted in Pakula pp. 290–1
40 Li, p. 135
41 '*Mui tsai* system in Shanghai', *The Guardian*, 23 February 1937
42 Sarah Paddle, 'The Limits of Sympathy: International feminists and the Chinese "slave girl" campaigns of the 1920s and 1930s', *Journal of Colonialism and Colonial History*, 4:3, 2003
43 Ibid
44 Chit Chat, *Western Mail*, 26 October 1933
45 Calvocoressi, Wint and Pritchard, p. 796
46 Ibid
47 Ibid, p. 798
48 Powell, p. 291
49 H. J. Timperley to Sir Hughe Knatchbull-Hugesen, 15 July 1937, Winston G. Lewis Papers

50 John Gittings, 'Japanese rewrite *Guardian* history', *The Guardian*, 4 October 2002

51 Ibid pp. 292–3

Chapter 19: Bloody Saturday

1   Farmer, p. 38
2   Hibbard, p. 136
3   'Round trip to Nanking', *New Yorker*, 18 September 1937
4   Sherwood, pp. 17–18
5   Gillison, p. 147
6   'Havoc in the streets', *The Times*, 16 August 1937
7   Ibid
8   Emily Hahn, 'Round trip to Nanking', *New Yorker*, 18 September 1937
9   Powell, p. 300
10 *North-China Daily News*, 15 August 1937; Sergeant, p. 299
11 Wheelhouse, pp. 52–3
12 Ibid, p. 301
13 Farmer, p. 43
14 Ibid, p. 45
15 Ibid, p. 46
16 'Japan and China', *Time* Magazine, 23 August 1937
17 'Scrambling over bodies', *The West Australian*, 18 August 1937
18 'WA woman wounded in Shanghai', *The Advertiser*, 19 August 1937
19 'Japan and China', *Time* Magazine, 23 August 1937
20 Sherwood, p. 13
21 Carl Crow, 'Farewell to Shanghai', *Harper's Magazine*, December 1937
22 Ibid
23 Shanghai Municipal Police report, 13 April 1942, quoted in Wasserstein, p. 178
24 Abend, *My Years in China*, p. 257 *passim*
25 Farmer, p. 55
26 Abend, *My Years in China*, p. 263
27 Selle, p. 340
28 Hahn, *The Soong Sisters*, pp. 219–20. Donald arranged for Hahn to interview Mayling Chiang who apparently told her this version.
29 Sergeant, p. 303
30 'Have lost prestige', *The Argus*, 16 October 1937
31 Marjorie Hunter, 'China will never forget them', *Courier-Mail*, Brisbane, 21 May 1938
32 Eleanor Hinder to Florence Rawlinson, 14 September 1937
33 Farmer, p. 85
34 'Doomed men: victory in defeat', *Canberra Times*, 2 November 1937
35 Farmer, p. 88
36 Sergeant, p. 310
37 John Gittings, 'Japanese rewrite *Guardian* history', *The Guardian*, 4 October 2002

38 Ibid; 'China faces the Crisis', *The Guardian*, 12 November 1937

39 Clune, p. 351

40 Alley, pp. 100–1

41 Ibid, p. 103

42 Calvocoressi, Wint and Pritchard, p. 803

43 W. H. Donald, 'Nanking raids: Mr Donald's vivid account', *Sydney Morning Herald*, 24 September 1937

44 'Tense day at Shanghai', *The Times*, 4 December 1937

45 Farmer, p. 94

46 Thompson, *Pacific Fury*, p. 37

47 'Present political situation in China', 20 January 1938, MLSMSS 7594/3/10, James M. McHugh Papers, courtesy of the Division of Rare and Manuscript Collections, Cornell University Library

48 Ibid

49 'The Doom of Nanking', *The Times*, 8 December 1937

50 Helen Fordham, 'Our Man in China', *The West Australian*, 28 October 2006

51 C. M. McDonald, 'Eye-witness in the *Panay*', *The Times*, 18 December 1937

52 John Gittings, 'Japanese rewrite *Guardian* history', 4 October 2002

53 C. M. McDonald, 'Terror in Nanking: Looting and murder', *The Times*, 18 December 1937

54 'Japan at Shanghai', *The Times*, 7 January 1938

55 Donald to Kenneth Cantlie, 21 January 1939, Winston G. Lewis. Despite the date, it is clear in the letter that Donald is referring to events that happened early in the invasion – ie, after August 1937.

56 Farmer, p. 156; 'Australian shot down', *The Argus*, 1 April 1938

Chapter 20: Celestial Twilight

1 M. Keswick (editor), p. 212

2 Sergeant, p. 319

3 Brunero, p. 152

4 'Japanese claims at Shanghai', *The Times*, 8 January 1938

5 Emily Hahn, 'A Reporter at Large', *New Yorker*, 3 December 1938

6 'Violence at Shanghai: British police assaulted', *The Times*, 8 January 1938

7 'Strong British protest', *The Times*, 10 January 1938

8 Timperley's original telegram said, '[A] survey by one competent foreign observer indicates [that] in [the] Yangtze delta no less than 300,000 Chinese civilians [have been] slaughtered, [in] many cases [in] cold blood.' John Gittings, 'Japanese rewrite *Guardian*, history', *The Guardian*, 4 October 2002

9 Timperley's telegram was published by the US National Archives and Records Administration (NARA) in September 1994.

10 'Present political situation in China', 20 January 1938, MLSMSS 7594/3/10, James M. McHugh Papers, courtesy of the Division of Rare and Manuscript Collections, Cornell University Library

11 Ibid

12 'Present political situation in China', 14 September 1938, MLSMSS 7594/3/10, James M. McHugh Papers, courtesy of the Division of Rare and Manuscript Collections, Cornell University Library

13 'Present political situation in China', 20 January 1938, MLSMSS 7594/3/10, James M. McHugh Papers, courtesy of the Division of Rare and Manuscript Collections, Cornell University Library

14 'Mme Chiang in Hong Kong', *The Times*, 14 January 1938

15 Gillies, p. 89

16 Thompson, *Pacific Fury*, pp. 39–40

17 Ibid, p. 104

18 Isherwood, p. 53

19 Ibid, p. 55

20 Ibid, pp. 64–5

21 'Present political situation in China', 14 September 1938, MLSMSS 7594/3/10, James M. McHugh Papers, courtesy of the Division of Rare and Manuscript Collections, Cornell University Library

22 Smedley, p. 149

23 Farnsworth, p. 398

24 Ibid, p. 399

25 Isherwood, p. 237

26 Ibid, pp. 240–1

27 Ibid, pp. 252–3

28 Clune, p. 348

29 Coulthard-Clark, p. 449

30 Ibid, p. 450

31 'Bomb outrages in Shanghai', *The Times*, 8 July 1938

32 Farmer, p. 165

33 Ibid, pp. 158–9

34 Agnes Smedley, 'The last days of Hankow', *The Guardian*, 28 October 1938

35 Donald to Kenneth Cantlie, 21 January 1939, Winston G. Lewis Papers

36 Woodburn Kirby, p. 19

37 Thompson, *Pacific Fury*, pp. 39–40

38 'China's tragic ordeal', *Sydney Morning Herald*, 23 January 1939

39 Selle, p. 348

40 Donald to Kenneth Cantlie, 21 January 1939, Winston G. Lewis Papers

Chapter 21: Goodbye Chungking

1 Mayling Soong Chiang to James M. McHugh, 16 June 1939, James M. McHugh Papers, courtesy of the Division of Rare and Manuscript Collections, Cornell University Library

2 Andrews, p. 99

3 Farmer, p. 229

4 Ibid, p. 247

5 Fenby, *Chiang Kai-shek*, p. 413

6   Wakeman, *Spymaster*, front matter

7   Wakeman, *The Shanghai Badlands*, p. 30

8   Jonathan Spence, 'Goodfellas in Shanghai', *New York Review of Books*, 20 April 1995; Wakeman, *The Shanghai Badlands*, pp. 32–3

9   Jean Armstrong to Civilian Internees' Trust Fund, Melbourne, 22 January 1953, Australian National Archives

10 'Relations between Great Britain and France and China', Memorandum of Conversation, Department of State, Washington, 2 April 1940

11 Harold K. Hochschild to Earl A. Selle, 31 January 1947, William Henry Donald Correspondence, Columbia University Library

12 Chennault, p. 34

13 Memorandum of Conversation, Chungking, 8 March 1939, Military reports and miscellaneous memos 1937–1942, James M. McHugh Papers, courtesy of the Division of Rare and Manuscript Collections, Cornell University Library

14 W. J. Timperley to Sir Hughe Knatchbull-Hugessen, 15 July 1937

15 Alan Willoughby Raymond, statement to Captain Wilfred Blacket, Shanghai, 5 December 1946, A4144/1, 244/1946, National Archives of Australia

16 'Australia and Japan: W. H. Donald criticises friendship', *Sydney Morning Herald*, 16 January 1941

17 McDonald, Wynette Cecilia, Bowden report on H. O. Lindquist, 10 September 1940, A6126, no. 1213, National Archives of Australia

18 V. G. Bowden to Colonel H. E. Jones, director, Investigation Branch, 27 December 1940, Australian Archives, Canberra. Enclosures: 'Report on Mr H. O. Lindquist', 10 September 1940; 'Report on Wynette Cecilia McDonald', 23 December 1940, A6126, no. 1213, Australian National Archives

19 McDonald, Wynette Cecilia, undated statement of Mrs Ruby Taylor and Bowden to Colonel H. E. Jones, director, Investigation Branch, A6126, no. 1213, Australian National Archives

20 Ibid

21 Pakula, pp. 339–40, quoting journalist Ernest O. Hauser

22 'Bigger US loan to China', *The Times*, 18 October 1940

23 Shaw, pp. 212–3

24 Ibid, p. 213

Chapter 22: Betraying Australia

1   'Statement of Baron von Puttkamer on Wynette McDonald', 1 May 1946, A1066/4 IC45/94/5, National Archives of Australia

2   Wasserstein, p. 179

3   *London Gazette*, 24 July 1915

4   'Husband in exile', *Sydney Morning Herald*, 15 December 1948

5   'Divorce sought from husband', *Canberra Times*, 14 December 1948

6   French Political Police report, 5 March 1941, Shanghai Municipal Police records, quoted in Wasserstein, p. 179

7   Jonathan Spence, 'Goodfellas in Shanghai', *New York Review of Books*, 20 April 1995; Wakeman, *The Shanghai Badlands*, p. 122

8   Ibid

9   Ibid, pp. 123–4

10 Donald to Herbert Elliston, 3 June 1941, quoted in Selle, p. 352

11 Selle, pp. 352–3

12 Thompson, *Pacific Fury*, pp. 198–9

13 *The Argus*, 2 September 1941

14 Osmond, p. 212

15 Ibid

16 Ibid, p. 208

17 Ibid, p. 228

18 Eleanor M. Hinder to A. Viola Smith, 9 October 1941, Eleanor M. Hinder Papers, Mitchell Library

19 Geoffrey Hutton, 'Chungking has taken it for 2 years', *The Argus*, 11 October 1941

20 H. W. Timperley to W. P. Crozier, 2 November 1941, Winston G. Lewis Papers

21 Author's interview with Elizabeth Fay Woodfield

22 A. Viola Smith to Eleanor M. Hinder, 9 October 1941, Eleanor M. Hinder Papers, Mitchell Library. This letter was returned to Ms Smith on 27 March 1942 as 'service suspended'.

23 Collar, pp. 18–19

24 Carey, pp. 33–4

25 Author's interview with Stephanie Sherwood née Fernandez

26 Helen Fordham, 'Our Man in China', *The West Australian*, 28 October 2006

27 'Japanese thrown back at Hong Kong', *The Argus*, 26 December 1941

28 Author's interview with Ivor Bowden

29 Ibid

30 'John Joseph Holland', A1066/4, IC 45/94/5, National Archives of Australia; A6119/79, Item 718, Director, CIS to Secretary, Department of Immigration, 16 June 1948

31 *Shanghai Times*, 13 March 1942; Longfield Lloyd to deputy director of security All States, 'The Independent Australia League', 5 May 1945, A1066/4, IC45/94/5, National Archives of Australia

32 Shanghai Municipal Police report, 13 March 1942, quoted in Wasserstein, p. 180

33 'Newscaster of Shanghai', *Time* Magazine, 29 July 1940

34 Director-general of security to acting secretary, Department of External Affairs, 5 October 1945, A1066/4, IC45/94/5, National Archives of Australia

35 'The Independent Australia League', H. S. Austin, Australian Security Service, Brisbane, 24 May 1943, Alan Willoughby Raymond file, Australian National Archives

36 A. V. Cattel statement, 1 December 1945, PRO, FO 369/3791, British Archives

37 'Report of interview with Miss Georgina Fuller', National Archives of Australia

38 *Shanghai Evening Post & Mercury*, 6 July 1942, A4144/1, 244/1946, National Archives of Australia

Chapter 23: Behind Barbed Wire

1 Collar, p. 29
2 Powell, p. 371
3 Jack Percival, 'The prisoner the Japanese could not find', *Sydney Morning Herald*, 11 November 1946
4 Donald to Muriel Donald, MLMSS 7594/11/2, Winston G. Lewis Papers, Mitchell Library
5 *Time* magazine, 25 November 1946
6 Author's interview with Stephanie Sherwood née Fernandez
7 Sherwood, p. 66
8 Hinder, p. viii
9 Carey, p. 39
10 Sherwood, p. 69
11 Mydans, p. 93
12 Raymond, Alan Willoughby, Volume 2, John J. Holland to Dr J. Holland, director-general Security to director, Military Intelligence, 11 February 1943, A6126/XMO, National Archives of Australia
13 Author's interview with Freda Ingham née Howkins
14 'W. H. Donald held by Japanese', *Sydney Morning Herald*, 5 August 1943
15 Letter from Mrs Irene Duguid Kilpatrick, *The Times*, 1 September 1984
16 *Daily Telegraph*, 23 February 1946; 'Report of interview with Miss Georgina Fuller', National Archives of Australia
17 'Nominal rolls – Lunghwa Camp' in Leck, p. 581
18 Between 1942 and 1946, a total of 27,000 people sailed in the *Gripsholm* in exchanges between the Allies and Japan.
19 'Australian on treason charge', *Sydney Morning Herald*, 6 March 1947
20 'Charge of treason: John Holland sentenced', *Sydney Morning Herald*, 26 March 1947
21 Author's interview with Catherine Cotterman; *Pacific Fury*, p. 467
22 The editors of *Time* apologised for this gaffe in the next issue.
23 'Russia to move against Japan, says W. H. Donald', *Canberra Times*, 17 May 1945
24 Creighton Burns, 'Chiang's adviser visits USA', *The Argus*, 17 May 1945
25 Tennant, p. 163
26 Long, p. 407; Donald to Muriel Donald, 18 June 1945, Winston G. Lewis Papers
27 David McNicoll, 'W. H. Donald discusses Japan's fate', *The Argus*, 12 July 1945
28 Donald to Robert Tierney, 4 August 1945, Winston G. Lewis Papers
29 Meo, p. 83
30 'Talk by Alan Raymond', 20 July 1945, Listening Post Report, Department of Information.

Chapter 24: Return to Shanghai

1 Donald to Robert Tierney, 29 August 1945, Winston G. Lewis Papers
2 Author's interview with Stephanie Sherwood, née Fernandez
3 Sherwood, p. 95

4   'Foreign property in Shanghai', *The Times*, 18 September 1945

5   H. Mishael, 'Surrender ceremony in Shanghai', *Sydney Morning Herald*, 8 September 1945

6   Twomey, p. 138

7   H. Mishael, 'Aiding Shanghai internees', *Sydney Morning Herald*, 21 September 1945

8   Twomey, pp. 79–80

9   Mary and Muriel Donald became American citizens in 1954. Mary died on 14 June 1972 in a convalescent hospital at Paradise, California, at the age of 90. Muriel died less than a year later on 21 April 1973 at the Feather River Hospital, Paradise, at the age of 63.

10 H. Mishael, 'China's iron man looks back at his achievements', *Sydney Morning Herald*, 23 October 1945

11 Lary, p. 172

12 Associated Press, 4 December 1945

13 'US policy attacked by Donald of China', *New York Times*, 28 January 1946

14 Professor Lewis commented that 'the claims made for Donald in that volume sometimes appear to verge on the fantastic . . . [they] suggest that he, almost alone, shaped the course of the history of modern China' (Winston G. Lewis, 'The Quest for William Henry Donald (1875–1946), that other Australian in China', *Asian Studies Review*, Volume 12, Number 1).

15 John Hersey, 'Letter from Shanghai', *New Yorker*, 9 February 1946

16 Tyn Li, p. 271

17 Alastair Morrison to Professor Lewis, 1 April 1980, Winston G. Lewis Papers

18 Mrs Ida du Mars to Muriel Donald, 11 July 1947, Winston G. Lewis Papers

19 Donald to Harold K. Hochschild, 15 April 1946, Winston G. Lewis Papers

20 Li, p. 276

21 *China Press*, 10 November 1946

22 *North-China Daily News*, 11 November 1946. The cemetery was vandalised during the Cultural Revolution and there is no sign of Donald's grave today.

23 'John Holland arrested in barber's chair', *The Mercury*, Hobart, 29 September 1945

24 Alan Willoughby Raymond, statement to Captain Wilfred Blacket, Shanghai, 5 December 1946, A4144/1, 244/1946, National Archives of Australia

25 Wynette Cecilia McDonald, statement to Captain Wilfred Blacket, 'Report on Shanghai Position Prior to Embarkation of Shanghai Detachment', 10 January 1946, MP742/1, 255/2/686, National Archives of Australia

26 US CIC interrogation of Ikushima Kichizo at Sugamo Prison on 20 March 1946, FOIA/USAISC, US Army Intelligence and Security Command, CIC: Counter-Intelligence Corps, quoted in Wasserstein, p. 179

27 Dai Li was killed in a suspicious plane crash on 17 March 1946.

Chapter 25: Mao's Triumph

1   Pakula, p. 547

2   James M. McHugh to his wife, 31 July 1946, James M. McHugh Papers, courtesy of the Division of Rare and Manuscript Collections, Cornell University Library

3   Marjorie Harper, 'Copland, Sir Douglas Berry (1894–1971)', *Australian Dictionary of Biography*, Volume 13, Melbourne University Press, Melbourne, 1993

4   D. A. Alexander, deputy director, Commonwealth Investigation Service, Canberra, to director, 23 September 1947

5   Memorandum from Ian Morrison to *The Times* foreign news editor Ralph Deacon, 19 November 1948, *History of The Times*, Volume V, p. 179

6   The Allied Intelligence Bureau (AIB) was set up by General MacArthur in 1942 as an umbrella organisation to control all American, Australian, British and Dutch special operations.

7   Barber, p. 62

8   'R. Williams, deputy director, to director, Canberra, 'John Charles Rookwood Proud', 18 October 1948, National Archives of Australia

9   'Calwell upholds firmly White Australia policy', *Shanghai Evening Post*, 24 March 1949

10 'Shanghai newspaper suspended', *The Times*, 26 April 1949

11 'Chinese civil war incident', *Cairns Post*, 27 April 1949

12 'Communists in Shanghai: The Bund occupied', *The Times*, 25 May 1949

13 'Communist Shanghai', *The Times*, 24 June 1949

14 Andrews, p. 142

15 Helen Fordham, 'Our Man in China', *The West Australian*, 28 October 2006

16 'Mr H. J. Timperley', *The Times*, 29 November 1954

17 *History of The Times*, Volume V, p. 94

18 'Mr Ian Morrison', *The Times*, 14 August 1950

19 Alastair Morrison, p. 156

INDEX